The Hare Krishna Movement

The Hare Krishna Movement

Forty Years of Chant and Change

Edited by
Graham Dwyer
and
Richard J. Cole
(Radha Mohan Das)

I.B. TAURIS

LONDON · NEW YORK

Published in 2007 by I.B.Tauris & Co Ltd
6 Salem Road, London W2 4BU
175 Fifth Avenue, New York NY 10010
www.ibtauris.com

In the United States of America and Canada distributed by Palgrave Macmillan
a division of St. Martin's Press, 175 Fifth Avenue, New York NY 10010

HB   ISBN: 978 1 84511 407 7

PB   ISBN: 978 1 84511 408 4

A full CIP record for this book is available from the British Library
A full CIP record is available from the Library of Congress

Library of Congress Catalog Card Number: available

Printed and bound in Great Britain by TJ International Ltd, Padstow, Cornwall
From camera-ready copy edited and supplied by the editors

To
Bridget and Maggie

and to
the family and friends of Radha Mohan Das

CONTENTS

PART 1 Origins, Developments and Organisational Patterns

PART 2 Dreams and Devotion

PART 3 Tradition and Modernity

PART 4 Identity and Perception

LIST OF PLATES

Plates follow page 118

Plate 1   Srila Prabhupada on a morning walk in San Francisco's Golden Gate Park with Malati Dasi, one of the early devotees who came to establish the Hare Krishna movement in Britain (1967). (Copyright: Bhaktivedanta Book Trust)

Plate 2   Srila Prabhupada on the *vyasasana* (elevated seat) leading a chant or *kirtana*. (Copyright: Bhaktivedanta Book Trust)

Plate 3   Srila Prabhupada during *arati* (worship), accompanied by devotees. (Copyright: Bhaktivedanta Book Trust)

Plate 4   Srila Prabhupada bathing an image of Lord Krishna at Bhaktivedanta Manor in the UK. (Copyright: Bhaktivedanta Book Trust)

Plate 5   Devotees escorting Srila Prabhupada down the stairs of Bhaktivedanta Manor on his *palanquin* (Summer 1977). (Copyright: Bhaktivedanta Manor Archives)

Plate 6   Mukunda Goswami talking with the late George Harrison in the corridors of Bhaktivedanta Manor (1996). (Copyright: Bhaktivedanta Manor Archives)

Plate 7   Marble *samadhi* (place of burial for a holy man) of Srila Prabhupada in front of ISKCON's Krishna Balaram temple in the holy town of Vrindavan, India. (Private Collection: The Editors)

Plate 8   Campaigners on a protest march in London to save Bhaktivedanta Manor from closure (1994). (Copyright: Bhaktivedanta Manor Archives)

Plate 9   Gauridas, Temple President of Bhaktivedanta Manor, greeting Gordon Brown MP, Chancellor of the Exchequer, at the Diwali function held at the House of Commons (October 2006). (Copyright: Bhaktivedanta Manor Archives)

Plate 10 Radha-Londonishvara, the first images of Radha and Krishna installed in an ISKCON temple, now on the shrine at the temple in Soho Street, London. (Private Collection: The Editors)

Plate 11 ISKCON's annual Ratha Yatra chariot festival, which involves a procession from Hyde Park to Trafalgar Square, London (June 2006). (Private Collection: The Editors)

Plate 12 The editors at the annual Ratha Yatra chariot festival in London (June 2006). (Private Collection: The Editors)

Plate 13 Kripamoya Das (and daughter Tulasi) preparing to perform a public fire sacrifice or *yajna* (1995). (Copyright: Bhaktivedanta Manor Archives)

Plate 14 ISKCON's lavish property in Mayapur, West Bengal, where Lord Chaitanya Mahaprabhu was born. It is this location that was chosen by Srila Prabhupada as the movement's world headquarters. In the background is the dome (*pushpa samadhi*), the magnificent cathedral-like structure built in honour of Srila Prabhupada. (Private Collection: The Editors)

Plate 15 Devotees photographed in June 2005 outside Twenty Six Second Avenue in Manhatten's Lower East Side. Opening in May 1966, it was the first ISKCON temple and also the place where ISKCON was legally established. (Private Collection: The Editors)

Plate 16 Deena Badhu Das (pictured wearing a *kurta* and Hari Nama scarf) with numerous community devotees of Bhaktivedanta Manor admiring the food offerings cooked in honour of Srila Prabhupada's Appearance Day, known as Vyasa Puja. (August 2005). (Copyright: Bhaktivedanta Manor Archives)

INTRODUCTION

Graham Dwyer and Richard J. Cole (Radha Mohan Das)

The Hare Krishna movement made its eventful first appearance in the Western world in 1965, the year in which the movement's founder, His Divine Grace A.C. Bhaktivedanta Swami Prabhupada, travelled from India to the West.[1] In 1966, the very next year, the International Society for Krishna Consciousness (ISKCON) became the movement's registered official title. New disciples soon joined the fold in America, where Bhaktivedanta Swami Prabhupada at the age of 70 started his missionary work, and a little later the movement attracted increasing numbers of recruits in Britain and in Europe as well as in other parts of the world, especially in the movement's homeland of India. One of the most prominent features of the tangible presence of the Hare Krishna movement during its early days in the West was its practice of chanting in public locations, the physical appearance of its members – with their shaven heads and exotic saffron robes – equally being conspicuous in the public domain. Although chanting bands of ISKCON followers are seen less on city high streets today, as this aspect of devotionalism, preaching and proselytising has become less pronounced and has given way to other trends, such as congregational activities and activities carried out in the homes of devotees, as well as the cultivation of practices that increasingly embrace the Hindu diaspora, chanting and hearing the names of Krishna still continue to be distinctive and indeed remain definitive of the Bengali Vaishnava tradition of devotion to God (*bhakti* or *bhakti-yoga*), which the founder of ISKCON transported to the West over four decades ago. Today, despite its relatively short history of 40 years of chanting in the Western world, the Hare Krishna movement still persists but has undergone and continues to experience a variety of challenges, transformations and developments as it endeavours to hold on to its members and to expand its Krishna Consciousness mission, not only in the West, but also further a field – in countries such as Russia and countries in Eastern Europe, which before the fall of Communism seemed almost impenetrable. It is these challenges, transformations and developments as well as the future prospects of the Krishna Consciousness movement that are analysed in this book, with attention to what is taking place inside the movement today being its central focus.

The Hare Krishna movement itself, a branch of the Vaishnava tradition established by Chaitanya Mahaprabhu (1486-1533), holds the saint Chaitanya to be non-different from Krishna and Krishna's consort Radharani combined, the Supreme Personality of Godhead;[2] and it is the particular practice of chanting and hearing the names of Krishna that Chaitanya popularised in medieval East India, a practice adopted by Chaitanya's intimate disciples, the six Goswamis of Vrindavan in Uttar Pradesh, north-west India, who both formulated and propagated the tradition's monotheistic theology, and whose theology and practices have continued to thrive in Vrindavan as well as in East India, being revived in more recent times through the efforts and zeal of two key figures: Bhaktivinoda Thakura (1838-1914) and his son Bhaktisiddhanta Saraswati (1874-1936). Indeed, it was the latter Bengali saint who not only founded a missionary organisation known as the Gaudiya Math (Gaudiya denoting the tradition of Vaishnavism inaugurated by Chaitanya), an organisation that established many temples throughout India but one which today has become fragmented as a missionary enterprise; it was he who also encouraged one of his foremost disciples, Bhaktivedanta Swami Prabhupada, to take up missionary activity outside India, resulting in the birth of the Krishna Consciousness movement in the West. Operating on Western soil, the founder of the Hare Krishna movement, in fact, explicitly viewed his spiritual lineage (*parampara*) as an uninterrupted, unified chain of spiritual masters extending backwards in time to include the figure of Chaitanya himself and, following Chaitanya, also considered devotion to God through the chanting and hearing the names of Krishna to be the recommended path to salvation in the current age (Kali Yuga, the age of irreligion or spiritual decline). In an important respect, therefore, this book provides an examination of a movement that is self-consciously a continuation of the spiritual heritage of Chaitanya Vaishnavism, a movement transplanted from Indian religious tradition that has put down roots in the West.

This volume offers novel perspectives on the Hare Krishna movement, perspectives which provide an account of what is taking place inside the movement today, as well as shedding light on the movement's status vis-à-vis the wider international social and religious landscapes in which it has attracted followers. Essays in this edited collection address not only problems and tensions affecting the movement since its foundation, many of which still loom large and which in some instances have taken different expressions and trajectories, particularly since the demise of the movement's founder in 1977; the essays also offer new approaches in terms of assessing challenges currently facing ISKCON, challenges shaping leadership as well as activities amongst grass roots members, involving devotional and outreach practices, scope and appeal of ISKCON today as well as challenges affecting ISKCON's sense of its own identity. Importantly, while the edited collection provides new understandings in terms of such challenges, it further casts light on many positive developments in ISKCON – developments internal to the dynamics of the Hare Krishna movement as it seeks to grapple with forces potentially destabilising to the movement and its attempts to expand its mission.

The essays in the collection are authored by two types of writer: (1) academics who have previously published seminal papers on the Hare Krishna movement and (2) members of the movement itself, including senior figures within it who are also scholars holding an internationally renowned publication record for their writings about the Hare Krishna movement. Current trends and developments within the Krishna Consciousness movement are key in the edited collection; and attention to ISKCON today is the common thread linking the essays, which explore a wide range of different themes and issues, including *inter alia* the politics and history of the Hare Krishna movement; membership patterns; recruitment strategies and practices; pedagogical and social factors impacting on or shaping the Hare Krishna movement; the importance of dreams and ritualism in the religious lives of many of today's adherents; as well as the movement's articulation of traditional theology (and even perhaps finding a place for a thealogy) in the modern context of the movement's evolving self-perception. ISKCON worldwide is considered in the book, though the Hare Krishna movement's members, its centres, practices and activities in Britain, America and parts of Europe are the subject of particular attention, as it is these geographical areas where the research experience, knowledge and expertise of contributors to the volume mostly lie.

Since the Krishna Consciousness movement was established in the West over 40 years ago, a large corpus of scholarly literature has emerged; yet, while the movement's origins, establishment and development from the mid-to-late 1960, through the 1970s and the 1980s have been well documented, what is taking place now is less well known.[3] With the exception of one notable publication, whose relevance needs to be outlined here, it is well over a decade since a comprehensive, book-length work on the Hare Krishna movement has surfaced, making the essays assembled here particularly timely, a way also of marking and commemorating the movement's 40 years of chanting in the West as well as its continued persistence in the modern world.

Most of the academic books dealing with ISKCON, in fact, were published in the 1980s but in very recent years attention of scholars has once again turned to the Krishna Consciousness movement, with many of them coming from religious studies and sociology backgrounds. A number of these academics, as well as a number of ISKCON members, ex-members and ISKCON opponents, have contributed to a recent important book edited by Edwin Bryant and Maria Ekstrand,[4] a work that is not centrally focused on ISKCON today but whose themes and concerns overlap in part with the themes and concerns of this book, each of the two books thus being of complementary value to the other. Bryant and Ekstrand's edited collection, which principally deals with events that took place immediately after the death of ISKCON's founder, and which traces the theology, history and legacy of ISKCON's fortunes and misfortunes, concentrates much of its attention on the politics of the Krishna Consciousness movement. But it also offers speculation about possible future paths the movement might take in the post-Enlightenment setting of the West, speculation which privleges Western rationalist discourse; for Bryant and Ekstrand stress that ISKCON must adopt a hermeneutics consistent with the sentiments of modern educated individuals or the intelligensia if it is to continue to survive as well as to attract new converts.[5] While such a rationalist emphasis offered in Bryant and Ekstrand's book is problematic [6] but not an invalid analytical framework, contributors to this volume who offer speculative comment on ISKCON's possible future adopt modes of analysis that tend to move away from a rationalist stance, seeing, for instance, a greater role for members of the Hindu diaspora in the Hare Krishna movement and increased development of home-centred and congregational practices as being key to its on-going as well as future prospects, as intiatives such as these allow opportunities both to access and to experience a form of spirituality that may be appealing to many in an otherwise disenchanted materialistic world characteristic of Western modernity. Moreover, the present work offers discussion and analysis of developments taking place inside the Hare Krishna movement not incorporated in the edited work of Bryant and Ekstrand, developments of major relevance involving factors such as ISKCON's ritual practices, the role dreams play in religious commitment, as well as discourse about feminine and feminist aspects of divinity. Thus, while what is on offer in the present work builds upon much of the excellent scholarship found in the valuable work of Bryant and Ekstrand, it also seeks to extend this, providing additional understandings and fresh insights, particularly in terms of what is taking place today inside the Hare Krishna movement.

The book's ten substantive essays have been divided into four major parts according to their principal themes. In Part 1 Steven Rosen's essay discusses the arrival in the West of the Hare Krishna movement's founder and, following an examination of the circumstances that facilitated Bhaktivedanta Swami Prabhupada's initial achievements in America, his essay goes on to identify events occurring 40 years on, events which Rosen views as an indication of ISKCON's continued, on-going success. This optimistic appraisal of the Krishna Consciousness movement's development over 40 years of its history is a view also articulated in Richard Cole's essay, though in his examination of ISKCON's origins and growth, Cole draws attention not only to the Hare Krishna movement's achievements but also to major schisms and crises that have occurred. In tracing the movement's history from its foundation to the present day Cole thus presents a nuanced assessment of ISKCON's fortunes and misfortunes, the features of its development it has reasons to celebrate while also not ignoring the failures and mistakes from which it undoubtedly has lessons to learn.

Following on from Cole's essay Ross Andrew analyses membership patterns, with a focus on Britain. In his essay (and in the brief note he gives about it in a separate comment on his work), Andrew outlines major phases in the development of ISKCON membership, showing how ISKCON has moved from being a relatively isolated, temple based community cut off from mainstream society during the early years of its formation to one that is increasingly congregational, with most devotees residing no longer in temples but living and working in the outside world and supported by a clergy trained to minister to them. Andrew further predicts this pattern will endure in the foreseeable future and, most crucial of all, sees education as well as training programmes offered to devotees as a natural progression and as a key organisational feature ISKCON should continue to embrace if it is to be proactive in terms of improving retention, expansion and quality of its membership.

Part 2 highlights the importance of dreams in the devotional lives of many ISKCON members, a subject that is for the first time given serious scholarly attention. Graham Dwyer demonstrates in his two essays that a focus on dreams is critical, not merely for understanding the spiritual orientation and religious commitment of many of today's adherents, but also key for understanding hitherto undocumented devotional trends and trajectories of Hare Krishna community members. In the essays by Dwyer dreams about the founder of the movement and dreams about Krishna are shown to be particularly significant, as well as being of importance in terms of comprehending issues of power or spiritual authority; for, as Dwyer's work reveals, messages puportedly given by ISKCON's founder in dreams may have led some devotees during crucial periods of leadership crisis and conflict to disregard, even to subvert, rulings or precepts put in place and sanctioned by those holding the reins of power. In this respect, Dwyer's work discloses how devotees' claims of receiving messages in dreams potentially can be devisive and can have a powerful impact on ISKCON's authority structure as well as on the wider politics of the Krishna Consciousness movement.

Part 3 focuses on the tension between tradition and modernity, and it examines problems faced by ISKCON in the modern world as it endeavours to institute and fully realise the traditional teachings and practices Bhaktivedanta Swami Prabhupada transported from India to the West. Such a task William Deadwyler argues in his essay was envisioned by ISKCON's founder as being nothing less than a strategy of "cultural conquest", a task involving a complete abandonment of what Deadwyler refers to as the failed project of modernity. From the perspective of ISKCON, Deadwyler contends rejection of modernity means a radical movement away from the phantasmagoria of scientific "progress" and the recognition that the modern project born of the Enlightenment is fundamentally misplaced human effort resulting in spiritual impoverishment. Yet Deadwyler readily acknowledges that in terms of appeal ISKCON's anti-modernist stance is not without problems, particularly as this involves attempting to convince would-be followers that scientific advancement merely brings "illusory happiness" and also requires adherents, for example, to accept the traditional guru-disciple hierarchical system of authority in ISKCON. Nonetheless, as an anti-modernist movement – a feature ISKCON shares with other increasingly successful anti-modernist movements, such as many New Age groups or communities – the attraction of ISKCON, Deadwyler holds, seems set to expand, particularly as in his estimation disillusionment with the project of modernity everywhere appears to be growing.

The tension between tradition and modernity is the main theme in Kenneth Anderson's essay, as well as a key issue in Anna King's first essay, which primarily deals with much neglected dimensions of ritualism in ISKCON. In Anderson's essay the mode of analysis utilised is largely similar to the kind of analysis adopted by Deadwyler, as Anderson, like Deadwyler, argues in favour of what he holds to be the merits of ISKCON's traditional spiritually informed approach to solving problems confronting the modern world. But Anderson, like Deadwyler, equally draws attention to difficuties presented with such an endeavour; for Anderson makes it clear that, despite ISKCON's explicit attempt to embrace the traditional teachings of its founder, the Hare Krishna movement itself has experienced (and continues to experience) many problems of the type it purports to be able to overcome – failings in the field of education, for instance, as well as failings of family breakdown, and failings in its attempts to provide a fully working economic alternative to what is on offer in modern capitalist society. Indeed, one encounters in ISKCON major features of the tension between the traditional and the modern that are perhaps essentially unresolvable King goes on to argue in her essay. Thus, in terms of her discussion of Bhaktivedanta Swami Prabhupada's directive to institute in ISKCON a form of the traditional Indian system of socio-religious organisation (*varnashramadharma*) King contends it is both inappropriate in an egalitarian post-industrial society and also viewed by some devotees as impractical and irrelevant in the modern world. Yet, on the other hand, King indicates there are signs too that ISKCON seems capable of overcoming certain aspects of the contadictory forces of tradition and modernity, as in ISKCON today (and indeed for a number of years now) one finds much emphasis given to education, training and graduation – a trend which, according to King, is very much in accord with the global expansion of Hindu priestly traditionalism coupled increasingly with the adoption of modernist values and attitudes.

Moving on from issues of tradition and modernity (though with some of the same or related themes still continuing to reverberate), Part 4 concentrates on ISKCON's evolving sense of its own identity and examines perceptions of the Hare Krishna movement from a range of perspectives. In Thomas Hopkins' essay ISKCON is analysed in terms of its struggle for self-expression and its own search for self-identity, with the author drawing upon a wealth of direct knowledge of the Hare Krishna movement and first-hand experience gained over the past 40 years. Presenting his reflections upon the movement as a historian of religions, and as a scholar of Vaishnavism (particularly Gaudiya Vaishnavism), Hopkins examines ISKCON's sense of itself as an international missionary organisation rooted in the spiritual heritage of the Chaitanya school of devotionalism, and he assesses the development of ISKCON from its very inception as an international movement through to the present day, as well as offering insight on how it may develop in the future. Hopkins compares aspects of the emergence and development of ISKCON with early Christianity and argues that such comparison is of particular value, not only for understanding major features of the dynamics of structure and sense of distinctiveness developing within ISKCON but, importantly, for understanding how ISKCON's leaders might learn from the lessons of the Christian experience. Just as the success of Christianity was, in part, achieved by rigorous effort expended in defining the central tenets of the faith coupled with the determination of its founders to be both clear and liberal regarding matters of religious practice, as well as inclusive, where possible, in respect of various interpretations of scripture, so Hopkins offers the suggestion ISKCON could benefit enormously as a religious organisation if it were to adopt a similar stance – one where essentials of doctrine are clearly defined while resisting fundamentalism or a literalist orientation. Indeed, Hopkins holds that if ISKCON hopes to flourish or endure it must not only avoid taking a literalist doctrinal stance; it needs also a long-term commitment to the kind of theological enterprise found at the heart of most religious traditions, involving critical assessment of the tradition's sources of authority and concomitant on-going evaluation of its practices.

This call for greater liberalism is also a central motif in Anna King's second essay, which is the final contribution to this volume. Here King explores feminine and feminist dimensions of deity with a focus on perceptions of the goddess Radha (the internal potency of Krishna), and she analyses the position of Radha in terms of the liberating (though not unproblematic) forces she embodies for aspiring devotees. In her highly original work (no scholar to date has focused in any in-depth way on the position of Radha in ISKCON) King argues that, although much of the identity of ISKCON has taken expression through a theology that has been largely the preserve of male gurus and scholarly devotees, a shift in emphasis to a thealogy of Radha could balance the orientation to the male divine, resulting in the greater recognition and incorporation of women's devotional experience. Indeed, while it appears there is some evidence such a shift might be occurring in ISKCON today, to be fully realised, King argues, this would require a revisionist outlook in ISKCON capable of enabling devotees to move beyond mere gender stereotypes, thus leading to a thealogy of Radha and Krishna devoid of gender hierarchy. As ISKCON becomes more mature and refines how it is percieved, King contends such a revisionist shift is not only highly desirable but critical also in terms of the future prospects of the Krishna Consciousness movement. King like the other contributors who engage in speculation about the future of the movement thus provides much food for thought, particularly in terms of its prospects as an international organisation.

As a final remark, however, it should be noted that, as the concerns of the essays in this volume concentrate primarily on the Hare Krishna movement in Britain, America and parts of Europe, the book's ability to shed light on the status of the movement globally inevitably has some limitations. This volume is unable in any significant way, for example, to offer an account of what is taking place today in India, where the Krishna Consciousness movement not only originated but where it still continues to thrive and where in many holy cities, such as ISKCON's world headquarters in Mayapur, West Bengal, evidence of the on-going achievement of the movement in the sub-continent is especially clear, both in terms of the grandeur and opulence of its many temples and other sacred monuments and also in terms of its flourishing ritual activities, its busy pilgrimage and festival events. In addition, this book is able to do little more than hint at what is taking place now in regions such as Eastern Europe or the territories formerly known as the Soviet Union. Comprehensive studies of the status of the Hare Krishna movement in all these geographical areas are very much needed in order to gain a clearer global picture of ISKCON today. However, despite such limitations of the book, it nonetheless offers, we hope, much in terms of understanding what is currently taking place inside the Hare Krishna movement in the West and will be of value to students and scholars concerned with issues of major import, not only in the sociology of religion and in the field of history of religions, but also, in particular, in the study of how a distinctive Indian religious tradition with 40 years of chanting in the West orients itself towards attaining a secure and successful future.

PART 1

Origins, Developments and
Organisational Patterns

1

1965 WAS A VERY GOOD YEAR
and 2005 is Better Still

Steven J. Rosen (Satyaraja Dasa)

Introduction

This chapter will explore the idea that the year 1965 served as a host, if you will, for three consequential events – emendations to the then-existing immigration laws, a papal decree, and the phenomenon known as the counterculture – and that these events helped facilitate the arrival of an Eastern religious/philosophical system of thought onto Western shores.[1] That system, known as Vaishnavism (an ancient form of monotheism that refers to God as Vishnu, or Krishna), was introduced to the West in 1965 by A.C. Bhaktivedanta Swami (later given the honorific "Srila Prabhupada" by his disciples), a monk in the long-standing Brahma-Madhva-Gaudiya lineage.

Sociologists and historians of religion have posited that this particular year was critically significant, that had Prabhupada made his journey either a year earlier or later, he would not have achieved the same degree of success. Needless to say, adherents to the faith take a different tack, seeing the successful unfolding of Prabhupada's mission as divine dispensation – the year not being particularly significant. Nonetheless, believers would have to admit that Prabhupada did come to Western shores at a time most appropriate for his work, a time when people would be ready to hear his message.

This chapter, therefore, focuses on the concatenation of the three events that occurred in 1965, rendering Prabhupada's appearance in the Western world exceedingly timely. It begins with a brief analysis of Prabhupada's place in the Gaudiya tradition and the predictions from within that very tradition which his mission appeared to fulfil. The chapter then proceeds with an exploration of the three events mentioned above, allowing both scholars and devotees critically to examine the circumstances and evaluate for themselves if there is not some "divine arrangement" at play here. The conclusion will show that Prabhupada's accomplishments live on and indeed continue to grow in the present day, suggesting that his work was everything he had hoped it would be, for it brought to life a spiritual phenomenon that is virtually unstoppable.

The Mission

On 13 August 1965, only a few days before the advent celebration of Lord Sri Krishna, on a dishevelled dockside in Calcutta, an elderly Indian monk – then known as A.C. Bhaktivedanta Swami – carrying only a small suitcase, an umbrella, and a bag of dry cereal, climbed up a steep gangway onto an old cargo steamship, aptly named the Jaladuta ("the Messenger from the Water"). After a rough voyage of 35 days (during which he suffered two heart attacks), the ship berthed in Boston at Commonwealth Pier on 17 September. The time, metaphorically appropriate, was sunrise, 5:30 a.m., to be exact.

The next day, the "Messenger from the Water" continued to New York, where the solitary monk disembarked onto a rugged Brooklyn pier and into the land of America. Although the monk's personal possessions were few and simple, his personal qualities of knowledge, renunciation, and devotion were immeasurable. He would share these spiritual riches with everyone he would meet, at first from a bleak Bowery loft, then while sitting on an oriental rug under a tree in a New York park, and finally from an unassuming shop located in the city's bohemian Lower East Side. Here he would make an impact, not for saavy marketing of "Hindu hocus-pocus" as the "anti-cult" critics liked to claim, but rather for authentically transmitting an age-old religious tradition, Gaudiya Vaishnavism, which was inaugurated by the Bengali ecstatic, Sri Chaitanya Mahaprabhu (1486-1533).

A pivotal figure in the lineage represented by Prabhupada, Sri Chaitanya revived the spiritual sentiments of Bengal in medieval times, even as Martin Luther (1483-1546) was instigating the Protestant Reformation in Europe. Chaitanya's wish was that his followers spread the doctrine throughout India and to every town and village of the world. Not only did this fail to happen in Chaitanya's time, but the tradition, by Prabhupada's time, had become moribund in its sub-continental milieu.

Aware of the increasing tendency on the part of his fellow countrymen to adopt Western ideas and practices, Prabhupada's intention in transplanting the tradition, besides benefiting its Western recipients, was to reinvigorate its original proponents in India. Indeed, some have likened Prabhupada's accomplishment to the first transplantation of a human heart by the South African surgeon, Dr Christian Barnard, in 1967. Just as that physician replaced an old, dysfunctional heart with a new and robust one in order to provide rejuvenated life, Srila Prabhupada revived an endangered religious tradition by transferring it to an alien culture. The "heart" of this Indian religion (bhakti), which had all but stopped beating, was given new life when Prabhupada performed his transplant. The transplant a success, the tradition thrived in its new home (and in its native land once again) and, ironically, became widely known in the West as a "new" religious movement. Although the "heart" analogy has certain limitations, it is clear that Prabhupada's transplantation was quite successful.

In fact, his success was a unique achievement amongst all the respected saints in the great succession of Vaishnava sages (*acharya*s). It is for this reason that Prabhupada became widely known as the West's first "ambassador of *bhakti*" and as the "Founder-*Acharya*" of the International Society for Krishna Consciousness (ISKCON).

A Mission Prophesied

Lending credence to the providential nature of Prabhupada's mission are a number of scriptural passages foretelling his coming, albeit obliquely, as well as prescient statements by sages in the tradition preceding Prabhupada.

To begin, Chaitanya Mahaprabhu is quoted as saying "My name – the name of Krishna – will spread to every town and village of the world."[2] This prophecy, from the 16th century, did not manifest in practical form until after Prabhupada's arrival on Western shores.

Prior to the *Chaitanya Bhagavata* reference mentioned above, the *Padma Purana* stated that *bhakti*, or loving devotion to the Lord, would be carried by someone from South India to Vrindavan, and then to "other lands." There are elaborate commentaries on this phenomenon, but it is clear that Prabhupada first went to South India, then Vrindavan, and from there he came West with his treasure of devotion to Krishna. A clear fulfilment of the *Purana*'s prophecy.[3]

In addition, there is the more often cited prediction of Bhaktivinoda Thakura (1838-1914), a saint in the tradition, in which he writes about a universal religion centred on the chanting of the holy name of Krishna. While he does not mention Prabhupada directly, his description of people from various countries joining together in *kirtana* did not take place until Prabhupada came West:

In the world now, there are so many religious communities, and in their purest, mature form they are the religion of singing the praises of the Lord. At the present time there is a great spiritual quest going on in the world, and it seems that the one unalloyed religion which is the essence of all religions will soon emerge. What is that religion? It is plain to see that in western countries and in Asia, religions are engaged in conflicts. There is no doubt that these religions will not be able to endure. Therefore, many of the established religions which harbour prejudiced, conflicting beliefs have become fragmented. When all of these contradictory dogmas are removed, it is then and there that all religions will be united. Let us consider the specifications the Eternal Religion would have: (1) God is one and is the all-knowing source of knowledge. He is devoid of all limitations and is the reservoir of all good qualities. (2) All living entities are His infinitesimal parts and parcels of consciousness, and the eternal function of all living entities is to serve the Supreme Lord.(3) To sing the glorious qualities of the Supreme Personality of Godhead and to establish the brotherhood of all men as pure religion.

Gradually the established religions will then be removed of all specific contradictions, and the secular or "party spirit" will not remain. Then all castes, all creeds, and men of all countries will be united in coexistent brotherhood under the Supreme Personality of Godhead, united by *nama-sankirtana*, the congregational chanting of the Lord's holy name.

Very soon the unparalleled path of *Hari-nama-sankirtana* will be propagated all over the world. Already we are seeing the symptoms. Already many Christians have tasted the nectar of divine love of the holy name and are dancing with *kartals* (hand-cymbals) and *mridangas* (drums). Educated Christians are ordering these instruments and shipping them to England. By the super-excellence of Lord Krishna's holy name and the grace of pure devotees, our consciousness gets purified...Oh, for that day when the fortunate English, French, Russian, German and American people will take up banners, *mridangas* and *kartals* and raise *kirtana* through their streets and towns. When will that day come? Oh, for that day when the fair-skinned men from their side will raise up the chanting of *Jai Sachinandana, Jai Sachinandana ki jai*, and join with the Bengali devotees.[4]

Bhaktivinoda states it even more directly: "Soon a personality will appear who will preach the holy name of Hari all over the world."[5]

1965: It Was a Very Good Year

We will now proceed to the central theme of our thesis, namely, that Prabhupada's historic journey from the East was precipitated by a series of legal, ecclesiastic, and sociological events in the Western world that would inadvertently make this a fertile ground for the reception of his message. Devotees generally relegate the significance of these events to the domain of "mundane considerations," and necessarily afford them a secondary position when compared to the more overtly spiritual reasons for Prabhupada's success, i.e. his lifetime of preparation (as delineated in Satsvarupa Dasa Goswami's *Srila Prabhupada-Lilamrita*); his exceptional personal character; his initiation in disciplic succession; his scholarship and pure devotion. Possessing these qualities gave Prabhupada access to divine beneficence, say his followers, which manifested, in this instance, in the three categories of "mundane" phenomena described below.

A. The Legal Dimension: Immigration

When the Jaladuta landed in Boston, the U S Immigration officials boarded it and processed Srila Prabhupada's entry as an American visitor. Asked how long he intended to stay, he replied "two months." His passport was duly stamped and the date of intended exit was entered. Although Prabhupada was hardly aware of it, he had entered the USA while prohibitive immigration laws were in effect. These laws reflected a protracted period of racial and religious hostility and suppression. J. Gordon Melton, the founder and Director of the Institute for the Study of American Religion, in a paper published in Krishna Consciousness in the West has uncovered the following facts.[6]

The turn of the 20th century saw a sudden increase in Indian immigrant workers, in particular the conspicuously turbaned Sikhs from the Punjab, who emigrated to America's Northwest coast, because they were attracted by the lucrative labour jobs in the expanding timber industry. The result was an ever-growing resentment among the local American population, who felt jobs were being lost to the new arrivals willing to work longer hours for lower wages. The year 1907 saw in half a dozen cities anti-Indian riots and violence. During World War I, there emerged an entrenched prejudice against Chinese immigrants. War-time politics, the Chinese communal habit of aloofness from other Americans, and the Chinese financial success, made them objects of suspicion and resentment. In general, America's reaction to the war was a strong isolationism and a refusal to accept outside ideas and cultures. An incipient racial sensibility for preserving America as an Anglo-Saxon bastion proliferated. This bigotry was a factor of the fundamentalism of the rural Protestants, who took the commanding position of America's social mix. Congress responded over the veto of President Woodrow Wilson with the passage of the Oriental Exclusion Act of 1917. This law created the Asian Barred Zone, which included India, and from which no immigrants were permitted. Indians who had previously resettled in America and who tried to gain citizenship were denied by a Supreme Court ruling in 1923, which conceded that Indians were "caucasians" (emphasis added) but could not be considered "white."

The Immigration Act of 1924 modified the prohibition by creating a quota system, which was fixed at one-sixth of 1 per cent of the total number of immigrants from each particular country living in America in 1920. This meant that the total number of Indians allowed entry was 100 per year. These laws prevailed for 45 years until they were suddenly amended by an act that abolished the quotas. This major reform of the immigration laws, which was first proposed by President John F. Kennedy, was ultimately signed by President Lyndon Johnson in a dramatic ceremony in New York at the foot of the Statue of Liberty on 3 October 1965 – only three weeks after Srila Prabhupada's arrival.

Professor Melton observes that:

> Between 1871 and 1965, only 16,013 Indians had been admitted to the United States. Between 1965 and 1975, more than 96,000 were admitted, and the 1980 Census reported 387,223 Indians in the United States...This change in the immigration also allowed a number of Hindu teachers to come to the United States and establish new groups consisting predominantly of new converts from among the general population...A.C. Bhaktivedanta Swami, having come to America on a tourist visa just before the immigration laws were changed, was able to stay in America because of the change.[7]

However, there were further immigration difficulties for Srila Prabhupada. He had initially intended to stay for only two months. However, after determining that there was an opportunity to spread the philosophy of Krishna Consciousness in America (and at the fervent urging of his new students), Srila Prabhupada applied for permanent residence, after having obtained several extensions to his tourist visa. The application for permanent residence was denied with the following reply: "You came originally as a visitor and later applied for residence, which means that you did not truly enter as a visitor."

Srila Prabhupada's followers sought legal help. The well-known though non-conformist poet, Allen Ginsberg, who personally knew Srila Prabhupada, was prevailed upon for advice and assistance. A lawyer specialising in immigration was hired. After a considerable number of visits, telephone calls, and meetings for which he naturally charged fees, the lawyer suggested he could lobby a Congressman to propose a resolution on the floor of the United States House of Representatives for specific residence for Srila Prabhupada by name. The late Adam Clayton Powell Jr of New York was mentioned as an appropriate lawmaker to do this – but it would all cost money, something of which Srila Prabhupada's early disciples, who were all inexperienced young men and women, had very little. Consequently, nothing was being done to solve the problem.

Prabhupada then obligingly complied with the order of the immigration department to leave the country. He went to Montreal, Canada, where the first preaching centre outside America, and the third after New York and San Francisco had recently been established, under his direction. This centre was set up with the initial effort of one of Srila Prabhupada's earliest disciples who was a French-Canadian. Being resigned to the fact that he might not be able to obtain permanent residency in the USA, Srila Prabhupada planned to stay in Montreal until the new Canadian centre was firmly on its feet; after that, he would go to London to establish his movement abroad. Srila Prabhupada reasoned that by opening centres in these four important cities, Montreal, New York, San Francisco and London, his mission would have been accomplished and he would then be able to return to India.

As fate would have it, Srila Prabhupada soon applied for residency in Canada. Obtaining residential status there afforded Prabhupada the opportunity to travel freely to the United States. This being the case, Srila Prabhupada planned to make Montreal his headquarters. He next applied to the American consulate in Canada for residential status in the USA, and this was finally granted in October of the same year. Thus perseverant, Prabhupada had strategically accomplished this first step, enabling him to stay in the country. He therefore became one of the first test cases to be granted permanent residency under the new immigration laws, which came into effect at much the same time as did his arrival in America. Thereafter, many Indians emigrated to the USA in a similar manner.

B. The Religious Dimension: A Papal Edict

After disembarking from the Jaladuta, Srila Prabhupada travelled to Butler, Pennsylvania, where, on the recommendation by a friend in India, he became the houseguest of an Indo-American family. Prabhupada found himself in a typical small town in provincial America. He delivered a few lectures at a local YMCA to assorted religious groups, curious college classes, and with his hosts he had friendly chats, but he knew this was not the purpose for which he had come to America, risking his life in the process. After a few weeks, Srila Prabhupada began to plan to go to New York, a place his small-town friends had politely suggested might provide a better audience for his teachings. At this time Pope Paul VI made a momentous visit to New York. America, still reverberating from the assassination of John F. Kennedy two years before, was injudiciously escalating its war with North Vietnam, and the Pope came to deliver a peace address to a special session of the United Nations General Assembly. Arriving on 4 October 1965 (the day after President Johnson signed the immigration law) the Pope made a whirlwind visit of only 15 hours, creating quite a stir.

It was the first visit by a pope to the Western Hemisphere. A 20 mile motorcade from the airport passed through New York streets lined with people totalling in the millions. The Pontiff was protected by a special police force of 18,000 officers, the largest force ever, larger even than the one for Khrushchev, who had visited New York some years earlier. The Pope's address at the United Nations, being the first papal appearance before a secular political body in centuries, was directed primarily to America; which had by then bombed North Vietnam with three times the entire tonnage of bombs dropped in World War II in all of Europe, Asia, and Africa, yet which failed to destroy Vietnam's military or economic infrastructure. This resulted in the USA increasing its forces to 200,000.[8] The Pope's ardently delivered plea for peace, broadcast live by television and radio to 20 nations, reached hundreds of millions. Fourteen days later, on 18 October 1965, Srila Prabhupada entered New York (from Pennsylvania) on a bus. Except for his unusual appearance in the saffron robes of a *sannyasi*, no one noticed.

A year earlier, in December 1964, Pope Paul VI had distinguished himself by being the first Pope to visit India. In fact, Pope Paul VI had left Italy only once previously on a pilgrimage to the Holy Land of Jerusalem, thus being the first Pope to leave Italy in over 150 years. Although his visit to India had been protested by militant Hindu groups, the Pope endeared himself to millions of Hindus by quoting (in translation) from their scriptures (the *Mundaka Upanishad* and the *Brihadaranyaka Upanishad*) in his arrival address. The Pope said:

This visit to India is the fulfilment of a long-cherished desire. Yours is a land of ancient culture, the cradle of great religions, the home of a nation that has sought God with a relentless desire in deep meditation and silence and in hymns of fervent prayer. Rarely has this longing for God been expressed with words so full of the Advent as in the words written in your sacred books many centuries before Christ: "From the unreal, lead me to the real, from darkness lead me to light, from death lead me to immortality."

This is a prayer that belongs also to our time. Today more than ever, it should rise from every human heart. The human race is undergoing profound changes and is groping for the guiding principles and the new forces that will lead it into the world of the future. Your country has also entered into a new phase of her history. And in this period of transition you, too, feel the insecurity of our age, when traditional orders and values are changed, and all efforts must be concentrated on building the future of the nation, not only on a stable material basis but on firm spiritual foundations...Are we not all one in this struggle for a better world, in this effort to make available to all people those goods that are needed to fulfil their human destiny, and to live lives worthy of the children of God? Therefore we must come closer together, not only through the modern means of communications...We must come together with our hearts, in mutual understanding, esteem, and love. We must meet not merely as tourists but as pilgrims who set out to find God, not in buildings of stone but in human hearts. Man must meet man, nation meet nation, as brothers and sisters, as children of God. In this mutual understanding and friendship in this sacred communion we must work together to build the common future of the human race.[9]

Striking the spiritual chords of the Indian people, the Pope became affectionately known as *burra guru*, or "great holy man." Even as the Pope was visiting Bombay and Delhi, Srila Prabhupada was in Vrindavan endeavoring by himself to complete the third volume of the mighty scriptural tome, *Srimad Bhagavatam*.

Having completed trips to India and New York and once again in Rome a document was issued from the Vatican entitled, "Declaration on the Relationship of the Church to Non-Christian Religions." This proclamation, an outcome of the three-year Roman Catholic Ecumenical Council sessions of Vatican II, was signed by "Paul, Bishop; Servant of the Servants of God, Together with the Fathers of the Sacred Council for Everlasting Memory." Although concerned primarily with relations with the Jews, the document included pertinent sections on Buddhism, Islam, and also on Hinduism, a religion which was characterised as follows:

> From ancient times down to the present there is found among various peoples…the recognition of a Supreme Being, or even of a Father. This perception and recognition penetrate their lives with a profound religious sense…In Hinduism men contemplate the divine mystery and express it through an unspent fruitfulness of myths and through searching philosophical inquiry. They seek freedom from the anguish of our human condition either through ascetical practices or profound meditation or a flight to God with love and trust.[10]

While asserting the spiritual authority of the Church, the document broadens the Catholic perception of non-Christian faiths as follows:

> The Catholic Church rejects nothing which is true and holy in these religions. She looks in sincere respect upon those ways of conduct and of life those rules and teachings which, although differing in many particulars from what she holds and sets forth, nevertheless often reflect a ray of that Truth which enlightens all men.[11]

In the views of many, this Declaration of Vatican II marked a watershed for the Roman Catholic Church. As such, numerous commentaries were written (both officially produced by the Church and otherwise) examining its significance.

Robert A. Grahman (S.J.), a Vatican authority, commenting on this extraordinary promulgation, says, "…[I]t is the first time an Ecumenical Council has expressed such an open approach to the other great faiths of the world."[12] And, as Karl Rahner and Adolf Darlap write:

> This document signified a break in the Church's history of its relationship with the non-Christian world. Thus, a new position was taken by the Church which opened the way for changes in the dealings with peoples of other faiths that had been guided by other criteria for a millennia and a half. For the first time there was official recognition that non-Christians were not pagans, that is, the followers of a religion that was invented by men, and thus sinful and unable to merit God's grace. The salvific function of non-Christian churches was recognised for the first time by Christian orthodoxy. This was not just a modern liberal mentality but an integral element of Christian conviction. The result was dialogue. [13]

As theologian Richard P. McBrien remarks:

> There was no more theological imperialism. One faith may be the truth but other faiths also have the right to exist which leads to syncretism that all religions may amalgamate together to create a new faith of the future. The traditional ecclesiastical isolation of the Catholic Church was broken for the first time with the result that the Church was brought into the modern world with a willingness for dialogue now a possibility.[14]

In his introduction and commentary to the "Declaration," John M. Oesterreicher writes:

> This Declaration holds a special place among the documents of Vatican II....In it a Council for the first time in history acknowledges the search for the absolute by other men and by whole races and peoples, and honors the truth and holiness in other religions as the work of the one living God....To that extent the Declaration is an acknowledgement by the Church of the universal presence of grace and its activity in the many religions of mankind.[15]

Also, in the official commentary (first published in 1967 in Germany, and in 1969 in America and England), Cyril B. Papali writes on the section of the declaration dealing with Hinduism, presaging Srila Prabhupada's mission:

> These words of the Council are not meant to be a description of Hinduism, but an indication of some of its outstanding spiritual values which may serve as spring-boards for a dialogue with it. And such a dialogue is of the utmost importance to the Church, for Hinduism is a religion that has moulded the spiritual destinies of a large part of humanity for thousands of years and still remains a living force. Having absorbed, during its long lifetime, the peoples and religions of the Indian sub-continent, and spread its philosophy and spirituality over the greater part of Asia, *it now stands knocking at the portals of the Christian world* (emphasis added). Since the turn of the (20th) century, Hinduism has grown increasingly missionary and keen on entering into a dialogue with Christianity.[16]

These momentous new directions undertaken by the Roman Catholic Church would inestimably alter Western receptivity to the religions of the East. The process of modifying centuries-old prejudice had now begun – religious exchange was in vogue. Rather than denouncements of Eastern religions as heretical, a new recognition of mutually-shared spiritual values was taking place by clerics and lay Christians alike. Thus, the initiative taken by the Vatican was, in effect, an official welcome invitation to just such a missionary as Srila Prabhupada. This declaration, issued on 25 October 1965, was exactly one week after Prabhupada's entry into New York.

C. The Sociological Dimension: Prabhupada and the Counterculture

Decades before Prabhupada's arrival in the West, other representatives from the Gaudiya Vaishnava tradition had come to these shores attempting to reach a Western audience. In an important essay, Gerald Carney discusses the sojourn West of Premananda Bharati at the turn of the century. In the 1930s several of Prabhupada's godbrothers, including Bhakti Pradipa Tirtha Maharaja and Bon Maharaja, came West; however, they were all relatively unsuccessful. The success of Prabhupada's mission, caused in part by the congruity of Prabhupada's arrival with the countercultural revolution taking place at the time, is described by Robert S. Ellwood, Bishop James W. Bashford Professor of Oriental Studies at the University of Southern California:

> Swami Bhaktivedanta arrived in New York in the fall of 1965. From the Krishna consciousness perspective, one could well regard that time of arrival as highly providential. For conceding all the cautions appropriate to historical speculation, it seems that had his mission in this country commenced even a few years – possibly a few months – earlier or later, it would have been farless fruitful. Bhaktivedanta's timing caught the powerful rising tide of what was called the counterculture, which included within its spectrum of concerns a fascination with India and an exceptional openness to exotic, consciousness-expanding spirituality. This countercultural tide carried with it many new boats, some of which have stayed afloat despite the receding of that wave.[17]

This unique slice of history called the "counterculture" was basically an unofficially declared revolution by a vast segment of the youthful population of America (and abroad) against what was called "the establishment," i.e. anything resembling authority – government, churches, institutions, parents. Nationally, it was a time of general social turbulence, discord and mistrust as evidenced by the racial struggle, the Vietnam conflict, the assassinations of popular public figures. And, globally, this period in time had given rise to the population explosion, resulting in a world population in which more than half of its individuals were under the age of 30 – and more widely educated than ever before. A vast fomentation of ideological exchange was occurring the world over due to the availability of increased global communications.

The *Weltanschauung* of an entire generation of young people was gradually changing. The big questions of life were being asked en masse by America's youth; dislocation from the cultural mainstream was rampant; alternative lifestyles and value systems were being explored. Conservative views on sex, politics, race, language, dress, drugs and codes of behaviour were increasingly frowned upon, and, for some, had become anathema.

Due to this growing dissatisfaction with Western culture, a particularly sharp focus on the East ensued. This was not something new. There had long been in America a tradition, both intellectual and popular, of interest in Eastern religion and spiritualism. For example, the early "Transcendentalists," such as Ralph Waldo Emerson (1803-82) and Henry David Thoreau (1817-62), were heavily influenced by Indian philosophy and religion. This was reflected in their writings, as well as in those of John Greenleaf Whittier (1807-92) and T.S. Elliot (1888-1965), among others. However, this attraction to the East seemed to reach a peak during the countercultural period of the 1960s, for it was reinforced by the stress of the times. Thomas Hopkins, who recently retired from Franklin and Marshall College as Emeritus Professor of Religious Studies, points out that:

[D]evotional movements have always sprung up, I think without exception, in periods of tremendous social stress and change. They've always been the answer to the collapse of society. In a sense they're ideally suited to, tried and proven in, periods of social disorder. That's what Kali-yuga is all about, isn't it? It's when everything falls to pieces, when the world is no longer a secure place and a source of satisfaction…The counterculture era was a period when the problems of society were so obvious and so visible that you couldn't ignore them. We were fighting a crazy war, we had a crazy president, the whole society was riddled with contradictions in values and standards, and nobody was providing any kind of guidance and discipline. So, obviously these conditions did lend themselves to creating a mood of receptivity to a movement like yours, which did provide meaning, guidance, and discipline…[18]

The sociological ramifications of the counterculture, especially in relation to Prabhupada's arrival in America, were insightfully expressed by J. Stillson Judah, Professor Emeritus of Religion and Director of the Graduate Theological Union Common Library at Berkeley. In an eloquent appraisal of just where history had taken us, Dr Judah lays bare the expectations of the 1960s youth scene, with special attention to aspects of society that were rejected by them:

(1) material success for themselves through competitive labor; (2) an education that promotes that end; (3) the accumulation of unneeded possessions for sense gratification; (4) authority, both civil and parental, that favors the status quo; (5) any war, such as the Vietnamese conflict, that is regarded as a product of imperialistic purposes with a selfish economic basis; and (6) the hypocrisy of many belonging to the establishment, especially regarding civil rights and racial relationships. In addition, some felt that they were trying to practise many of the ideals upon which their former religious faiths were founded, but which they felt were so little

practised by other churchgoers...The devotees [of Krishna] sought a transcendental, spiritual solution to...[these] problems.[19]

Interestingly, Judah points out that those who converted to Krishna Consciousness were not only disenchanted with the materialistic world, but the countercultural subculture itself was a great source of disenchantment because here they found the same hypocrisy, exploitation, hedonism, and selfishness. Thomas Hopkins points out that devotee countercultural youth were not *ipso facto* opposed to all authority but only hypocritical or deficient authority – those who did not practise what they preached. In Steven Gelberg's *Hare Krishna Hare Krishna*, Larry Shinn, then Professor of Religion at Bucknell University, says that the young people who became devotees felt a need for ethical mores and structure, which seemed to be lacking in the countercultural world. An intellectual as well as emotional fulfilment was desired and found in the form of the community of devotees and, more importantly, in the person of Srila Prabhupada, who was seen to be nothing less than a saint. Here was someone who could be trusted, who followed the same standards he set for others. He gave guidance and instruction and taught by example.

Collectively, the youthful rebels of the 1960s embodied the condition of Arjuna, who lovingly submitted to Krishna on the battlefield as depicted in *Bhagavad Gita*. Confused as to their duty and purpose in life, some sought refuge, solace, and instruction from Prabhupada, Krishna's representative; others did not.

The countercultural 1960s was brief, virtually half a decade long – a kind of deep social spasm – and during that brief interval a Vaishnava devotional movement took hold in the West. But, as Shinn points out, the movement was not in itself a result of the counterculture, because, at least in India, it existed millennia before the counterculture and, even with the demise of the 1960s youth scene, the movement continued to evolve and transform itself well into the 1970s, 1980s and 1990s. Hopkins goes further: "But now the movement is much broader and wider in scope and vision so...that it is no longer just a peer-group defence community against the world, but something that is a world – a world that has its own kind of lifestyle, standards, and vitality at every level."[20]

Preliminary Conclusions

We have shown that due to unusual legal, ecclesiastical, and sociological events a door to America swung open in the year 1965, which allowed for the admittance of a venerable monk from an Eastern tradition, Srila A.C. Bhaktivedanta Swami Prabhupada. Whether coincidental or providential (depending on one's perspective), these three factors provided a workable environment for the birth of the Vaishnava *bhakti* movement in the West. The suitability of this environment, however, may have proven negligible in the hands of one not qualified to rise to the task at hand. A stage may be beautifully set, but unless the player possesses the proper qualifications, the part will not come to life. Srila Prabhupada was just such a qualified player, and not the least of his qualifications was the profound yet simple synchronicity of his actions with service to the divine. This consideration cannot be overestimated. In the introduction to the first volume of Satsvarupa Dasa Goswami's *Srila Prabhupada-Lilamrita*, resident Christian theologian at Harvard Divinity School, Harvey Cox, eloquently expresses this thought:

> Yet, it must be added, Srila Prabhupada was also a unique person. To say that the teachings of the ancient ones come to us through a series of teachers does not mean that the teachers are themselves interchangeable. If they were so faceless, there would be little point in writing a biography of any of them. But this life of Srila Prabhupada is pointed proof that one can be a transmitter of truth and still be a vital and singular person, even – in a sense I now feel safe to use – in some ways "original." Srila Prabhupada lived through a particularly critical period in Indian history, that of British colonial rule and its aftermath. He worked with and among dozens of people who befriended, opposed, supported, or ignored him. He initiated *Back to Godhead* magazine. At what almost anyone would consider an advanced age (70), when most people would be resting on their laurels, he hearkened to the mandate of his own spiritual master and set out on the difficult and demanding voyage to America. Srila Prabhupada is, of course, only one of thousands of teachers. But in another sense, he is one in a thousand, maybe one in a million.[21]

Ultimate Conclusion: 2005 Is Better Still

Prabhupada's success can be ascertained by starting backwards, that is to say, we can look at his devotees' current accomplishments, as of 2005, and, by this, we can draw certain unmistakable conclusions about his secure place as the inspiration and, indeed, the fountainhead of everything that is now occurring in his movement. By evoking this method, we can again see how the timing of his appearance was orchestrated by Krishna Himself – for it bore fruits that could only come from a godly tree.

Though educated people around the world are somewhat aware of ISKCON's difficulties,[22] particularly those that have arisen since Prabhupada's demise, we need only review a few of the movement's current successes effectively to neutralise any lingering idea that the institution may have failed. In fact, the good far outweighs the bad, even if the bad is considerable.

Let us look, for example, at the fact that many temples keep opening in Prabhupada's name throughout the world, affecting people's lives for the better, or at the massive Food for Life International programme – a praiseworthy free food initiative that feeds and educates literally millions throughout the world, largely in Third World countries. Or consider the success of Radhanath Swami, one of Prabhupada's Western-born disciples and a saintly person respected by the mass of ISKCON devotees today. The Bombay temple project, which was completed after Prabhupada "left the planet" (an ISKCON colloquialism for death), was taken on by Radhanath Swami and expanded beyond anyone's wildest dreams. More – and his godbrother Lakshmi Nrisimha says it best:

> He [Radhanath Swami] has attracted thousands of the city elite to his congregation in Chowpatty Bombay. Their *ashram* is also constantly expanding with qualified and dedicated monks, although they refuse candidates unless they finish their university studies and work at least one year in their respective careers. So many medical graduates and established doctors have come forward that their congregation has opened the International Occupancy Standard (IOS) Bhaktivedanta Hospital, with over three hundred resident doctors, half of them initiated ISKCON members.[23]

Prabhupada's followers in India have also given us impressive projects in Baroda, Dvaraka, and Ahmedabad, while Prabhupada's main projects on the subcontinent, those in Vrindavan and Mayapur, have been developed by devotees far beyond where they were when their guru was still here: Vrindavan now includes the Mayapura-Vrindavan Trust (MVT), an international guest house and restaurant facility that can easily accommodate devotees from around the world, and two new establishments, at Govardhana and Vrinda-Kunda, which make Vrindavan a very ISKCON-friendly place. Mayapur, for its part, is a virtual Disneyland for serious devotional Westerners, and is every bit as luxurious as its Vrindavan counterpart.

Delhi, too, has been transformed from a small *ashram* to a major temple complex, complete with restaurant and museum. But why only focus on India? Indradyumna Swami, another ISKCON luminary, has, in the mood of his spiritual master Srila Prabhupada, taken Krishna Consciousness around the world. A particularly newsworthy aspect of his travels brings us to Poland, where a yearly "Woodstock" of sorts, has him setting up a tent as large as a football field, and literally thousands come to join him for chanting the Holy Name and taking *prasadam*, vegetarian foods that have been offered first to Krishna.

Add to this the massive expansion in the former Soviet Union and even in China, and the numerous books and scholarly studies published by Prabhupada's disciples, coupled with the many inroads made in academic circles, such as the Mayapura and Vrindavana Institutes of Higher Education, Bhaktivedanta College and the Vaishnava Theological Seminary in Belgium, and one has to admit that Prabhupada is still very much present. People continue to be nourished by his philosophy, personal example and institution.

As of 2005 there is every sign that the expansion of Prabhupada's movement will continue for years to come. Though 1965 was a special year indeed, particularly for the reasons mentioned above, it is clear that now, 40 years later, we are embarking on a new era, one in which Prabhupada and his followers will remain a strong presence.

FORTY YEARS OF CHANTING:

A Study of the Hare Krishna Movement from its Foundation to the Present Day

Richard J. Cole (Radha Mohan Das)

Introduction

This chapter considers key developments in the International Society for Krishna Consciousness (ISKCON), commencing with an assessment of its early establishment and evolution and focusing, in particular, on its status today in the West as well as further afield, including Eastern Europe and the former Soviet Union. The early days of the founder's organisation in America will be described, as will the extension of ISKCON to Britain. Issues and activities in Britain are the subject of special attention in this chapter and largely so because it is here where both my own understanding of, and my own relationship with, the movement mostly lie.

The Mission of Chaitanya Mahaprabhu in Britain [1]

Britain has always been significant in the eyes of two very exalted and powerful Indian saints: Srila Bhaktivinoda Thakura (1838-1914) and Bhaktisiddanta Sarasvati Goswami Thakura (1874-1936). This is not surprising perhaps, given that India was under British rule between 1776 and 1947. Bhaktivinoda Thakura was a high court magistrate and government officer in Bengal and in Orissa, which were among the highest posts an Indian could hold under British occupation. Some of his writings, such as "Caitanya Mahaprabhu, His life and Precepts"[2] were accepted into the library of the Royal Asiatic Society in London, the library of McGill University in Canada and other institutions. Bhaktivinoda Thakura composed, edited, and published more than 100 books in Sanskrit, Bengali and English, and revived the mission of Gaudiya Vaishnavism: the teachings of Sri Chaitanya Mahaprabhu, a divine personality born in Bengal in 1486 who is believed to be an incarnation of Lord Krishna and His consort Radharani.

Bhaktisiddhanta Saraswati Goswami Thakura, the son of Srila Bhaktivinoda Thakura and founder of the Gaudiya Math, which established 64 temples across India, kept a map of London and meditated on how to preach there. Bhaktisiddhanta's mission was truly international in spirit. On 20 July 1933 the first of his disciples entered Britain, including a *sannyasi* (renounced holy man) known as Bhakti Hriday Bon Maharaj. Not long afterwards, after a concerted effort, the first European preaching centre of any Hindu denomination was established in South Kensington, London under the name "Gaudiya Mission Society of London". Lord Zetland, the English Secretary of State, was the president of this Society. For four years the temple was run by Gaudiya Math members from India, but after lecturing in various places in England and Germany, and after posing for photographs with a number of aristocrats, they returned to their homeland. The property in London was then taken over by an English follower, Miss Daisy Bowtell (Vinode Vani Dasi).

Although a Gaudiya Math centre was indeed established in London, some of his Indian *sannyasi* disciples returned to India, adopting "Western ways" of eating with a knife and fork, even having taken up some of the English diet. Overall, their visits had not been altogether successful. However, this was not going to be the case with A.C Bhaktivedanta Swami Prabhupada, known at that time as Abhay Charan De. During most of Abhay's student days at the acclaimed Scottish Churches College in Calcutta, he was a supporter of the anti-British Gandhi movement. Yet this was not to last. The first time he ever heard Bhaktisiddhanta speak, he asked him: "How can these teachings of Caitanya Mahaprabhu spread around the world when India is occupied by the British?" Bhaktisiddhanta replied that whether one power rules or another, that was temporary and then requested: "…Why don't you preach Lord Caitanya's message throughout the whole world?"[3] Abhay was highly impressed with Bhaktisiddhanta and his instructions remained with him. Years later, in December 1931, Bhaktsiddhanta wrote a letter to Abhay repeating the same message. In 1933, the same year that the first pioneer preachers left India, Bhaktisiddhanta was to initiate Abhay, making him one of his disciples.

After Abhay's family life had come to a natural end, he took to the holy order of renunciation (*sannyasa*), dedicating the rest of his life solely to preaching Krishna Consciousness. Importantly, in 1965 Abhay, then known by his *sannyasi* name of A.C Bhaktivedanta Swami Prabhupada, climbed aboard the Jaladuta cargo ship bound for America.

The Slums of New York [4]

It was 5.30 a.m. on 17 September 1965. The Jaladuta had just docked at Boston's Commonwealth Pier. where it was briefly stopping before proceeding to New York City. The vessel had arrived following a 35 day journey from Calcutta. This was nothing particularly out of the ordinary, apart from one passenger. The small, elderly gentleman with an aristocratic demeanour took his first steps onto Western soil. He wore the traditional saffron robes and had the shaven-head of an Indian holy man. Around his neck were beads made of sandalwood, and in his right hand he carried a small cotton bag, which contained his *japa mala* beads (a type of rosary). A short ponytail hung from the back of his head and he had two parallel vertical lines made from sacred yellow clay on his forehead, the traditional *tilak* or mark of a Vaishnava.

Although he had been born in the middle class suburbs of Calcutta, much of the years spent before his arrival in the West had been in temples of the simple holy town of Vrindavan. Therefore, it is not surprising he found it difficult to relate to his environment whilst passing through US customs and wandering around the commercial area of Boston, which included lobster stands, office buildings, bars, tawdry bookshops, nightclubs and restaurants.

It had already been difficult. Along the rough and painful sea-journey he had barely survived two heart attacks and suffered repeated sea-sickness. Therefore, upon his arrival in America he was feeling physically weak. Two days later, the Jaladuta sailed into New York Harbour and docked at Brooklyn Pier. Swami Prabhupada was on his own and had come to the West against all advice. After all, he was approaching 70 years of age and traditionally members of the *sannyasi* order rarely leave holy places, let alone journey outside India.

After Swami Prabhupada stepped off the ship for the final time, he said: "I didn't know whether to turn left or right."[5] He passed through the dockside formalities. Those in the travel office were struck by the unusual passenger's dress, simple belongings and lack of financial resources, as he only possessed a few hours worth of spending money. His initial plans were to leave after about two months' stay in Butler, Pennsylvania, with his one and only American contact. Instead, after deciding there was sufficient potential to preach in America, he moved to New York and gained a following from his presentations at Dr Mishra's Yoga Society in Uptown Manhattan. After braving a bitter winter wearing his uncompromising robes and continuing to live in abject poverty in the spring of 1966 he moved into a loft space within the notorious Bowery slums.

It could not have been easy for him: drunken tramps lined the streets and drug addicts lay virtually in every crevice. Yet Swami Prabhupada remained aloof, gaining the respect of all who came his way. He was prepared to live wherever his mission would take him, but a reckless young man with whom he was sharing facilities simply became too much: the youth's behaviour under the influence of LSD was intolerable. Disgusted, Swami Prabhupada stormed down the rickety stairs and into the street. Now without even a place to live, he asked one of his followers to move him elsewhere. With the help of a small number of his followers, including Michael Grant (Mukunda Goswami), a property was soon obtained in a relatively better area.

By the summer of 1966 Bhaktivedanta Swami Prabhupada, more affectionately known today as Srila Prabhupada, appeared in front of his congregation in a small former shop-store at 26 Second Avenue in the Lower East Side of Manhattan. This facility had been converted into a small temple with the hard work of interested local inhabitants, mostly young men who had embraced the counter-culture. Amongst the congregation was Allan Ginsberg, the famous poet and icon of the hippy scene. Srila Prabhupada sat down on a thin mat and began playing his small hand cymbals and singing the Hare Krishna mantra, requesting everyone to follow. His audience was more than ready to obey. The world was advancing in science and technology at a rapid pace and cinema, television, fashion, pop music and cars were becoming increasingly accessible to the public. Meanwhile, the cold war, the space race and, most significantly for Americans, the threat of being drafted for Vietnam hung over their heads. This shaped the social conditions out of which the counter-culture emerged and which led many of America's youth to experiment with drugs, often as part of a search for some kind of spiritual experience. Now, some of these youth were sampling something quite unique, for they were chanting the Hare Krishna mantra, the *mahamantra*. Hare Krishna, Hare Krishna, Krishna Krishna, Hare Hare, Hare Rama, Hare Rama, Rama Rama, Hare Hare.

Afterwards Srila Prabhupada began to talk. Despite the busy street outside many stayed to the end of the lecture and intelligent questions often ensued. This was the humble beginning of a brand-new, yet most ancient society. After the lecture, everyone present would be treated to Krishna *prasadam*, sanctified food first offered to Lord Krishna. In the very early days, *prasadam* was simple, but in a short period of time guests were consuming sumptuous vegetarian Indian meals. With Srila Prabhupada overseeing and personally preparing multi-course feasts, news of the delicious sanctified food spread quickly. The availability of free *prasadam* was, and continues to be, one of the most noteworthy reasons for the movement's ability to attract people.

Srila Prabhupada was planning for the long-term future. He was serving his spiritual predecessors and beginning to fulfil the prediction of a spiritual movement prophesised to last for the next 10,000 years.[6] His mission was designed to promote the well being of society by preaching the science of God or Krishna Consciousness in accordance with teachings of the *Bhagavad Gita*, *Srimad Bhagavatam* and other ancient scriptures.

The Hare Krishnas Enter the UK

After gaining a foothold in New York, Srila Prabhupada left for other parts of the United States as well as for Canada, and with the help of his faithful followers he quickly established centres, festivals and communities of disciples in San Francisco, Columbus, Ohio, West Virginia and Montreal. He then returned to India for health reasons as well as to preach with his American disciples. There he asked one of his earliest disciples, Kirtanananda Das, to go to London and seek support from Miss Bowtell. However, Kirtanananda Das chose not to comply, but this minor set back did nothing to hamper Srila Prabhupada's mission.

Soon after he had returned to the West in 1968, whilst he was in Montreal, Srila Prabhupada summoned three married couples who had begun their work at the temple in San Francisco: Mukunda and Janaki, Syamasundar and Malati (with their infant daughter, Sarasvati), and Gurudas and Yamuna. Prabhupada had selected them to set up an ISKCON centre in London and they were most eager to help.

Thirty-five years later, in the summer of 2003, Syamasundar Das, Malati Dasi and Gurudas attended a 30th Anniversary Festival at Bhaktivedanta Manor, the main Hare Krishna temple in the UK. Much of the festival was dominated by remembrances by these pioneer devotees. During one of his talks before hundreds of eager listeners, Syamasundar Das recalled the time when Srila Prabhupada gave them specific instructions:

> ...(I)n 1968 our spiritual master asked us to go to London...The scene, the centre of activity, was shifting from San Francisco to London...There were the Carnaby Street fashions and the Beatles and the Rolling Stones...Prabhupada had always wanted to have a centre in London because he was an Indian in the British Empire. He always thought about London as (a) Wizard of Oz type of city that should have a Krishna temple. So we took off![7]

In the beginning the team of American devotees were so poor that they could not afford to enter Britain in one group: once one couple had entered, they would send their money back to the others. Finding themselves living as separate couples in different parts of London, the young devotees found great inspiration from Srila Prabhupada's regular letters of encouragement. During that time the devotees made a point of attending numerous fashionable venues and distributing thousands of leaflets in Oxford Street. Domestic circumstances, however, were difficult: the devotees being foreigners were not allowed to earn a proper salary and Srila Prabhupada had said he would come to London only when they had opened a temple. After months of living in squalid conditions and relying on members of the local Indian community, an English philanthropist offered rooms in a warehouse complex in Covent Garden. There was no heating, and later often the devotees would recall the cold. Amidst the light-hearted presentation of the

memories of the 30th Anniversary Festival, at one point Malati Dasi stopped
laughing and gravely commented:

> There were indeed many special memories, but actually we should not
> forget something which wasn't so funny. Most of the time in the early days
> it was very hard: often we would go hungry. (We had) hardly any
> possessions, no money, no protection. It often got very cold. We had
> nothing. All we had was love for Srila Prabhupada.[8]

However, despite their austerities eventually good fortune came their way: out
of the blue Syamasundar Das had a call from Rock Skully and members of the
Grateful Dead – his high profile popular music contacts from San Francisco. They
were on their way to a function with the Beatles. Immediately Syamasundar Das
asked if he could come along, and Rock Skully agreed.

After describing how Yoko Ono helped him pass through security,
Syamasundar Das recalled the time when he first met George Harrison:

> (I saw) all famous kinds of people and Ken Keezy and the Hells Angels and
> all these people waiting around to see the Beatles...Suddenly, at one point,
> the door opened and George Harrison stuck his head out, looked around
> the room, put it back...Then he looked out again and saw me over there
> and just walked right through all those people. He came over to me and sat
> down and he said, "Where have you been? I have been waiting to meet you
> people!"[9]

It turned out that Harrison had already heard of the Hare Krishnas on   one of
his visits to San Francisco. He quickly went on to explain that he was chanting
Hare Krishna whilst aboard a plane that was dangerously spiralling downwards.
As soon as he began chanting out loud, the plane safely levelled off again.
Harrison went on to introduce Syamasundar Das to the other Beatles and he was
later to produce the "Radha Krishna Temple" album. Because of this the devotees
sang on Top of the Pops, made a video and even toured pubs and clubs across
Europe. The singles of "The Hare Krishna Mantra" and "Govindam" became hits
across Europe, in Japan, in Australia and even in Africa. Practically overnight the
chanting of Hare Krishna had become world famous.

But Harrison helped ISKCON in so many other ways also. He was later to pay
for the publishing of *Krsna: The Supreme Personality of Godhead*, Srila Prabhupada's
beautifully illustrated book about the activities of Lord Krishna. He even helped
the devotees gain the lease of the first ISKCON temple in Britain, a seven story
building in London's Bury Place near the British Museum. Initially, the Bury Place
property was in a terrible state; so John Lennon asked the devotees if they would
like to stay at his home in Tittenhurst Park near Ascot in Berkshire.
Unsurprisingly, the devotees agreed, and soon they moved into the servants'
quarters and helped with John Lennon and Yoko Ono's revovation projects. Later

the same devotees also spent considerable time at Harrison's Friar Park in Henley-on-Thames and helped with his gardening chores.

After much effort Bury Place was converted into a temple and all the exciting news about the record was more than sufficient to encourage Srila Prabhupada to enter the UK. After landing at Heathrow Airport in September 1969 he was driven to John Lennon's home in a limousine belonging to Apple Records. During his stay on the estate Lennon, Ono and Harrison would meet him. According to Syamasundar Das, Srila Prabhupada was so charming and alluring that he deeply impressed them all.

As the months and years went by more devotees came from America to help with the UK mission, most notably Tamal Krishna Das (soon after to be known as Tamal Krishna Goswami). Copious quantities of books and leaflets were distributed around central London; lectures were organised and much singing and dancing across the West End took place. Meanwhile, many young people moved into Bury Place following all the strict rules incumbent upon devotees.[10] Also with a growing regular congregation it became apparent that the building was much too small.

Yet, once again, Harrison generously assisted, offering to buy the devotees a much larger property in the countryside within easy reach of London. The search for a suitable building got underway. After viewing a number of properties with the devotees Harrison realised that the owners were immediately increasing the price, knowing that the former Beatle could afford it. Not wishing to be cheated Harrison asked devotees to search for a property on their own.

It was a Scottish devotee called Dhananjaya Das, an early British disciple, who discovered Piggotts Manor in Aldenham, four miles from Watford in Hertfordshire. The impressive 17 acre estate was to be renamed Bhaktivedanta Manor after Harrison donated it in 1973. For this most generous donation, as well as for everything else he had done, Srila Prabhupada was extremely pleased with Harrison. The significance of ISKCON acquiring Bhaktivedanta Manor was to have a lasting and profound impact on ISKCON in Britain and beyond, as will be explained later in this chapter.

Although a substantial property was now in the devotees' hands, it was a very expensive building to maintain. By 1974, according to Kripamoya Das, there were still little over 50 full time members who had very little money between them and circumstances were austere.[11] As with the many ISKCON temples opening around the world at that time it was the devotees' love of Srila Prabhupada that made them persevere.

The Hare Krishnas in the 1970s

What initially began as a group of counter-culture youth who had decided to "opt out" of mainstream society quickly developed into a complex and sophisticated world-wide institution. Travelling and preaching continuously, Srila Prabhupada was extraordinarily empowered as well as determined. Yet he was also known to be caring and sensitive, showing respect to everyone. Due to his natural charisma, including a spiritual effulgence, he was able to attract loyal and hard-working followers virtually everywhere he went.

Preaching, austerity, spiritual surrender and solid commitment were high on the lifestyle agenda of ISKCON members. It is reasonable and also unavoidable to say that over the years the movement attracted its fair share of those living on the fringes of society. However, among those joining were highly qualified individuals who were devoted, competent, creative and above all willing to do almost anything for their spiritual master. Some individuals were wealthy too, such as Alfred Ford (Ambarisha Das), great grandson of the legendary Henry Ford of the car company. Srila Prabhupada had a mission to build a foundation for a dynamic spiritual movement on a global scale within a very short time frame. Meanwhile, he was all the time writing and publishing books, which he encouraged his disciples to distribute widely. Sometimes up to 70,000 of Srila Prabhupada's books were distributed in one week in Britain, at one time attaining the highest figures in the ISKCON world. However, it was the Californian Radha Damodar Party, equipped with a fleet of buses and a strong team, who had the highest overall figures. And also in America, it was not only the city streets where the Hare Krishnas were known for distributing books but also in airports all over the country.

Srila Prabhupada knew he did not have long to live and he wanted his more senior disciples to take more responsibility. When he saw evidence of their competence and sincerity he tried to turn affairs over to them so he could concentrate on his mission of presenting all 12 cantos of the *Srimad Bhagavatam*, altogether including 18,000 verses as well as purports (commentary). Out of some of his most committed disciples, Srila Prabhupada created ISKCON's international Governing Body Commission (GBC).

Whoever was sincere, Srila Prabhupada gave him or her a chance, but as the 1970s drew on he sought to tighten standards according to Vedic tradition, especially when elaborate purpose-built ISKCON temples started opening in India. There is much fame and admiration for ISKCON in India today, but initially, when young white devotees entered the country, local inhabitants and even officials sometimes suspected them of being CIA agents in disguise sent to spy on one of the former Soviet Union's allies.

In the first five years of Srila Prabhupada's movement, a remarkable 60 centres in America and Europe had opened. By 1977 there were 108 temples across six continents of the world, including farms with bulls and cows, restaurants, schools, a scientific institute and a book company – the Bhaktivedanta Book Trust. He also inspired a free food distribution programme to the poor and needy across the world: Hare Krishna Food for Life. He established in many major Western cities the Ratha Yatra festival, which originated in ancient Orissa, involving huge decorated chariots that are pulled through the streets.

Srila Prabhupada made over 5,000 disciples of all nationalities, had circled the globe at least 12 times, and countless tapes of his lectures and conversations were made and are still very widely distributed in all media forms. Meanwhile, he was managing and overseeing the entire movement, giving lectures, meeting disciples, journalists, intellectuals, politicians, religious leaders, pop artists and indeed anyone who had the fortune to encounter him.

That in itself was achievement enough, but undoubtedly his most impressive accomplishments were his books. A staggering 62 books have been written by or attributed to him (four of them in Bengali), consisting of English translations and commentary from the original Sanskrit and Bengali texts. His books included the *Bhagavad Gita As It Is*, *Srimad Bhagavatam* (12 cantos), *Caitanya-caritamrita* (in nine large volumes), "Nectar of Instruction" (as *The Nectar of Devotion*) and numerous smaller books. His *Bhagavad Gita As It Is*, is now available in over 60 languages around the world and some of his other books are available in over 80 languages. In addition, his *Back to Godhead* magazine, originally published during the Second World War period in Calcutta, is now a bi-monthly international magazine available in 66 countries, with a distribution of about 570,000 annually, including the Indic language versions.

Towards the end of February 1977, around the time Tamal Krishna Goswami began his secretarial work for Srila Prabhupada,[12] his health was not strong. Even though the 81 year old was still taking walks across ISKCON land in Mayapur, West Bengal,[13] it was not for long. Then Srila Prabhupada's health noticeably deteriorated, as a very serious illness became manifest. Naturally his disciples took shifts to be with him constantly and served him in all ways possible. During that time he could no longer even talk with the devotees. Soon he was left with no strength and was in constant need of help and various medications. Yet, remarkably, as his condition relatively improved he continued to travel, preach and translate the *Srimad Bhagavatam* with great determination.[14]

On 27 August 1977 Srila Prabhupada arrived at Heathrow Airport, "demonstrating miraculous strength to withstand the exhausting ordeal of a 24 hour journey."[15] This was to be his final trip to Britain, and, in fact, anywhere outside India. For the devotees who had been at the airport to meet him it had been a heart-rending experience. Srila Prabhupada himself was composed as ever, but the devotees were shocked to see him extremely thin and carried everywhere on a *palanquin*.

The next morning the temple room of Bhaktivedanta Manor was packed with about 300 disciples and well wishers from all over Europe, waiting to be with Srila Prabhupada. As his frail body was carefully carried down the main stairs of the Manor and into the bustling temple room the devotees began chanting and dancing energetically. As Srila Prabhupada admired the temple room's shrine, which included the deities of Radha Gokulananda, streams of tears emerged from behind his sunglasses which he was wearing due to his condition.

During Janmashtami (when Krishna's birthday or appearance day is celebrated) that year, two weeks after landing in Britain, a Rolls Royce transported Srila Prabhupada to the Bury Place temple in central London. Entering the building, Srila Prabhupada came before Radha London-Ishvara, the first deities of Radha and Krishna in ISKCON. Slowly, he removed the sunglasses and once again his eyes flooded with tears, as all around him devotees danced and chanted. In the last crucial chapter of Srila Prabhupada's life, he was to show enormous affection not only for the deities, but also for his faithful disciples who served him to the very end.

The next day, back at the Manor, Srila Prabhupada's health suddenly became worse and instead of going on to America as planned, he now requested that he be taken back to India. He was particularly eager to see the progress at the impressive temple project in Bombay, which he and his disciples had fought so hard to establish. Soon after that, he was taken to the holy town of Vrindavan. There Srila Prabhupada's body became so weak he could not even move by himself. Yet, with a Dictaphone held close to his mouth, he miraculously continued to translate and comment on the *Srimad Bhagavatam*. Then, as the devotees solemnly chanted, Srila Prabhupada departed this world at 7.25 p.m. on 14 November 1977.

Two Major Splinter Groups since the Demise of Srila Prabhupada

After the demise of such a personality as Srila Prabhupada, naturally many devotees were completely devastated. For many, life would simply never be the same again. Bearing these circumstances in mind, it was perhaps inevitable that leadership controversies in ISKCON would follow and Srila Prabhupada himself predicted this. Much has been documented on the subject and it is discussed by Tamal Krishna Goswami.[16] However, the main points of this topic are worth summarising in this chapter because of their significance in the movement's history.

Six months previous to his departure, Srila Prabhupada had announced that he would appoint 11 of his disciples to perform initiations on his behalf. It was clear that Srila Prabhupada intended these 11 devotees to become gurus in their own right after his departure, but what was not so clear was whether or not he wanted them then to become the only initiating gurus in ISKCON. Although it is now felt this was not his intention, that was the way things developed. At the time it was believed that Srila Prabhupada had selected the 11 most senior and qualified devotees in the movement more or less jointly to inherit the position of *acharya*.

Shortly after Srila Prabhupada's passing, the 11 gurus continued to initiate but this time the new disciples were their own. As a result, managerially they assumed an extraordinary position above all others, including the non-guru GBC members. This was based on charismatic and autocratic systems of authority in separate zones in the world. For example, Bhagavan Das' (then Goswami's) zone included Britain, Belgium, France, Spain, Greece, South Africa and, because of his origin, the city of Detroit. In the temple communities within the respective zones, their status was practically elevated to that of Srila Prabhupada's.

For a time the systems were successful. Within their respective areas, zonal gurus managed to increase ISKCON's growth and create a sense of unity between devotees, which, in some ways, is still unmatched today. Also, the chanting processions in the cities of Britain and other Western countries were most orderly and frequent.

Whilst most disciples of the new gurus found nothing strange with the new arrangement, many disciples of Srila Prabhupada who were not gurus became increasingly alarmed. The zonal *acharyas* were still young men with much less spiritual and material status than their predecessor. Their spiritual status in the institution also gave them considerable managerial power. Although their contributions to ISKCON's mission were immense, when some of them had spiritual shortcomings the impact was devastating because large numbers of disgruntled devotees left the movement. For example, when in 1986 the disciples of Bhagavan Goswami learned that their spiritual master had given up his *sannyasi* and guru status, it damaged many devotees' faith in the movement as a whole.

After a global policy adjustment in 1987 gurus were then free to initiate in any zone, but their authority was tied to the GBC. The move was designed to re-establish Srila Prabhupada, via the GBC, as the head of a unified ISKCON. Thus, the vast majority of initiating spiritual masters (*diksha* gurus[17]) – and there are now around 70 worldwide – presently work under local management, and the reverence they receive is considerably less than before.

The Ritviks

However, despite the series of adjustments that have been steadily taking place since 1987, for some it appears too late to restore their faith in the GBC and any kind of ISKCON leadership. The guru troubles of the 1980s led some disgruntled former members to adapt what is informally known as the *ritvik* philosophy. Adherents of this theory currently identify themselves as the ISKCON Revival/Reform Movement or IRM. Their position is that Srila Prabhupada can continue to initiate disciples even after his demise. This view claims that by appointing *ritvik* priests (those who preside over a Vedic ceremony on their spiritual master's behalf), Srila Prabhupada meant that he did not want any of his disciples to become gurus at any stage in the future; and the IRM endeavour to support their position by quoting from ambiguous conversations and correspondence of Srila Prabhupada, particularly a letter written in July 1977 by Tamal Krishna as Srila Prabhupada's secretary.[18] ISKCON's GBC, however, adheres to the traditional understanding of the principle of disciplic succession, a principle expressed throughout Srila Prabhupada's books, involving the ongoing process of initiation through a physically present guru. It is significant that the *ritvik* position, namely that only Srila Prabhupada should be an initiating guru, has no genuine backing in Vedic tradition as interpreted by ISKCON. Senior members of the Gaudiya Math once organised a meeting to discuss the validity of the *ritvik* position, but it was dismissed after just ten minutes. The principle of having a physical guru is a cultural necessity in the *bhakti* tradition and not a topic for extensive theological discussion.

To those familiar with the principle of *parampara* (disciplic succession), the philosophy indeed appears odd, given that Srila Prabhupada would have made it obvious if he wanted to invent a new system. The GBC have also pressed the point that Srila Prabhupada consistently said that disciples would themselves one day become spiritual masters. The book *100 Deviations of Ritvikism* authored by the disciples of Jayapataka Swami[19] goes into detail about the flaws in the IRM position. But from the point of view of ISKCON leadership, it is slanderous and over-critical behaviour that discredits the IRM most: it appears many members outside of India are more preoccupied with fault-finding and dissention than with practically assisting in Srila Prabhupada's mission.

From the ISKCON standpoint it is believed that Srila Prabhupada was potent enough to create disciples to be *diksha* or initiating gurus. If some of his more advanced disciples have only been able to capture a small fraction of this potency, it is sufficient to qualify them to perform initiations. Suffice it to say, there are thousands of disciples of successful *diksha* gurus today; and their role is to keep Srila Prabhupada's mood, his personality and his teachings at the forefront of the mission. In fact, ISKCON temples, such as in Chowpatty (Mumbai) and the Hungarian farm community, are extremely successful because of the presence of a local spiritual master, demonstrating devotees benefit from the presence of strong local leadership, especially since they oversee standards and provide unity and guidance.

The GBC itself has developed a great deal since its early days. Today there are 36 main members and 20 deputies, with a wealth of experience, who have managerial authority over all the gurus. If or when there is a need for further adaptation it is felt the GBC will be able to act accordingly.

Narayana Maharaja

The IRM is not the only group that has branched away from ISKCON: 15 years after Srila Prabhupada's departure there was one personality who became particularly controversial: Bhaktivedanta Narayana Maharaja, a disciple of Srila Prabhupada's *sannyasi* guru. Learned, austere and a long-time resident of Vrindavan, he has disclosed how Srila Prabhupada asked him to help ISKCON devotees after his departure. However, today ISKCON devotees are not encouraged to take his association or the association of many of his followers.

Irvin Collins writes in some depth about the issue concerning Narayana Maharaja in "The Routinization of Charisma and the Charismatic: The Confrontation between ISKCON and Narayana Maharaja."[20] His concluding reflections suggest that the institution of ISKCON is possibly being counter-productive by not being more open to the likes of Narayana Maharaja. However, it can be argued that ISKCON has highly valid reasons to keep him at a distance; for in the aforementioned essay Tamal Krishna Goswami describes how Narayana

Maharaja became a problem for ISKCON:

> When invited by ISKCON to a number of public functions, (Narayana
> Maharaja) frankly proclaimed that ISKCON devotees should not remain
> neophyte, clinging simply to rules and regulations, but should follow the
> path of spontaneous devotion. His emphasis on *gopi-bhava*, the mood of
> Krishna's amorous cowherd lovers, particularly disturbed his ISKCON
> audiences who were conscious of so many warnings from Prabhupada.
> Prabhupada had stressed that the path of spontaneous devotion was only
> for liberated souls...Once a practitioner became purified of all material
> inebriates, spontaneous devotion would automatically manifest [itself]...

Furthermore, correspondence by Srila Prabhupada, such as a letter written in
1974, increased caution over Narayana Maharaja within some ISKCON circles:

> Actually amongst my God brothers no one is qualified to become *acarya*. So
> it is better not to mix with my God brothers very intimately because instead
> of inspiring our students and disciples they may sometimes pollute
> them...We shall be very careful about them and not mix with them. This is
> my instruction to you all. They cannot help us in our movement, but they
> are very competent to harm our natural progress...[21]

Tensions came to a head when Narayana Maharaja publicly stated there were
many higher teachings that Srila Prabhupada did not give, and ISKCON devotees
were now ready for a more advanced stage of Krishna Consciousness, which he
could give. In addition, some ISKCON devotees had claimed to have identified
differences in Narayana Maharaja's position regarding certain details of the Vedic
accounts, as well as his global perspective in general. The GBC concluded that
Narayana Maharaja's teachings were in danger of eclipsing those of Srila
Prabhupada and decided matters had gone too far. But the controversy increased
even further when Narayana Maharaja began to tour the West in the late 1990s.
His first visits to Britain and Holland were arranged by disenchanted former
members of ISKCON. Evidently, the functions were solely aimed at attracting an
ISKCON audience because Narayana Maharaja would often lecture close to the
temple communities.

Although Narayana Maharaja praised Srila Prabhupada's remarkable
achievements and expressed his desire to unify ISKCON, temple presidents
everywhere as well as the GBC considered his tour to be anything but unifying. By
the time his first tour had ended dozens of ISKCON members had aligned
themselves with him in Europe, in Australia and in North America. From
ISKCON's perspective, there is nothing technically wrong with Narayana
Maharaja acquiring followers; after all, he is undoubtedly qualified. Yet, he would
not only adopt disciples of ISKCON gurus who had fallen, he would adopt
rebellious disciples of gurus in good standing, as well as disciples even of Srila

Prabhupada. Often this led to Narayana Maharaja giving them a new spiritual name, apparently involving some form of re-initiation. Yet, if some type of re-initiation has been carried out, this would be a gross transgression of etiquette according to Vedic tradition, even if the disciple's original *diksha* guru is no longer present. However, at the time of writing tensions between the ISKCON and the Narayana Maharaja camps appear to be dwindling. Today it seems likely that they will be able to co-exist and in a condition of mutual respect.

Some Concluding Thoughts on ISKCON's Guru Issues

It is sometimes tempting to compare the Narayana Maharaja issue with the IRM issue. After all, most members of both groups are not likely to have emerged were it not for ISKCON's existence in the first place. Members of both groups in their own ways are clearly missing the personality of Srila Prabhupada. Both groups have certainly lost faith in high-level ISKCON management, and yet to some they may paradoxically appear to be the same as ISKCON.

Today ISKCON's approach to addressing the existence of the two splinter groups is further to centralise the position of Srila Prabhupada. The movement was, after all, founded by him and ISKCON leaders have faith that he taught everything necessary to achieve Krishna Consciousness. As a way of securing Srila Prabhupada's position but also maintaining the disciplic succession, some have referred to examples from within other Vaishnava traditions. One example being suggested as a source of ideas is the position of Ramanuja, a great figure of the Sri Sampradaya who passed away in the 10th century CE. Despite the fact that there are many other *diksha* gurus who succeeded him, Ramanuja himself retains the position of spiritual master and principal teacher to the current disciples of that tradition.

This mood placed within the context of ISKCON would mean Srila Prabhupada is seen as the unquestionable *shiksha* (transmission of spiritual instruction), the pure devotee guru of the community, with ISKCON members initiating and creating followers for his movement. Therefore, whether or not an initiating guru is held to be fallible or infallible is not the central issue because Srila Prabhupada's original teachings are available to all, and it is the mission of the relatively advanced devotees to follow and to present such teachings to their juniors. (It must be added, however, that the teachings of Ramanuja naturally differ from the Gaudiya Vaishnava tradition; thus mimicking other successions such as this one is not likely to provide the complete solution to ISKCON's guru issues.)

In the future the reverence given to ISKCON's *diksha* gurus is likely to lessen somewhat further, mainly because the role of *shiksha* leaders or local figures of spiritual authority is more practical and consequently is likely to become more prominent. With more "approachable" gurus in the movement's system it will become easier for senior devotees with guru potential outside of the everyday management structure to be able to step forward and make disciples, thus helping to fulfil some of ISKCON's local ministerial obligations. It is interesting to note here that during the GBC meetings of March 2005 no objection was expressed regarding the principle of having female gurus. But, regardless of the gender issue, as the number of lay members increases relative to full time temple residents, all *sannyasi*s, all gurus, as well as senior temple managers and temple residents themselves, will remain under pressure to be particularly exemplary as well as to work under the authority of the GBC. If the right processes of selection, standardisation, accountability and training continue to develop at the present rate, there is every reason to believe ISKCON will augment its effective guru system in the future. However, some experienced devotees believe a good deal of work still needs to be completed in this area.

Trials Specific to ISKCON in Britain: Two Leadership Case Studies

This section concentrates now on two significant episodes within ISKCON's history in England, which occurred since Srila Prabhupada's demise. These two examples, I believe, in many ways represent the contrast between the autocratic system that was in place throughout the early-to-mid-1980s, and a "flatter", localised management system, which has become dominant today.

The first example, Case One, is the account of ISKCON's temporary possession of Croome Court which, I would argue, exposes how an entire community suffered because of one or two individuals possessing a disproportionate amount of power over a property utilised by a wide community of devotees. In contrast, Case Two is a description of the campaign to save Bhaktivedanta Manor from closure, which involved not only a responsible temple president, but also teams of ISKCON managers working together to empower the congregation for a clear and unified purpose. Needless to say perhaps, Case One was an unsuccessful project whilst Case Two was not only successful but is often held responsible for placing ISKCON in Britain in a far stronger position that it had experienced previously. Perhaps much can be learnt from these case histories, particularly if one is to understand how the movement might continue to prosper in the future.

Case One: ISKCON's Former British HQ: Chaitanya College

By 1979, as recruitment increased, conditions for devotees were getting far too crowded at Bhaktivedanta Manor. Sri Pati Das, an early Srila Prabhupada disciple, recalls how the devotional community dealt with this problem:

> By 1979 lots of people were joining as a result of a vibrant recruitment programme in London. Jaya Tirtha, the UK zonal *acharya* of the time, found Croome Court near Worcester. The building was historically famous because it had been constructed by Lancelot "Capability" Brown in the mid

18th century and has been the residence of former Earls of Coventry. The impressive estate included a chapel, a stable, a walled garden containing fruits and flowers from around the world, and historical paintings of former earls adorned the main building.[22]

The property was for sale at a good price and Jaya Tirtha Swami liked it. The funds were available so ISKCON quickly snapped it up. Devotees had found a gap in the British market for importing oil paintings, and high book sales added to the income. Croome Court very quickly became ISKCON's British headquarters and was renamed Chaitanya College. The chapel was immediately turned into the temple room. The printing press was moved to the site, as were the Bhaktivedanta Book Trust, the ISKCON British administration, including a novice training programme and a school. Naturally all the householders moved from the community around Bhaktivedanta Manor to the Worcester area, since their children were attending the new school. In one part of Croome Court, the devotees even installed a television editing studio. In the city of Worcester itself some devotees ran a branch of the International Spiritual Sky company, selling incense, oils and candles. Meanwhile, the Manor was left as a preaching centre and continued to cultivate the Indian community.

About 150 devotees lived on the premises of Chaitanya College, including *brahmcharis* (monks), *brahmacharins* (nuns) and some married couples. Most married couples lived in the suburbs of Worcester. At the weekends hundreds of Western guests would go there to view the historical buildings, but they were also taken on tours of impressive exhibitions focused on Krishna Consciousness. The preaching initiative was looking very good. Around that period, pop singer Boy George began to befriend the devotees, who later helped him to become free from his heroine addiction.

But the dream was not to last, for in 1982 Jaya Tirtha was asked to leave ISKCON for behaving most inappropriately. He took many of his disciples with him, which resulted in a shortage of manpower and funds for ISKCON in Britain. Rukmini Ramana Das recalls the sequence of events that followed:

> When Jaya Tirtha left Bhagavan came along as the new zonal *acharya*, but inheriting a depleted community. Bhagavan then decided to shift many of the operations taking place at Chaitanya College to other parts of the country.

An anonymous devotee felt that the reason why Bhagavan decentralised Chaitanya College was because a growing number of members there did not fully accept his authority. Rukmini Ramana Das, who did not necessarily agree with that hypothesis, makes mention of the financial difficulties experienced at the time:

> Meanwhile, the lucrative painting sales explosion had taken a dive because of growing competition. The devotees had made a major investment in a large fleet of expensive cars in order to make a good impression to customers. When sales declined, young devotees were burdened with a whole fleet of these expensive-to-run cars! To make matters worse, some bright spark had the idea of making a big investment in carpet sales, but the business failed miserably!
>
> Chaitanya College gradually became too great a financial weight to maintain...and so, despite all the valiant fund-raising efforts, regretfully, in June 1984, ISKCON withdrew from the property. I can't remember how much we sold it for, but we made a significant loss in the deal. With the closure of the school, many families tried to move back to...(Bhaktivedanta) Manor... but that proved difficult for some and not only was the community scattered, morale was severely damaged.[23]

Case Two: The Indian Community and Bhaktivedanta Manor

Undoubtedly, one of the most significant developments in the history of ISKCON in Britain is the massive cultivation of the Indian community. The 2001 Census[24] reveals there is a Hindu population of 559,000 in the UK, though according to the National Council of Hindu Temples (NCHT)[25] the actual figure is as high as 600,000. (Interestingly, the Census states that 1.3 per cent of Hindus are white indigenous persons.) According to 1991 estimates, about 70 per cent of Hindus in the UK are Gujarati,[26] many of whom are brought up to revere Lord Krishna as their principal Deity. This fact has been fundamental to ISKCON's expansion in Britain.

In an important article on the topic Malory Nye[27] gives reasons why the Indian community began to attend the festivals at Bhaktivedanta Manor, and impressively in their tens of thousands. He correctly indicates that the temple is within good driving distance of north London. There are about 40,500 Hindus living in nearby Harrow, and about 40 per cent of the Manor's congregation are resident in that area. Also, the Manor's facilities outmatched Hindu temples more local to them and the rural location is an attractive feature. Moreover, Nye adds that the commitment of the white British devotees also impressed the Indian community. In another key article Nye acknowledges the significance of deity worship at Bhaktivedanta Manor:

> On the level of public worship, the worship at ISKCON temples is of an extremely high standard. Because of the training facilities at Bhaktivedanta Manor and...(ISKCON's)...high number of full-time followers (supported by ISKCON without any other work commitments), there is a pool of well

trained *pujari*s who have the ability to serve the temple deities very well throughout the day.[28]

Indeed, presently there are about 15 full and part time devotees who work throughout the week on an activity directly connected to the Manor's altar or *pujari* service. If the volunteers are included, there are some 25 devotees on any given week. Nye further states:

> ...(W)hen young British Hindus of Indian ancestry go to ISKCON temples, the devotees... can talk to them in depth about their religion in English...[29]

Yet, despite Nye's important observations here, in "Hare Krishna and Sanatan Dharma in Britain: The Campaign for Bhaktivedanta Manor", he says, "...for various reasons (not all of which are clear) they were drawn to the style of ISKCON worship."[30] In terms of my own experience at the Manor over the last 12 years I would suggest three additional reasons for its on-going appeal to the Indian community, an appeal which remains very highly pronounced:

1) The lively *kirtan*s (singing and chanting in praise of a deity) and *bhajan*s (hymns or classical religious songs) create a happy and enthusiastic atmosphere of worship.

2) Organising festivals has always been a strength for ISKCON practically anywhere in the world. Especially when there is land and resources, generally devotees know how to merge spirituality and entertainment with drama, dance, multi-media presentations, *prasadam* (sacred food) distribution and so on.

3) Pro-active and extensive preaching to the Indian community by means of mail-outs, door-to-door calls, house visits, leaflets and messages relayed by word of mouth have been fundamental. In particular, the Manor–based Indian preaching department under the headship of Sruti Dharma Das and Pranabandhu Das stands out.

The Campaign to Save Bhaktivedanta Manor

By the late 1970s attendance at Bhaktivedanta Manor began to increase very significantly. For example, only 253 pilgrims were counted at the Janmashtami festival in 1975. However, by 1979 the figure climbed to about 3,000. Tension between ISKCON and the local Hertsmere Borough Council began soon afterwards, when Hertsmere officials issued an enforcement notice banning all public festivals at the Manor. An agreement was signed allowing six events a year, which involved more than 1,000 visitors.

But, as numbers steadily continued to increase, some local villagers of Letchmore Heath and the Council itself felt uneasy with this arrangement. In 1986 there was a count of 2,600 cars and coaches driving through the village, bringing over 12,000 visitors over the two day festival period. In 1987, it rose to at least 16,000 visitors. Clearly intimidated, the following year the Council issued an enforcement notice with the aim of preventing all visitors to the Manor.

Such action by the Council seemed extreme from ISKCON's perspective, especially considering it was a successful place of public worship. Yet on the six major festival days the residents of Letchmore Heath were experiencing miles of traffic jams outside their own front doors, leading to major congestion in the country lanes. Other reasons most likely to have contributed were diminishing house prices in the village, ISKCON's dress code and cultish image, festival noise levels and elements of racial prejudice. Also, what contributed towards the local paranoia was the fact that a few Indian and Western devotee families moved into the area, which culminated in the devotees running the only shop in the village.

Public Inquiries over the use of Bhaktivedanta Manor were held in 1988 and in 1989, with temple president Akhandadhi Das bearing the legal brunt. After the then Secretary of State for the Environment, Chris Patten MP, favoured the Council's position, circumstances were looking bleak for the temple. However, support from the Indian community and some indigenous community members meanwhile grew stronger by the day. For example, in 1990 the Hare Krishna Temple Defence Movement (HKTDM) was formed. By 1991 Janmashtami festival attendance had more than doubled in four years, reaching some 36,000 visitors to the Manor.

ISKCON decided to take their case to the Court of Appeal, but that too proved fruitless. Thus, the Manor was given a two year grace period, after which, on 16 March 1994, public worship at the Manor would be illegal. Yet by this time MPs had received hundreds of letters from the Hindu community and over 100 MPs of all parties had joined the list of Manor supporters. There were protest marches and some temple devotees even fasted for days. There was also activity abroad, including massive demonstrations of Indians taking place outside British embassies around the world: in India, USA, South Africa, and Australia.

With the build up to, and in the aftermath of, what become known as the Campaign March, the tables started to turn in ISKCON's favour. Politicians, including Tony McNulty MP, Glenys Kinnok (wife of Neil Kinnok, Leader of the Labour Party at the time), and Keith Vaz MP openly supported the campaign. Local Hertsmere Councillor Frank Ward played a crucial role, putting his full energy into the campaign to save the temple. In early 1994, the youth wing Pandava Sena (meaning the army of the Pandavas – heroes of the *Mahabharat*) was set up to mobilise young Hindus to support the campaign. The very concept of having their beloved place of worship closed was abhorrent to the Indian youth, especially given that most of them were born in the UK.

Then, in the middle of March 1994 36,000 people gathered in central London. People came from all over the country, including 150 coaches from Hindu temples. The young and the old, Hindus, Jains, Sikhs and ISKCON devotees marched together in a powerful statement of solidarity behind ISKCON. It was the birth of a different Hare Krishna movement in Britain. This was certainly no minority religious cult: this was something for the British government and the world to take notice of. The march was acknowledged as the first historical large scale Hindu protest outside India. Outside the Houses of Parliament many members of the crowd, including the elderly, blocked the traffic by sitting in the road. Mike Wooldridge, the BBC Religious Correspondent at the time, gave a live broadcast on Radio 4. "This is an historical event", he announced, and then added: "I've never seen anything like it – it's the first time I've ever seen Hindu ladies being dragged across the road by policemen in front of Parliament". One devotee present was Bhavesh Patel, a young recruit of the Pandava Sena. He recalled the experience:

> I felt it was the most amazing day of my life...I have never been in such an atmosphere of absolute unity. Everyone had one thing in mind, "deal (with) and eradicate this travesty of justice!"...Everywhere I looked I could see people shouting and screaming, old ladies crying and even attacking police, not due to their malice but due to their fear that their place of worship was going to be removed from them...Without doubt I was fortunate enough to be part of history that day.[31]

In Trafalgar Square, Akhandadhi Das addressed the vast crowd with good news: "The Council has bowed to you. They are feeling the pressure...Last night they told me that the gates of the temple can remain open until they consider our application for a new access road!" [32] There was roaring cheer as well as applause.

By then ISKCON had entered into negotiations to purchase adjacent land with a view to building an access road. The idea was to link the Manor to the A41, therefore diverting the flow of festival traffic away from the village of Letchmore Heath. After great endeavour and considerable expense, the land for the new driveway had been acquired. Yet, despite what the planning experts recommended, still the politicians at Hertsmere rejected it. To make matters worse, the temple was prosecuted for observing the Janmashtami festival in 1994. This made ISKCON the first religious community in England in the last 300 years to be prosecuted for observing a rite of worship. Meanwhile, sympathetic national and international media attention was given to the issue, especially from the BBC, and from Asian and local press.

The following year ISKCON entered into yet another appeal to the Department of the Environment. This was followed by a Public Inquiry which took more than six months to be completed. By that time, the temple had explored every avenue it could and effectively its very existence hung on the result.

Then, on one ordinary day in May 1996 Akhandadhi Das and other members of the temple management arrived at Bhaktivedanta Manor from Hertsmere Borough Council offices, all of them appearing with broad smiles on their faces. After Akhandadhi Das had hastily gathered key devotees, they all entered Srila Prabhupada's personal quarters and bowed down to his *murti* (sacred statue).

Akhandadhi Das, letter in hand, then declared the news: the Department of the Environment John Gummer MP had granted planning permission for Bhaktivedanta Manor to construct an access road and to remain a place of public worship and religious festivals!

Today, an astonishing figure of some 60,000 pilgrims flock to Bhaktivedanta Manor during the Janmashtami festival period and without hindrance. With the new land, the estate has grown from the initial 17 acres to a generous 97 acres (including 20 acres of rented land). The campaign itself also increased the fame of ISKCON and has won the respect of the media, politicians, interfaith groups and Hindu communities across the world. It is also significant that today the temple community has a much improved relationship with the Hertsmere Council. Because of the faith, hard work and unity of the devotee community, victory was finally achieved and ISKCON took a major step forward in its remarkable history.

ISKCON Today: Some Key Global Patterns and Trends

Despite the challenges ISKCON has faced since the passing of the immense figure of Srila Prabhupada, his movement has continued to grow around the world in a variety of ways. ISKCON today is a worldwide confederation of more than 400 centres, including 60 farm communities (half of which are aiming for self-sufficiency), 50 schools and 60 restaurants. In India expansion has unsurprisingly perhaps been the most rapid. Today there are about 60 temples and some 10 farm communities in the sub-continent, the largest temples being in Mayapur (ISKCON world headquarters in West Bengal), Vrindavan, Delhi and Mumbai. A member of the temple community informed me that on an average day, the Mayapur complex receives about 5,000 guests. At weekends and on public holidays he said the numbers passing through increase to 75,000. On its main festival days, such as Gaura Purnima, Lord Chaitanya's birthday, as many as 150,000 pilgrims are expected – about 5,000 among them travelling from abroad to stay at the site. It is also culturally significant that ISKCON Mayapur is now helping to renovate and revitalise the local Gaudiya Vaishnava temples.

Moreover, according to reliable estimates given to me by a member of the Krishna Balaram temple in Vrindavan, the temple receives between 15,000 and 20,000 visitors during Janmashtami, 12,000 during Diwali and an average of 4,000 visitors every Sunday. The Mumbai figures provided to me by a member there are truly huge: he suggests a figure of 700,000 for the number of guests who flow through the temple premises to pray during Janmashtami, and 40,000 for Sundays and other festivals. Given these figures, it is hardly surprising that in 1988 the former Prime Minister of India, A.B Vajpayee stated in his inaugural address at the opening of the ISKCON temple in New Delhi:

> The ISKCON movement has few parallels in the world in terms of its rapid
> global spread; its transnational, transethnic, and transprofessional appeal; its
> outward simplicity; and the devotional energy of its followers. In the less

than three and one half decades since its inception it has established temples in practically all parts of the world and many of them are marvels of beauty, such as the one that is being opened in Delhi today.[33]

Furthermore, Food for Life, ISKCON's free vegetarian food distribution programmes for the homeless and disadvantaged, served at least 900 million meals between 1966-95 in 60 countries. Today it averages about 50,000 plates per day globally. That figure does not include free meals served at public festivals, at temples, or during substantial relief operations such as in Sri Lanka and Tamil Nadu following the Tsunami wave disaster that struck at the end of 2004. One of the most active Food for Life programmes is within the ISKCON temple in Vrindavan. Twice a day, seven days a week, many poverty-stricken inhabitants are treated to a free meal at the temple. In addition, devotees visit local villages where there are no doctors or medical facilities. Also, sweet drinking water is supplied to villages, benefiting more than 40,000 people.

Between 1965 and 2004, according to Bhaktivedanta Book Trust (BBT) calculations, a staggering 448 million of Srila Prabhupada's books have been distributed worldwide. Bhaktivedanta Library Services (BLS) based in Belgium have just over 2,000 separate items available in their catalogue, 636 of which are Srila Prabhupada's books and include literature produced by various ISKCON authors. Other items regularly sold by ISKCON include the likes of CDs, CD ROMs, audio-tapes, instruments, incense, clothes, images of deities and many other devotional items.

Other ISKCON assets include a hospital near Mumbai, smaller meeting centres, the Bhaktivedanta Institute (started in 1974 and comprised of high academic achievers, particularly in scientific fields), and other notable academic institutions. Adding to the hospital's credentials is the large team of doctors and other specialists who have taken part in much important relief work in India, for instance in the immediate aftermath of the Gujarat earthquake in 2001 and Tsunami disaster in 2004.

Public festivals of all types also continue to be organised or attended by ISKCON members. Notably, devotees are always present at the UK's largest rock festival of Glastonbury, which in June 2004 was attended by 150,000 participants. At this event, "Hare Krishna" is nearly always associated with free vegetarian food. This is not surprising given that thousands of plates are served there every year. The same team of devotees have toured east Africa extensively and have opened schools in Kenya and in Uganda.

In the USA ISKCON youth (mostly graduates from the movement's schools) complete an annual 13,600 mile journey over two months. In 2004 they toured 18 ISKCON temples and set up nine Ratha Yatra public festivals in cities across the country. Today Ratha Yatra is celebrated in 200 cities around the world. For example, about 3,000 people join the annual procession from London's Hyde Park to Trafalgar Square, and about 10,000 attend the festival events in Trafalgar Square itself.

The British Isles

No longer an insular monastic-based society, temples in Britain tend to prioritise receiving guests from a variety of backgrounds and levels of commitment. In the remote Inisrath community in Northern Ireland, Open Days can receive upward of 1,000 paying visitors. In fact, I was told by a community member that in the days when the tension between Catholics and Protestants was at fever-pitch, the ISKCON centre was perceived as a peaceful "neutral ground" and attracted considerable numbers to their festivals.

Devotees from the strategically placed temple on Soho Street in central London host thousands of people who make frequent visits to the temple or restaurant there. However, as indicated earlier, it is the festival of Janmashtami at Bhaktivedanta Manor which is particularly noteworthy. Such is the significance of this event that in September 2004 the House of Commons held a function in this connection, and it was attended by 300 leaders and representatives from ISKCON and the British Hindu community, along with the Deputy Prime Minister, Ministers, MPs, Peers, the Indian High Commissioner and the Mayor of London. This is in addition to the annual Diwali function that is also observed in the House of Commons and in which ISKCON plays a dominant role. In 2003 Prime Minister Tony Blair himself inaugurated proceedings by lighting the Diwali candles.

In the summer at Bhaktivedanta Manor there can be thousands of Sunday guests visiting at some time on the day, and there are special Open Days, courses and workshops, aimed mostly at local indigenous people who can now be attracted in their hundreds. On a week day in summer sometimes hundreds of guests receive a free lunch, as do the thousands of people who attend the many civil traditional Vedic weddings. Moreover, there is an average of 60 school children at any one time on 150 separate annual visits to the Manor. Today ISKCON has one of the loudest voices in Hinduism when it comes to the British school curriculum. For example, about 1,000 schools across the country possess ISKCON's *Heart of Hinduism* educational resource pack.[34]

Across the UK today the Pandava Sena youth group have listed around 5,000 names on their database. Of these 500 are regularly participating in Krishna Consciousness functions, and between 50-75 represent the core group. This makes the Pandava Sena the largest religious Indian youth group in Europe, with most of its members based in and around London and Birmingham. There are branches abroad, including in countries such as Holland, the US, South Africa, Malaysia, Australia and Singapore. It is also noteworthy that, although most members of the Pandava Sena are Asian, the number of Western members is steady increasing.

For many years ISKCON prioritised the distribution of Prabhupada's books on the street and elsewhere. This was construed to be more pleasing to Srila Prabhupada and it is estimated that over 25 million of Srila Prabhupada's books have been distributed in Britain.[35] To date, if one includes magazines and pamphlets and such like there have been about 50 million pieces of literature distributed in Britain. Book distribution in Britain and in other Western countries has slowed down since the early days, but that has been replaced by many other activities, such as ministerial outreach, communications work, education, training and farming. It is noteworthy, however, that Scottish devotees have gained the reputation for the largest book distribution in the UK, and it seems many of them continue with similar vigour today.

In British Homes

In chapter one of Kim Knott's *My Sweet Lord*, one finds a description of the stereotypical Hare Krishna chanting party:

> ...(A) movement in the crowd a little further on, the strains of a melody, a flash of orange...here they are, the Oxford Street chanting party, the men in orange robes, their heads shaved but for a topknot or ponytail of hair...[36]

Her words will be striking to many devotees today because she highlights what so many are aware has changed: the "flashes of orange" on the processions represent only a tiny minority of Hare Krishnas and the processions themselves are less frequent than before. Although the stereotypical Hare Krishna image remains, the fact is that ISKCON members have become far more family-orientated and household-based. Labelling the Hare Krishnas as shaven-headed monks in saffron is perhaps akin to the regular Catholic being labelled a member of the Benedictine order: it is quite simply out of date and inaccurate. At any function today, unlike the early days of the movement, people are not in any way obliged to join a temple themselves. "There is no need to live in a temple," devotees will say, "as you can practise Krishna Consciousness anywhere."

In Britain today there are literally thousands of devotees and former devotees, many of them coming from Western backgrounds who have spent some time in an ISKCON temple in the past 30 or so years. It is also widely acknowledged that there are ISKCON sympathisers about whom little is known. There are also those who have read Srila Prabhupada's books, met devotees at festivals or eaten *prasadam* (sanctified food) and who greatly respect ISKCON's philosophy, but who have perhaps never even visited a Hare Krishna temple.

Naturally, today there are various levels of involvement. Amongst the more than 1,000 people who have so far undergone initiation in Britain, there has always been a core of temple regulars, but it is true to say there are also hundreds of initiates who are rarely seen in a temple. There are also many who do not necessarily strongly identify themselves with any particular temple or devotee peer group but who still believe in Krishna as presented by ISKCON, individuals who may also chant the Hare Krishna mantra and who may remain vegetarian. Indeed, to state that they are spiritually redundant would be seen as a great insult to a devotee who lived a distance from a temple community. Here one could be accused of having a narrow and superficial view of Srila Prabhupada's mission.

As well as temples, there are groups of devotees who meet in each other's houses on a regular basis. Today it hardly raises an eyebrow if a devotee moves out of the temple to get married or to do otherwise. It is not seen as reprehensible in any way regarding the institution's mission. After all, devotees with jobs can potentially bring in money for projects, have skills and better understand the psychology of the general public and how to share some degree of Krishna Consciousness with them – and these are all very much respected in ISKCON today.

Exploring the subject of congregational activity within Britain, Kripamoya Das has stated that there are about 40 groups of devotees in England that meet together called *nama hatta*s (literally meaning house-based groups of people who come together to chant and to hear the Holy name of Krishna).[37] Most of such groups are in towns and cities, and the average size of regular attendees is ten who meet once a week. However, within Indian groups, or within Indian dominated groups, figures sometimes rise to 40 or 50 people. For the Indian groups, many of which are based within Greater London, ISKCON is often seen as a form of revivalist Hinduism. To the indigenous folk it comes as something new, seeking to add certain philosophical principles and practices to their lives as well as offering what will help them spiritually. Naturally it involves a change of lifestyle for them and consequently there is a higher turnover of indigenous members; yet some of the most committed *nama hatta* leaders are non-Indian devotees.

Baring in mind the extent of the *nama hatta* groups, as well as general temple congregations and ISKCON's status in Britain today, I asked Kripamoya Das some important questions to which he offered illuminating responses. These can be summarised here.

Question:

"About how many people in the UK today would you estimate to have ISKCON/Hare Krishna as their 'main faith'?"

Answer:

"I would say about 10,000, including the Indian community."

Question:

"How many in the UK identify with Krishna as a name for God (including those who are not necessarily affiliated to ISKCON)?"

Answer:

It's not possible to put a figure to this one. But I can say there's a certain section of the UK population largely with an Eastern/Buddhist/New Age tendency...and amongst those people many would identify Krishna

Consciousness as one of the streams flowing into their ocean of reality. These days it seems few people want to be counted as exclusive members of any particular group. The "religion" of today is to allow yourself to be influenced to some degree from all different quarters. We have our part to play in that.[38]

The Former Communist Block

Having discussed key ISKCON patterns of development in the West as well as in India, mention should also be made of some patterns of growth and development in former communist countries. Since the decline of communism in the former Soviet Union and Eastern Europe, a huge part of the world became fertile preaching ground for religious movements. This fact is of particular note because ISKCON was among the groups which acted rapidly to expand their missions in these regions. From ISKCON's perspective, the two most successful former communist countries arguably include Russia and Hungary.

In Poland there is an annual summer tour, which includes one of the largest and most exciting ISKCON festivals today. The "Woodstock" festival held near the German border is the biggest music festival in the country, where an estimated 350,000 young people attend. Over the three days of the festival most of them visit "Krishna's Village of Peace" there. At any one time one may find some 5,000 people within the area, an area nearly the size of a football stadium and which is exclusively run by ISKCON. In 2004 an estimated 100,000 plates of *prasadam* were served over the course of the event.

There is much evidence to indicate that Srila Prabhupada knew that the former Soviet Union, the great communist empire of atheism (as it was known), was an important strategic part in his mission. He wanted his disciples to go there so much that he even expected them to compromise their diet, if necessary, to establish a foothold in Moscow. It was in 1971 when Srila Prabhupada made an official visit to Moscow at the invitation of Professor Kotovsky, head of the Indian and South Asian Studies Department of the former USSR's Academy of Sciences. However, under Russia's communist regime ISKCON devotees were forced to operate underground due to severe persecution, which included imprisonment and even murder. However, since Glasnost and the fall of communism in the late 1980s open membership soared. In April 2004 Bhakti Vijnana Swami, a senior Russian guru and *sannyasi*, estimated in a meeting in which I was present that there are about 10,000 devotees of Russian origin alone. It was also estimated that there are as many as 8,000 Russian devotees scattered around the world.

The first ISKCON temple was opened in Moscow in 1990 and today there are 100,000 members and sympathisers, 97 registered communities, 22 *ashram*s/monasteries and some 250 groups or centres across Russia, as well as a radio station. Since 1994, however, the devotees had been fighting to keep the Moscow temple open because the land was wanted for commercial development.

After much campaigning and political wrangling, in January 2004 the Mayor of Moscow announced to ISKCON that they would receive as a donation two and a half acres of land near the heart of the city, just seven minutes drive from the Kremlin. Some have said this offer is due to long-term Russian political ties with India, Moscow's 15,000 strong Indian community and pressure exerted by Western democracies, including Britain. After considerable resistance from other local faith groups (especially the Russian Orthodox Church), in June 2005 there was a major breakthrough for ISKCON: the Moscow Architectural Committee and the Moscow Religious Committee each gave approval to the temple project. However, in October 2005 the Mayor of Moscow then withdrew the offer of the land and left the ISKCON devotees without any suitable property at all. At the time of writing the matter is yet to be resolved, but it now appears the Mayor of Moscow has conceded to pressure from the Indian and British governments, and ISKCON will be given land a little further from the city centre. Despite the challenges, ISKCON has undoubtedly experienced success in Russia and in other former communist countries, as in other parts of the world.

Conclusion

Briefly outlined, this chapter has described the humble beginnings of an ancient Vedic tradition which took root in America and then in Britain, followed by its rapid growth throughout the world due to the efforts of A.C. Bhaktivedanta Swami Prabhupada and his disciples. The chapter has identified some of the challenges the movement has faced since the demise of Srila Prabhupada and has made mention of the main splinter groups which emerged as a result. By using examples of significant events in ISKCON's UK history, I demonstrated how an international and hierarchical guru-based management system (referred to as the zonal *acharya* system) was unsuccessful, whilst a system with a much "flatter" or localised management system was able to relate to as well as empower lay members, increase ISKCON's resources and bring it into the realm of social acceptability – not only within the Hindu community and political circles, but also among many indigenous folk. In this context I also discussed the status of *nama hatta* groups in Britain and the seemingly natural growth away from temple centred communities, resulting in the movement's far greater integration with the rest of society. The activities of ISKCON around the world today have also been briefly discussed, which demonstrate activities after just 40 years the movement has, in many respects, been successful. Importantly, in this regard, I have shown that seemingly against all odds, ISKCON has become a movement that is continuing to spread its influence and in a variety of ways. Not only has the movement been successful in terms of many Indian groups around the world, but in more recent years growth has been particularly noticeable in the former communist countries. Despite the fact that Srila Prabhupada himself did not spend much time in former communist countries, a significant number of the indigenous populations of these countries have taken an active interest in Krishna

Consciousness, confirming that the movement carries natural broad appeal. It seems as long as ISKCON learns to build on its internal relationships and gives greater emphasis to the value of marriage, family life and employment, there is every sign ISKCON will increasingly become both socially acceptable and attractive as well as prosper in the foreseeable future.

(COMMENT ON) MOVING INTO PHASE THREE:

An Analysis of ISKCON Membership in the UK

Ross Andrew (Rasamandala Das)

Comment

In 1995 I wrote an article (a version of which is reprinted below), an article entitled "Moving into Phase Three: An Analysis of ISKCON Membership in the UK." The article was originally published in *ISKCON Communications Journal* and postulated that that the Hare Krishna movement in the mid-1990s was on the threshold of a third phase of development. The first phase, I argued, had concentrated on recruitment and core membership, while the second phase had involved a major congregational focus. The future I envisioned – the third phase – would be characterised by a fundamental change in the role of temple life, shifting from what was essentially a workplace to a residential training centre. With this in mind, recruits – or, more precisely, enrolees – would no longer join monastic communities for an indefinite period (leaving, often unceremoniously, after an average of five years, which an unpublished survey I conducted in the early 1990s revealed); they would enrol for systematic education with clear periods of commitment and assessment, and with the vision of continuous progress and successful "graduation". Although that analysis was based on membership patterns in the UK, it is important to note that inadequate record-keeping at the time meant that figures were often only approximate. Nonetheless, I believe that much of the analysis of the original article remains significant now and that it may also be of interest to scholars exploring societal and theological developments in ISKCON.

Here in this brief comment on (as well as extension to) the original essay, I wish briefly to evaluate to what extent my prognosis was correct. As one might expect, in some areas it was right, in others wrong. There is no doubt that education has now become a significant word in ISKCON and the subject of a number of academic studies (Davies 1997; Das 1997). More importantly, a number of adult educational projects have started over the last decade. It was somewhat earlier, in the late 1980s, that the Vrindavana Institute for Higher Education started a major initiative, offering casual courses for devotees on pilgrimage to the holy town of Vrindavan in north India. The project relied heavily on charismatic leadership, drawing teachers from the ranks of gurus and *sannyasi*s (renouncers). Although leadership challenges contributed to a decline in the popularity of its courses, it may have been pivotal in raising awareness of the need for adult education. In 1992, an initiative called Vaishnava Training and Education (VTE) proposed that formal education was not only much needed but was congruent with ISKCON's theology. Three years later it launched its first teacher training course and subsequently published over ten courses, on topics ranging from leadership and management (Vaishnava Training and Education, 2002) to marriage enhancement (Vaishnava Training and Education, 2005). In 2000, the Society's worldwide headquarters in West Bengal founded the Mayapur Institute for Higher Education (MIHE), concentrating on *shastric* (scriptural) study and teacher training. By this time, Bhaktivedanta Manor in the UK had already established the College of Vedic Studies. In Britain today young devotees are largely discouraged from abandoning their university studies (unlike in the counter-culture period of ISKCON'S inception) and some initiatives have positively encouraged such education. For example, from 1997 onwards over 15 devotees have studied Sanskrit or theology at Oxford University, supported by The Oxford Centre for Hindu Studies, an independent project started by an ISKCON member. Throughout the world, moreover, there are now several other educational initiatives focussing on adult education. These include the Bhaktivedanta College of Education and Culture in South Africa, the Bhaktivedanta Theological College in Belgium, and the Raganuga Vedic College in Kansas City, USA.

However, contrary to what I had first anticipated, these developments have occurred much nearer the periphery of the ISKCON world. Most temples, with their *brahmachari* (celibate monk) residents at the centre, and with a conservative style of leadership, continued largely as before. In many places, most notably in the USA, there has been severe atrophy, so that many temples or *ashram*s have no more than a handful of residents, some now quite elderly. In the UK's Bhaktivedanta Manor, although the number of *ashram* residents remains relatively high compared to the rest of the world, most of the voluntary single staff have been replaced by employed householders receiving a stipend. Many *ashram* bunks are occupied not by local recruits but by devotees migrating from India, Russia and Eastern Europe. Furthermore, the economic dependence on single temple residents, through book sales and fund-raising, has been replaced with programmes seeking support from the ethnic Hindu community, contributing to what Carey (1987) calls "the process of Indianisation." The educational initiatives at Bhaktivedanta Manor are increasingly aimed at congregational members.

Significantly, in addition to the core and congregation communities identified in my original *ISKCON Communication Journal* essay, a third target group has emerged. They have been termed "common interest groups" and consist of people with no faith commitment but who are interested in subjects such as yoga, ox-power and vegetarian cooking. Throughout these changes, the *brahmachari ashram*s at the core of most ISKCON communities have remained largely unchanged, and most educational initiatives retain a high degree of independence from ISKCON'S management.

The pioneers of these educational initiatives tended to proceed with relatively little active support from the administrative leadership, who were under constant pressure to collect funds, secure man-power for daily chores as well as tackle other management issues and crises. Educationalists were thus forced to develop self-resourcefulness. There is a case for suggesting that their struggles have been a positive step towards developing a class of self-reliant thinkers, being also financially and emotionally independent of the institution. As the educational initiatives have progressed, however, there are signs today that the healthy changes are becoming accepted nearer to the "core" and that some temple managers value and support education rather than perceiving it as a threat to the dominant discourse (Baumann 1996). For example, at Bhaktivedanta Manor, the temple president was previously a teacher, and many of the residents are first sent for training in the exemplary ISKCON temple in Chowpatty, Mumbai. Indeed, this appears to be one temple where changes have happened at the core, and where the *brahmachari ashram* operates much differently than in many other ISKCON temples; and it enjoys considerable success. In addition, UK devotees seeking first or second initiation are required to sit written examinations. At the main temple in Belgium, the president fully supports the associated college, which offers residential courses in Vaishnava Theology leading to degrees awarded by the University of Wales.

Despite these changes, some devotees remain wary, even critical, of education, and particularly of any interaction with non-devotees or "outsiders". Nonetheless, the capacity for critical and reflective thinking is a part of ISKCON's tradition. Research conducted by the VTE suggests that there has been insufficient reflection on scripture, and that it has been misappropriated in many ways. It is clear that the desire to create conformity and to maintain mission merely by legislation, or by invoking fear of transgression, has clearly failed, and there is dissatisfaction both with leadership, and within the leadership itself.

As indicated above, in my original essay two initial phases in ISKCON's development were identified. The first phase meant that joining the faith was largely synonymous with joining the temple, and there was a tendency for highly dichotomous thinking. The second phase featured a very significant growth of the congregation but increasing uncertainty about ideas of right and wrong. These two phases each lasted some 13 years. According to the same time scale, the present phase – phase three – is nearing its end. It has indeed included major strides in education, if not quite in the way I had first anticipated. If I were asked to predict a fourth phase, I would envision a period of enlightened leadership, with managers and educationalists working together for the long-term benefit of its core temple members as well as the general public. ISKCON leadership, I contend, can no longer continue to squeeze the world into an isolated community. ISKCON must allow itself judiciously to enter the wider world. The ability to walk in the world while maintaining one's dignity calls for spiritual integrity: to be in the world, but not of it. A mature leadership must recognise the role of systematic education as a powerful tool in this process. If it does, then I believe ISKCON will reap the benefits and will be recognised, not just for its theology, nor merely for its noble intentions, but for its ability to transform lives and to make concrete contributions to society at large.

MOVING INTO PHASE THREE:
An Analysis of ISKCON Membership in the UK

Introduction

In this chapter I intend to explore the expansion of ISKCON in the UK within the context of the various sections of its membership. By analysing the different trends, I have identified two principal phases of growth so far and suggest we are moving into a third. I have expressed each phase diagrammatically in terms of the main categories of membership. I have then used these models to examine further characteristics of the first two phases, specifically in terms of the movements of the individual, the predominating worldview, and the corresponding value system.[1]

For the third phase (of which we are on the threshold, I believe) I propose a new model which may help devotees realistically analyse and meet the Society's needs. Primarily it is intended as a basis for determining appropriate "paths of involvement" for the individual. This study may further assist in clarifying the values and attitudes we wish to nurture in our members and in establishing policies, standards and strategies for future growth. Rather than unconsciously reacting to circumstances, we can use this phase three model deliberately and purposefully to chart a successful course for ISKCON.

The first two phases become evident from a quantitative analysis of the two broadest categories of our society, namely "core membership" and "congregational membership."

Core membership

By "core membership" I refer to temple residents and those living outside the temple with full-time devotional engagement. Although statistics have not been consistently maintained, I propose that the diagram below fairly represents the trend in the numerical strength of core membership (see also Appendix 1).

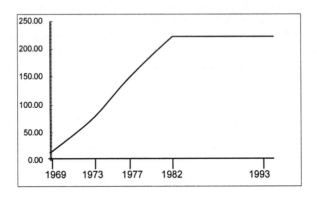

FIGURE 1

As is evident from the above graph, we experienced a steady anduninterrupted[2] growth in temple membership in the successful 1970s. This continued even after Srila Prabhupada's traumatic departure. Then, in 1982 came the change, the sudden levelling off. The outlook today may appear rather bleak, until we consider the other main category of membership, namely, congregational membership.

Congregational membership

The term "congregational member"[3] refers to a devotee not included in the category of core membership, as defined above. We have no detailed records of congregational membership. Nevertheless, it is widely accepted that in the 1970s it was relatively small and considered quite insignificant.[4] In the early 1980s, with the beginning of FOLK (Friends of Lord Krishna) and the subsequent *Nama Hatta* Programme (home-centred congregational activities), it began to increase substantially. This is demonstrated in the graph below.

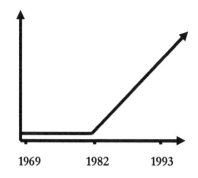

1969   1982   1993

FIGURE 2

Two Phases

From the above analysis, I will infer that so far there have been two broad stages of development. These are as follows:

Phase	Period	Focus
One	1969-82	Recruitment/Core Membership
Two	1982-95	*Nama Hatta* / Congregational Membership

I will later refer to evidence which suggests we are moving into phase three. For now, though, let us examine the first two phases in terms of membership patterns.

Phase One

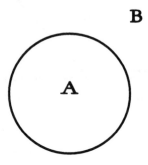

The model of the 1970s was simple. In the above diagram "A" (within the circle) represents core membership and "B" (outside the circle) the non-devotee world.[5] The structural development of ISKCON at this time was largely confined to opening temples. These were quickly filled with (largely) immature devotees, expected to demonstrate an extremely high level of renunciation in contrast to their previous lives. This gave rise to a highly dualistic worldview[6] by which spiritual merit was measured in terms of where one lived – whether in the *ashram* or outside.[7] Devotees identified members of the respective camps with corresponding descriptive words or phrases,[8] some of which are listed below.

A	B
Us	Them
Devotee	*Karmi*/Demon
Supra-human	Sub-human (hogs, dogs…)
Going up	Going down
Vishnudutas	Yamadutas
No bad qualities	No good qualities
Associate with	Avoid/Preach to

These sets of diametrically opposed terms can be identified withcorresponding values and attitudes fostered within temple communities.[9] Suffice it to say that these often questionable values became enshrined within our language, even endorsed by scripture, and most vividly demonstrated in our dealings with ourselves and others. For example, there was little room for individual or collective introspection, and open and honest dialogue was discouraged, if not condemned. This had significant implications on the way in which the individual decided to join the institution, and also on their subsequent involvement.[10] I will therefore examine how this paradigm, and its associated value structure, worked in respect of movement of members between the Society and the outside world, as represented below.

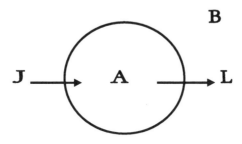

FIGURE 4

Joining ISKCON (Represented by Arrow "J")

Joining the faith was largely synonymous with joining the temple. It was on a non-contractual basis, with no clear definition of respective rights and responsibilities. For example, as soon as one joined (or shortly afterwards) it was expected (or taken for granted) that one would willingly dedicate 24 hours a day to service.[11] Enlistment was assumed to be forever, or at least until the end of this life, without consideration of future prospects. For example, within my generation[12] most *brahmacharis* (monks) – I cannot speak for *brahmacharins* (nuns) – never considered the possibility of marriage. Students were implored "to just depend on Krsna."[13] In addition, joining was relatively soon after initial interest in Krishna Consciousness. Members then took initiation, with its lifelong and irretractable vows, usually within another six-to-twelve months. There was a sense of urgency, often at the expense of long-term vision. Core devotees were enthusiastic that prospective candidates join them as soon as possible, often citing the possibility of an early demise.

Leaving ISKCON (Represented by Arrow "L")

Leaving the temple was termed "blooping". Devotees usually "blooped" unannounced in the middle of the night, sneaking out with their few belongings and with a large burden of guilt. Such events created waves within the community, who considered that the blooped devotee might now be destined for the "hot place" and needed saving from at least a severe "singeing". Such events stirred devotees to search their hearts for the cause of such a calamity. Full responsibility was usually apportioned to the absent devotee. I will not explore these features in detail here.[14] They will, however, no doubt prove useful in analysing trends and in establishing policies for the individual's course of involvement with the Society.

The Balloon Principle

I will now examine the basic principle which, I suggest, was behind ISKCON's initial rapid expansion. The diagram below is based on the phase one model and compares ISKCON to a balloon.

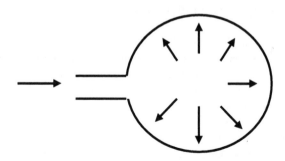

FIGURE 5

Observation reveals that a balloon gets bigger provided it meets two criteria, namely (a) that air goes into it and (b) there are no leaks. The ISKCON of the 1970s operated on a similar principle. Expansion of the Society was based on (a) making more devotees and (b) preventing them from leaving or blooping.[15]

This analogy can be extended further. For example, in blowing up a balloon all attention is concentrated on the nozzle. Similarly, most attention in phase one was on recruitment. Devotees openly demonstrated care and affection for the public who showed interest in Krishna Consciousness, but often sadly neglected the welfare of community members. As with the burst of a balloon one becomes aware of a drastic leak; similarly a devotee's sudden and resounding absence would often be the first recognised symptom of any personal difficulty. Nevertheless, for some time this principle worked well and ISKCON expanded rapidly. The early 1980s, however, saw significant changes which precipitated phase two in ISKCON's development.

Phase Two

The 1970s paradigm gave core members a considerable degree of commitment, enthusiasm and clarity of purpose; its shortcomings only became apparent in the early 1980s. The reasons for this are significant. Most notable of all perhaps was the growing awareness (at least for some individuals) that ISKCON had serious internal problems. Joining the Society did not necessarily provide the promised smooth transition to the spiritual realm. This awareness was fuelled by leadership problems[16] and the recurring difficulties devotees faced in successful transference to the householder or married stage of life (*grihastha ashram*). Consequently, throughout the 1980s preachers became increasingly reluctant to recommend that potential candidates join the community. Rather, they encouraged or commanded them to stay at home and there pursue the principles and practices of Krishna Consciousness.

The Congregation

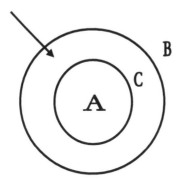

FIGURE 6

The significant increase in "the congregation" (represented in Section C of the diagram above) challenged the simple paradigm of the 1970s. Its shortcomings became apparent in trying to establish the identity of congregational members. In simple terms – are they "us" or "them?" Do we validate their commitment (even though apparently it may be of a lower order) or, by so doing, are we to be thought of as compromising our standards of purity?[17] Despite these tensions the 1980s saw a growing awareness of the need to include non-core devotees within the bounds of ISKCON and to validate their existence and their contribution. Non-core membership, however, was comprised of various sections, each identified by the way in which members joined. I have identified two main ways (see Fig. 7 below) by which a person tended to enter the congregational community, namely: (1) from the non-devotee world (represented by Arrow X), which usually was either through the *nama hatta* programme (dealing mainly with the indigenous white population) or through United Kingdom Life Membership (UKLM),[18] also embracing the Asian Hindu community; and (2) from the core community (indicated by Arrow Y). The latter occurred in two principal ways: (a) devotees got married (and few remained in full-time service), or (b) devotees "faded out"[19] (but the sudden "bloop" was becoming increasingly rare).

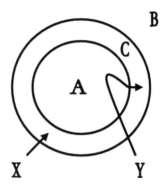

FIGURE 7

Although the *nama hatta* and the UKLM programmes faced their own challenges, more significant to this study were the often insurmountable hurdles faced by devotees making the apparently downhill transition from core membership to congregational membership, either through marriage[20] or by "fading out."[21] It is essential, I suggest, to explore these issues in depth. Nevertheless, for the moment it is enough to recognise that the vast majority of devotees have passed through Section A (representing core membership). In fact, from 1982 onwards the rate at which devotees left the core community was equal to the rate at which they joined ISKCON. Despite this fact, it appears that only those few who remained as core members received full validation from the Society.[22] I would like to propose a new model which exhibits two essential and highly significant features. Firstly, it acknowledges the transience of the celibate student *ashram*s. Secondly, it validates all devotees who have or keep some connection with ISKCON through practising the principles of Krishna Consciousness. At the same time it will, if properly implemented, ensure maintenance of the highest standards.[23]

Phase Three

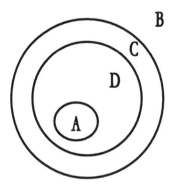

FIGURE 8

For our new paradigm (expressed above) it is convenient to change our definition of Section A (the reason for which will become evident later). This grouping still refers to temple residents (i.e. *brahmacharis* and *brahmacharins*) but now excludes householders in full-time service. The latter fall within the new category, Section D, which represents what I have loosely termed "the clergy." Its members consist of those devotees who have completed initial training[24] and who are now concentrating on actively spreading Krishna Consciousness, whether as householders or as renunciates.[25] They will have specific functions catering to both the congregation (Section C) and to the temple/student *ashram* (Section A).

Let us now study the possible options concerning the flow of personnel.

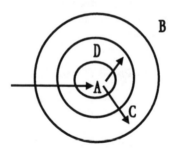

FIGURE 9

What is immediately clear is that anyone "joining the temple"[26] (or more precisely, the student *ashram*) does not stay there indefinitely. Even lifelong celibates move into band "D" – our newly-founded "clergy". Student life is a temporary allocation, dispelling the misconception of joining the temple and staying there forever. The temple *ashram* is now a place where the student enrols for training, with prospects that fall within two broad categories, namely: (i) joining the "clergy" or (ii) joining the congregation.[27] Although option (i) may be considered to be preferable, option (ii) is also valid, and thus should be validated through encouragement, practical support, and so on.

What we see now, in contrast to the balloon principle of the 1970s, is an acceptance of the reality that the *brahmachari/brahmacharin ashram* is a stage of life one almost always passes through (largely irrespective of encouragement to do otherwise). According to our model, even lifelong celibates, move out of the initial stage of training by joining the clergy. In other words, *everyone* [28] graduates from Section A within a finite (and hopefully specified) period of time.

In phase one (and to a lesser degree in phase two) attention was largely on recruitment. Now, I suggest, we should focus upon "graduation" and mould everything accordingly, right back to enrolment policy itself. In other words, we should "keep the end in mind". We may consider what we expect of devotees upon graduating from Section A. Specifically we may ask:

1) How should they be? (That is, what values and attitudes do we want them to exhibit?)

2) What should they know? (What knowledge should they possess?)

3) What will they be able to do? (With what skills should we equip them?)

This "graduation" concept, I propose, identifies our two most important areas for development. Firstly (though this chapter does not directly concern itself with this) the need for a thriving[29] householder community[30] into which graduates can move is indicated. Secondly (and this is the focus of my essay) a systematic and pro-active training and education to prepare temple residents for householder life (or, in some cases, for a life of renunciation) is needed.[31] In addition to this, with residential training it is apparent that the congregation needs similar support. In fact, I have identified the end of phase two not only in response to various successful training initiatives,[32] but also in view of the apparent inertia within the *nama hatta* programme.

Phase two is drawing to a close. Phase three will see the development of systematic training and education, both for core and congregational members.[33] These improvements will help the Society to synergise its needs with those of its most important resource – the individual devotee. Furthermore these initiatives will enable ISKCON to establish a clear vision and a defined strategy for the future, by providing the means for corresponding personal development. We must evolve from hunters and gatherers into cultivators.[34] As we do this, I believe we will move into a new and dynamic phase of development, synthesising the success, confidence and enthusiasm that typified phase one with the maturity, experience and thoughtfulness that emerged during phase two.

Appendix 1

ISKCON UK – Core Membership 1969–93[35]

1969	6
1973	75
1977	150
1982	225 (125)*
1993	225

* This second figure represents mid-March after the leadership crisis. The first figure represents membership before that.

PART 2

Dreams and Devotion

4

DREAMS OF PRABHUPADA
and Devotional Life in the Hare Krishna Movement

Graham Dwyer

Introduction

Based on research at Bhaktivedanta Manor, the UK headquarters of the Hare Krishna movement or, more precisely, the International Society for Krishna Consciousness (ISKCON), this chapter explores the significance of dreams in the religious world of a faith community now very well known to many students and scholars of religion as well as known to many in the public at large (the latter usually having been made aware of ISKCON as a result of encountering chanting Hare Krishna devotees on city high streets or in shopping malls and market squares).[1] Since April 2002, the date my research at Bhaktivedanta Manor commenced, and throughout the entire period of the research, which is still on-going, I came more and more to learn, not only about the importance and value attributed to dreams by Hare Krishna devotees, especially dreams of the their movement's late founder-*acharya* (spiritual leader), His Divine Grace A.C. Bhaktivedanta Swami Prabhupada, but, crucially, the manner in which dreams of the founder of the movement are considered deeply to affect, shape and direct much of the devotionalism of ISKCON members. This chapter will focus directly on dreams of the founder of ISKCON, affectionately known in the Hare Krishna movement as Srila Prabhupada, and it will endeavour to disclose the spiritual relevance of the dreams for devotees, assessing in particular the impact such dreams have on current devotional trends and trajectories within ISKCON. However, to do this, as well as to contextualise the analysis this chapter provides, some introductory comments relating specifically to the much discussed topic of ISKCON leadership, as well as the topic of the guru concept on which leadership itself is predicated, are in order. Indeed, some attention to leadership issues and to issues relating to the guru concept in the Hare Krishna movement is necessary, as consideration of them reveals precisely why dreams of Prabhupada are critical today in the religious lives of many ISKCON members.

Currently, the bureaucratic organisation Prabhupada established "to act as the instrument for the execution of the will of His Divine Grace" (Goswami 1993 [1980], vol. iv, pp.103-04) – an organisation put in place before Prabhupada passed away known as the Governing Body Commission – determines by means of democratic process all major ISKCON rulings, strategies and policies in collaboration with, and after consulting, spiritual heads or gurus, temple presidents and other senior devotees in the movement. This is the power base and structure of authority in ISKCON today, a structure now quite stable and continuing to evolve but one that was preceded by a profound leadership crisis.

Following the demise of ISKCON's founder-*acharya* in 1977 the Hare Krishna movement, which Prabhupada had founded a little over a decade earlier, encountered major difficulties and challenges in the domain of leadership. Of course, challenges to leadership in the movement had occurred long before 1977, for Prabhupada witnessed several direct attempts at usurpation himself (see Tamal Krishna Goswami 1997); however, a variety of challenges for, or squabbles about, leadership – squabbles linked particularly to arguments within the movement over matters of succession, doctrine regarding the nature and role of the guru, as well as concern to ensure the survival of the Gaudiya Vaishnava tradition Prabhupada had brought to the West – took on fierce expressive aggression after 1977, reaching a peak in the early-to-mid-1980s when a large number of aggrieved and disillusioned devotees elected to leave the movement altogether. (For a recent in-depth account of these issues, see the essays edited by Bryant and Ekstrand [2004].)

Within this great ferment of challenge, conflict and disillusionment, the concept of *guru-parampara* (literally, "uninterrupted series") was pivotal, with much disagreement centring on the issue of whether, or to what degree, any member of the movement, especially one invested with authority to initiate others and/or possessing charisma, could himself assume the role of guru or spiritual leader in some manner comparable to Prabhupada, and thereby take up the very mantle of the movement's founder. Indeed, although Prabhupada never named any single individual to succeed him (and "purposely" so, according to Tamal Krishna Goswami [1997, p.9]), there have in fact been well recognised efforts by certain ISKCON members to do just that, with such attempts not only always ending in failure, but sometimes in excommunication as well. Debate about the concept of the guru in ISKCON is a complicated matter; yet an important point that should be noted here is that within ISKCON today one who possesses authority to initiate others and who acts as a guru or spiritual guide to them is expected to view himself and also to be viewed by his initiated disciples, as well as by others in the movement, as being less exalted in spiritual status, authority or leadership when compared with Prabhupada. Thus, while it is frequently stated that a guru or spiritual master's initiates in a sense are "his" disciples, they are simultaneously, and more significantly, Prabhupada's grand-disciples, the main understanding here being, as Tamal Krishna Goswami (1997, p.9) writes, that "Prabhupada's position was unique and not to be imitated". Indeed, this is no doubt a crucial reason today's "new converts are trained (first to) accept Prabhupada's shelter exclusively for at least six months before being advised to select (an) initiating guru (and one) who reminds them most of Prabhupada" (Tamal Krishna Goswami, 1997, p.10). The same point has recently been underscored in *Plain Vanilla*, an ISKCON publication in which one of the volume's contributors, Drutakarma Dasa (2002, p. 9), states that "Srila Prabhupada, as the founder-*acarya* of ISKCON, is the primary source of guidance and instruction, for all members of ISKCON."

Now, as indicated above, the issues of leadership, succession and challenge, and in particular the thorny one of the guru concept at the centre of debate on these matters, have been the subject of much discussion, not only amongst leading figures within ISKCON itself (e.g. Drutakarma Dasa 2002; Gelberg [Subhananda Dasa] 1985, 1988; Tamal Krishna Goswami 1997; Jayadvaita Svami 2002a, b, c; Ravindra Svarupa Dasa 1994), but also amongst writers or scholars outside the movement (e.g. Knott 1986, 1997; Muster 1997; Rochford 1985 and Shinn 1987, 1996). A little less attention in the academic domain, however, has focussed directly on what may aptly, I believe, be termed Prabhupada's uniqueness within the Hare Krishna movement, with the different writers which have concentrated on him, in fact, articulating a variety of viewpoints, as recently indicated by Knott (1997). Yet, most surprising of all, very little attention has been given to the continuing relationship Hare Krishna devotees frequently claim to have with Prabhupada in their night visions or dreams, dreams in which Prabhupada may not only "appear" but in which he may also give a message, a word of encouragement or a word of chastisement and, most important of all, offer spiritual direction that critically affects the devotional lives and spiritual trajectories of many ISKCON devotees. No academic, as far as I am aware, has investigated this phenomenon, though within ISKCON itself some devotees have recently begun to research it.[2]

In this chapter I hope to demonstrate that, although the phenomenon of Prabhupada's "appearance" in the dreams of Hare Krishna devotees has been much neglected, examination of the phenomenon is crucial, not merely for shedding light on his perceived uniqueness or on his on-going centrality within ISKCON, but, importantly, for gaining major insight or a key to understanding some significant trends in the devotional lives of many of today's ISKCON members. In an attempt to do this, I will give examples of devotees' dreams of Prabhupada as well as the meanings they themselves attributed to the dreams, information devotees have enthusiastically provided during my research at Bhaktivedanta Manor. This chapter will also situate the dreams of informants and the interpretations they provided within the framework of their on-going devotional experience and commitment, experience and commitment in which, as I will attempt to illustrate, Prabhupada plays a direct role, despite none of the informants having ever physically seen or met the founder-*acharya* of ISKCON.

In privileging the authority of respondents' own interpretations of their dreams, it is clear the approach adopted in this chapter is opposed to classical Freudian approaches or other similar methods of examining dream texts and dream phenomena. Rather than appeal to mystical notions of unconscious mind, unconscious motivations, wishes, drives, desires and so forth, which for Freud (1998 [1900]) are expressed in dreams and require psychoanalytic modes of interpretation Freud himself developed to unlock their so-called secrets, the dreams I documented are explored in terms of their explicit content, privileging understandings constructed within a world of shared beliefs and common religious conceptions. More precisely, the approach this chapter engages is phenomenological, an approach emanating from the philosophy of Edmund Husserl (1964, 1967) and closely associated with the sociology of writers such as Alfred Schutz, (1967, 1970), Peter Berger and Thomas Luckmann (1967). The principal merit of the method of phenomenology, and one of the main reasons it is employed in this chapter, is that it does not attempt to dominate or loom over the materials to which it attends but rather seeks to give them voice, a voice subordinated to no other authority except its own. In this regard, the essay moves away from and also provides an alternative to Freudian and other psychological explanations, as the dreams it examines both avoids compromising the religious authority or religious logic of informants' experiences and testimonies, disclosing the full value of their perceived import.

Dreams and their Relevance for ISKCON Members

In ISKCON literature a number of references can be found on the subject of dreams generally. Some important ones might include, for example, those found in the work of Swami Krishnapada (also known as Bhakti Tirtha Swami) (1996). In his book, entitled *Spiritual Warrior: Uncovering Spiritual Truths in Psychic Phenomena*, one chapter, "Dreams: A State of Reality", considers the value of dreams for those within the ISKCON community. Thus, commenting on the significance of dreams for devotees, Swami Krishnapada writes:

> The dream medium can...provide the opportunity for advanced beings to chastise you...If there are messages you should receive, the impressions will always be there...If a communication is really meant for growth, even though you may forget it or may not be able to understand its significance, it will still have an effect on your consciousness. (Swami Krishnapada, 1996, pp.17-9)

Again the same author writes:

> Some of you will be given spiritual guidance through dreams. A very significant dream of this calibre occurs between the disciple or student and the mentor or spiritual master. Often, there is a need for the spiritual master

to warn the disciple or to give certain types of lesson that may not be easy to receive under normal circumstances. In such a situation, the communication will occur through the medium of the dream. Because you have been made aware of the opportunity for spiritual growth provided by dreams, you will now automatically receive more assistance from your spiritual guides when you are dreaming. (Swami Krishnapada, 1996, pp.24-5)

The belief that a disciple may receive guidance from a spiritual master by means of dreams is widespread within ISKCON, as is the related belief that the spiritual master may further aid his disciple in dreams through the destruction of the disciple's sins or *karma* (cf. Brockington, 1991, p.150), a point recently examined by Drutakarma Dasa (2002), who offers some discussion of the doctrine, a doctrine emphasised, of course, by Prabhupada. On this doctrine Prabhupada himself says,

A devotee sometimes accepts a sinful person as his disciple, and to counteract the sinful reactions he accepts from the disciple, he has to see a bad dream. Nonetheless, the spiritual master is so kind that in spite of having bad dreams due to the sinful disciple, he accepts this troublesome business for the deliverance of the victims of Kali-yuga (the age of irreligion or spiritual decline)...(Prabhupada, 1972-80, *Srimad Bhagavatam* 8. 4. 1, purport)

Prabhupada has commented on, or taught, how dreams may be of benefit or help to a devotee of Krishna in other ways too. An example of one such benefit is evident from a dream Prabhupada had during his arduous sea-voyage at the age of 70, a voyage he undertook in order to carry out and establish his mission in the West. As reported by Satsvarupa Dasa Goswami (1993 [1980]), the biographer of Bhaktivedanta Swami Prabhupada, at one stage of his journey to America by sea Prabhupada became acutely ill. Goswami writes:

He noted in his diary: "Rain, seasickness, dizziness, headache, no appetite and vomiting." The symptoms persisted, but it was more than seasickness...In two days he suffered two heart attacks...(and)...he thought that if another were to come he would certainly not survive. On the night of the second day, Prabhupada had a dream. Lord Krsna, in His many forms, was rowing a boat, and he told Prabhupada that he should not fear, but should come along. Prabhupada felt assured of Lord Krsna's protection, and the violent attacks did not recur.(Goswami, 1993, p.2)

For purposes of this chapter, however, there is one reference to dreams in the literature of the Hare Krishna movement that is of particular importance and should be mentioned here, a reference which, once again, is found in Goswami's biography of the movement's founder:

One night Abhay (or Prabhupada) had a striking dream, the same dream he had had several times before, during his days as a householder. Srila Bhaktisiddhanta Sarasvati (Prabhupada's guru) appeared, just as Abhay had known him, the tall, scholarly *sannyasi* (renouncer), coming directly from the spiritual world, from Krsna's personal entourage. He called to Abhay and indicated that he should follow. Repeatedly he called and motioned. He was asking Abhay to take *sannyasa* (renunciation). Come, he urged, become a *sannyasi*. (Goswami, 1993, p.224)

What is noteworthy about this dream is not merely that Prabhupada is visited in it by his spiritual master, the latter inviting the former to renounce the world and become a *sannyasi*; the telling point is that the dream actually occurred sometime after the demise of Bhaktisiddhanta Sarasvati, after Prabhupada's guru had passed away. Thus, a key step or development in Prabhupada's own devotional life and commitment – the decision to renounce the world and become a *sannyasi* – is itself contingent upon a dream, and one in which the instruction given to Prabhupada comes from beyond the grave. Here, then, one discovers not only a major precedent for the kinds of religious testimony I documented during my research at Bhaktivedanta Manor, findings to which I now turn, but, in addition, it is clear when one compares the findings with an account of Prabhupada's own experience just cited, that there is much resonance, particularly in terms of themes of devotion and religious commitment.

Dreams of Prabhupada and Devotional Life

Although it seems surprising little investigation within ISKCON (and no research in the academic domain) has directly focused on dreams of Prabhupada or the way in which such dreams may dramatically affect the devotional lives and spiritual trajectories of ISKCON members, in the case of ISKCON there are good reasons perhaps for this. For such dreams are both common place for many in the Hare Krishna movement and largely taken for granted by them; and it is precisely because they are so common or frequently experienced that they have perhaps tended to escape attention. Indeed, within any community or society, including ISKCON itself, whenever experience and understanding, as well as belief or practice, are largely taken for granted, they typically remain submerged in the sense that they evade, even resist, the mind's gaze. This is not only because such experience and belief are not in any doubt or question, but also because they are essentially routinised and quotidian. Yet, as I have demonstrated elsewhere (Dwyer, 2003), it is precisely because such phenomena tend to remain beneath the threshold of direct conscious attention, because they are so taken for granted or quotidian, that they simultaneously provide an avenue for a scholar from outside the community with an effective means of comprehending it; and this is indeed the case regarding dreams of Prabhupada, dreams which foster devotional life or commitment as well as reflect it.

It should be pointed out, however, that, while dreams of Prabhupada tend to be common and essentially taken for granted, it is unlikely that this was the case immediately following the demise of Bhaktivedanta Swami Prabhupada. Thus, Nori Muster, an American former ISKCON member who became disillusioned with the movement in the wake of the tumultuous events of the early 1980s, particularly events that led to much discord and schism within ISKCON leadership,writes:

> ...(A)n American from Calcutta, Amogha-lila...claimed to receive messages from Prabhupada through dreams, trances, and visions. ISKCON doctrine rejects the possibility, but a *sannyasi* named Trivikram became interested in Amogha-lila's writings and circulated them on the insiders' grapevine. Amogha-lila (channeling Prabhupada) added fuel to the anti-guru fervor with statements like, "I never wanted this big fanfare for (the) eleven disciples (I appointed). Now you stop treating them as special. That is their own concoction. You are all gurus, as much as you repeat my instructions and follow them." (Muster, 1997, p.87)

It is clear from Muster's comment that reports of messages received from Prabhupada by means of dreams or visions potentially could be extremely divisive, especially in terms of ISKCON's authority structure and in terms of the wider politics of the Hare Krishna movement; and with regard to the alleged occurrence of such dreams or visions, Muster's claim that "ISKCON doctrine rejects the possibility" appears to reflect this concern as well as to reflect evident condemnation of reports of dreams of Prabhupada Muster may well have frequently heard expressed in the context of leadership challenge and ferment during the early 1980s. Indeed, given that the 11 gurus Prabhupada selected to provide leadership after his death had in the view of many devotees seriously come to abuse the authority invested in them (a criticism which also brought the appointed gurus during the 1980s into much conflict with ISKCON's Governing Body Commission [GBC] Prabhupada additionally put in place to provide his movement with leadership), devotees strongly opposed to the chosen 11 may well have attempted to express their disgruntlement, and even subversion, by claiming they received instructions from Prabhupada that would then enable them to disregard rulings or precepts created or sanctioned by the appointed gurus. However, although Muster states that reports of dreams or visions of Prabhupada in which the founder-*acharya* gives a message to the devotee are not considered possible or genuine from the standpoint of ISKCON teaching, I have been unable to find any comment to support Muster's claim in the publications endorsed by Prabhupada (despite making a thorough search of references to dreams in all Prabhupada's works: books, lectures, conversations, etc.); furthermore, it is equally noteworthy that respondents at Bhaktivedanta Manor stated Muster's view should be treated as a personal one, one that has neither been officially propounded by ISKCON, nor one with any basis in ISKCON doctrine. Nonetheless, Muster's negative comment should not be completely dismissed in the sense that there may still be some ISKCON members who reject or contest testimonies of these kinds of dreams, seeing them as problematic or as having the potential to undermine ISKCON's authority structure. Further extensive research would be needed, particularly at other ISKCON centres and, importantly, involving how ISKCON's existing gurus and GBC members currently respond to claims of messages purportedly emanating from ISKCON's founder-*acharya* in order to ascertain whether or not there may be any continued resistance to, or contestation of, alleged dream messages. But it must be emphasised that investigations at Bhaktivedanta Manor have so far revealed no problems of this kind, neither conflicts nor contestation in any form. Indeed, attention should be drawn here to the finding that a little under two-thirds of monks interviewed in November 2003 at the Manor claimed to have had such dreams. Of the 32 monks, who were resident at Bhaktivedanta Manor in November 2003, eight of them could not be approached for certain reasons (some, for example, had only recently become resident at the time and interviewing them was not deemed appropriate); however, of the 24 monks actually questioned 15 of them (62.5 per cent) stated they had experienced dreams of Prabhupada. In addition, in the light of much discussion on the topic with many other devotees who not only spend time at Bhaktivedanta Manor, but who also regularly visit other ISKCON centres, it appears that the kind of opposition to claims of receiving messages from Prabhupada Muster encountered in the early 1980s was peculiar to that particular tumultuous decade of ISKCON's history.

To develop and demonstrate the claims made about dreams of Prabhupada and devotional trends within ISKCON today, I now consider three separate examples or case studies. The three selected here for discussion from a large collection of devotees' dream stories or texts recorded at Bhaktivedanta Manor have been chosen primarily for two reasons: (1) they are good examples of the typical dream narrative or case study I have documented, and (2) the actual dream narratives I consider were reported by devotees from quite different socio-cultural backgrounds, with the backgrounds being less important in terms of the interpretation of the dreams, it seems, than the application of meanings derived from the religious world of ISKCON itself, meanings whose accent has a focus on the uniqueness of Prabhupada.

Case 1: Shalini[3]

Shalini, a devotee in her sixth decade of life, became a committed member of ISKCON in 1985. She was born into a *brahman* Vaishnava household in Tamil Nadu, south India. Shalini informed me that Krishna was the focal deity of the household, a household in which the *Bhagavad Gita* was a scripture frequently read and discussed. As a member of the household, Shalini also consulted her family's guru from time-to-time, the guru himself being a devotee of Krishna from whom Shalini gained much devotional understanding as well as spiritual direction. However, although Shalini had grown up in a setting in which religious life was most pronounced, and while this had had a marked effect on her, she informed me that her religious commitment started to wane as she entered adulthood. As a young adult Shalini also married and came to live in England, which, she claimed, further led to the erosion of her spiritual life.

Now, Shalini informed me that one day as she was going about her daily business, she met a Hare Krishna devotee on a street close to her home and was given some ISKCON literature by the devotee, including a copy of Prabhupada's translation of the *Gita*, as well as information about Bhaktivedanta Manor, which, to Shalini's surprise, was located close to her own home. Shalini stated that she was extremely impressed by the piety of the white British devotee she had met and impressed also by the ISKCON literature she had received. When she returned to her house, she not only read through the literature, but started to chant the *mahamantra* (the Hare Krishna *mantra*), which soon became a daily practice. Indeed, Shalini not only started to chant the *mahamantra* on a daily basis; she told me that she completed the 16 *mala* rounds (a total of 1,728 recitations) prescribed within ISKCON on a daily basis too.

A few months after she had commenced chanting 16 *mala* rounds each day, her first dream of Prabhupada (she eventually had three dreams altogether of ISKCON's founder-*acharya*) took place. Shalini commented that in the dream she had a vision both of Prabhupada and of Raghavendra Swami, the latter being the holy man who had been her guru in India and who had since died. In the dream, her former guru walked over to the place where Prabhupada was standing and started to have a conversation with him. Shalini said that she tried desperately to hear the subject of their discourse but, unfortunately, could hear nothing. After conversing together for some time, her former guru, Raghavendra, gave Prabhupada a drink of water from a pot he was carrying. Prabhupada refreshed himself with the water, following which the dream ended.

Shalini understood the main message of the dream to mean that she should become more committed to Krishna and also that she should find out more about ISKCON. Consequently, at the earliest opportunity she visited Bhaktivedanta Manor and then started regularly to attend *arati* (a major rite of worship) and other rituals and events held at the Manor. Moreover, as a way of expressing and demonstrating her new-found faith in, and devotion to, Krishna, she volunteered time and assistance here by working at the Manor's bakery and shop, service she gave (and still gives) as a way of expressing and extending her devotional commitment. Shalini, in fact, currently works in the bakery and shop at Bhaktivedanta Manor two mornings every week, a job she has been doing for many years. Yet, despite the deepening of her religious faith and devotion, Shalini told me that during the first few months of her attendance at the Manor she had many misgivings. She commented that she had many anxieties or concerns about

ISKCON, though she could not easily explain why. It was just an unsettling feeling she experienced without knowing the reason for it. This is when she had a second dream of Prabhupada and one which, for Shalini, was the most crucial, both in terms of the sense of certainty about her decision to remain within ISKCON and in terms of the growing conviction of the importance of her renewed devotionalism.

In her second dream, Shalini stated that she found herself in a strange building in which there was a very tall, winding staircase. At the top of the staircase stood Prabhupada, holding his familiar walking stick or cane (*danda*). Yet Prabhupada seemed to be quite some distance away. Shalini started to climb the stairs, but each step was arduous and hard to take, largely so because of the difficult, winding structure of the staircase. Eventually, however, Shalini said she managed to reach the top of it and, when she got there, she looked into the face of Prabhupada. At that very moment, Shalini told me Prabhupada gave her the most welcoming smile imaginable. In the dream Prabhupada did not speak, though my informant said that his smile was unforgettable. Shalini then woke up from the dream, with her fears, anxieties and concerns dispelled; and from that time onwards, Shalini informed me she became a most fervent devotee.

But, while this second dream undoubtedly removed many of Shalini's anxieties, fears and concerns, particularly those that arose in the early period of her involvement with ISKCON, there were still other occasions when she claimed to experience moments of anxiety, though no longer as intensely or as frequently. To be sure, Shalini informed me that the third and final dream of Prabhupada she had after many years of being a member of ISKCON suggested to her that certain, albeit minor, anxieties may always remain with her to some extent; but in this dream, too, she holds that the feeling of being a member of the ISKCON community and the importance of Prabhupada in her spiritual and devotional life are clear and particularly strong, the dream also aptly expressing the close bond she feels she has developed in relation to ISKCON as well as in relation to Prabhupada.

In her third dream, Shalini told me that Prabhupada paid a visit to her house. When he arrived, together with a large number of his disciples, Shalini said that she felt anxious and irritable, for she realised there was nothing to eat there. She had no food to offer Prabhupada and the devotees accompanying him. After a short while, the devotees went outside into the garden of the house for a walk and to take in some fresh air. However, the devotees shortly came back into the house, and Shalini commented that she now started to feel even more disturbed, being thoroughly miserable and upset at the prospect of having to announce she could not offer them or Prabhupada a single morsel to eat. But, as the devotees filed into her home, one of them suddenly called to Shalini, saying "There are some baked potatoes here." At that very moment, Shalini felt relieved and much at ease. Here the dream ended.

As already indicated, in Shalini's dreams in which Prabhupada appears, it is apparent there is much evidence of anxiety, the anxiety itself being the informant's own interpretation of her concerns and worries about her spiritual life as well as her involvement with, or commitment to, ISKCON, particularly during the early period of her membership of the community. Yet, despite the clear anxiety displayed in the dreams, a more impressive feature of them is the way in which the anxiety itself is dispelled, which Shalini sees as being an analogue or representation, not only of her spiritual development and its growing enrichment, but also of increasing recognition of the value ISKCON holds for her, recognition involving religious commitment and devotionalism to which Prabhupada is central and in which Prabhupada himself undoubtedly plays a most important role. Indeed, it seems that Shalini's dreams of ISKCON's founder-*acharya* have not merely enabled her to experience renewed faith in Krishna, as well as to return to the tradition of Vaishnavism into which she was born, albeit now within a Gaudiya framework; it is clear, too, that, for Shalini, Prabhupada is the key figure orienting or directing her devotional life, with his appearance in her dreams evidently having a powerful moulding effect on it.

Prabhupada's powerful shaping and orienting effect on the devotional lives or devotional trajectories of Hare Krishna devotees, the effect itself being realised or made possible through the medium of dreams, equally is much in evidence in other dream texts and case studies I have documented, as revealed by the case of Radha Mohan (and the case of Jaya Krishna) I now briefly outline.

Case 2: Radha Mohan

Radha Mohan, a university graduate, is a white, British *brahmachari* (celibate monk) in his mid-30s who currently resides at Bhaktivedanta Manor. He informed me that he began seriously to develop an interest in spiritual matters during his teenage years, a pursuit that led him to explore a number of religious traditions or faiths until finally he became a member of ISKCON in his early 20s. Throughout the whole period of his quest to find a suitable religious community or tradition in which he could feel comfortable and appropriately situated spiritually, as well as on some occasions before this time, Radha Mohan had a number of dreams with marked religious content and imagery. However, the vast majority of these dreams occurred after he entered the Hare Krishna community. Since becoming a member of ISKCON, Radha Mohan has had very many dreams of this kind and often involving a variety of major sacred figures, including Jesus Christ, the Buddha, Shiva (the Hindu god of destruction), Vishnu (the Hindu preserver deity), Lord Krishna, Lord Chaitanya (the 15th-16th century saint held by those in ISKCON, as well as by all other Gaudiya Vaishnavas, to be non-different from Krishna and His consort Radharani combined), and, of course, Prabhupada himself, the latter being especially prominent in the dreams. Indeed, in Radha Mohan's own personal diary in which he records the dreams – a diary he keeps and has kept since 1998 specifically for documenting these important dreams and which he also kindly made available in order to facilitate my research – Prabhupada appears on no less than 15 separate occasions. In the dreams,

Prabhupada sometimes appears simply in the form of a vision, but in the vast majority of the dreams Prabhupada gives a message, a message extended sometimes in response to questions put to him by Radha Mohan within the dream itself and sometimes spontaneously, as it were, without any kind of prompting on Radha Mohan's part. The actual words uttered by Prabhupada in the dreams are harsh sometimes, typically involving here some kind of chastisement; and on other occasions the words spoken are given in order to offer encouragement. However, whether the words uttered by Prabhupada in Radha Mohan's dreams are offered to chastise, to encourage or to provide answers to specific questions, Radha Mohan informed me that they have always been critical in his devotional life, enabling him to deepen and to develop this as well as to direct and enrich his commitment as an ISKCON member.

A number of the dreams, in fact, turn around clearly identifiable themes, notable ones involving Radha Mohan's status as a *brahmachari*. To begin with, Radha Mohan not only elected in 1999 to take initiation (the *nama-initiation*, or first rite of passage within ISKCON, which involves making vows and taking a new name) after having a dream in which Prabhupada instructed him to do just that, but his choice to reside at Bhaktivedanta Manor as a monk and his choice to continue living a strict, disciplined life there, are decisions very much contingent upon his dreams of Prabhupada. In one dream, Prabhupada rebukes Radha Mohan, saying:

> You must always be committed to the (early) morning programme, especially as a *brahmachari*. If you cannot make the effort, just live outside...

Yet, in another dream, Prabhupada offers much needed words of encouragement:

> Temple life is good. It's not like a prison. (Prabhupada then laughs.) What else are you going to do? There's nothing wrong with living in the temple.

In a context of particular hardship experienced by Radha Mohan while remaining a monk, as well as maintaining the strict discipline this entails, especially the importance of celibacy and managing libido or sexual drive, Prabhupada frequently enters into Radha Mohan's dreams. In one of them, Prabhupada utters the words:

> So we are making (spiritual) progress. However, you will have to control your genitals; otherwise just go into white.[4]

The words "just go into white", according to Radha Mohan, were not simply uttered by Prabhupada as a way of impressing upon him that he was faced with a choice involving the possibility of giving up the austere life of a monk (and thus sooner or later becoming a householder or *grihastha*, a married man who is distinguished in ISKCON by the donning of white garments); for Radha Mohan, it was essentially Prabhupada's way of making him aware of the importance of remaining a monk, and specifically because of the spiritual benefits it is held to bring. Indeed, in this dream, as in a number of other dreams like it, Radha Mohan told me that Prabhupada has been a potent orienting force, a force enabling him to remain a temple resident and one wholly committed to ISKCON as well as to its principles, practices and teachings. It thus seems clear that Radha Mohan's steadfastness and his committed stance have been much benefited by dreams of ISKCON's founder-*acharya*, with Prabhupada offering a great deal of guidance and direction through the medium of dreams.

Case 3: Jaya Krishna

Jaya Krishna is a senior devotee at Bhaktivedanta Manor who became an active member of ISKCON in the early 1970s and who received initiation into the Hare Krishna movement in the latter part of the same decade. Jaya Krishna was born in Kenya, east Africa, into a Hindu family. Although for a variety of reasons I was only able to carry out an interview with him on one single occasion, the information he gave concerning a dream he had of Prabhupada is most noteworthy and particularly instructive in terms of the aims and purposes of this chapter.

The dream of Prabhupada Jaya Krishna informed me about took place soon after his initiation into the ISKCON community. The circumstances which led to the dream are especially relevant, as the dream itself was occasioned by the complete withdrawal from ISKCON of the very guru or spiritual master who only a few months earlier had initiated Jaya Krishna and who had thus been appointed the role of spiritual guide to him. His guru's falling away from ISKCON, in fact, caused Jaya Krishna a great deal of anguish and much spiritual turmoil.

Now, it should be made clear here that the guru-disciple relationship in ISKCON is a core feature of spiritual and devotional life, a relationship that is established during the rite of initiation into ISKCON itself. As Knott points out in her discussion of initiation within the Hare Krishna movement:

It is (an) event which binds the disciple to the guru for life, and which marks the beginning of a serious commitment. The guru not only becomes responsible for the instruction of the disciple, but also takes on the effects of this person's actions...In exchange, the devotee promises to practise the minimum requirements of a life of true Krishna consciousness...The initiation of the disciple by the guru is complete when the guru gives the initiate a set of *japa* beads on which he has previously chanted the Hare Krishna *mantra*. (Knott, 1986, p.66)

Yet it is well recognised, of course, that in any faith community its members, however senior they may be or may have become, occasionally back-slide or withdraw from religious life; and here ISKCON is no exception. But for one who finds himself in Jaya Krishna's unsettling position, it is not at all surprising that much anguish or turmoil would be a likely, even perhaps an inevitable, consequence. Within ISKCON Tamal Krishna Goswami has examined the kind of difficulties this typically involves. Thus, commenting on the problem, and with particular reference to a letter he received from one devotee who found himself in a similar (though not identical) situation to Jaya Krishna, he writes:

> ...(T)he following (correspondence sent to me by) an aspiring initisate after learning that the guru of his choice had recently renounced his duties, becomes entirely understandable:

> "After building a relation with 'X' Maharaj on a guru/disciple relation and then receiving the fax of the bad news, it really hits hard. Now I can see why some devotees lose faith in ISKCON *sannyasi*s. You have to realise that Srila Prabhupada is our true guru and that his instructions are always there for us to fall back on. After all, he is our *acarya*, our master. I owe everything I have and everything I will have in Krishna consciousness to Srila Prabhupada for saving me from this material world of repeated birth and death."

> Such comments are not rare. Similar letters requesting re-initiation are also received from initiates whose gurus have fallen. (Tamal Krishna Goswami, 1997, p.10)

Jaya Krishna did not request re-initiation, though a key comment in the letter of the devotee cited above, namely, "I owe everything I have and everything I will have in Krishna consciousness to Srila Prabhupada" are words which Jaya Krishna very much echoed when I interviewed him; and this is evident from what Jaya Krishna told me about his dream of Prabhupada.

Now, I have already indicated that, on discovering his guru had withdrawn from devotional life and commitment, Jaya Krishna was distressed and suffered a great deal spiritually. And I have also pointed out that it was precisely these circumstances that preceded and occasioned his dream of Prabhupada. With regard to the dream itself, Jaya Krishna stated that one night when he was feeling much depressed as well as spiritually vulnerable due to his guru's decision to leave ISKCON, Prabhupada came immediately to aid and to rescue him. In the dream, Jaya Krishna said he first heard what seemed to be some kind of faint methodical tapping sound. The sound, however, soon became more and more audible. Then, suddenly, Prabhupada appeared. The rhythmical sound he heard was the tapping of Prabhupada's cane (*danda*) as he approached and drew ever closer to Jaya Krishna. When Prabhupada arrived at the place where Jaya Krishna was standing,

Prabhupada raised his walking stick or cane into the air until it was finally level with Jaya Krishna's chest. Prabhupada pointed the cane to the region of his chest where the heart is located. Then, following this action, Prabhupada uttered the words: "I am very much alive in ISKCON, and those who read my books will understand." After uttering the words, Prabhupada simply turned around and departed. The dream ended and Jaya Krishna woke up.

On waking from the dream, Jaya Krishna told me all his anxieties and fears had been completely removed, that he felt fully at peace. He explained that the dream involved Prabhupada's direct intervention at a crucial and decisive time in his religious life, a time when he most needed spiritual help and assistance. Indeed, Jaya Krishna emphasised that his encounter with ISKCON's founder-*acharya* in the crucial dream he had is clear indication that Prabhupada does not merely still continue to watch over members of the Hare Krishna community today, but that he equally continues to intervene in their lives as well as give them the guidance they need, particularly during moments of difficulty or hardship. In addition, for Jaya Krishna, Prabhupada is also still very much doing the spiritual work in which he was engaged before he departed from this world in order to return to the abode of Krishna. Despite having left his body, he is still, according to Jaya Krishna, the true and dependable, ISKCON's unique, irreplaceable guru.

Conclusion

In the introduction to this chapter, attention was drawn to a recent ISKCON publication, entitled *Plain Vanilla*, a publication in which one contributor, Drutakarma Dasa (2002, p.9), states that "Srila Prabhupada, as the founder-*acarya* of ISKCON, is the primary source of guidance and instruction, for all members of ISKCON." This statement appears to carry much conviction and force for those in the Hare Krishna community I have interviewed. Prabhupada is undoubtedly not only viewed in this manner by all those with whom I have discussed the subject at Bhaktivedanta Manor, but the dreams of Prabhupada cited in this chapter seem to demonstrate it too, and in a most telling fashion. Indeed, as a final comment, it is worth noting here that one key informant, Radha Mohan, whose dreams have been discussed in this chapter, told me that, although during his initiation in 1999 he made the "promise to remain faithful to ISKCON and to put Srila Prabhupada at the centre of ISKCON", he emphasised that it was his dreams of the founder-*acharya* which actually enlivened the words of the promise and which also imbued the words with deep spiritual value, meaning and purpose for him. To be sure, it has been demonstrated that all the dream texts presented in this chapter, as well as the meanings attributed to them by informants, potently reveal that, even beyond the grave, Prabhupada is still continuing to play a major role in the religious experience of ISKCON members and is still very much at the centre of their religious lives, with the highly pronounced experiential dimension having an important moulding effect on religious behaviour as well as on religious belief itself (cf. Bowman, 1992, p.13 and *passim*). Not only is it clear that the memory of Prabhupada remains most vivid, but through the medium of dreams this chapter has shown that he is held to exercise a force whose power profoundly shapes and directs his disciples, both in terms of their devotionalism as well as in terms of their spiritual orientation. Given that no figure within ISKCON has ever succeeded in taking up the mantle of the movement's founder-*acharya*, though not without attempts being made to achieve this very goal, it is entirely understandable why Prabhupada's uniqueness is still stressed and why dreams and visions of him loom large in the religious world and devotional discourse of Hare Krishna devotees today. The phenomenon of devotees' dreams of Prabhupada provides a new analytic focus this chapter has emphasised, one which offers fresh understandings, and one which students and scholars concerned with devotional beliefs and values or with devotional practices and developments in the Hare Krishna movement should not ignore.

THE CONSCIOUSNESS OF SURRENDER AND THE SURRENDERED CONSCIOUSNESS:
Ecstatic Dreams of Lord Krishna

Graham Dwyer

Introduction

It is difficult to find any religious system or faith community, whether ancient or modern, whether grounded in historical or mythical tradition, whether orthodox or popular in expression, that does not celebrate or recognise in some form the importance of dreams. In many religions dreams are the actual medium through which a transcendental being, a God, even, perhaps, a whole pantheon of gods and goddesses, as well as various types of lesser supernatural agent, are frequently believed to reveal themselves (Kilborne 1987). In the Judeo-Christian tradition, for instance, as in Islam, it is by means of dreams or visions that God is often held to make known His very identity, giving messages, disclosing His will or issuing particular demands through dreams. I note too that in Hinduism the belief that a temple should be established at a particular site immediately following a divinely inspired dream in which a god or goddess is said both to reveal itself and to express its desire for a shrine to be erected in that specific location is also a common occurrence, as well as being another important example of divine revelation through dreams (Dwyer 2003, pp.14-5). Moreover, in Buddhism, although the concept of a supreme God is rejected *in toto*, one can equally find accounts of supernatural or transcendental beings appearing in dreams, as in the celebrated dream of the Buddha's mother, Queen Maya, who during the course of the dream is said to encounter multitudes of divinities precisely at the moment when the as yet unborn Buddha enters her womb in the form of an elephant and is thus conceived (*Lalitavistara Sutra* 1983, p.95 ff.). But most notable of all, perhaps, in shamanic traditions found throughout various parts of the world divine or supernatural beings are widely thought to communicate their wishes and to be contactable through dreams.

The widespread belief that deities or *extra*-mundane entities may intrude upon the human world and are contactable through dreams is also one shared by members of the Hare Krishna movement. Investigations I have been conducting since April 2002 amongst converts to the Hare Krishna movement, or the International Society for Krishna Consciousness (ISKCON), reveal that such dreams are both common place for Hare Krishna devotees and considered by many of them to bring the devotee into an immediate as well as desirable relationship with divinity. During research at Bhaktivedanta Manor, ISKCON's UK headquarters, I came more and more to learn about the importance and value devotees attribute to their dreams (also see Dwyer's earlier chapter in this volume), both to their dreams of ISKCON's late founder, His Divine Grace A.C. Bhaktivedanta Swami Prabhupada, and, crucially, to dreams of Lord Krishna, who within ISKCON is held to be the Supreme Personality of Godhead.[1] In fact the subtitle of this chapter was originally suggested by one key informant, Radha Mohan, a celibate monk (*brahmachari*) and full-time resident at Bhaktivedanta Manor. During numerous interviews with him, this informant provided a wealth of information about his religious dreams, especially his dreams of Krishna. Importantly, the vast majority of his dreams have a clearly marked ecstatic expression and force, an expression and force that lie at the heart of much devotional discourse in the Hare Krishna movement, as well as being a major theme of many of its publications, most notably the publications authored by the movement's founder (see Prabhupada 1982 [1970]). Radha Mohan's ecstatic dreams of Lord Krishna, which are types of dream also reported by other Hare Krishna devotees I interviewed at Bhaktivedanta Manor, are this chapter's primary focus; but in it I hope to demonstrate that the phenomenon of ecstatic dreams reveals a particular orientation and mode of consciousness, namely: (1) a consciousness of surrender that is also at the same time (2) a surrendered consciousness.

In this chapter the first of these terms is employed to refer not merely to the broad theme of selfless surrender to God, a complete yielding of oneself to God as an act of pure devotion known in ISKCON as *bhakti-yoga*, which is central to ISKCON's religious ethic and philosophy; more precisely the term is used to denote a particular application of the practise of this philosophy, one that aims at its realisation or fulfilment through the medium of dreams. The second of the two terms, on the other hand, is used here to denote a specific structure of consciousness, a structure Jean-Paul Sartre (2001 [1940]) calls "fascinated consciousness" or "captivated consciousness"; that is to say, a condition of consciousness in repose. In his early philosophical work, *The Psychology of the Imagination* (2001), Sartre identifies two variants of a captivated consciousness: one variant being the consciousness of the dreamer during moments of deep sleep, the other being a condition of consciousness during the process of falling asleep (or, alternatively, during moments of arousal from sleep). And it is the latter mode of consciousness, the so-called hypnagogic condition, with which I am chiefly concerned, though I argue attention to each of these modes of consciousness is critical, as it aids understanding of and indeed sheds much light on the dynamics of the ecstatic dreams this chapter explores, as well as enabling one to gain understanding of crucial aspects of devotional life in ISKCON. Thus, while the chapter is mainly concerned with the dreams of one committed Hare Krishna devotee – a single case study – much of the analysis it provides is directly applicable to the religious dreams of other Hare Krishna devotees. To be sure, by engaging concepts rooted in Sartre's work on dreams and on the generative forces of human imagination, the chapter hopes to show this provides students and scholars with a helpful model for interpreting ecstatic dream narratives in the Hare Krishna movement.

Dreams, Consciousness and the Life-World

Major insights in the writings of Sartre this chapter engages – in particular key dimensions of his approach to dreams, consciousness, and the anchoring of consciousness in the lived-in world (*lebenswelt* or "life-world" as Husserl [1970] designated it) – are largely a product of Sartre's early explorations in phenomenology. In *The Psychology of the Imagination* (2001[1940]) Sartre aims explicitly to introduce into French intellectual life the work of the German philosopher Edmund Husserl; and in the book Sartre makes much use of concepts employed by Husserl (as well as concepts later used by Heidegger), central to which is the notion of *intentionality*. This term of major import in phenomenology has a technical application quite different from its use in every day parlance, as it is used to denote the manner in which consciousness attends to objects, that is to say, the way in which it is *directed onto* or *constructs* them (Dwyer 2003, pp.41-3). In this regard, therefore, objects are not thought passively to present themselves to consciousness; rather they are viewed as a construction of consciousness, consciousness itself positing them; and Sartre, closely following Husserl, holds that this property of intentionality is not merely peculiar to mental phenomena but common to all such phenomena. Thus, according to Sartre (2001, p.9), "(t)he intention is at the centre of the consciousness: it is the intention that is aimed at the object, that is, which makes it what it is."

Now, in terms of the constitutive work of consciousness, Sartre examines three ways in which consciousness constructs or intends its objects: an object, he states (2001, p.6 ff.), can be given to consciousness by means of (i) a perception, by means of (ii) a concept or an idea, and by means of (iii) an image. Throughout *The Psychology of the Imagination*, however, Sartre is largely concerned with the way in which consciousness posits or intends its objects imaginatively. And just how the structure of the imaginative consciousness can be grasped is made clear, Sartre holds, when one considers the mental state in relation to the apprehension of objects like photographs. He says,

> If someone suddenly shows me a picture of Peter...the photograph is but a paper rectangle of a special quality and colour, with shadows and white spots distributed in a certain fashion...If I see Peter by means of the photograph *it is because I put him there*...(I)t needs a certain intention, the one that turns it into an image. (Sartre 2001, pp.18-9)

Sartre in fact develops his exploration of the imaginary with reference to a range of different types of image in his analysis of the imaginative consciousness, though his treatment of dreams and related or similar phenomena, such as hypnagogic images, is, as Mary Warnock comments in her brief introduction to Sartre's celebrated work, especially noteworthy and even "of absorbing interest for its own sake" (Warnock 2001, p.xvii). According to Sartre, the imaginary consciousness in dreams functions in a fundamentally *noetic* way. This term, yet another of import in phenomenology and earlier employed by Husserl to denote pre-reflective thought (as opposed to *noematic* or reflective thought), is applied to the imaginative consciousness in dreams by Sartre because he explicitly rules out the possibility of genuine self-reflection here. For Sartre, it is not possible for the dreamer to be aware of him or herself. He contends that, correctly understood, there can be no true consciousness of "I" or "self" in the world of dreams. While this thesis may perhaps seem difficult to defend, Sartre, I believe, offers a convincing argument to support the claim, providing numerous examples to demonstrate how the dreamer cannot be likened to one who is awake precisely because "the reflective consciousness destroys the dream by the very fact that it presents it for what it is" (Sartre 2001, p.188).

Since Sartre maintains true self-consciousness cannot emerge in dreams, he considers the consciousness of the dreamer to be captivated, consciousness itself having fallen into a kind of enchanted world. With the arising of a reflective consciousness, on the other hand, which for Sartre is concomitant with the actual awareness of dreaming, with arousal from sleep, consciousness is freed from the captivity of the dream. Paradoxically, however, he also maintains that, even when the reflective consciousness escapes the enchanted world of the dream, there is still a sense in which it may continue to experience a form of captivation; and this occurs, crucially, when consciousness permits itself by an act of will actually to remain enchanted or fascinated by the imagery or content of the dream. It is this condition and similar mental states to which he applies the term hypnagogic. According to Sartre, while the hypnagogic condition typically develops its structures during the process of falling asleep, it also occurs in moments of arousal from sleep, as well as at moments when, during half-sleep, one allows one's eyes, for example, slowly to glide over marks on wall paper, descend on to a blot on a cloth or settle upon the flames of a fire. Commenting on the condition, he says,

> ...(W)e no longer feel capable of *animating* our body...This is a condition of very slight auto-suggestion...It will be noticed that here we have an entirely new way of thinking... The paralysis of my limbs and the fascination of my thoughts are but two aspects of a novel structure: consciousness in bondage... In this condition ...I have the power to decide whether or not to permit myself to be fascinated...If I become fascinated then hypnagogic images will appear. (Sartre 2001, pp.47-51)

The key point of these remarks centres on the highly creative force of the fascinated consciousness in the hypnagogic condition, a creative force of a consciousness that constitutes or intends its objects imaginatively in an immobile body. But the manner in which it constructs them hypnagogically is different to the way consciousness posits objects by means of photographs, and Sartre endeavours to disclose how the imaginative consciousness functions here as well as how its intentional dynamic displays itself in quite unique ways. But it must be emphasised that, with regard to the hypnagogic state, as in all other aspects of the work of consciousness, the very positing of objects for Sartre is not and never can be a creation *ex nihilo*. Thus, according to Sartre, all hypnagogic images, and the very material or content of dreams, cannot in any way be conceived as existing apart from the life-world; since, following Husserl (as well as Heidegger), he holds that an imaginative consciousness is inseparable from the actualities of the lived-in world: "every image rests on a layer of real existences", he writes, "and it is this we have called the imaginative consciousness" (Sartre 2001, p.156).

Sartre's approach to the imaginative consciousness, however, is not without problems (Dufrenne 1973; Kapferer 1997; Scruton 1995; and Warnock 2001). Importantly, while he maintains every image is built upon a realistic foundation, he problematically opposes the imaginary to the real, arguing that the imaginary is less real than the real (Sartre 2001, p.161 ff.). Yet, as Kapferer comments:

> ...(A)lthough the imaginary of consciousness may derealise the real, it is through the imagination that human beings adhere to or grasp the real...The imagination...is part of the real (rather than being less than real). It is constituted (as Sartre himself in fact recognises) on the basis of the lived-in world and (thus) is the means by which the reality of this world is realised as real in experience. (Kapferer 1997, p.231)

Nonetheless, despite difficulties such as this Sartre's original contribution is of genuine value, as many of his critics readily acknowledge. Thus, Kapferer says,

> Despite my reservations about Sartre's approach to the imagination...his notion of the "chained consciousness"...is important for extending an

understanding of the dynamics of ...consciousness...and...the body..., (a) chained consciousness...(in which the) imagination...assumes its particular inventive and phantasmagoric character... (Kapferer 1997, p.231)

Spiritual Dreams – Radha Mohan's Ecstatic Dreams of Lord Krishna

Having summarised key ideas in Sartre's work this chapter draws upon, I wish to turn now to the creative forces of the imagination in relation to the ecstatic dreams of Lord Krishna reported by my informant Radha Mohan. And I further wish to point out at this juncture that the dream experiences he described are essentially hypnagogic in form, as he indicated that in many of his dreams he is not only acutely aware of dreaming but also sometimes employs particular techniques actually to facilitate or maintain a reflective consciousness. Indeed, these types of dream experience as examples of the kind identified by Sartre where a reflective consciousness allows itself to be fascinated, reveal a chained consciousness that does not merely permit itself to be enchanted by ecstatic imagery, but also discloses itself as a consciousness oriented towards the ecstatic. To be sure, the very willingness and effort exercised on the part of Radha Mohan actually to become fascinated or enchanted in this manner is a crucial dimension of his devotional stance and commitment, involving a surrender to Krishna that extends beyond the everyday religious duties incumbent upon him as a monk. But to demonstrate how a Sartrean phenomenological approach can be fruitfully applied to his experiences (experiences I will refer to simply as ecstatic or spiritual dreams) an account of the particular Krishna dreams this chapter focuses upon is needed, as is a brief account of the informant's biographical details.

Radha Mohan is a white, British Hare Krishna devotee in his mid-30s who became a member of ISKCON in his early 20s. A number of years before his conversion to the Hare Krishna movement he became deeply interested in pursuing a religious life. During his teenage years he read many religious texts as well as many books about religion, particularly books about mysticism and Eastern faiths. And by the time he entered his final year as an undergraduate at Salford University his spiritual yearnings further developed. He thus made an effort at this time to find a religious community that could offer what he needed. Initially, the particular community he thought likely to be most suitable would be a Buddhist one. Radha Mohan thus found out about various Buddhist centres in Manchester and decided to visit some of them. The first centre he went to, however, turned out to be completely inappropriate: it seemed culturally too distant and alien to Radha Mohan. He looked elsewhere, therefore, and, after identifying another Buddhist centre, decided to go there. To get to it he had to take a bus journey, and what happened en route to this centre was of major import, not only in terms of his eventual conversion to the Hare Krishna movement, but also in terms of how he first became involved with the movement. According to my informant, he fell asleep on the bus journey and had a dream of the Hindu god Vishnu (who in ISKCON is held to be a manifestation of

Krishna). The dream was short and difficult to recall in any detail, however; but when Radha Mohan awoke he realised he had missed the bus stop he needed. Having gone past the Buddhist centre, he then looked out of the bus window and saw a road that led to a Hare Krishna temple, which he decided to investigate; and on entering the temple he stated he knew he had found his "spiritual home."

From this brief account of how Radha Mohan first became acquainted with ISKCON, it is readily apparent from the testimony that he attributes much significance to spiritual dreams. Indeed, he stated that such dreams have always been of enormous importance to him, the dreams being especially central in his devotional life. During interviews with Radha Mohan I not only learned about the many spiritual dreams he has had; I was told prominent sacred figures frequently have appeared in them, including Jesus Christ, the Buddha and numerous Hindu deities. Furthermore, I was told he has had many dreams of ISKCON's founder and, most important of all, many dreams of Krishna. A number of dreams of Prabhupada and Krishna were further claimed to have occurred at key points in the spiritual development of my informant. Thus, he not only decided to take initiation (the *nama-initiation* or first rite of passage within ISKCON) after being instructed in a dream to do so by Prabhupada; he stated that, after a period of doubt, he also decided to remain as a monk at Bhaktivedanta Manor following Prabhupada's instructions in dreams as well as after receiving similar messages in dreams from Krishna and from supernatural entities said to be acting on behalf of Krishna.

Although Radha Mohan commented such dreams sometimes occur spontaneously, as, for example, on the bus journey when he had the dream of Vishnu (or Krishna) that was so critical to his religious conversion and decision to become a member of ISKCON, he stressed that most of his spiritual dreams take place because of techniques he engages. One technique Radha Mohan sometimes employs (a technique, it seems, that is peculiar only to his practice, as other interviewed devotees claimed to have no awareness of it) was said to have been discovered by him before he became a Hare Krishna devotee. It is a technique culled from books such as Carlos Castaneda's *The Art of Dreaming* (1993 [1931]), and one my informant claimed to use specifically to "meet" with Krishna in dreams. Whether the purpose of this "meeting" is to enter into dialogue with the deity (as when, for instance, Radha Mohan feels he requires answers to questions relating to his religious commitment) or whether it is sought purely so as to enter into mystical union with Krishna, the procedure my informant observes was outlined by him in the following way:

> I first place pictures or images of Hindu divinities in the bedroom and, before getting into bed at night, set an alarm clock to ring after three or four hours of sleep. On waking, I immediately get out of bed, go to the bathroom and splash cold water on to my face. I then return to the bedroom and lie down again on the bed, allowing myself to descend into a semi-state of sleep. In this condition of half-sleep I next begin to think of

myself actually lying on the bed, with the body possessing an imaginary invisible axis running length ways through it such that one end of the axis protrudes out from the head and the other end of it extends outwards from the feet. Keeping my eyes closed and positioning my arms so that they are both close to and directly parallel with the body, I further imagine myself turning clockwise on the axis. After a very short while one's "astral body" or "subtle body" (*sukshma deha*) becomes detached from one's "gross body" (*sthula deha*), the former being free to wander and the latter being left motionless behind on the bed. In this condition of dissociation or state of self-hypnotic trance it then becomes possible temporarily to commune with Krishna and with other sacred beings who may appear or present themselves via the images previously assembled in the bedroom.

The application of this technique, leading to a hypnagogic state and facilitating a reflexivity in an imaginative consciousness directed on to the object of its devotion, Krishna Himself, has, according to Radha Mohan, enabled him to have a number of powerful ecstatic experiences. One of the most potent of these, indeed on his own admission one of the most significant in his spiritual life, involved seeing a painting of the deity and entering into it. This ecstatic dream of the deity my informant claimed actually occurred on two separate occasions, the second occurrence of it essentially being a repeat of the first. But the two versions of the dream, which I now outline and analyse, are separated in time by almost three years. Thus, according to the informant's dream diary, the experience of entering a picture of Krishna first took place in October 1998, recurring again in April 2001.

Dreaming of Entering a Painting of Lord Krishna

On the first occasion of Radha Mohan's dream of entering a painting of Krishna the deity, I was told, is seen standing close to his beloved brother, Balarama, in the sacred land of Vrindavan. Both in terms of his narration of the text of this powerful dream and in terms of his comment on its religious import, my informant emphasised the environs framed by the painting in the dream should not be understood simply as familiar geography, as merely delineating the Vrindavan situated in the north Indian state of Uttar Pradesh, but rather should be grasped as being at once an image of Vrindavan's physical location, as the land where Krishna appeared in this material world, as well as being a truly celestial domain. And on entering into the canvas my informant testified to being given a genuine "taste" of the divine. Yet it is notable that the painting into which Radha Mohan is taken in the dream was described by him as possessing all the familiar characteristics of typical paintings featuring Krishna in ISKCON's iconic repertoire, paintings which adorn the walls of Bhaktivedanta Manor where Radha Mohan resides. Indeed, this observation, one which underscores the point made earlier that dreams are not separate from, and in fact are grounded in, the actualities of the lived-in world, Radha Mohan himself stated he found particularly striking, though equally understandable given their place in his everyday familiar environment.[2] I was told the painting in the dream, like the paintings found at the Manor and found also in reproduced form in much ISKCON literature, manifested itself as an idyllic landscape in which Krishna's flower-garlanded body emanated divine light, the very force, according to Radha Mohan, that drew him within the canvas. But on entering the painting my informant said everything became "black." He could see nothing beyond or outside it, as though the world beyond the picture had vanished. Radha Mohan claimed that in the midst of the dream he now experienced a sense of being at "one with Krishna", located in a sacred landscape in which direct communion with the deity ensued. However, just as the light of the realm beyond the canvas had been extinguished, so too the light within it disappeared. Radha Mohan now could see nothing at all, the blackness that came, a blackness confounding all sight or vision, being the actual moment of transcendental union with God, the very moment, according to my informant, Krishna kissed him on the lips in a blissful embrace of divine rapture. However, the blackness here should not be interpreted as indicating some kind of void in any sense whatsoever my informant stressed but rather should be understood as an expression of the informant's own profound feeling of humility in Krishna's presence, as though the deity was revealing to Radha Mohan he was spiritually deficient and thus not "qualified" to see God.

It is this dream experience that is once more repeated almost three years later, the main difference being that in the second version of it Krishna is said to kiss Radha Mohan on the cheek rather than on the lips. In his dream diary account of it, he writes:

(It is the) most wonderful dream I ever had...In the dream, I entered an empty building. It was quite large – a bit like an art gallery that was yet to be opened. On one wall was a painting of Krishna in Vrindavan. At that moment my dream became lucid, i.e. I realised that I was dreaming and my "real" body was lying on a bed in the Hare Krishna temple. Then I had an idea: to introduce (the) technique that I had developed since reading *The Art of Dreaming* by Castaneda...

In my dream, I decided to enter into the Krishna painting on the wall as a way of meeting Him! It worked! Climbing on to the bottom of the frame of the painting, I then took an extra step into the painting itself. To a degree, once "inside", I was disappointed because I couldn't see anything. I had the impression that Krishna was trying to tell me that I wasn't "qualified" to see Him yet. But then, amidst my blindness, Krishna got closer to me. I put my hands on His waist and then He lent forward and briefly kissed me...

At that moment I woke to find myself lying on my bed in the *ashram* (of Bhaktivedanta Manor). I couldn't move my body – (it was) as if I hadn't properly "landed" (i.e. my subtle body had not yet fully settled back into my gross body). It was a beautiful dream...Especially at that time, I felt as if Krishna really had kissed me. The experience, I think, was a droplet from the reservoir...a taste (of the divine)...

Now, one of the most striking features of this dream, especially from the standpoint of Sartrean phenomenological analysis, turns around the constitution of Krishna in an imaginary consciousness that has its seat in a paralysed body. While Radha Mohan suggested physical immobility as a genuine function of the separation of the subtle body from its outer, gross form is both apparent here and should not be ignored, it is also notable such paralysis in the presence of Krishna is itself the focus of much attention in the devotional literature of the Hare Krishna movement. In *The Nectar of Devotion*, for example, Prabhupada says,

It is explained in *Srimad Bhagavatam* that when Brahma understood that (the) cowherd boy (Krishna) was the Supreme Personality of Godhead Himself, he became stunned. All of his sensory activities stopped...Lord Brahma was so stunned that he appeared to be a golden statue... (Prabhupada 1982 [1970], pp.224-5)

Crucially, in *The Nectar of Devotion* paralysis of the body in Krishna's presence is itself said to be a genuine expression of ecstatic love for the deity as well as one of the greatest manifestations of the ecstatic. Prabhupada writes:

Out of many ecstatic symptoms...the symptom of being stunned is especially significant...Unlike the shedding of tears and faltering of the voice (which are also ecstatic manifestations), the condition of being stunned is spread all over the body. The shedding of tears and faltering of the voice are simply localized symptoms. (Prabhupada 1982, p.229)

In the light of ISKCON doctrine, then, Radha Mohan's own experience may be viewed as an example of some degree of ecstatic rapture, his physical immobility (as well as the tears he sheds) being at once "symptoms" of ecstatic love for Krishna as well as being a register and embodiment of a consciousness in a state of spiritual submission. Here there is both a consciousness of surrender (a wilful giving of himself on Radha Mohan's part as an act of devotion expressed in his yearnings and in his search for Krishna as well as expressed in the emotionality of his attraction to the deity), and here also is a surrendered consciousness, one that permits itself to be captivated, indeed one that is oriented towards the image of Krishna, the object of fascination, which the surrendered consciousness itself intends or constitutes.

Further on the theme of embodiment vis-à-vis religious ecstasy and spiritual submission to the deity in a surrendered consciousness – what is also striking about the dream is the canvas itself as the site of transcendental union with God. Here it is believed a sacred space opens into which Radha Mohan enters, a space in which the deity is also present, Radha Mohan and the deity thus being enclosed within the body of the painting. In a sense the whole canvas itself *as* body uniting devotee and deity is a profound metaphor of becoming one with Krishna. Yet it is also more than mere metaphor for Radha Mohan, since for him it is the locus of genuine and immediate communion with divinity. However, this communion or transcendental union, which is ultimately expressed in the dream in the ecstatic embrace, particularly when Krishna bestows a kiss, never destroys their separateness or individuality, a point my informant stated is crucial to the interpretation of the dream. For, although in the ecstasy of the dream there is a consciousness of surrender to Krishna, a consciousness that remains captivated by the image of Krishna in an intending consciousness oriented towards the divine image, the unity that is held to occur leads to a condition of absorption that also allows for distinctness, a condition my informant, who, invoking the devotional philosophy of ISKCON, described as "inconceivable simultaneous difference and non-difference." In other words, the dream of entering a painting of Krishna for Radha Mohan signifies unity as well as plurality. This philosophical conception known as Bhedabheda or Dvaitadvaita Vedanta (Brockington 1991, p.151; Knott 1986, p.27) has its origins in the work of the 13th century theistic saint Nimbarka, a philosophical conception also adopted by the saint Chaitanya, who championed the doctrine of identity-in-difference and who popularised the very tradition of devotional practice seen in ISKCON today. The doctrine of *dvaitadvaita* (literally, "dualistic non-dualism") here is thus a theistic philosophical stance which holds God to be both the same as and different from individual souls; and because in ISKCON Krishna is viewed in this manner, because He is held to be a personal God who in an important sense is separate from the souls of His disciples, the latter are believed to be able to offer service and worship to Him (Knott 1986, p.24). In the context of my informant's dream, his own individuality or separateness from Krishna, which enables Radha Mohan to stand in a devotional relationship to the deity, is maintained by means of the very reflexivity of the devotional consciousness itself, a reflexivity that is disclosed in his account of the dream narrative already cited and evident particularly where he states: "*I* realised that *I* was dreaming." Moreover, the erotic features of the dream suggested by Krishna's kiss as well as by the deity's loving embrace, are, perhaps, especially significant as illustration of the inconceivable simultaneous difference and non-difference (*achintya bhedabheda tattva*) Radha Mohan claimed to experience, the joining together of Radha Mohan and Krishna in the loving embrace being symbolic of it, as well as being a prominent theme of much devotional discourse throughout Vaishnavism (Brockington 1991, p.162).

But most important of all here is the reflexive consciousness. For it is this which permits Radha Mohan to become captivated by the image of Krishna, which permits the consciousness in the imaginary of the ecstatic dream to be directed on to the divine image. And in view of this it is little wonder Radha Mohan actually employs techniques to facilitate a reflective consciousness in dreams: self aware of self in its own intentional structure of willing captivation to the divine image is in Radha Mohan's dream a powerful manifestation of devotionalism, a dynamic expression of the consciousness of surrender in a surrendered consciousness. Indeed, as a way of experiencing or meeting with the deity it is for Radha Mohan both powerful and supremely devotional, a potent means of augmenting his devotional commitment. In effect his spiritual dreams have enabled him to develop a spiritual dimension that complements and enriches other devotional practices to which I was informed he remains committed, practices involving daily *mantra* recitation (*japa*) and worship (*puja*), for example. It is entirely understandable, then, why Radha Mohan attributes much significance to his spiritual dreams and why they are central in his devotional experience. To be sure, just as for this servant of Krishna the dreams command much attention and are of immense religious import, so too they provide an important focus for the student or scholar of spiritual dreams who seeks to comprehend the meaning and value such dreams possess within the framework of devotional life; and utilisation of concepts rooted in the work of Sartre, in particular the concepts developed by him in *The Psychology of the Imagination*, appear greatly to facilitate this.

Concepts and understandings developed by Sartre clearly help illuminate the dream phenomena reported by Radha Mohan in a number of ways, enabling one to gain insight into the major processes and dynamics of the structure of the intentional consciousness of the religious dreamer; for it reveals precisely how this Hare Krishna monk is mentally directed during his spiritual dream experiences. It shows how the intentionality of the monk as dreamer is oriented in an imaginary consciousness, a consciousness whose origination and focus (Lord Krishna) are constituted by that very consciousness. With Radha Mohan the mental state of the dreamer – a mental state of willing captivation or surrender – is, as Sartrean analysis discloses, not passive but active, and in the particularly creative manner Sartre considers peculiar in such a consciousness. Such a consciousness itself, as Sartre indicates, is essentially hypnagogic in form, a form of consciousness generated in the case of the monk because of the kind of techniques he employs. As is evident from the devotee's own account of their use, they make it possible for him to meet with Krishna, that is, to cultivate dimensions of devotionalism in dreams that offer unique and novel possibilities of a wholly *extra*-mundane order, a crucial reason why the monk actually uses techniques to generate a hypnagogic condition. That Radha Mohan's dream experiences in fact are hypnagogic in form, and thus helpfully examined from a Sartrean standpoint, is further made clear in terms of other key features Sartre identifies in his account of the condition. Of particular note is Sartre's point that the unique, creative force of consciousness in the hypnagogic state typically develops its structures in an immobile body. Paralysis of the body together with these novel aspects of imaginary thought, it will be recalled, are in Sartre's view the condition's primary features, each being a concomitant of the other. They are also key defining features of the dreams of entering a painting of Krishna Radha Mohan claims to have experienced, as is evident from his diary record cited earlier. In the dream narrative it is clear that the physical immobility of the dreamer and the powerful imagery that ensues in consciousness within the dream are inseparable; that is, they are two interconnected or interrelated dimensions of the whole experience. As the Hare Krishna monk indicates in his testimony of the ecstatic dream experience, it is only during that moment of consciousness of physical immobility that the same consciousness becomes focused on Krishna, the moment when the imaginary scene of Krishna in the sacred land of Vrindavan emerges, together with the unfolding of the events that are said to result in mystical union with divinity. Moreover, the other major defining feature of the hypnagogic state in terms of the manner in which Sartre has analysed it, namely, the presence of the reflective consciousness, is, as already emphasised, central in Radha Mohan's account of his ecstatic dreams of Krishna too. The monk's stated ability to maintain this in the dreams and, importantly, his claim that it is the actual presence of reflexivity that helps ensure the spiritual benefit such dreams bring, enabling the monk both to develop and to extend his devotion to Krishna by means of them, equally makes it clear that a Sartrean approach has much to offer in the interpretation of Radha Mohan's dreams. Thus, the approach developed by Sartre is evidently not only of relevance here but of great value, both in terms of assessing and in terms of understanding this Hare Krishna devotee's ecstatic dreams.

Conclusion

Radha Mohan's ecstatic dreams of Lord Krishna – types of dream also commonly reported by other members of the Hare Krishna movement I have interviewed – are amenable, no doubt, to a variety of analytical perspectives other than the one engaged in this chapter. Psychoanalytic and similar or allied psychological approaches, for instance, particularly the approaches developed by Freud (1998 [1900]) and Jung (1978, 1979 [1961],1995 [1938]), are now classic examples of the kinds of perspective frequently utilised in the study of religion that could also perhaps be used to interpret the dreams this chapter has presented. However, the main difficulty with such approaches, and a major reason for refusing to employ them here, is that they move away from, indeed in the case of Freud deliberately eschew, the meanings the dreamer ascribes to his or her spiritual dreams. That is, in such types of analysis, the way the dreamer comprehends dreams or the way the dreamer interprets them is forced into terms removed from the dreamer's own conceptions and understandings, involving appeal to mystical notions of unconscious mind, unconscious motivations and so forth. While such approaches may not in themselves be seen as incorrect or invalid ways of accounting for dream phenomena, they are nonetheless problematic precisely because they loom over (and in Freud's work seek fully to dominate) the dream texts to which they attend. Here, then, there is a reductionism, one that privileges the authority of theoretical arguments and concepts to which the voice of the dreamer ultimately is subordinated.

In contrast to these problematic ways of assessing dream narratives, this chapter provides an alternative approach, a phenomenologically oriented approach anchored in the work of Sartre, one that, in turn, emanates from the philosophy of Husserl (as well as from the philosophy of Heidegger). One of the chief merits of this approach, and an important reason it has been engaged in this chapter, is that it does not attempt to undermine the authority of the interpretation or the meaning spiritual dreams hold for the dreamer; nor does it seek to compromise the integrity of the religious logic that underpins the dreams. On the contrary, it endeavours to reveal the value of spiritual dreams for the one who experiences them, focusing on their overt, explicit content within the framework of the dreamer's own religious conceptions and beliefs. It is these understandings the chapter's engagement of a Sartrean model has hopefully demonstrated in its examination of the Hare Krishna monk's ecstatic dreams I have discussed. In addition, I hope to have shown that a Sartrean phenomenological approach has much to offer, as it not only enables the full force of the dreamer's own voice to be given recognition but also discloses the religious or spiritual import the dreams themselves have in the religious or devotional life of the dreamer.

PART 3

Tradition and Modernity

6

BRINGING THE LORD'S SONG TO A STRANGE LAND:
Srila Prabhupada's Strategy of "Cultural Conquest" and Its Prospects

William H. Deadwyler (Ravindra Svarupa Dasa)

Introduction

In September of 1965, A.C. Bhaktivedanta Swami Prabhupada, a solitary 70 year old missionary monk, took in his first view of America, his freighter having made landfall in Boston Harbour. In a Bengali poem he composed on the occasion, Prabhupada called the place he found himself *ugra-sthan* – "terrible land" – and wondered how the people here, covered by passion and ignorance, would be able to understand his talk about Krishna.[1] Later, alone in a Manhattan winter – it was the first time he saw snow – he must have presented an entirely incongruous figure, clad as he was in the traditional saffron robes of a mendicant *sannyasi*, walking among the soaring glass and concrete towers of that endlessly hustling, trafficking city.

Manhattan! – Prabhupada had unerringly set himself in the beating heart of the modern enterprise, the vital centre of the empire of "getting and spending" that in its inexorable global expansion was sedulously ingesting all the traditional cultures of humanity. Among those mortally threatened was in fact the spiritual culture that Prabhupada himself represented. What is more, Prabhupada's journey to the West expressed his tradition's bold response to this threat – a response crafted by two prior generations of preceptors in Prabhupada's spiritual lineage. The response was not a strategy of mere survival by withdrawal and isolation, by passive or active hostility. Prabhupada did not plan merely to survive; he planned to prevail.

Prabhupada called his strategy "cultural conquest." This phrase first appears in an unpublished article he composed years before his Western journey.[2] Reporting on his meeting with the Governor of Bihar, Prabhupada set forth his vision for a

world-changing mission, presented to the Governor as a kind of spiritually
surcharged Gandhism:

> Gandhiji in the latter part of his life began this transcendental chanting of
> the Name of the Lord and his famous chorus singing of RAGHUPATI
> RAGHAVA RAJA RAMA is quite well known to us. Lord Chaitanya did
> not put any barrier to any caste, creed or color for joining this
> transcendental chorus of chanting the Lord's name and he blesses all men
> to achieve the highest spiritual realization by this simple method. By this
> method of chanting every one will attain to the plane of pure consciousness.
> They shall be relieved of the pangs of a mechanical life of repeated birth,
> death, old age and disease. By this method of realization the supreme life of
> perfection by realizing God as He is, will (be) usher(d) in.
>
> (Certain Gandhian programmes) if systematically carried on will help
> very much in the spiritualizing process. They can be given a real spiritual
> shape in accordance with the principles of *Bhagwat Gita* and other authentic
> scriptures. And by doing so India's original culture will not only be revived
> and re-established but also will foster India's indigenous culture in other
> parts of the world. That will be a sort of cultural conquest of all (the) world
> by India. By such conquest the people of the world will get relieved of the
> so-called material prosperity terrorized by atomic bombs.

In India, Prabhupada had painstakingly prepared an arsenal for his campaign
of "cultural conquest," and it accompanied him on his voyage: a metal trunk
packed with three-volume sets of the First Canto of *Srimad Bhagavatam*. Working
single-handedly in Vrindavan and New Delhi, he was the sole translator,
fundraiser, publisher, and distributor. The preface to the first volume in the trunk
began with a mission statement expressed in Prabhupada's characteristic voice,
here unmuffled by the normalising of subsequent editing:

> We must know the present need of the human society. And what is that
> need? The human society is no longer bounded by geographical limits of a
> particular county or community. The human society is broader than that in
> the middle age, and the world tendency is to belong to one state or one
> human society. The ideals of spiritual communism according to *Srimad
> Bhagwatam* are based more or less on oneness of the entire human society,
> nay, the entire Energy of the living being. The need is felt by great thinkers
> how to make it successful ideology. *Srimad Bhagwatam* will fill the gap of
> human society and it begins, therefore, with the aphorism of Vedanta
> Philosophy as *Janmadyasya yatah* to adjust the ideal of common cause.
>
> The human society, at the present moment, is not in the darkness of
> oblivion. It has made rapid progress in the field of material comforts of life,
> education and economic development of the entire world. But it suffers a
> pin-prick somewhere in the social body at large and therefore there is large

scale quarrel even on less important issue(s). Therefore there is the want of a clue as to how they can become one in peace, friendship and prosperity by the common cause. *Srimad Bhagwatam* will fill this need, for it is a cultural presentation for re-spiritualization of the entire human society.[3]

I wish to take these statements about cultural conquest and respiritualisation as a starting point for exploring the nature of the tradition Srila Prabhupada brought with him to the West in order to understand how he expected it to take root and flourish in the inhospitable soil of modernity and ultimately to prevail. In less than a year after his arrival, Prabhupada incorporated the International Society for Krishna Consciousness (ISKCON) in New York, an organisation intended to embody that tradition – "India's original culture" – and to carry out the project of "cultural conquest" in the West.

Srila Prabhupada's Perspective on Modern Society

The struggle between modernity and tradition has had, of course, a long history before the recent headline-generating assaults on modernism by jihadist Islam and politicised Christian fundamentalism – both focused in or on the United States of America. ISKCON itself can also be classified among the anti-modernist movements. Yet this is a widely disparate class, since it includes not only the various fundamentalisms, but also the profusion of "New Age" political, religious and social groups. The resurgence of the anti-modern, or the stubborn persistence of the pre-modern, in all their various forms, may seem surprising just when digital technology, igniting an explosion of world-transforming innovations, has propelled the modernist endeavour to even greater triumphs. Yet much is happening – global warming and environmental degradation head a long list – to lend credence to the position that the current modernist efflorescence may yet be, as Debussy remarked of Wagner's music, "a beautiful sunset mistaken for a dawn."

Prabhupada certainly thought of modern technological civilisation as an artificial, dangerous, rickety affair that created problems rather than solved them. Interestingly, his introduction to life in Manhattan included the famous blackout of November 1965. He described his experience in a letter dated 13 November to Sally Agarwal:

> Yes there was all darkness in New York on the 10th instant and it was not a happy incident. I learn(ed) that many people remained in the elevators and in the subway trains for more than seven to eight hours in darkness...That is the way of material civilization too much depending on machine. At any time the whole thing may collapse and therefore we may not be self complacent depending so much on artificial life. The modern life of civilization depends wholly on electricity and petrol and both of them are artificial for man. You will be surprised to know that I had to take help of

the old crude method of lightening by burning some vegetable oil and (to) use the small bowl as lamp to save myself from the extreme darkness...Yes in India we...experience failure of electricity but I was surprised to see the same thing in America...Even in such an advanced country there may be possibility (of) such failure but failure in America is more dangerous than that in India.[4]

For Prabhupada, people urgently needed to be delivered from the sufferings of "so-called material prosperity terrorised by atomic bombs." To him, the Enlightenment project is a massive misplacement of human effort, and "progress" is a phantasmagoria:

The history of the world has factually proved that attempts to increase economic development for bodily comfort through the advancement of material civilization have done nothing to remedy the inevitability of birth, death, old age and disease. Everyone has knowledge of huge empires throughout the history of the world – the Roman Empire, the Moghul Empire, the British Empire and so on – but all the societies engaged in such economic development...have been frustrated by the laws of nature through periodic wars, pestilence, famine and so on. Thus all their attempts have been flickering and temporary...All such positions of economic development, although created with great endeavor and hardship, are vanquished very soon. (*Srimad Bhagavatam* 7.7.39, purport)[5]

Prabhupada's writings and lectures abound in jeremiads against modernity:

Human prosperity flourishes by natural gifts and not by gigantic industrial enterprises. The gigantic industrial enterprises are products of a godless civilization, and they cause the destruction of the noble aims of human life. The more we go on increasing such troublesome industries to squeeze out the vital energy of the human being, the more there will be unrest and dissatisfaction of the people in general, although a few only can live lavishly by exploitation. The natural gifts such as grains and vegetables, fruits, rivers, the hills of jewels and minerals, and the seas full of pearls are supplied by the order of the Supreme, and as He desires...The natural law is that the human being may take advantage of these godly gifts by nature and satisfactorily flourish on them without being captivated by the exploitative motive of lording it over material nature. The more we attempt to exploit material nature according to our whims of enjoyment, the more we shall become entrapped by the reaction of such exploitative attempts. If we have sufficient grains, fruits, vegetables and herbs, then what is the necessity of running a slaughterhouse and killing poor animals?...If the human civilization has sufficient grains, minerals, jewels, water, milk, etc., then why should it hanker after terrible industrial enterprises at the cost of the labor of some unfortunate men? (*Srimad Bhagavatam* 1.8.40, purport)

One of Prabhupada's stated purposes for ISKCON was to "create a simpler, more natural way of life." Using a phrase from Wordsworth as his slogan, Prabhupada called this "plain living and high thinking."[6] He advocated the return to an agrarian economy as an ideal and encouraged the establishment of wholly self-sufficient rural communities, where oxen pull the plows. Such is the natural, simple way of life that best fosters true cultural development and human progress.

Yet all this did not inhibit Prabhupada from writing:

One should not give up anything which can be utilized in the service of the Lord. That is a secret of devotional service. Anything that can be utilized in advancing Krsna consciousness and devotional service should be accepted. For instance, we are using many machines for the advancement of our present Krsna consciousness movement, machines like typewriters, dictating machines, tape recorders, microphones and airplanes. Sometimes people ask us, "Why are you utilizing material products if you condemn the advancement of material civilization?" But actually we do not condemn. We simply ask people to do whatever they are doing in Krsna consciousness. This is the same principle on which, in *Bhagavad Gita*, Krsna advised Arjuna to utilize his fighting abilities in devotional service. Similarly, we are utilizing these machines for Krsna's service. With such sentiment for Krsna, or Krsna consciousness, we can accept everything. If the typewriter can be utilized for advancing our Krsna consciousness movement, we must accept it. Similarly, the dictating machine or any other machine must be used. Our vision is that Krsna is everything. Krsna is the cause and effect, and nothing belongs to us. Krsna's things must be used in the service of Krsna. That is our vision.[7]

The policy of liberally employing material resources for Krishna's service, even to confute the way of life that produced those resources, is certainly not without dangers. People make tools, but the tools tend in turn to remake their makers. To avoid such dangers, the Amish – withdrawing from world to retain their own "plain living and high thinking" – are well-known for eschewing modern technology. Prabhupada knew the risks. He was, for example, famously reluctant to use the telephone; he much preferred to employ the post to supervise his far-flung movement. It is said that he blamed over use of the telephone for an abortive 1970 leader's "conspiracy" to marginalise him. In 1977 he wrote to his disciple Gurudasa: "The installing of telex communications for our main temples is not required. Then they will gossip more through the telex." One can well imagine what he would have thought of e-mail and the internet.

Clearly, any material facility used for Krishna's service offers opportunity for misuse. Prabhupada was confident enough to run the necessary risk. His aim, after all, was not to withdraw from modern society, but to transform, to "respiritualise" it. And that required engaging with that society by living within it and using its products. How, we may ask, did he expect to do that and at the same time preserve the integrity and purity of his tradition?

Tradition forms the foundation of Prabhupada's teachings and actions. "Tradition" here refers to the divinely instituted culture of spiritual teaching and practice that is transmitted faithfully from generation to generation. Prabhupada came to the West as a person formed through-and-through by tradition, as one who veritably embodied it, and as one with the warrant and power to transmit it to others intact and without compromise. And those who received it from him – though formed in a degraded "cat-and-dog society" – had to become themselves sufficiently reformed so they could in turn transmit it purely to the next generation. They had to become just like him. As Prabhupada wrote on 16 June 1972 to Madhudvisa (a member of the Governing Body Commission):

> I am successful only because I am following strictly the orders of my Guru Maharaja, and I do not deviate. Therefore people respect what I am saying and they listen because I do not say one thing and do another. So now you are doing my work and you shall be like me and be yourselves the worthy representatives of our disciplic succession.

Disciplic Succession: the Transmission of Spiritual Authority

"Disciplic succession" is Prabhupada's regular English rendering of the Sanskrit *parampara*, a word that literally means "one after another." "Disciplic succession" makes it clear that it is the succession of guru and disciple who in turn becomes a guru. *Parampara* denotes the core mechanism of tradition, by which what is bestowed aboriginally by divinity is received, preserved, and perpetuated by humanity in full potency through the ages. Although *parampara* entails a temporal sequence, it is a sequence that, rightly carried out, collapses time into an eternal present – and presence.

A close reading of Prabhupada's commentaries on a pair of *Srimad Bhagavatam* texts (1.3.44, 1.4.1) will illustrate this feature and convey in depth the theology and practice of disciplic succession. It will also show how ISKCON itself was constructed to be the medium for a viable *parampara*.

Srimad Bhagavatam contains within itself an account of its own composition and first disciplic transmissions at the beginning of this present age of Kali. These events are paradigmatic for the later tradition. *Bhagavatam* tells how its author, Vyasadeva, the "literary incarnation of God," was instructed by his guru, the sage Narada Muni, to correct the insufficiency of Vyasa's literary endeavours (dividing the Vedas and reducing them to writing; composing the Puranas, the *Mahabharata*, and the *Vedanta-sutra*) by writing *Srimad Bhagavatam* and thus providing a more complete and confidential account of the pastimes of Krishna. Vyasa's son Sukadeva heard the *Bhagavatam* from his father, and Sukadeva afterwards recited it to Maharaja Pariksit, the great emperor of the world, who was fasting while awaiting his death on the bank of the Ganges. On that occasion a host of sages sat in audience, among them Suta Goswami, the speaker of this verse, who now prepares to deliver the second public recitation to a convocation of sages at the sacred Naimisaranya forest. He says:

O learned *brahmanas*, when Sukadeva Goswami recited *Bhagavatam* there (in the presence of Emperor Pariksit), I heard him with rapt attention, and thus, by his mercy, I learned the *Bhagavatam* from that great and powerful sage. Now I shall try to make you hear the very same thing as I learned it from him and as I have realized it.

Srila Prabhupada's commentary will focus on the qualifications of speaker and hearer for a successful transmission of *Srimad Bhagavatam*. He begins in a startling way by abruptly stating the characteristic of a perfect reception:

One can certainly see directly the presence of Lord Sri Krsna in the pages of *Bhagavatam* if one has heard it from a self-realized great soul like Sukadeva Goswami.

Behind this claim for a direct vision of God we find a theology: because God is absolute or without duality, there is no difference between God and his veridical representation in the form of proper name or of description of actions or features. Though God's audible representation appears in what may seem to be the material medium of speech, the actual transcendent meaning will be revealed only when both speaker (guru) and hearer (disciple) are qualified. Under those conditions, although there is a verbal medium, it becomes a transparent enabler of unmediated perception of what is described. Such direct spiritual experience is called "realised knowledge." It is as if we found a travel guide that magically transported us to whatever city it described. Here, with "transcendental literature," such direct perception of the divine requires special conditions to take place. The speaker must be fit – a "self-realised" person, whom we must distinguish from the unfit:

One cannot, however, learn *Bhagavatam* from a bogus hired reciter whose aim of life is to earn some money out of such recitation and employ the earning in sex indulgence. No one can learn *Srimad Bhagavatam* who is associated with persons engaged in sex life. That is the secret of learning *Bhagavatam*. Nor can one learn *Bhagavatam* from one who interprets the text by his mundane scholarship. One has to learn *Bhagavatam* from the representative of Sukadeva Goswami, and no one else, if one at all wants to see Lord Sri Krsna in the pages. That is the process, and there is no alternative.

In India, talented orators earn their livelihood by reciting *Bhagavatam*, and they regularly move audiences to tears. In universities erudite scholars dazzle the mind with exegetical speculations about *Bhagavatam*. However, although the text may be read, *Bhagavatam* does not take place. No one sees Krishna "in the pages" – not unless the orator or scholar be initiated into the "secret of learning *Bhagavatam*." The required "process" is called "secret" because not everyone will appreciate it – perhaps because it requires continence. In any case, one has to hear in a proper way from the proper person, the "bona fide representative":

> Suta Goswami is a bona fide representative of Sukadeva Goswami because he wants to present the message which he received from the great learned *brahmana*. Sukadeva Goswami presented *Bhagavatam* as he heard it from his great father, and so also Suta Goswami is presenting *Bhagavatam* as he had heard it from Sukadeva Goswami.

Here Prabhupada recounts the disciplic succession from Vyasa to Suka to Suta. Suta is "bona fide" because he has placed himself under the discipline of the succession, and he is thereby enabled to present *Bhagavatam* "as he had heard it." Prabhupada here points to the essential feature of *parampara*: absolute fidelity in representation. Even though the "message" may pass through a long succession of members, it remains unchanged. This claim, utterly incredible to modern historical consciousness, is so important to Prabhupada that he incorporated it into the title of his *Bhagavad Gita As It Is*. Now, Prabhupada explains how such fidelity is possible:

> Simple hearing is not all; one must realize the text with proper attention. The word *nivista* means that Suta Goswami drank the juice of *Bhagavatam* through his ears. That is the real process of receiving *Bhagavatam*. One should hear with rapt attention from the real person, and then he can at once realize the presence of Lord Krsna in every page. The secret of knowing *Bhagavatam* is mentioned here.

Notice the two occurrences of the word "realize" in the passage above: "realize the text" and "realize the presence of Krishna in every page." Both denote the experience of unmediated spiritual perception. The word *nivista* – "being intent on" – indicates the "secret" of the process. *Bhagavatam* must be heard with "rapt attention" from the "real person." It is clear that the "real person," the qualified speaker, is one who has first been a qualified hearer – that is, able to listen with intensely concentrated attention. This degree of attention is uncommon, for, Prabhupada now will explain, it is attained only by a life of complete purity:

No one can give rapt attention who is not pure in mind. No one can be pure in mind who is not pure in action. No one can be pure in action who is not pure in eating, sleeping, fearing and mating. But somehow or other if someone hears with rapt attention from the right person, at the very beginning one can assuredly see Lord Sri Krsna in person in the pages of *Bhagavatam*.

As Krishna teaches in the sixth chapter of the *Bhagavad Gita*, fixed concentration in yoga practice is achieved by controlling the mind, and for this the mind must be made peaceful, undisturbed by material attractions and aversions. This purity of mind, Prabhupada here points out, cannot be attained unless the actions of the senses are pure – so pure that even the most basic animal drives are conducted in a pure way. Prabhupada is alluding here to the "regulative principles" of devotional practice – *bhakti-(vidhi) sadhana* – established for members of the tradition. Followed with dedication, they effect a total sanctification of life – rising daily before dawn for chanting and worship, reading scripture every day, offering all the results of one's labour to Krishna, eating only the vegetarian food that had been prepared for and first offered to Krishna, restricting sex strictly to procreation in marriage, taking no intoxicants – not even coffee or tea, and so on. Then it becomes possible to become a qualified hearer and speaker of *Bhagavatam*. Srila Prabhupada brought the *Bhagavatam* with him to America, and he founded ISKCON to create the necessary conditions under which *Bhagavatam* could actually take place.

Srila Prabhupada concludes his discussion of this text (1.3.44) in his commentary on the text (1.4.1). There he writes how the leader of the gathered sages "stood up to congratulate Sri Suta Goswami when he expressed his desire to present *Srimad Bhagavatam* exactly as he heard it from Sukadeva Goswami and also realized it personally." Now Prabhupada elaborates further on the idea of realisation:

Personal realization does not mean that one should, out of vanity, attempt to show one's own learning by trying to surpass the previous *acarya*. He must have full confidence in the previous *acarya*, and at the same time he must realize the subject matter so nicely that he can present the matter for the particular circumstances in a suitable manner. The original purpose of the text must be maintained. No obscure meaning should be screwed out of it, yet it should be presented in an interesting manner for the understanding of the audience. This is called realization.

"Personal realization" makes possible what may seem a union of opposites: undeviating adherence to the previous *acharya*s (exemplary teachers) and the responsiveness and adaptability to changing time and circumstance to convey it compellingly to new audiences. When there is realisation, traditional teaching is not passed on by superficial rote repetition. Rather the teaching is fully assimilated by the hearer – one takes it in and directly experiences the truth of what has been heard; having thus made it one's own, it is brought out again into the world, expressed with the urge to convey that same truth to the new audience. Such teaching will be well-spiced with a particular and personal flavour; it will have all the compelling attractions of novelty and freshness, yet it will be the same unchanging and immutable teaching of old.

Realisation alone makes the difference between a living and a dead tradition. Realisation is the foundation of inspired and inspiring teaching, and it makes *parampara* the conveyance of an unbroken flow of the spiritual energy (*chit-shakti*) that illumines our understanding and provides immediate perception of divinity.

The volumes of *Bhagavatam* in Prabhupada's trunk themselves exemplify the above instructions. When Prabhupada composed them, he had before him the Sanskrit text accompanied by the verse-by-verse commentaries of nearly ten centuries of previous *acharya*s. Prabhupada studied and assimilated them, and then in his own distinctive voice typed his English "purports." With this in mind, we can understand Prabhupada's question in his arrival poem – "Will they be able to understand talk about Krishna?" – to mean: Will they be able to understand his own presentation of *Srimad Bhagavatam*? We can also see that this implied the further question: Would Srila Prabhupada be able to create fit hearers so that *Bhagavatam* could actually take place? Otherwise, his labour would be fruitless; there would be no continuance of *parampara*. The "standard of recitation" had to be met, as Prabhupada noted in concluding his comments on the paradigmatic *Bhagavatam* recital at Naimisaranya:

> So the speaker and the audience were bona fide in this meeting where *Bhagavatam* was being recited for the second time. That should be the standard of recitation of *Bhagavatam*, so that the real purpose can be served without difficulty. Unless this situation is created, *Bhagavatam* recitation for extraneous purposes is useless labor both for the speaker and for the audience.

For this reason, Prabhupada wanted his student trained in spiritual culture so they could perpetuate the living tradition. In the 1972 letter to Madhudvisa already quoted, Prabhupada had written, "So now you are doing my work and you shall be like me and be yourselves the worthy representatives of our disciplic succession." He immediately continued to instruct his Australian GBC secretary how to institute a daily *Bhagavatam* class:

> I am very much stressing at this point that all of my students shall be very much conversant with the philosophy of Krishna consciousness, and that they should read our books very diligently at least one or two hours daily and try to understand the subject matter from varieties of angles. We are holding our morning class here in Los Angeles in the temple and I am speaking from 7 to 8 a.m., and the process is that we are going through

some chapters of *Srimad Bhagavatam* by taking one *sloka* each day, and reading the Sanskrit aloud, each word is pronounced by me and repeated by the students and then altogether we chant the *sloka* several times until we have learned it. And then we discuss the subject matter very minutely and inspect it from all angles of approach and savor the new understandings. So you introduce this system in all of the centers in your zone, and you will discover that everyone becomes very much enlivened by these daily classes. Read one *sloka* and discuss and then go on to the next *sloka* on the next day, and so on, and even you discuss one verse each day it will take you 50 years to finish *Srimad Bhagavatam* in this way. So we have got ample stock for acquiring knowledge. And if the students get knowledge more and more, they will automatically become convinced and very easily perform their duties for *tapasya* or renunciation of the material bondage, and that will be their successful advancement in Krishna Consciousness. So I want that advancement amongst all of my students, so you are responsible that the standard will be maintained.

All this was necessary for Prabhupada's disciples to "be like me and be yourselves the worthy representatives of our disciplic succession." Prabhupada knew his spiritual culture would be established only when his successors could perpetuate it from generation to generation. That is why, from the earliest days on, Srila Prabhupada instructed his Western disciples to become gurus after him. For example, on 5 September 1969 in Hamburg, Germany Prabhupada spoke to the small band of disciples who had gathered to celebrate his appearance day:

So to understand the spiritual master...Spiritual master is not a new invention. It is simply following the orders of the spiritual master. So all my students present here who are feeling so much obliged (to me)...I am also obliged to them because they are helping me in this missionary work. At the same time, I shall request them all to become spiritual master. Every one of you should be spiritual master next. And what is their duty? Whatever you are hearing from me, whatever you are learning from me, you have to distribute the same *in toto* without any addition or alteration. Then all of you become the spiritual master. That is the science of becoming spiritual master. Spiritual master is not any...To become a spiritual master is not very wonderful thing. Simply one has to become sincere soul. That's all...Vedic knowledge is called *sruti*. One has to hear it properly, assimilate it, and then practice (sic) it in life and preach the same thing. Then everyone becomes spiritual master. Caitanya Mahaprabhu says, *amara ajnaya guru hana tara 'sarva-desa.* ("O My dear disciples, I tell you that you, all of you, become spiritual master. Simply you carry out My order. That's all...The order is the same"): *yare dekha, tare kaha 'krsna'-upadesa* ("Instruct everyone to follow the orders of Lord Sri Krsna as they are given in the *Bhagavad Gita* and *Srimad Bhagavatam*".). (Cc. Madhya 7.128)

Over the years, Prabhupada repeatedly instructs his disciples to become gurus after him, in much the same language and citing the same text. A late instance of this occurs in an address to his disciples in Vrindavan (7 April 1976), in which Srila Prabhupada exhorts them: "So Caitanya Mahaprabhu says you, all of you, to become guru and deliver. Because there are so many innumerable fallen souls in this age…we require hundreds and thousands of gurus. But not cheaters. This is the time when (it) requires hundreds and thousands of gurus."

Only one month before this public talk, Srila Prabhupada had held a discussion on the same topic with the members of the GBC, who were holding their annual meeting in Mayapur. Hari Sari Dasa, Prabhupada's personal servant, made a record of this discussion in a diary he was keeping. First, Prabhupada broaches the topic to Hari Sauri alone:

> Prabhupada surprised me when I entered his room at about 11 a.m…to prepare for his massage. For almost half an hour he preached to me, explaining that he wants all his disciples to become gurus. Each of us is to make thousands of disciples just as he has and in this way spread Krsna consciousness all over the world.
>
> He didn't seem to be speaking in general terms either, but directly to me. He seemed very enlivened at the prospect of spreading Krsna consciousness in this way.
>
> In the evening, when the GBC men filed into his room to make their report about their day's meeting, he brought up the same topic, before discussing their resolutions. He asked me to explain to everyone what he had said earlier. But when I hesitated, he did it himself, repeating in brief this principle of becoming guru.
>
> He told them that just as he had made thousands of disciples he wants each one of them to make ten thousand each. He encouraged them to become increasingly more qualified and rise to the position of being spiritual masters. He stressed that this can be done only if they maintain spiritual strength by strictly following the four regulative principles and chanting the prescribed number of rounds.
>
> It is all dependent on enthusiasm, he told us. At seventy years he had left Vrndavana with no money or men, nor any facility. He had done everything simply on this principle of enthusiasm. Without directly saying it, Srila Prabhupada made it clear that all internal arguments and disputes can be resolved by turning our attention to the higher ideal of preaching Krsna consciousness to the world.[8]

The next day, Prabhupada returned to the topic. That morning Prabhupada had dealt with a controversy regarding a prominent leader named Siddha Svarupa. He had been leader of a yoga group in Hawaii, but he became Prabhupada's disciple, and he and his followers all joined ISKCON. There were tensions. Hari Sari writes:

> ...I questioned Srila Prabhupada again on the criticism that Siddha Svarupa's men are more attached to him than to Prabhupada.
>
> Prabhupada shrugged it off, saying it is all right, it is not harmful. He said that each of us has to become a guru and accept many disciples. But as a matter of etiquette, one should wait until his own spiritual master has departed before doing so.
>
> After lunch, I questioned him further. He told me that having a following is not such a serious offence. But if someone thinks that he is qualified, and accepts disciples in the presence of his own spiritual master, that in itself would be his disqualification.
>
> Replying to my question whether one has to be a pure devotee to make disciples, he said that one has to be strictly following the principles. That is the requirement. Then he can be considered to be on a pure platform.[9]

"Strictly following the principles" is Prabhupada's consistent instruction on the qualification for his disciples to act as guru after him. During a recorded conversation in Bombay on 22 April 1977 with Tamal Krishna on that issue, Prabhupada said, "Caitanya Mahaprabhu wants that. *Amara ajnaya guru hana.*" (You become guru.) Prabhupada laughs: "But be qualified. Little thing, strictly follower." The "little thing" is ironical. Tamal Krishna responds: "Not rubber stamp." And Prabhupada agrees: "Then you'll not be effective. You can cheat, but it will not be effective."

During a walk with Dr Patel in Bombay (4 January 1977), the topic turned to the necessity of receiving knowledge from a liberated person. Prabhupada makes the case that if a person is strictly following the orders of Krishna he is liberated. Prabhupada says:

> If you take Krsna's instruction, then you are liberated. If you manufacture your own idea, then you are conditioned...Anyone who has surrendered to Krsna and strictly follows what Krsna says, then he is liberated. Otherwise not. If he manufactures idea, then he's conditioned...Yes, and it is very easy: "Henceforward I shall simply follow what Krsna says." That's all. You become liberated immediately. It is one minute's task, simply to decide that "No more my concoction, my imagination." Then he is liberated.

Dr Patel raises the problem of *vartma*s, subtle mental impression in the mind from past births. Prabhupada replies:

> Mind may be, but if I ask the mind that "You cannot do anything except what Krsna says," then you are liberated. Very easy. You see? We are doing

the same thing. We are not liberated. I am not liberated. But I am presenting *Bhagavad Gita* as it is. That's all. That's my doing.

Later in the conversation Prabhupada returns to the issue of what it means to be liberated:

And, therefore, our proposition is you take direction from Krsna and His representative. That's all. That will help you. Try to understand this point. Our system, *parampara* system, is that I am just like disciple of Bhaktisiddhanta Sarasvati. I don't say that I am liberated. I am conditioned. But because I am following the instruction of Bhaktisiddhanta, I'm liberated. This is the distinction between conditioned and liberated. When one is under the direction of a liberated person...The same thing: Electricity. The copper is not electricity, but when it is charged with electricity, if it is touched, that is electricity. And, similarly, this *parampara* system, the electricity is going. If you cut the *parampara* system, then there is no electricity. Therefore it is stressed so much.

Here, by asserting "I don't say that I am liberated," Prabhupada dramatically draws our attention to the essential characteristic for liberation: that one is strictly following in *parampara*. "But because I am following...I'm liberated." It is not necessary for one to make any further claims for himself. The implicit teaching here is that even a liberated soul will always consider himself a conditioned soul who is nevertheless enabled, by the mercy of guru, to act as a liberated person. And if one is indeed a conditioned soul, his strict following in *parampara* will make him liberated for all practical purposes.

This teaching, given in informal conversation, has also been more formally presented by Prabhupada in *Srimad Bhagavatam*. One place is in the commentary on *Srimad Bhagavatam* 4.18.5. The text states: "A foolish person who manufactures his own ways and means through mental speculation and does not recognize the authority of the sages who lay down unimpeachable directions is simply unsuccessful again and again in his attempts." Srila Prabhupada comments:

At the present moment it has become fashionable to disobey the unimpeachable directions given by the *acaryas* and liberated souls of the past. Presently people are so fallen that they cannot distinguish between a liberated soul and a conditioned soul. A conditioned soul is hampered by four defects: he is sure to commit mistakes, he is sure to become illusioned, he has a tendency to cheat others, and his senses are imperfect. Consequently we have to take direction from liberated persons. This Krsna consciousness movement directly receives instructions from the Supreme Personality of Godhead via persons who are strictly following His instructions. Although a follower may not be a liberated person, if he follows the supreme, liberated Personality of Godhead, his actions are naturally liberated from the contamination of the material nature. Lord Caitanya therefore says: "By My order you may become a spiritual master." One can immediately become a spiritual master by having full faith in the transcendental words of the Supreme Personality of Godhead and by following His instructions.

Chanting and Hearing the Name of God

It should be noted that the process of cultivating *Srimad Bhagavatam* is identical with the process of cultivating the Hare Krishna *mahamantra*. In the first place, a proper name of God denotes in every case one of the divine qualities, pastimes, or relationships. "Krishna" means "all-attractive," "Syamasundara" means "dark blue and beautiful," "Radha-Syamasundara" means "Syamasundara who is controlled by Radharani", and so on. Names become long: "Yamuna-tira-vana-cari" means "He who wanders in the woodlands on the bank of the Yamuna River." In principle, names can be unlimitedly extended, and on that principle we may think of *Srimad Bhagavatam* as a very long name of the Lord. Chanting and hearing the Hare Krishna *mantra* and reciting and hearing *Bhagavatam* are both modes of *sankirtana*, the congregational glorification of God. And both require cultivation through spiritual discipline. Ultimately, one has to come to chant the Hare Krishna *mantra* and hear *Srimad Bhagavatam* with the same quality of "rapt attention." The two practices, executed together, become mutually reinforcing and enriching.

The result of such practice, Prabhupada claims, is that one gains direct experience of the divine, or "realised knowledge," *vijnana* in Sanskrit. The information received from scripture through disciplic succession is called *jnana*, but the practitioner's experienced realisation of that knowledge through practical application is called *vijnana*, or scientific knowledge. Therefore Prabhupada frequently uses expressions like "science of self-realization" "science of God," "science of *bhakti-yoga*" and so on. The process he taught reliably gives the ability to acquire direct perception when properly applied by a serious student.

The Science of the Spirit

This spiritual science should not be confused with "religion" as we understand it today. Spiritual science has reference to *dharma*, wrongly translated as "religion." "The *dharma* of Vedic culture," Prabhupada says, "should not simply be considered Indian or Hindu in a sectarian sense." He goes on to explain:

Often the word *dharma* is translated to mean religion, but to conceive of *dharma* as a religion is to misconceive the word. In general usage, the word religion refers to a particular type of faith. The word *dharma* does not. *Dharma* indicates the natural occupation of the living entity. For example, wherever there is fire, there is heat and light, so it may be said that heat and light are the *dharma* of fire. Fire cannot change its *dharma*. In the same way, liquidity is an intrinsic quality of water, and this quality cannot be changed. If it is, it can no longer be considered water. The *dharma* of the individual soul can never be changed, and that *dharma* is the occupational duty of rendering service unto the Supreme Lord. Faiths and religions can be changed. Today I may be a Hindu, but tomorrow I may become a Christian or Moslem. In this way faiths can be changed, but *dharma* is a natural sequence, a natural occupation or connection.[10]

Prabhupada raised the prospects of a spiritual science when he addressed students at the Massachusetts Institute of Technology on 5 May 1968. Prabhupada said:

You are all students of technology. This Krsna consciousness movement is also another technology. Unfortunately – In the modern state of civilization there are different departments of knowledge. There is department of teaching medical science, there is department of teaching engineering, there is department of educating – so many other departments of knowledge. Unfortunately, there is no department for distributing knowledge in the science of the soul. But that is the important, most important thing, because the soul is the mainstay, is the background of all our movements.

After giving a brief account of the current sciences of the body and mind, Prabhupada continues:

And above this mind, mental science, there is the science of intelligence. And above the science of intelligence, the background is the soul. Unfortunately, we have got technology for the bodily senses, we have got technology for psychology, but we have neither any technology for intelligence nor for any technology in the science of the soul. The Krsna consciousness movement is the technology of the science of soul.

Prabhupada acknowledges: "The idea is that we are making progress, certainly, in technology, in economics, in so many other departments of human necessities." But he goes on to explain in detail that "If you are intelligent enough, then you should see the real problem is birth, death, old age and disease," and that in spite of all advancements of modern technology there is no remedy for these real problems. "But because these problems cannot be solved by the modern scientific advancement of knowledge, they have practically set aside or neglected (them)." He continues:

Unfortunately, we have no time, neither we have desire to understand actually what I am, why I am suffering, what is this world, what is my

PLATE 13 Kripamoya Das (and daughter Tulasi) preparing to perform a public fire sacrifice or *yajna* (1995). (Copyright: Bhaktivedanta Manor Archives)

PLATE 14 ISKCON's lavish property in Mayapur, West Bengal, where Lord Chaitanya Mahaprabhu was born. It is this location that was chosen by Srila Prabhupada as the movement's world headquarters. In the background is the dome (*pushpa samadhi*), the magnificent cathedral-like structure built in honour ofSrila Prabhupada.
(Private Collection: The Editors)

PLATE 15   Devotees photographed in June 2005 outside Twenty Six Second Avenue in Manhatten's Lower East Side. Opening in May 1966, it was the first ISKCON temple and also the place where ISKCON was legally established. (Private Collection: The Editors)

PLATE 16   Deena Badhu Das (pictured wearing a *kurta* and Hari Nama scarf) with numerous community devotees of Bhaktivedanta Manor admiring the food offerings cooked in honour of Srila Prabhupada's Appearance Day, known as Vyasa Puja. (August 2005). (Copyright: Bhaktivedanta Manor Archives)

relationship with this world, what is God, what is my relationship with God. These questions are very important questions, and there is technology to understand these questions. And the *Srimad Bhagavad Gita* or *Srimad Bhagavatam, Vedanta-sutra,* all these literatures are there. If you kindly, of course, see to these literatures, you'll find the solution of the problems of life. But we are not interested. That is the difficulty. We are thinking that we are happy, we have no problem, although there are so many problems and we are not happy. This is called *maya*...We are thinking that we are happy, but actually we are not happy. And even if we are happy, how long we are happy?

America, as they say in psychology, is "in denial" – massive denial. Prabhupada came to wake America up to reality.

Wrapped in his saffron monk's robes, delivering a plea laced with lines of ancient Sanksrit, intent on relieving all the anguish of the most advanced nation on earth, Prabhupada made an impassioned case for the truth and efficacy of a science of the spirit to students at the Massachusetts Institute of Technology.

Concluding Remarks

Reflecting upon the great work of Srila Prabhupada, let us consider the prospects for the success of his mission 40 years after ISKCON's founder first set foot on a Boston pier.

Prabhupada had only 11 years to perform his Herculean task. After his demise in November 1977 his movement – not unexpectedly – began to undergo a series of travails. There is no need to rehearse them here.[11] In my judgment as a disciple of Srila Prabhupada and as an ISKCON member who has lived through these difficulties, all of them spring from a single cause: shortcomings in the matter of that "little thing, strictly follower."

If we who are Prabhupada's followers desire his effort of "respiritualization of the entire human society" to succeed, we need to take his instruction very seriously, and engage ourselves in the "science of Krishna" as he so clearly taught it. As that happens, we will gain that realised knowledge which bring direct vision of God and the concomitant cessation of all material miseries. Our teaching will increase in the compelling power that is given by realisation, and others will become persuaded to take it up; and they will also experience the scientific truths of transcendence.

This is the first condition for success. The second, I suspect, is that the modern world must, in one way or another, get "out of denial." To the extent that the world realises how the science of material advancement by itself brings only illusory happiness, to the same extent it will become receptive to the science of spiritual advancement. Now the disillusionment with the modern project seems to be growing everywhere. Under that circumstance, if Prabhupada's followers continue to become worthy of his legacy, we may look forward to a time when religion will become recognised as a science, and science will become truly religious.

7

SPIRITUAL SOLUTIONS TO MATERIAL PROBLEMS:
ISKCON and the Modern World

Kenneth Anderson (Krishna Dharma Das)

Introduction

It is not uncommon for Hare Krishna devotees appearing in public (at least in the West) to be accosted with jibes of "Get a job!" Even many of those favourably inclined toward the devotees are moved by their "other-worldly" appearance and behaviour to wonder if their practices have any relevance at all to everyday life. Those joining the Krishna Consciousness movement are well accustomed to hearing how they have "escaped" from normal life. When I moved into a Krishna *ashram* I remember my own friends saying, "I am sure it's good for you, and we wish you well, but we have many responsibilities and can't afford to opt-out and lead such an isolated existence."

However, according to Vaishnava theology, these are misconceptions. As far as the devotees of Krishna are concerned, they are certainly working meaningfully, even as they chant and dance, engaging themselves in what the Vedas sometimes describe as the "highest welfare work" for all beings. Devotees do not see themselves as being in any way irrelevant or disconnected from the world. In fact they would argue that their engagement is more connected to reality than that of anyone else, at least in terms of the Vedic definition of reality, which considers everything to be a part of God. In this chapter I would like to explore this argument, to examine the relevance of ISKCON to the modern world, drawing on the Vedic teachings as presented by ISKCON's founder, Srila Prabhupada. I would also like to discuss some of ISKCON's activities that have been directly targeted at societal problems, as well as the movement's ongoing aims in this regard.

Vedic knowledge in general covers many diverse subjects, from martial arts and diplomacy to house design and cooking, and these have relevance to almost all areas of human endeavour. ISKCON, however, is mainly based upon the spiritual teachings found in Vedic writings such as the *Bhagavad Gita* and *Srimad Bhagavatam* (*Bhagavata Purana*).[1] These texts also claim to be presenting a timeless philosophy that has relevance to all people at all times. The *Srimad Bhagavatam* declares itself to be intended to "bring about a revolution in the lives of the world's misdirected population."[2] From its very beginning the text states that it can "uproot all the miseries of life."[3]

Indeed, it was with this in mind that ISKCON's founder, Srila Prabhupada, set off from India to start his spiritual movement. Inspired by the words of his spiritual master, Bhaktisiddhanta Sarasvati, who said that Krishna (God) Consciousness was an "urgent requirement" for humanity, Prabhupada underwent great personal difficulty in his old age to travel to the West to deliver the Vedic spiritual messages. He was convinced these messages would benefit everyone who heard them, as he showed in a poem of prayer that he wrote upon arriving in Boston in 1965:

> I am sure that when this transcendental message (of the *Bhagavata Purana*) penetrates their hearts they will certainly feel engladdened and thus become liberated from all unhappy conditions of life.[4]

But spiritual leadership is key here, and it is this issue the essay will first focus upon.

Spiritual Leadership

Prabhupada saw Krishna Consciousness as the solution to all ills, whether individual or collective. Immediately upon arriving in America, although he had practically no resources whatsoever, he began making grand plans to open a large temple in New York, attempting to secure funds from wealthy donors in India. Whilst living in India he had made many previous efforts to present Krishna Consciousness on a broad stage, writing letters to such figures as Gandhi, Nehru and various other political leaders, exhorting them to adopt the principles of Krishna Consciousness in their leadership. He had already begun his magazine, *Back to Godhead*, in which, as early as the 1940s, he had presented many articles addressing social issues, such as "Solution of Present Crises by *Bhagavad Gita*", "Mr Churchill's 'Humane World'," and "Human Welfare Activities".[5]

Without doubt Prabhupada wanted ISKCON, which was the culmination of all his previous efforts in India, to engage with the issues of the day and make a difference. He made this clear throughout his writings. For example, in the *Srimad*

Bhagavatam, in the First Canto – which he wrote in the early days of ISKCON – he stated:

> …(I)t is the duty of all executive heads of states to see that the principles of religion, namely austerity, cleanliness, mercy and truthfulness, are established in the state, and that the principles of irreligion, namely pride, illicit female association or prostitution, intoxication and falsity, are checked by all means.[6]

He then went on to present a detailed list of specific items that he said should be adopted by any state that wanted to "eradicate corruption by the majority."

Similar statements abound throughout Prabhupada's writings, which he wanted ISKCON to distribute widely, teaching people how to follow the principles they espoused. As such statements show, Prabhupada was particularly concerned about the state of government and leadership in human society. He strongly desired to establish the ancient system of *varnashramadharma* – the God-centred system of four spiritual and four occupational orders – in human society. He considered this the only organisational structure capable of bringing peace and "sanity" to mankind:

> According to Vedic principles, there must be divisions of human society. There should be *brahmana*s (priests), *ksatriya*s (administrators and warriors), *vaisya*s (tradespeople) and *sudra*s (workers), and everyone should learn to worship the Supreme Personality of Godhead. This is real human society, and without this system we are left with animal society.[7]

Many times Prabhupada criticised "godless" governments who failed to train their citizens in the principles and practices of *varnashramadharma*:

> In the name of secular government, unqualified people are taking the supreme governmental posts. No one is being trained to act according to the principles of *varnashramadharma*, and thus people are becoming increasingly degraded and are heading in the direction of animal life. The real aim of life is liberation, but unfortunately the opportunity for liberation is being denied to people in general, and therefore their human lives are being spoiled. The Krishna consciousness movement, however, is being propagated all over the world to re-establish the *varnashramadharma* system and thus save human society from gliding down to hellish life.[8]

Literatures such as the *Mahabharata* and *Srimad Bhagavatam* describe a time when great theocracies based upon Vedic teachings were the norm, when kings would lead highly religious lives and take all guidance from their priests or *brahman*s.[9] This was the ideal vision presented by Prabhupada to his followers, although on some occasions he admitted that in the present climate it may no longer be possible to re-institute such a society:

> The *varna* and *ashrama* society was considered to be the best institution for lifting the human being to the spiritual platform, but due to *Kali-yuga* it is not possible to execute the rules and regulations of these institutions.[10]

Nevertheless, even in the absence of a perfect *varnashrama* system, Prabhupada was still convinced that Krishna Consciousness, if properly practised and applied, could provide solutions to all of society's ills:

> The Krishna consciousness movement was started to convince the general populace to adopt the best process by which to satisfy the Supreme Personality of Godhead and thus solve all problems.[11]

Solving all Problems

In 1974 he asked devotees to write a book called *How Krishna Consciousness Can Solve All The Problems of Life*. At this time he asked his disciples to present a new problem to him each day and he would explain how Krishna Consciousness could deal with it. On one day he talked about how Krishna Consciousness can solve economic problems, and then on another he presented a solution to the oil crisis of the time. Various vexing social dilemmas were discussed, with Srila Prabhupada offering a spiritual solution in every case.

Inspired by this, the devotees eventually compiled a book called *The Science Of Self-Realisation*, in which there is a section headed "Spiritual Solutions to Material Problems". This featured a conversation Prabhupada had with Lieutenant Mozee of the Chicago Police Department, where he outlined ways in which Krishna Consciousness could solve the crime problem:

> No civil state wants this criminality. That's a fact. But the leaders do not know how to stop it. If they listen to us, however, we can give them the answer.[12]

In the course of this conversation Prabhupada suggested that the government give ISKCON a "large facility" to enable them to achieve their spiritual solution. This was a suggestion he repeated on practically every occasion that he met with any civic authority or dignitary. While in Chicago he also met with the Mayor of Evanston and requested that ISKCON be given the use of a building that had been earmarked for use as the city hall. He told the Mayor that it would be better if ISKCON were given the building, arguing that, "...this is more important. City service is going on, but criminals are increasing. So why not give us little opportunity?"[13] Sadly the Mayor was unable to offer the building to ISKCON, but

Prabhupada remained undeterred in his efforts for his movement to achieve wide societal influence, and he frequently encouraged his disciples in this direction.

Prabhupada did not feel that spiritual life and politics were in any way mutually exclusive, as long as the politics were used to further the cause of Krishna Consciousness:

> There is no need to eradicate politics, economics, sociology, etc., which are mundane to the mundaners. To a pure devotee, who is actually related with the Lord, such mundane things are transcendental if dovetailed with the Lord or with His pure devotees.[14]

ISKCON and Politics

In 1974 Prabhupada encouraged his disciples to get directly involved with politics. In one letter he said:

> Your entering politics is good. You should make political propagation on the basis of reforming the whole human society. The leaders must be an ideal class of men, with ideal character, free from the four sinful activities: no meat eating, no gambling, no illicit sex and no intoxications, as well as chanting. They should chant the names of God. This is essential for leaders. Leaders must be ideal men so others will follow them. So make propaganda on this basis.[15]

Around this time, with Prabhupada's approval, ISKCON formed a political party with the unlikely name of the "In God We Trust Party for Purified Leaders." They contested civic elections in Los Angeles and were hoping to put up candidates for US Congress. A similar attempt was also made in Australia in the same year, with a devotee standing for election to the House of Representatives. However, the devotees involved had little success and eventually they gave up on the idea as they found the association of political circles degrading to their consciousness. In the end Prabhupada remarked: "We don't mind getting the post, but not at the cost of our God consciousness."[16]

But Prabhupada still wanted ISKCON to influence society's leaders. He roundly castigated administrators who took no heed of divine direction, particularly when they allowed animal slaughter:

> In the age of Kali, the poor helpless animals, especially the cows, which are meant to receive all sorts of protection from the administrative heads, are killed without restriction. Thus the administrative heads under whose noses such things happen are representatives of God in name only. Such powerful administrators are rulers of the poor citizens by dress or office, but factually they are worthless, lower-class men without the cultural assets of the twice-

born. No one can expect justice or equality of treatment from once-born (spiritually uncultured) lower-class men.[17]

He pointed out that war and so many other "awkward" problems in human society were linked to animal slaughter:

The material world is itself a place always full of anxieties, and by encouraging animal slaughter the whole atmosphere becomes polluted more and more by war, pestilence, famine and many other unwanted calamities.[18]

Of course here he is thinking of *karma*, and this was a recurrent theme in his directions on leadership; namely, that any leader who did not understand the framework of divine law within which he was working could do little to help his citizens. His so-called solutions to a particular problem may just make things worse if he has not understood the real cause of the problem. For example, abortion, which Prabhupada also greatly criticised, is said by Vedic texts to be the cause of many serious problems in human society. If this is true then a government that tries to solve societal difficulties such as single parents by making abortion more easily available is acting most foolishly. This is the kind of message that Prabhupada wanted ISKCON strongly to advocate.

Prabhupada especially felt that India should adopt a God conscious approach to leadership and on one occasion met with Indira Gandhi while she was the Prime Minister of India. He went to the meeting with a list of suggestions that included: "only Brahmins as MP's, closing all slaughterhouses, and a requirement for all government officers to join congregational chanting at least twice a day."[19] Unfortunately, the meeting was rushed and in the end he was unable to present his proposals.

An Ambitious Agenda

In the early 1990's ISKCON's International Communications Ministry came up with a mission statement that enumerated many key issues of the day that ISKCON hoped to tackle. This was as follows:

The Hare Krishna movement benefits the individual and society by offering practical solutions to today's material and spiritual problems. These problems include:

1) Ethnic, racial and cultural conflict
2) Religious intolerance
3) Hunger
4) Disregard for animal and human life (including the unborn)
5) Health, diet and disease

6) Environment
7) Drug and alcohol abuse
8) Crime
9) Economic imbalance
10) Family breakdown
11) Decline of ethics and morality
12) Stress and anxiety
13) Failure of education
14) A mechanistic worldview

This "Universal Mission Statement", as it was known, set out an ambitious agenda for ISKCON, or at least for its communications department. The movement had at that time (and still has) few programmes that specifically address these issues. Furthermore, the question of how and even if ISKCON should get involved with charitable work can raise polemic within the movement. There are statements from Prabhupada to the effect that "mundane" welfare work divorced from spirituality does not have much value, as it only benefits the temporary material body and not the eternal soul. Prabhupada would compare it to saving the coat of a drowning man:

> Just like my Guru Maharaja used to say, that a man has fallen on the water, and one brave man came. He said, "I shall save this man." And he also jumped in the water and brought out his coat and shirt, and said, "Now the man is saved." Is it saving the man? So similarly, the service of humanity means they are serving the body. Where is the soul?[20]

For Prabhupada, real welfare work meant delivering spiritual knowledge and helping people progress in Krishna Consciousness. For this reason ISKCON devotees only perform charitable and welfare work that is directly connected with the movement's core spiritual mission. For example, "Hare Krishna Food for Life," a free food distribution programme, has been set up in many branches of ISKCON. Its main aim is to give out *prasadam*, which is the sanctified food that has been offered to Krishna. *Prasadam* distribution is a prime missionary activity of ISKCON, strongly advocated by Prabhupada. However, by styling it as "Food for Life", the movement has successfully created a welfare programme that addresses a major social problem, hunger and poverty. This programme draws inspiration from a statement of Prabhupada's that "no one should go hungry within ten miles of any ISKCON temple," and in fact in 1974 Prabhupada himself started a programme in India called "ISKCON Food Relief", with the purpose of feeding the poor, but again only with *prasadam*.[21]

Chanting as Therapy

Another important aspect of ISKCON's missionary work that easily lends itself to addressing modern social issues is the core activity of chanting. Various studies have been made as to the efficacy of the chanting in relieving the symptoms of stress and depression. One such study was made by Dhira Govinda Das, for his doctoral dissertation. He describes the results:

> For the period from pre-test to post-test, statistical analyses revealed – for the *maha-mantra* group compared with the other groups – a significant decrease in stress, depression, and the mode of ignorance, and a significant increase in the mode of goodness.[22]

In the light of this kind of experience ISKCON will sometimes advertise its chanting programmes as *"mantra* therapy". In my experience almost everyone who joins with a chanting session reports that he or she feels more peaceful afterwards.

Another particularly knotty and growing social problem that Prabhupada would often say could be solved by the practices of Krishna Consciousness is drug abuse. He liked to mention how his disciples had renounced all forms of intoxication, even tea and coffee:

> In the Western countries, many young boys and girls who had been addicted to drugs and who had other bad habits, which they could not give up, abandoned all those propensities and very seriously engaged in chanting the glories of the Lord as soon as they joined the Krishna consciousness movement.[23]

Projects specifically aimed at this particular problem have been developed in various parts of ISKCON. One such was "Mukunda's Drop-in" in Auckland. Its success in dealing with the drug problem was noted by Dr Fraser McDonald, Chief Medical Superintendent at Auckland's Carrington Hospital, who said:

> Medicine as it has been practiced in the West concentrates far too much on the purely mechanical, physical aspects of healing. Little attention is paid to the psychological aspects, and absolutely no attention is given to the religious or spiritual part of a person's being, for a variety of reasons. However, the result of this was that we at the Drug Clinic had to look around for people with expertise in a spiritual way of life so that we could offer this to our recovering drug addicts. And the Hare Krishna people gave us a warm welcome. We discovered that the combination of our medical care and the spiritual care from the Hare Krishna philosophy results in a very powerful tool indeed for the treatment of drug addiction, and for this we are very grateful.[24]

Mukunda's is no longer open, although similar "drop-in" style projects still operate in London (where drug counselling is available) and in Melbourne.

The problem of crime has also been directly addressed with the formation of the "ISKCON Prison Ministry", which as the name suggests visits offenders within prisons, teaching them the practices of Krishna Consciousness. As well as Prabhupada's many statements as to how Krishna Consciousness can rectify the criminal mentality, this programme has drawn inspiration from one of the aims of the "League of Devotees", an organisation set up in India by Prabhupada before he travelled to the West:

> To take charge of moral upliftment by spiritual process even for the criminals and prisoners of the state, and to accept all kinds of help and facilities from the police and government concerned.[25]

Although this programme, which is active in a number of countries, has yet to receive official recognition and support, it has received many hundreds of letters from prisoners who attest to the positive effects of ISKCON's spiritual practices.

Challenging Atheism

One particular area that Prabhupada focussed upon in making his movement relevant to the issues of the day was modern mechanistic science, whose theories and concepts underpin much of modern life. He spent a great deal of time discussing with his disciples how to challenge scientific atheism, and a series of these discussions was eventually transcribed into a book entitled *Life Comes From Life*. Prabhupada sums up the aim of this book early on in his talks:

> The whole world of science and technology is running on the false idea that life is born from matter. We cannot allow this nonsensical theory to go unchallenged. Life does not come from matter. Matter is generated from life. This is not theory; it is fact. Science is based on an incorrect theory; therefore all its calculations and conclusions are wrong, and people are suffering because of this.[26]

Soon after this Prabhupada formed the Bhaktivedanta Institute, who styled themselves as "A body of scientists and scholars who have recognized the unique value of the teachings of Krishna consciousness brought to the West by His Divine Grace A.C. Bhaktivedanta Swami Prabhupada."[27] Their mission is to establish the scientific basis of theism, and conversely the non-scientific position of atheism. In this regard they have published a number of books challenging the modern scientific position, such as *Forbidden Archaeology*, which looks at Darwin's theory in the light of much contradictory evidence, and also *Consciousness, the Missing Link*, which examines the key underlying concepts of the modern life sciences.

The current environmental crisis we are experiencing is another area where ISKCON feels it can make a direct contribution. Prabhupada was keen to establish self-sufficient farming communities that evinced a simple and natural lifestyle, as he made clear with the sixth of the "Seven Purposes of ISKCON", which states: "To bring the members closer together for the purpose of teaching a simpler, more natural way of life."[28]   Numerous communities have been started, although none have yet reached full self-sufficiency. However, it remains a key aspect of ISKCON's mission. Devotees have recently compiled a book, *Divine Nature*, that addresses many environmental issues from a Krishna Consciousness perspective, and describes the natural alternatives to modern farming and energy generation that are being pursued on ISKCON projects around the world.

Many Problems, One Remedy

Ultimately all these problems and so many more like it have one solution, according to Vedic wisdom. Prabhupada describes this in his conversation in Chicago with Lieutenant Mozee:

> Unless he cleans the heart, you cannot stop criminality simply by laws. Laws are already known. The professional thief, he knows the law. The professional murderer, he knows the law. But still, he commits because heart is unclean. And our process, to cleanse the heart. *Ceto-darpana-marjanam*, it is Sanskrit, "Cleansing the heart." *Bhava-maha-davagni-nirvapanam*, "Then all the troubles of this material world will be solved".[29]

Krishna Consciousness philosophy sees all human problems as stemming from "impurities" in the heart. Specifically these impurities manifest as lust, greed, anger, envy and illusion. These base qualities influence us to become sinful and to misbehave in various ways. By chanting God's names one becomes purified of these influences due to the "transcendental potency" of the sound vibration. An analogy is given to explain how this works. Just as the sun can purify a dirty place by its powerful rays, so by approaching God through his holy name a person can purify his consciousness and become free of all bad behaviour.

Prabhupada taught that the real problem we face is that we are trapped within a material body that is fast growing old, becoming diseased and about to die. Vedic teachings tell us that we do not belong in this world and that all our endeavours should therefore be aimed at gaining spiritual emancipation, thereby solving all our problems in one fell stroke. It is therefore with this in mind that the Vedas suggest that anyone who is working to assist people toward this aim is, as this chapter began by saying, engaged in the "highest welfare work." Chanting the holy names in public (not necessarily accompanied by dancing) serves to purify the hearts of everyone who hears the sound.

Of course, such a spiritual solution – purifying the heart – takes time and thus the Vedic literatures also show us how we can minimise "bodily disturbances" – which includes all societal problems – while we pursue the ultimate answer to our awkward material situation. Prabhupada would often speak about the need for a peaceful life before spiritual practices are possible, and his teachings include many directions about how this can be achieved. He frequently condemned the materialistic mindset that has led to the development of our industrialised society, which he saw as the very antithesis of a peaceful, God-centred life, and to which he wanted ISKCON to show better alternatives:

> Human prosperity flourishes by natural gifts and not by gigantic industrial enterprises. The gigantic industrial enterprises are products of a godless civilization, and they cause the destruction of the noble aims of human life. The more we go on increasing such troublesome industries to squeeze out the vital energy of the human being, the more there will be unrest and dissatisfaction of the people in general, although a few only can live lavishly by exploitation.[30]

Spiritual life provides a solution to this problem by freeing us from the desires that lead to excessive exploitation of the earth's resources, and of the concomitant difficulties that arise from this abuse. Through spiritual practices one becomes peaceful within and satisfied with minimal material possessions. Prabhupada would often talk about giving up "unnecessary necessities" – items produced by the advancement of technology that gradually become indispensable, even though man has done perfectly well without them for thousands of years.

Challenges to ISKCON

However, it is not always entirely straightforward to see how the "ultimate" solution of purifying the heart connects with a specific problem, and this is a challenge faced by ISKCON devotees today in making the movement relevant to the dilemmas of an increasingly complex society. For example, the oil problem mentioned above is a key issue. It was a crisis when Prabhupada addressed it, and even today it is problematic. Increasingly Western society (at least) is becoming dependent on limited supplies of oil that it needs to import from other countries. Western economies thus become vulnerable to the vagaries that might beset the oil producing nations, as well as to the failures of their own infrastructures, which is another fast looming threat. Prabhupada gave the following solution:

> So this problem will be solved as soon as we are localized. Petrol is required for transport, but if you are localized there is no question of transport. Petrol is not required.[31]

Prabhupada went on to say that one could utilise the bull for transport and farming needs. He advocated a return to ox-power in place of tractors and other petrol driven vehicles. It is a simple solution, but its implementation would be far from simple. To go from the heavily industrialised, completely oil and electricity dependent society of today, to the simple, agrarian society suggested by Prabhupada and indeed the Vedic teachings presents many steep problems. Those problems are yet to be fully solved on even a small scale by the ISKCON projects that are striving for self-sufficiency. As well as this, it requires some careful thought to see how the spiritual practices of ISKCON would in any event enable such a solution – how it is that a lack of spirituality lies at the heart of our never-ending movement toward increased industrialisation and technology. Prabhupada contended that this movement toward technological "advancement" was actually retrogression:

Rameshvara: (Localization is) possible in India but not in America.
Prabhupada: Why?
Rameshvara: The American people...consider it backwards.
Prabhupada: That has to be educated, that backward is real life.[32]

For this reason devotees might be accused of hopeless idealism, although in their defence they might point to the largely industry-free, self-sufficient, agrarian lifestyle (based upon Vedic spiritual principles) still found in rural India, where it has existed for many millennia. Prabhupada would often cite this as an example to be emulated, although sadly India's leaders are now more and more embracing Western values and industrialisation. No doubt unemployment, hitherto a hardly known problem in greater India, will soon begin to appear there, as Prabhupada himself points out:

Now this machine, this machine nonsense means unemployment. One machine will work for hundred men. So hundred men become unemployed, and one technician, he gets all the salaries.[33]

Implementation

Perhaps though the main challenge to ISKCON in showing the relevance of its spiritual solutions lies in its ability to evince the efficacy of those solutions among its own members. In particular *varnashramadharma*, the Vedic social model, has yet fully to manifest itself within ISKCON. It is generally accepted among the members that ISKCON has a long way to go in even understanding how to implement this model. In a recent discussion with an ISKCON leader I heard how he had met with government leaders in the Ukraine. They had told him that they had no faith in either communism or capitalism and were open to other alternatives. Naturally the devotee thought of *varnashramadharma*, but upon further thought realised that he had little idea how to advise the Ukraine government of ways they might begin practically to implement the system. He remarked: "It is doubtful whether we, at present, would be able to actually construct the entire system, even theoretically."

Going back to the Universal Mission Statement, there are other issues listed there where ISKCON is struggling to get its own "act together." The failure of education for example; ISKCON has yet to provide a fully working alternative, although it does have a few successful small schools. Family breakdown is another area of struggle, with ISKCON divorce rates still matching those found in greater society. And to show a fully working economic model that could operate on a large scale certainly will not be simple.

Clearly there are many challenges, but there are also encouraging signs. It is a fact that many people, the author included, have taken to the practices of Krishna Consciousness and as a result experienced a diminishment of the base urges that drive us to seek destructive so-called solutions to our problems. The alternatives it offers are surely worthy of a careful study, and this chapter is really only a summary. Hopefully, as the movement continues to grow and mature it will be able more and more to show how its spiritual practices are indeed a real solution to the many material problems we now face.

8

For Love of Krishna:
Forty Years of Chanting

Anna S. King

Introduction

As a missionary, proselytising movement, ISKCON defines itself not only in terms of what it is, but what it is not. It understands itself in essentialist terms (as teaching unchanging truths). In historical terms ISKCON identifies itself as an important denomination within Gaudiya Vaishnavism, accepting the bona fide guru and particular sacred texts as authoritative. Theologically it proclaims that Krishna is the Supreme Personality of Godhead, and attacks Western representations of Hinduism in terms of polytheism or *advaita Vedanta*. In ritual terms it follows the principles of *bhagavata-dharma* and rejects impersonalism, *brahmanical* ceremonial, the Vedic worship of the demi-gods (*devtas*) and of the ancestors *(pitris)*.[1] Its authoritative texts challenge the fact that *smarta* ceremonies were accepted as *Vaishnava* and argue that non-*Vaishnava* practices are inimical to pure devotional service. Culturally ISKCON challenges the supremacy, materialism and secularism of Western society. It defines its identity in opposition to the "casteism" and ritualism of Hinduism and to certain Vaishnava *sahajiya* sects. Yet ISKCON has always existed within the dynamic of cultural and religious pluralism both in the West and East, and during the past decade it has turned inward, becoming in the process self-reflexive and self-critical, with an active commitment to inter-religious and theological dialogue.[2]

The principal aim of this chapter is to throw a steady stream of light on the practices of ISKCON.[3] It argues that in the postcharismatic phase of the movement the priestly aspect of ISKCON is inextricably intertwined with the ecstatic, that the structured performance of major daily, periodic and "epic" rituals *are* the high points of transcendence. It emphasises the dialectic between the esoteric *bhakti* of love and the exoteric *bhakti* of ritual.[4] Love of Krishna cannot be expressed except in intentional, meaningful activities, which give delight to Krishna. Just as one cannot easily separate text and image, one cannot easily separate *pancharatrika-vidhi* or *vidhi bhakti* (rule-governed *bhakti*) and *bhagavat* or *raga* (emotion-governed *bhakti*). While ritual propriety and purity may be held as ultimately inferior to *raga* and the cultivation of ethical virtues such as love, purity, selflessness and humility, it is in fact Chaitanyite Vaishnava practices, codified by Gopala Bhatta, one of the six Vrindavan Goswamis, which nurture ISKCON's Krishnaite devotion (cf. Klostermaier 2000a, p.122). Deity-worship, *mantra japa*, *sankirtana*, full prostration (*dandavat*s), the offering of light and incense, a strict vegetarian diet, feasts observed in honour of Krishna, observance of *vrat*s like fasting on *ekadasi* are the main means of winning God's grace. Such activities delight Krishna who is the *akhila rasamritamurti*, "the complete embodiment of the nectar of all feelings." Even Chaitanya and those "pure" devotees who enter ecstatic or mystical states are believed to maintain exemplary standards of practice so that neophytes do not "fall." Kripamoya Das speaks of devotees who fail to understand the importance of ritual in their lives as: "like the goldfish who, when asked what the water was like in his bowl, replied: 'What water?' They are so completely immersed in ritual they don't even realise it's there."

Engaged Theology

ISKCON's rich and complex rituals and doctrine of *seva* (divine service) are embedded in and explained by a theology of *achintya-bhedabheda tattva* (inconceivable simultaneous oneness and difference with Krishna). Prabhupada follows Chaitanya in teaching that Krishna descends as *avatara* in His holy name, in the form of sound vibration, and in his images (*murti*). Hearing and chanting the names of Krishna leads to the experience of ecstatic spiritual emotion (*bhava*) and transcendental pleasure. Prabhupada (1982 [2003], p.6) reflects that in this age all of the perfections of yoga "can be realized through *bhakti-yoga*, the sublime process of Krsna consciousness, specifically *mantra-yoga*, the glorification of Sri Krsna through the chanting of Hare-Krsna."[5] The Hare Krishna *mantra* is sufficient for one's perfection and liberation (Prabhupada 1997, p.44). *Nama-sankirtana*, congregational chanting of the holy names of God, remains the main devotional practice.[6]

Prabhupada teaches that the bliss of the devotee lies in service, and that this bliss is realisable *now*. However, he also proclaims that traditional *Vaishnava sadhana* takes the devotee back to Godhead and that *seva*, which includes the ritual worship of images, is one of the foremost, lifelong duties of a Vaishnava. Devotion and "ritual" must be balanced. Transcendence is experienced in this body. One devotee (personal communication: 18.11.04) asked about the purpose of ISKCON's mission simply said: "We serve God. We gain happiness by serving God." Since Krishna is physically present in space and time, everything must be perfect: the *arati*s (rituals of worship), the *bhog* (food) offerings, the sumptuous dresses for the deities, the *samskara*s (purificatory ceremonies/rites of passage), etc. Major ritual events require months, even years, of preparation. *Pujari*s (priests), cooks, garland makers, seamstresses, *nitya-sevak*s (constant attendants) are always engaged in caring for Govinda. Devotees and volunteers work ceaselessly to maintain buildings, garden, care for guests, protect Krishna's cows and work on organic farms, etc.[7] Bhaktivedanta Manor's own flowers, vegetables, sweets, food, milk, *tulasi* leaves, are pure offerings to Krishna. *Seva* or service in a material sense not only enables ISKCON's institution building but provides the multitude of actors who are behind the exquisite ritual performances. Gelberg once commented (1989, p.155) that: "The greater the devotion with which work-for-Krishna is performed, the more powerful its potential to purify and elevate the worker."[8]

British Hindus are attracted in their thousands to ISKCON's major festivals by religious performances: the *prasadam* (sanctified food) distribution, fasting and feasting, congregational singing and chanting, sacred art, drama, music and dancing. Vertovec points out correctly that the larger Hindu community, particularly the majority East African Gujaratis, show exceptional respect for "the strength of ISKCON members' devotion, their knowledge of Sanskrit, their strict vegetarianism, and their elaborate, detailed rituals" (Vertovec 2000, p.101). Festivals, *yatra*s (pilgrimages) and *yajna*s (sacrifices) encourage volunteers with a range of skills to use them in Krishna's service. Contemporary newsletters, journals and media reports give insight into the very diverse ways in which ISKCON's rituals and festivals are becoming institutionalised within mainstream British civic society. The London Ratha Yatra of Jagannath is now an annual traffic-stopping event, while Janamashtami and Diwali are celebrated in the House of Commons.[9] As ISKCON has established a reputation for integrity, hard work and faithfulness in Britain it has lost many of its defensive sectarian features and become a broad-based institution.

Shaunaka Rishi Das commented: "Prabhupada was a man in a hurry. He just wanted to get things going, and let Krishna sort everything out. And He has!" Prabhupada's devotees negotiate their religious identities in a movement which is still maturing; systematising its teachings, writing books, establishing temples, installing deities, founding a social system, directing self-sufficiency, and forming an institutional structure with a suitable hierarchy that will facilitate and perpetuate all those things (cf. Sivarama Swami 1999, p.130). Visitors continually move in and out of the organisation. Identities are hybrid, shifting, intercultural. Ritual activities not only sanctify this diversity, but enable devotees to transcend their past social identities. The daily devotional practices establish emotional stability and orderliness by absorbing devotees within the reality of Vrindavan, nurturing the devotional moods of *bhakti-yoga*, and preparing devotees for God's grace.

Dialectical Tension: The *Bhakti* of Love and the *Bhakti* of Ritual

The devotional love of God, or *bhakti*, is the very substance of life for the *bhakta* (or devotee). The internal world of the devotee is governed by the grace of God (*kripa*) (Schweig 2004, p.377). Yet Prabhupada insists that *bhakti* develops by *strict adherence to* prescribed Vedic practices, Vedanta philosophy and *brahmani*cal principles and values. Although *bhakti* is the process *and* the goal, a major part of Prabhupada's legacy lies in the puzzling teaching that ISKCON as a whole should have a *brahmani*cal role within society. Prabhupada insists on orthopraxis: consistency of behaviour, correct, authentic practice.[10] Ritual performance based on "Vedic" sources becomes one of the most important ways in which ISKCON presents itself as an authentic and distinctive Vaishnava *sampradaya* (or tradition). Observers of the early movement, whether sympathetic or not, uncritically describe ISKCON as differing from other new religious movements and "cults." They claim that it is "uniquely" rooted in ancient Indian spirituality and is a successful implantation of a whole religious tradition – philosophy, theology *and* ritual – in a completely alien culture.[11] Brockington (1992, p.184) observes:

> The Hare Krishna movement…is simply the transplantation to the West of patterns of worship long known in India. The movement is basically a branch of the form of Bengal Vaishnavism established by Chaitanya (1486-1533) and in most of its doctrines and its ritual is indeed impeccably orthodox by the standards of that *bhakti* tradition, a point that is endorsed by the extent to which ISKCON has been accepted as a spokesman for Hinduism by Hindus living in Britain.

Klostermaier tells us that the Hare Krishna movement is "the most genuinely Hindu of all the many Indian movements in the West" (2000a, p.278). Hopkins makes the huge claim that no other non-Western tradition has managed to transplant successfully its authentic tradition (cf.1983, pp.101-61). Ellwood similarly (1983, p.12) stresses that Hare Krishna is the *only* successful transplant of *bhakti* devotionalism in the West and that the transmission has occurred practically without acculturating changes. The "authentic" practices required by Prabhupada are contrasted by both devotees and scholars with the minimal ritual, ascetic, linguistic and cultural demands made by other Hindu missionary movements. Such legitimations in the early years defended ISKCON from anticult crusades and media attack. However, a new generation of scholars and textualists are beginning to emphasise the uniqueness of ISKCON's spiritual culture and the many ways in which Prabhupada stamped his own personality, authority and teachings on ISKCON. Today also liberal devotees who are completely committed to ISKCON's theology, nevertheless challenge any kind of excluding metanarrative which implies that other Hindu-related missionary movements are somehow less authentic, or that the Chaitanya movement as a whole is homogeneous and monolithic (cf. Goswami 1983, p.253).[12]

Prabhupada proclaims that after Krishna's advent and the coming of Chaitanya (an incarnation of Krishna and Radha), the essence of religion no longer lay in *brahmanical yajnas*, but in the loving response to the full presence of God. However, Prabhupada himself was extremely cautious about the path of *ragunaga bhakti* (love for God in the feminine mood of the *gopis* of Braj). His writings are full of earnest, heartfelt warnings against the mundane eroticising of Krishna's pastimes. *Rasa* (profound emotional loving spirituality) is the goal of devotional life and for the totally surrendered devotee more blissful than *vidhi bhakti* (following the rules and regulations of scripture) (cf. Rosen 1996, p.125). Yet it is the exoteric, prudent path of *sadhana bhakti*, preaching and outreach projects that Prabhupada advocates for his movement as a whole. Srila Narayana Maharaja's narrations of Krishna's "transcendental *lila*" led to controversy and to a major confrontation with ISKCON. Revisionist devotees, Thomas Herzig and Kenneth Valpey among them, have advocated a balanced return to attraction (*raga*) but the cultivation of *raganuga bhakti* is still regarded by many devotees as a spiritual path which should remain confidential and private.

Scholars, Saints and Disciples

The fascination of this particular topic is so obvious that it seems curious that ISKCON's rich heritage of ritual resources, the role of the "clergy" and the transmission of revitalised Vaishnava spiritual practices are only now receiving scholarly attention. Why? Is it perhaps because poetic *rasa* is more appealing than normative ritual? Chaitanya (1486-1534) is considered to embody a Vaishnavism that is principally concerned with feelings and emotions. Klostermaier (2000a, p.115) says: "(Chaitanya's) religion consists in 'taking the name' and expresses itself as disinterested *bhakti*, accompanied by signs of highest emotion like tears, choked voice, horripilation, etc., and making very intense the desire for union with God." Scholars and devotees focus upon the devotional and ecstatic intentions of the movement, upon what Basham (1983, p.165) calls "simple, Indian *bhakti*" and Gelberg "simple, guileless devotion" (1989, p.145). The Chaitanya tradition, of which ISKCON is a branch, is portrayed as giving full expression to religious emotion, as discouraging ritualism and caste, and as dispensing with the traditional, complicated *yajna* (or sacrificial) rituals, viewing them as unnecessary for salvation (cf. Basham 1983, pp.180-3). The *brahmanical* stress on *havan* (fire ritual), on *yajnas*, the ritual chanting of *mantras* or elaborate sacrifices is described as giving way (cf. Goswami 1983, p.217) to the rise of genuine, spontaneous, selfless love, *bhakti*, and to "more natural, simple, devotional acts."

This stress on simplicity and spontaneity does not adequately represent Prabhupada's disciplined spiritual approach. After 40 years of chanting perceptions are changing. ISKCON devotees with academic training are making significant contributions to scholarship in the area of *Vaishnava-vedanta* ritual and deity worship. While liberal, progressive devotees urge a shift from institutional to individual realisation, those with the interests of the greater congregation in mind are eager to transplant all Vaishnava rituals to Britain. The practical need to conduct marriages, death ceremonies, to install deities, to celebrate *puja* (worship), to site new temples, to train *brahman*s or priests, etc., has led to a recognition that Prabhupada introduced devotees not only to Chaitanya *bhakti* and the experiential dimension of Bengali Vaishnavism in its bewildering variety, but to overarching Hindu ideas of ritual purity and auspiciousness, the efficacy of chanting and the power of *mantra*.

Human Flourishing in ISKCON: The Ritualisation of Life

While some ISKCON gurus have placed emphasis upon a doctrine of grace as the sole means of salvation, others have recognised the rituals of *bhakti* as essential for human flourishing. They view ISKCON's ritual tradition against a background of the spiritual impoverishment and barrenness of ritual life in America and the West. Tamal Krishna Goswami, Swami Prabhupada's personal secretary, contrasted the stark, decimated tree of his biological birth with the healthy luxuriant spiritual tree of Gaudiya Vaishnavism: "Ritual practice is the art of making life sacred. Its strength lies in its apparent simplicity, yet profound meaning." He says (1998, p.48):

Traditional cultures – including the Vaishnava Hindu tradition to which I now adhere – are ritually enriched. Apart from enshrining the periodic rituals of the life cycle and life's crises (illness, disaster, drought, etc.), as well as seasonal rituals (and important dates on the sacred calendar), traditional cultures often elevate ordinary daily activities to a sacramental level. In the Vaishnava world view, this life literally prepares us for the next: we practice here for the eternal performance hereafter. Even the simplest act is pregnant with transcendence.

Goswami asks rhetorically whether a culturally rich mythical tradition, one that appreciates the significance of every moment enough to substantiate it ritually, creates a congregation of weirdos. He exclaims that it is not the devotees, but everyone else who is crazy:

Yes, we are crazy – crazy for Krsna. In that uncivilized long-ago when God was still an acceptable myth, when mystics were still in touch with the heavens, and when rituals had not yet lost their sacramental powers, to be crazy was normal. I am now fifty and I've lived through initiation, marriage, burial, and birth not once, but twice (just in this life!). Both life cycles were crazy in their own way, but I much prefer the craziness of the second.

Gelberg, an ex-devotee, also writes perceptively of the importance of ritual:

> (W)e should remember that religious experience is itself largely constituted
> of precept and ritual deeply interiorized and "felt" and then concretized
> into distinct, affectively powerful ways of perceiving and conceiving reality
> (just as, conversely, doctrine and ritual, are, in an important sense, the
> rational and symbolic externalization and codification of core religious
> experience). (1989, p.156)

Kripamoya Das reminds us that:

> Ritual is the external extrapolation of inner consciousness; the body
> language of someone at prayer; the external body language that moves the
> devotee into the area of religious theatre. (personal communication:
> 04.10.04)

ISKCON's Ritual Authenticity

One of the great functions and responsibilities of ISKCON is to perform
devotional rituals correctly as an aspect of spiritual discipline. Shinn and Bromley
(1989, p.14) remark that: "...from his first days of preaching...Bhaktivedanta
confronted his young listeners with traditional, undiluted devotional teachings
and practices from the ancient Indian Krishna scriptures (e.g. *Bhagavad Gita* and
Bhagavata Purana) as interpreted through the ecstatic devotionalism of Chaitanya."
Hopkins (1983, p.105) observed that in the early years, "Newcomers were taught
the *mantra* and were given chanting beads and taught how to use them. That was
about it as far as ritual practice is concerned." He found however that only two
years later (1969) a formal ritual structure had developed:

> Disciples now know far more about the Vaishnavite scriptures than they did
> a year ago, and their ritual practices have become much more complex and
> sophisticated. A major effort has been to introduce and perfect the full
> range of traditional Hindu rituals associated with the worship of Krishna.
> (1983, p.107)

The deity worship which is central to Gaudiya Vaishnavism had become one
of the principal means by which devotees expressed their commitment to the
association of devotees and their love of Krishna and his personal representative,
Prabhupada. ISKCON's rituals had also become powerful expressions of
continuity. They brought the worshipping community together in celebration.
Frequent public ritual provided a strong contrast with secular degenerate society:
it created Vrindavan in a culture steeped in materialism (cf. Goswami 1983,
p.243). ISKCON devotees believed (and many still believe) that the present age of
the world is the age of Kali Yuga, a "demonic era of especial corruption,

materialism, sensuality and spiritual desolation" (Whitworth, Shiels 1982, p.159); from the beginning they saw themselves as bringing transcendental wisdom to "the especially benighted West…embedded in the slough of spiritual ignorance and materialism" (ibid. p.157).

Devotees Talking

Shaunaka Rishi Das once joked: "There are as many theologies as devotees in ISKCON."[13] Ordinary acts of worship on the other hand often go unremarked. Their very familiarity makes them almost invisible. There are therefore many methodological pitfalls in asking devotees to reflect reflexively on "ritual." Devotees acknowledge the authority of approved texts such as the *Hari-bhakti-vilasa* (the authorised scripture for *arcana*) or the *Sat-kriya-sara-dipika* (the authorised manual for *yajna* and *samskara*), but few read them. Moreover devotees associate "ritual" with the very formal practices of *yajna*. They talk, not of ritual (a generic and outsider term used by scholars and priests), but of *sadhana, mantra, japa* or *kirtana, yajna,* etc. Many are unfamiliar with the term *karmakand,* and those who understand its meaning often reject what it stands for. Devotees when first interviewed reiterate Swami Prabhupada's principal teaching that chanting the *mahamantra* is sufficient for salvation. They suggest that Prabhupada taught that all rituals except chanting the holy names could be jettisoned. Many emphasise divine grace and supreme will to the exclusion of systematic rules and displayed a strong hostility to "*brahmanical*" ritual.[14] Several devotees warned me of the dangers of concentrating on rituals without an understanding of the subjective consciousness within. They noted Prabhupada's attacks on Hindu ritualism and casteism. A much respected senior disciple distinguished the "pure" teaching of ISKCON from that of Hinduism on the grounds of ritual transcendence: "Hinduism is just another fossilized religion. Totally rule bound. It stops at the level of ritual."

Paradoxically, however, *all* devotees, whatever their theoretical perspectives and whether connected with a temple or not, celebrate their individual and community life in terms of meaningful formalised practice. They talk of Vaishnava ritual which pleases Krishna and sanctifies those who surrender to him. This includes the disciplined daily life of the temple, the periodic feast days and festivals, the theory and practice of chanting the names of God and of image worship, the magnificent welcoming ceremonies connected with the installation of deities, the activities linked with devotee association (*sadhu sanga*) and devotional service, especially *bhajana, kirtana, sankirtana, prasadam* distribution, the performance of *samskaras, yajnas,* the rituals of pilgrimage, etc. Devotees insist that all these spiritual practices contribute to the power of *Hari-nama sankirtana* and to individual and community transformation. The *mahamantra* is still invoked as the principal *yajna* of this age, but ISKCON's *pujas* and *samskaras* are interpreted as transformative and purifying. Many devotees feel indeed that the entire life of the surrendered devotee becomes ritualised. The pure devotee becomes "Krishnaised and divinised." Krishna showers down his grace where he is remembered and worshipped.

The Soho Temple

In Govinda's Restaurant in London's Soho Street, customers, many Asian, drift in from Oxford Street to buy "Vedic" vegetarian *thalis*, *lassi*, ice cream, smoothies, *gulab jaman* and *burphi*. At first sight this looks like any other professionally-run restaurant. Yet ladling out food, sweeping the floor, cleaning the lavatories, taking money are assistants wearing Vaishnava *tilaks*, robes and saris. One or two are in jeans and T-shirts. *Chant and Be Happy: The Power of Mantra Meditation* featuring "exclusive" discussions with John Lennon, George Harrison and Yoko Ono is propped up on nearby tables. From upstairs comes the sound of *kirtana*. The food is *prasadam*, vegetarian *satvik* food prepared purely in Vaishnava kitchens and ritually offered to Krishna. As such it is auspicious and beneficent for all who eat it. A German devotee who had been clearing plates and wiping tables pauses. I ask whether his *sikha* and white *dhoti* mean that he has been initiated. "No. We are advised for the first six months to concentrate on the founder-*acharya* and then only to think of approaching a guru." I asked if he would eventually seek *brahmanical* initiation. "Absolutely." "Why?" "*Brahman* or second initiation is like becoming a doctor. In ISKCON it is like getting a doctor's certificate." I then asked him about the distinguishing qualities of a *brahman*. He talked about ethical qualities rather than prescribed duties or purificatory rites: compassion, gentleness, truthfulness, etc. Questioned about the relationship of ritual and devotion, he observed:

> It is only by following rules and regulations that the mind can be controlled...It is like learning to make a cake. For a perfect cake you need to have the exact ingredients...In music you need the notes and the technique to play them but you also need inspiration. Only then is the music alive. Similarly *bhakti* requires s*adhana* – ritual discipline.

In the shop upstairs two young Croatian devotees in blue saris were selling books and *puja* items. ISKCON is growing fast in Croatia, and they tell me that they have come to England to learn how they can further Krishna Consciousness. They live in the Soho Street temple, and one remarks: "From the moment I step across the door I feel joy. Krishna is here!" I ask the women about the interdependence of devotion and ritual. They reply with bubbling enthusiasm:

> Swami Prabhupada teaches that chanting the *mahamantra* is the *only* sacrifice appropriate for the Kali Yuga. Chanting transforms our material world. It creates auspicious *karma* to counter the illness, genocide and terrorism created by bad *karma*.

I probed further: "Why do we need to think of *karma* when Vaishnavas can take refuge at the feet of Lord Krishna? Isn't it Krishna's grace that saves those who surrender to him?" The devotees praise this as a very high teaching for the spiritually advanced, but respond that actually *karma* (justice) and grace work together.

The temple priests or *pujaris* are responsible for regular public worship (*puja*) of the deities. They perform the daily rituals of the temple, often lead hymn singing, and distribute the food offered during the worship as *prasadam*. They maintain the temple's ritual cycle, which includes periodic festivals. One of their most important duties is to ensure the purity of the temple complex.[15] The *pujari* of the Soho temple commented:

> In this Kali Yuga *brahman*s no longer have the knowledge to perform the great *yajna*s. ISKCON's rituals have been adapted and simplified for the West. Like all initiated *brahman*s, I am able to serve the deities at the altar, but the position of *pujari* is in no way superior to that of the devotee who sweeps the temple floor...It is not necessary for *pujaris* to understand Sanskrit to worship the deities...I myself have not performed particular rites of passage (*samskara*), but at the time of death, I with other devotees visit and comfort the dying man or woman, read the second chapter of the *Bhagavad Gita* and chant the *mahamantra* so that the patient feels tranquil and calm. The patient dies knowing that: "I am not the body. All that love Krishna go back to Godhead."[16]

Bhaktivedanta Manor

At Bhaktivedanta Manor everything was being made ready to receive the vast crowds of *Krishnajanmashtami*, Krishna's birthday. Outside Radharani's Bakery a devotee was waiting peacefully for his guru. He wore the white robes and *sikha* (pony tail) of the *grihastha* (householder), and told me that he was at a Scandinavian university studying social psychology. His only goal, he remarked, was to become a pure devotee of Krishna. He had been diagnosed with a brain tumour four years previously. Chanting had taken away fear. By the grace of Krishna he had fully recovered. The devotee reiterated that the greatest *yajna* of the Kali Yuga was the *Hari-nama-sankirtana*:

> This is the sacrifice of controlling the mind and fully focusing it on the sound vibrations. Since Krishna's holy names are non-different from him, chanting benefits and purifies the conscious and unconscious minds of all who hear. It sanctifies the world. If the *mahamantra* is chanted in a pure way that is pleasing to Krishna, it is more spiritually effective. The focus on purity of intention avoids a mechanical, routine approach to daily ritual. *Samskara*s like marriage, initiation and *sannya*sa should be done with devotion. The goal of *all* rituals should be to please Krishna.

In answer to the question who *could* or *should* perform *samskara*s, the devotee replied:

> In this age we are all born *shudra*s (servants). *Shudra*s don't have the qualities
> to perform ritual. Only those who are genuine *brahmana*s can. In the Vedic
> age *brahman*s were able through their sacrifices to call the demi-gods down
> from heaven. This is no longer possible…Whilst *brahmanical* initiation
> enables me to perform the service of the deities, the *mantra*s I recite I have
> memorised by heart and I don't have the knowledge to perform the
> different *samskara*s.

He went on to explain:

> ISKCON wants to train priests to perform all the Vaishnava *samskara*s. I
> have come to Bhaktivedanta Manor for just this purpose. Today I am
> meeting my guru and tomorrow I am flying to India. I am going to study
> ritual in Mayapur under a very great master, Bhaktividyapurna Maharaja.
> Since the Indian congregation is growing…there is a social need for
> *samskara*s. The need is strong. Before the movement consisted of celibate
> monks, now it is a lay congregation. Rituals enable us to be more, not less,
> Krishna-centred. We will perform the same *samskara*s as other Hindus, but
> with Krishna Consciousness.

Krishnajanmashtami

Vertovec (2000, p.101) points out there has been a process of Iskconisation
within the British Hindus, that ISKCON's magazine *Back to Godhead* is widely
read by Indians, the *Bhagavad Gita As It Is* has become perhaps the most common
translation of the *Bhagavad Gita* in Britain and ISKCON's powerful, pro-active
preaching has proved very influential.[17] However, I had long been fascinated to
know whether birth Hindus would have very different attitudes to ISKCON's
rituals, and how they would accomplish the religious duties that domestic priests
(*kul purohit*s) traditionally perform at home on behalf of their *jajman*s or clients.[18]
Opportunity came at the great *Janmashtami Festival* in September when the whole
culture of Krishna Consciousness is displayed to tens of thousands of pilgrims,
and also to inter-faith representatives, diplomats, community leaders and media.
Over 700 volunteers help with the preparations.[19] For two days the loving
pastimes of Krishna and Radharani are told through the expressive arts of ritual,
dance, drama and music, while the attitudes of hospitality are symbolised by the
free distribution of *prasadam*. There are *bhajan*s, *kirtana*s and *pravachan*s in Hindi
and English given by ISKCON priests. South Asian visitors from all over Britain
and abroad vastly outnumber the very few initiated devotees present. Some were
twice migrants from East Africa, many with considerable experience of temple
building. Some were visiting Bhaktivedanta Manor for the first time; others were

seasoned volunteers, youth leaders and fundraisers. As expatriates they emphasise the religious and national aspects of their culture. A volunteer putting up direction signs said that he was not a devotee and was not initiated into ISKCON. A young software engineer, he spends weekends "helping out" and "helping Krishna." Asked if "Western" priests were respected for their ritual knowledge, he looked at me incredulously:

> They are very religious, very pious. The devotees have a hundred times more knowledge than I have. I am a *brahman* and have been initiated with the *janeu* (sacred thread) in India, but these people have more knowledge than me. They know *all* Vedic rituals. As for the caste system, it has been resolved. You see that girl over there! I am working with her and I have no idea of her caste. There is no caste here. The caste system has been perverted. In Vedic times it was based on qualities and virtues, not birth. Today it is the same here.

I asked whether a Hindu who worshipped Shiva or any other deity could perform rituals in the temple. He replied that: "Shiva is the greatest devotee of Vishnu, and all the demi-gods are created by Krishna. So *of course* the priests perform rituals for everyone."[20]

This confidence was not shared by every visitor. Two Bengali doctors, one living in Milton Keynes, the other in South London, drew attention to ISKCON's sectarianism and the language of "demi-gods" as uncharacteristic of Hindu flexibility and adaptability. Both were training to be surgeons and had come straight from a course in key-hole surgery. Devendra was accompanied by his wife, Bhavana. They told me that they had never been to the Manor before but had come for *darshan* ("viewing" of the deities) and *prasadam* because "as Hindus we worship Krishna." Jyoti had been influenced by Vivekananda's "clear, logical" teachings about Hinduism, and emphasised that ISKCON was a particular Vaishnava *sampradaya*, with sectarian ritual practices. Devendra said:

> We can go to any temple and any church or *gurdwara* – even to a mosque. You know Hinduism is tolerant. It respects all religions, all gods. Images are just symbols to direct the worshipper to God. They are for the people. The real devotee can worship without temples and images. The important thing to remember is God.

I asked Bhavana whether she and her husband would ever contemplate calling a priest to perform ritual in Britain. Bhavana replied: "We have no family with us here so we perform all rituals in India. No one thankfully is of the age to die in the family but in general any relative would like to have the death ritual performed in India."

A young accountant promoting subscriptions to *Back to Godhead* explained that he too spent all his weekends helping out at the Manor, but that he took initiation far too seriously to contemplate it yet. Work and family commitments meant that he would have little time to chant and fulfil all the other vows. He was certain that it was only the chanting the name of Krishna, "the one who attracts", that was important in this age:

> How will rituals help you on a desert island? Rituals are essential but very, very secondary. Just as I have a daily discipline of going to work, so in the same way rituals must be there to maintain discipline. It is too easy in the Kali Yuga to slide into materialism, to slump into a chair after work and watch Eastenders!

Older Indian visitors, whether Gujarati, Punjabi or "East African", seemed much more comfortable using the term "ritual" to designate *karmakand*, family *samskaras*, temple worship, etc. They pointed out that Bhaktivedanta Manor was famous in the Hindu community precisely for its high standards of *puja*, for the decoration and ornamentation of the deities. Large numbers of visitors (young and old) had participated (clapping, swaying, singing, waving arms) in the prolonged *aratis* and extended chanting of the *mahamantra*. They spoke of their joy at the devotional atmosphere (*bhavana, bhav*), but also of the importance of cultural continuity, of keeping faith with ancient practice. Elders were happy that their children and grandchildren were able to enjoy "Indian" festivals. They praised ISKCON's clergy for transmitting "traditional" Hindu values and customs to the younger generation. The idea that ISKCON affects as well as represents tradition was not voiced as a concern. Yet the rituals of ISKCON undoubtedly *do* construct tradition and *do* implicate and address "others" (cf. Baumann 1992, p.98).

Transmission, Mission and Mediation in the UK

In the UK the training for the priesthood is now an essential requirement for ministry. Bhaktivedanta Manor, originally envisioned by Prabhupada as a training centre for ISKCON *pujaris*, became, according to Malory Nye (1997, p.9), "the only institution where Hindu priests are formally trained." Both within the movement and within the Hindu diaspora it is often a taken for granted fact that ISKCON priests set the ritual standard for all other Hindu temples in Britain. An ISKCON information leaflet, *Bhaktivedanta Manor as a Place of Pilgrimage*, observes: "The priests are trained to perform all the ritual exactly according to Vedic custom." This situation is contrasted with the situation in Britain as a whole "where most large temples employ priests from India and the standard of worship in most Hindu temples is necessarily a compromise."[21] The same leaflet comments significantly: "Because of the spiritual atmosphere at Bhaktivedanta Manor, many families choose to hold important family ceremonies such as weddings and first hair cuttings (*mundan*) at the Manor."

Why is such an internationally influential culture of education and training for the ministry developing in Britain? Answers are readily available. Firstly, ISKCON in the UK has been remarkably successful (cf. Radha Mohan Das' chapter in this volume). Bhaktivedanta Manor has become a place of pilgrimage (*tirtha*) for a relatively large Hindu population. Indeed, Knott points out that Krishna is the most worshipped god in Britain today.[22] Their political influence and financial support during the ten-year campaign to save the Manor not only gave ISKCON a high national and international profile but also created enduring trustful relationships. Secondly, Bhaktivedanta Manor serves a diverse congregation of householders. An increasing preoccupation of the Governing Body Commission (GBC) and initiating gurus is to ensure that the ritual and devotional resources offered by ISKCON reach families at times of crisis or transition. Thirdly, the large congregations of today are often birth Hindus from very different devotional traditions.[23] Malory Nye (1997, p.7) points out that the large majority of Indian Hindus who worship at ISKCON temples and centres (most particularly Bhaktivedanta Manor) were of Gujarati ancestry and came from a region and culture far removed from the Bengali roots of ISKCON. For many, interaction with ISKCON does not entail any high degree of commitment to ISKCON's ideals or teachings. However, the high quality of worship is important to individual devotees:

Consistent, rigorous and efficient worship by the *pujari*s in the temple has the result that the deities (*murti*s) are pleased, and will be more likely to intervene in human affairs. In particular the *murti*s of Radha-Gokulananda (Radha-Krishna), that are the main focus of worship at the temple at Bhaktivedanta Manor, are considered by many Hindus to be very powerful, and highly effective if prayed to.

Fourthly, priesthood in ISKCON is becoming professionalised, the commitment to ministry and pastoral care increasingly articulate. The 17 international recruits to the 2004 training programme for priests in Bhaktivedanta College in Belgium are in the main educated, older second generation Western devotees who are choosing priesthood as a vocation (Shaunaka Rishi Das: personal communication: 29.11.04). The transmission of spiritual instruction (*siksha*) is given a contemporary energy at an earlier stage with the formation of the youth group, Pandava Sena and the Krishna Club, the Sunday school for 5-18 year olds, and ISKCON's primary school.[24]

The final point is general. Many religious traditions in the UK share the same basic requirements in the 21st century: a trained clergy, a theologically educated laity and a strong pastoral programme. ISKCON is well placed to mediate between concepts of Hinduism as a way of life and Hinduism perceived as a discrete faith in the modern Western sense (cf. Baumann 1999, p.71). As Brockington comments (1992, p.188): "...the nature of Hinduism is inevitably beginning to change in Britain – and no doubt in other countries – as it becomes something consciously learnt about rather than absorbed naturally, with the concomitant shift from practice to doctrine." For these reasons alone educated ISKCON devotees rooted in British cultural values are in a position to mediate both the kind of teaching and rituals required by "Western" devotees and by an expanding Asian congregation. They are also well placed to explain those rituals to the wider British public.

As ISKCON matures reflective devotees recognise that the movement cannot isolate itself from social and intellectual trends within the wider society. It can only thrive by engaging with them. Shaunaka Rishi Das and Kenneth Valpey pointed out to me (personal communication: 30.11.04) that it is possible and highly acceptable within the Christian tradition to have a particular denominational or church commitment, but to recognise and interact with Christians and members of other faiths. In the same way ISKCON members can honour the plurality of Hindu and Vaishnava traditions without compromising deeply held beliefs and practices.

ISKCON's very terminology suggests intercultural hybridity. Words now used regularly in ISKCON literature – priest, clergy, ministers, ritual, liturgy, congregation, pastoral care, worship, sacrament, prayer, missionary practice, God, deities, etc. – have their roots in Western cultural history.[25] Prabhupada's own very distinctive language which has become the shared vocabulary of devotees shows cultural miscegenation. There is the creation of culture in the choice of terms such as The Supreme Personality of Godhead, the Supersoul, demi-gods and *bona fide* spiritual master. Shaunaka Rishi suggested to me that the reframing of beliefs and actions, indigenisation and simplification of ritual may simply be a passing phase, an establishment phase in which cultural translation is essential. Certainly in its founding stage ISKCON attracted early Western converts partly *because* it had elements that were missing in Western society. Nevertheless, recent books (e.g. Bryant and Ekstrand 2004) show very clearly the porousness of different intellectual and spiritual worlds within ISKCON.

Swami Prabhupada: ISKCON's High Priest

Swami Prabhupada was an outstanding figure of the 20th century, combining the roles of ascetic, prophet and priest. Tamal Krishna Goswami writes that Prabhupada's own self-designation – founder-*acharya* – has resonances with the categories of founder, prophet and priest, but does not fit neatly into any one. In the early days of the movement, it was Prabhupada's personal charisma which was most in evidence, lending support to the view of him as founder or prophet but as the movement progressed – as his "flock" stabilised and from the clergy, a growing laity emerged – it is his office as priest which came to the fore. By "prophet" Goswami means a person whose authority is based on personal revelation and charisma. A "priest" on the other hand derives authority from his office. He comments (1998, p.260):

> Wach's category of the priest, while not necessarily an accurate indication of
> Prabhupada's temperament, does accommodate the sweeping reach of
> Prabhupada's accomplishments better than the categories of either prophet
> or founder. Although less original, spontaneous, and intense than the other
> two, the priest's personal religious experience qualifies him to mediate
> between God and man.

Goswami (ibid. p.261) argues that in readying himself for his mission and in the
similar training later of his disciples, Prabhupada exhibited the preparation and
education which has come to be associated with the priesthood. This included
ascetic practices, meditation and prayer, instruction and study. In order to create
the well-organised priesthood needed to perform the exacting *brahmanical* rituals
and elucidation of scripture, he became the movement's first and foremost priest.
Goswami (ibid.) declares that Prabhupada was "...in Wach's terms,
simultaneously its high priest, guardian of traditions, keeper of sacred knowledge,
custodian of the holy law, chief justice, administrator, teacher, scholar, patron of
the arts, and theologian."

Prabhupada envisaged that ISKCON would give Western society a head and
perform the *brahmanical* function for the rest of society (Ravindra Svarupa Dasa
1999, p.35ff). The class of *brahman*s created by Prabhupada together with the
renouncers became "the clergy." He encouraged *sannyasi*s, *brahmachari*s and
*brahman*s to adopt both ascetic and priestly ideals, to understand the importance
of unremitting discipline, the practice of austerities, and the study of sacred
literature. After Prabhupada's death ISKCON's ascetics became associated with
leadership. The *ashram* of the householder became devalued. The present explicit
valuing of the *grihastha ashram* seems likely to elevate the function of the
householder priest, and indeed this is exactly what we find.

Varnashramadharma and Bhagavat-dharma

Throughout the *brahmanical* tradition there has been tension between the utopian
representation of *brahman*s as a superior social class and challenges to this caste-
based construction which define *brahman*hood in terms of personal qualities and
conduct. Brian Black (2004, p.11) argues persuasively that the composers of the
Upanishads and early Buddhist texts replace the construction of "Brahman"
based on birth with the notion of a "true Brahman", a status reached by means of
one's conduct. Prabhupada's teachings on *varnashramadharma* do little to resolve
these age-old tensions.[26] Prabhupada who was himself born a *vaishya*
(Klostermaier 2000a, p.279) teaches on the one hand that all Vaishnavas, whether
brahman, *kshatriya*, *vaishya* or *shudra*, *transcend* the *varna* system but engage with it for
the purposes of a harmonious society. However he teaches on the other hand that
the majority of humans have qualities fitting *shudras* and that *brahman*s have

qualities that fit them to be the guru of all social orders. The ethical dilemmas implied in determining the appropriateness of *varna* allocation in an egalitarian post-industrial society are never pragmatically faced.[27]

Prabhupada also understands *varnashramadharma* as *process*. Its aim is to turn "a crude man into a pure devotee of the Lord, or a Vaishnava" (1989, p.89). Just as the sacraments (*samskaras*) purify and support devotees from birth to death, so *varnashramadharma* offers the spiritual and practical *means* by which Vaishnavas are produced. *Varnashramadharma* therefore is not about heredity, but about developing the intrinsic qualities and intellectual abilities of the Vaishnava. Prabhupada explicitly contrasts this "godly" system with the standard Hindu caste system, in which birth is the sole determinant of membership.[28] In this Prabhupada followed the teaching of his predecessors in the lineage – Bhaktivinoda Thakura and Bhaktisiddhanta Sarasvati – that *brahman*hood is not a matter of birth, but of personal qualities.[29]

Prabhupada remains cheerfully optimistic that an intellectual, educated class can be created in this life; he therefore retains the hierarchical social principle but one based upon "natural" tendencies and inclinations.[30] His ideal *varna* system has as its apex a class of *brahman*s exhibiting transcendental and intellectual virtues. Only true *brahman*s by definition pure devotees of the Lord, are authorised to become teachers, priests and recipients of charity (1989, p.388). However, Prabhupada, concerned by the ignorance of many disciples, also offers a definition of the *brahman* more in keeping with modernity. This relies not primarily on innate goodness (*sattva*) but on success in a graduated system of examinations.[31]

Prabhupada's directive to establish *varnashramadharma* in ISKCON has been controversial.[32] Some devotees find it unthinkable, impractical and irrelevant in modern society. Others see in the *varna* system the ideal framework of society, and believe that Prabhupada's teaching about *varnashramadharma* is a valuable legacy for all humanity.[33] Radha Mohan Das suggests (personal communication) that the *varna* system is desirable because it would return to the priestly, educated class the social influence, respect and power which secular capitalism has removed. Ravindra Svarupa Das (1999) argues that the creation of "genuine" *brahman*s is ISKCON's unfulfilled mission.[34]

Many ISKCON leaders accept the principles of *varnashramadharma* but prudently link them with career choice and aptitude. A small illustration will suffice. The mission of ISKCON Youth Ministry is "(t)o inspire youth to take up the preaching mission of ISKCON; to help youth in ISKCON become peacefully situated in their vocation (*varna*) and social role (*ashram*), and develop Krishna consciousness to their fullest potential" (ISKCON Youth Ministry.com accessed 01.09.04). And to achieve its mission, ISKCON Youth Ministry promises to "**guide** youth in career (*varna*) and social roles and duties (*ashram*); **engage** youth in Krishna's service according to their nature, propensities, talents and abilities" (ibid).

The Embodiment of Divinity: Deity, Guru and *Tirtha*

ISKCON devotees have a long tradition of reflecting upon and articulating Hindu, and especially Vaishnava understandings, of *murti*-worship. Their willingness to explain deity-worship publicly has had a major influence in nurturing the second and third generation of Hindus in ritual practices, and encouraging diasporic Hindus to feel pride in their traditions. Gelberg writes: "God stands, quite literally, within the community of devotees, allowing Himself to be approached in an immediate and personal way" (1989, p.145). Shaunaka Rishi Das argues (personal communication: 17.09.04) that deity worship is the heart of ISKCON:

> The greatest jewel in the crown of ISKCON is the deity worship…but the devotees don't yet know it…Krishna, Lord of senses, is worshipped with the senses. It is deity worship rather than book distribution or any other activity that that is the real jewel of ISKCON.

Prabhupada teaches (*Sri Isopanishad,* Mantra 8 commentary) that Krishna and other deities visibly materialise as *archavatara,* images which are expanded forms of Krishna and nondifferent from the Lord. Indriyesha Das (18.11.04) told a group of my students that the temple *murtis* are the actual forms of God: "This is what God actually looks like. God appears like this to accept our love." Indriyesha Das enters the temple each day to have *darshan* of the Lord: "like a child, a young kid, at Christmas. It's all so simple." Kripamoya Das commented: "What you see in *darshan* is a replication of ultimate spiritual reality."

Bhaktivedanta Manor's daily ritual routine contains the same elements found in all Hindu temples. However, its ritual is notable for its elaboration: the deities are richly dressed and ornamented. Other ISKCON temples may have a more explicit *Vraja* mood or a simpler way of dressing the *murtis*, but all will regard the adornment of Krishna and Radha as essential to *darshan* and as rooted ultimately in the *Bhagavata Purana* and in a whole tradition of poetry, painting and theatre. Temple ritual is the living re-enactment of Krishna and Radha's eternal *lila* (play) in the sacred basil forest of Vrindavan. Krishna performs all his pastimes just for the fun of it (cf. Case 2000, p.6). He wakes up, goes to herd the cows, plays with his cowherd friends, has a siesta, spends the evening in dance and games, and finally retires with Radha for their ultimate union. The day is therefore punctuated by regular worship (*arati*), and the offering of food (*bhog*).[35]

Devotees on waking purify themselves by Vaishnava adornment and *mantra*. They then assemble in the temple for *mangala arati* at 4.30 a.m. While the *pujari* at the altar ritually bathes, anoints (*abhiseka*), and dresses the deities, offering them food, water, light, incense and flowers, worshippers jubilantly chant the names of Krishna, and sing and dance before the deities (cf. Gelberg 1989, p.150). From 5.00 a.m. there is *japa* meditation when devotees individually recite the Hare Krishna *mahamantra*. At 5.15 a.m. the devotees congregate in the temple for *tulasi puja*. Then at 7.00 a.m. the deities are greeted. Following this devotees at 7.10 a.m. gather before Prabhupada's seat of honour (*vyasasana*) and observe worship of the guru (*guru puja*). While one devotee performs *arati* to the sculpted image of Prabhupada, others offer flowers and perform *kirtana* – responsive singing of a Bengali song by Narottama Dasa Thakura, a 16-17th century Gaudiya Vaishnava poet-saint, *Sri Guru-vandana* (Prayer to the Guru) from *Prema-bhakti-candrika*. At 7.30 a.m. there is a *Srimad Bhagavatam* class conducted by a senior member of the temple community.[36] At 12.30 p.m. *Raj Bhoga Arati* takes place after which (1.00 p.m.) the deities rest until 4.20 p.m. when there is *Dhupa Arati*. Devotees may also attend an optional evening *Sandhya Arati/kirtana* (7.00 p.m.) followed by a *Bhagavad Gita* class. *Sringar Arati* is at 9.00 p.m. and at 9.30 p.m. the deities rest and the temple closes. In addition to these daily *puja*s devotees hold Sunday feasts, large public festivals such as the Jagannatha Ratha-yatra (Festival of the Chariots) and public distribution of sanctified food (*prasadam*). Religious festivals occur throughout the year. The most important are Janmashtami and Diwali, held for Krishna and Rama.

The Guru

The guru/disciple relationship in ISKCON is central theologically, ritually and socially (e.g. Shinn 1985, p.106; Baird 1995, p.518). Every human being is believed to need the grace of a spiritual master who comes in a chain of authentic teachers. One of the essential requirements of the disciple is the ritual worship offered to the guru, and numerous conventions and protocol govern the devotee's relationship to the spiritual master. Prabhupada teaches that the spiritual master in ISKCON is to be regarded as non-different from Krishna – the guru must be worshipped as Hari, God (*sakshad-hari*) (ibid. p.238).[37] Prabhupada himself as the founder-*acharya* who revitalised the mission of Sri Chaitanya is uniquely honoured. He is believed to be directly empowered by Chaitanya; other gurus receive empowerment through him. Sivaram Swami states that Srila Prabhupada's worship is a regular function of all Vaishnavas and should exceed the homage offered to all others (1999, p.257).[38]

Both the instructor and the initiator are "equal and identical manifestations of Krsna" (cf. Sivaram Swami 1999, p.36). The *siksha-guru* awakens the devotee to the activities of devotional service known as *abhidheya*, actions one is duty-bound to perform (ibid. p.166). The devotee who first gives *siksha* is the *vartma-pradarsaka-guru*, and those who give general instruction in devotional practice are known as *sadhus* or *siksha-gurus*. The *diksha-guru* takes charge of the disciple, instructs him in the process of devotional service and initiates with the holy name and Gayatri *mantra*. After initiation, he continues to train the disciple in the knowledge of the Vedas and the worship of the Deity. "In the mood of a protective father, the initiator takes charge of guiding his disciple back to Godhead." (ibid. p.170). The spiritual master, as the eternal manifestation of

Krishna, takes on the sinful reactions of the disciples that he initiates (Baird 1995, p.527).[39]

For the argument of this chapter what is significant is that all the central relationships in ISKCON (divine-human, guru-disciple, etc.) are expressed through transformative rituals, and governed by detailed rules, regulations and etiquette.[40]   All gurus (and indeed all Vaishnavas) are manifestations of the Supreme Lord who must be served as representatives of Krishna. Although the relative degrees of worship shown to them will vary according to their stature, from the absolute point of view they are to be venerated as Krishna (ibid. p.124). The disciple should therefore serve the spiritual master by revering his orders and if possible offer him bodily comforts, helping him in bathing, dressing, sleeping, eating etc. "The general attitude should be that a disciple serves the spiritual master as a menial servant" (ibid. p.179).

The role of the guru creates hierarchies. However, the initiating guru should not be a law unto himself; he is within a strong disciplic succession and his authority should be scrutinised and rejected if his teachings and observance do not accord with scripture. While Guru service and worship may have led to hardness of hearts and the subordination of people to principles (Gelberg 2004, p.397), disciples claim that it has also transformed lives. Tamal Krishna Goswami took intimate care of his guru during his final illness and ministered devotedly to his own cherished devotees. In turn when he was diagnosed with cancer his devotees showered him with round the clock nursing and dietary care. Many devotees told me that they had come to God only through their guru. A Polish married devotee who devotes his entire life to chanting the names of Krishna accompanied by drum (*mridanga*) and cymbals (*kartala*s) in central London, exclaimed: "My Guru Maharaj is a wonderful Guru for me. He is very free. He encourages me to do what I want and although learned, he is very humble."

Pilgrimage

Devotees, through prodigious displays of energy and skill, have replicated worlds sanctified by the living presence of Radha-Krishna, Chaitanya and his companions, and Swami Prabhupada. It is curious to contemplate that Hindus now make pilgrimages to British *tirtha*s and find in Bhaktivedanta Manor's temple, lake and cow shelters the timeless realm of Krishna. Pilgrimage, which has always been integral to Hinduism, is increasingly integrated into ISKCON's global networks. The ritual of pilgrimage provides continuity of tradition through the generations, conveys implicit values and sets the boundaries of devotees' sense of identity. The Braj area surrounding Mathura (Krishna's birthplace) and Vrindavan (Krishna's forest home) where Krishna and his beloved Radha are always present is the spiritual home of devotees. It is a reflection of Goloka Vrindavan, which offers the freedom to enjoy Krishna in the familiarity of unrestricted love. Van der Velde writes of a secular Vrindavan of corrupt *brahman*s and "broken images, withered trees and dried up wells" (2004, p.126). Seeing the "true (V)rindavan" demands spiritual training and vision. It requires a transformation of character, a "refinding" of an original lost or forgotten innermost self. Only then will Krishna's dwelling places make themselves known:

> If one were to visit the groves, the bowers, the riverside where [Krishna] danced with his beloved *gopi*s, the *lilasthala*s, the places where he performed his miracles, in that pilgrimage site one would be sure to be at that very moment a partner in his eternal games… (ibid. p.125)

Rites of Initiation and Renunciation

Just as the cycle of the day and of the year are profoundly marked by ritual in ISKCON so too are the stages of the life cycle and devotional life. The spiritual initiations are ritual processes which take the devotee back to Godhead. They are generally considered more important than the rites of passage which are often connected with social transformation rather than liberation. In fact both sets of rituals have aspects which are spiritually, socially, psychologically and personally transformative. There are three formal initiations.

Hari-Nama Initiation

Hari-nama (initiation into the holy name) is a second birth, and is undertaken by devotees after a novitiate period in the movement. Literature on the movement generally puts the period of novitiate at between six months to a year, but today it usually lasts considerably longer. Traditional Vaishnava teaching is that the guru provides knowledge to the disciple and helps to remove the obfuscation of pride and ego. Since humility is considered to be one of the prerequisites of spiritual life, a healthy working relationship between guru and disciple is essential.

The candidate must adopt Vaishnava culture by regularly studying the scriptures and developing the qualifications of a disciple (*sadhaka*). She is then formally initiated into the tradition of the Brahma-Madhva-Gaudiya *sampradaya* by a spiritual master (*diksha-guru*) of her own choice or of the temple she is joining (cf. Gelberg 1989, p.146; Deadwyler 2001, p.57; Knott 1995, p.47). She is also initiated into the actual association of devotees. Prabhupada teaches that in this age the desire for spiritual realisation is pursued more effectively in community than in solitude. Disciples make vows before the Deity, before the fire and before Vaishnavas to avoid intoxication, illicit sex, meat eating and gambling and to chant 16 rounds of the *mahamantra* daily. They are given a spiritual name ending with *dasa* (*dasi* for women) and a set of *tulasi* beads for chanting. After this they are said to have become either *brahmachari*s/*brahmacharin*s or *grihastha*s.[41] Initiation is often deferred for years by those who work in the world and maintain families. Even those who wear the robes of a *brahmachari* may not be initiated for six or more years (Radha Mohan Das: personal communication).

Prabhupada is often quoted as saying that unless the devotee is initiated by a bona fide spiritual master, all his or her devotional activities are useless. However, Kripamoya Das (personal communication: 20.10.04) points out that this teaching has been taken out of context. Prabhupada is paraphrasing Srila Rupa Goswami who cautioned devotees against the assumption that one could please God without taking wise counsel from another saintly practitioner – without going through the "pure devotee of God." Kripamoya Das is concerned that the misinterpretation of Prabhupada's words may have deterred fledgling aspirants from the path of Krishna Consciousness:

But again, in a (W)estern context where trust in authority figures – including gurus, sadly – has been almost completely eroded it would be disadvantageous for anyone to state that only the formalities of initiation – the rigorous disciplines of which might be unattainable for many people – would validate the aspirant's sincere spiritual activity.

Brahman or Second Initiation

The second initiation takes place after several years as a full-time initiated devotee.[42] Men and women, either celibate or married, may undergo this ceremony in which they are given the Gayatri *mantra* and invested with the sacred thread. In this sense *brahmanic* initiation can be likened to the Vedic initiation (*upanayana*) of the twice-born *dwija varna*s. Candidates for second initiation must be recommended by the temple authorities and undergo a philosophical test. Initiates are then allowed to worship Krishna's *archa-vigraha* form in the temple (*archane-vidhi*), perform *arati, puja*, fire sacrifices, *abhisheka* during festivals, cook for the deities, etc., and to operate as "a kind of priesthood" (Knott 51).[43]

*Brahman*s are encouraged to have priestly, scholarly and teaching roles. They are increasingly graduates of the kind of training programmes suggested by Prabhupada. Candidates for *brahman* initiation study foundation texts like the *Bhagavad Gita*, the *Bhagavata Purana* and the *Isopanishad*. They acquire some knowledge of Sanskrit and of *mantra*. According to Prabhupada, the Vaishnava stage is "the postgraduate status of a *brahmana*." A Vaishnava is a "self-realised, learned *brahmana*" (1989, p.89).

What does it mean to be a Vaishnava *brahman* in Britain today? During conversations at Bhaktivedanta Manor several full-time devotees who have dedicated themselves to the movement for much of their lives identified themselves as *brahman*s. Some said simply that *brahman*s are those who have received the Gayatri *mantra* and "follow requirements." Others spoke of the second initiation as a qualification to worship at the altar, to take classes and to cook for the deities (service which requires a state of intense ritual purity). Many related the initiation to the maintenance of fundamental *brahmanical* principles of Vedic culture. One devotee commented: "By these we mean the practices of restraint, purity and self-discipline." On the other hand, I met male and female initiates who described themselves as *shudra*s simply because they were engaged in manual activities such as cleaning dishes and mopping floors.

Sannyasa Initiation

Only those (male) devotees who have received the *brahman* initiation may take *sannyasa*, and *sannyasi*s are respected as the gurus of both spiritual and social orders, including the *brahman*s. Prabhupada taught (e.g. 1989, p.307) that *sannyasa* involves the renunciation of social intercourse and the devotion of life exclusively to the Lord. However, in ISKCON generally the service of the renunciants is to participate in spiritual family-building, and to offer spiritual leadership and direction. They often spend their lives travelling and preaching. Renouncers (including three or four British *sannyasi*s) should be treated with profound reverence by the entire community of devotees. Gurus who were close disciples of Prabhupada receive particular homage.

ISKCON's initiated ascetics are "saffron cardinals", priestly office-holders, rather than homeless holy men. They are administrators, members of the GBC and missionaries located in the very heart of social life, heading the global institution that is ISKCON. Their role as ascetics has more to do "with endorsing and supporting *dharma* than the traditional world-negation that one would find amongst *sannyasi*s in India. Therefore they are more priests and preachers than rootless mendicants. *Sannyasa* has…become something of an ecclesiastical position" (Kripamoya Das: personal communication: 12.10.04).

The Initiation of Women

ISKCON has had a contentious and sometimes fiery engagement with the whole issue of gender. Swami Prabhupada's broad generalisations about women would seem sexist and offensive if delivered today (cf. Lorenz 2004, p.123), but devotees suggest that Prabhupada's words have been taken out of their cultural context and insist that Prabhupada treated women with equal kindness and compassion. Women were able to preserve the traditional female cultural roles but live simultaneously the principles of equality of spiritual service. Devotees claim that in its origins ISKCON was a reformist movement. It initiated women as *brahamana*s (though they do not wear the sacred thread) and permitted them to conduct ritual as *pujari*s, servants of the temple deities (cf. Knott 1995, pp.34, 47).[44] In the mid-1970s the situation began to change. The householder or *grihastha ashram* as a whole was criticised. Some *sannyasi*s wanted to see the initiation of women stopped. Knott comments (ibid. p.44) that: "One practical effect of their preaching was the reorganization of worship such that in many temples women were made to stand at the back of the temple room behind the male devotees." Radha Devi Dasi notes that women in ISKCON face enormous difficulties in eliminating the "women in the back policy" in some gender segregated temple rooms and pleads for equal rights (1998a, pp.7-14). She states (1998b, p.33) that the belief that women are inferior is often reflected in ISKCON's policy and practice. Women are told (ibid. p.34): "Don't act", "don't dance in the temple", "don't stand in front of the Deities", "don't give class", "don't lead *kirtana*", and "do not participate in many other activities."

My own conversations with ISKCON devotees led me to think that the changes that have taken place in ISKCON have led to women having very different experiences of being Krishna Conscious in the secular world. Young Romanian women devotees at the Soho Temple indicated that they were attracted to ISKCON precisely *because* they believed that it gave them spiritual and material equality. They gave numerous examples where women with ability had become head priests and temple presidents, members of the GBC (the first was installed in 1998), and revered lifelong renunciates. They claimed that women could become initiating gurus "if their spirituality was powerful enough." However, at Bhaktivedanta Manor I met other women (including the wife of the head priest) who argued, just as strongly, that women naturally seek the shelter of men. They therefore rule out as unnatural positions of ritual authority for women, regarding feminism as a damaging inversion of the spiritual and biological order. A feisty second generation (unmarried) devotee in her late twenties challenged me: "Come on! You know what women really, really want! They want a man and to look after kids. All they want is to get married." Admitting that women today cannot find men strong enough to protect them, she argued that in this Kali Yuga men have become weak and abdicated their responsibilities. Thus the idea that women are emotional, vulnerable and in need of male protection and guidance persists. That men also require the shelter of women is not stressed.[45] The difficulties ISKCON experiences in reconciling Prabhupada's teachings and traditional models of gender complementarity and difference with modern realities has led to some uncompromising analysis. In Indian urban areas where priesthood has become a profession like any other, the gender of the practitioner is increasingly irrelevant. In ISKCON the debate continues.

Rites of Passage

Rick Jarow (2003, p.74) writes: "The ethos of *bhakti* is said to transcend fruitive acts, elevationist proclivities, and even liberation itself." The weight given to *samskaras* in ISKCON by individual devotees is extremely varied. Some devotees with a lifetime's commitment behind them believe that they are ultimately inessential. Others insist that far from being "merely" rites, which legitimise social order and uphold social institutions, ISKCON's rites of passage involve spiritual as well as social transformation. Such attitudes place ISKCON more or less directly within mainstream Hinduism. At the other end of the spectrum there are gurus and scholars who stress divine grace and reciprocal love (cf. Schweig 2004, *passim*) and decry any obsession with Hindu ideas of *karma* or ritual. All these readings can be legitimated by an appeal to Prabhupada's teachings which were attuned to time, place and circumstance. He taught both that rituals were unnecessary *and* that the *samskaras* were purificatory processes. He followed the path of many Hindus in seeing that the pure devotee is created by a series of rituals starting in the womb and proceeding to maturity and death.[46] Such *samskaras* included the *garbhadhana-samskara* ("spiritual family planning"), the sacred thread ceremony, the marriage ceremony and the death rituals.

Prema Rasa Dasa and Sandipani Muni Dasa in *The Book of Samskāras: Purificatory Rituals for Successful Life* (dedicated to Srila Prabhupada) contend that, the benefit of performing *samskaras* is undeniable provided their rules are applied in conjunction with *Hari-nama-sankirtana*. Even in this troubled Kali Yuga, society can only benefit from Vaishnava rituals. They are part of the primeval tradition emanating from Krishna Himself and they bring prosperity and harmony to all citizens. *Samskaras* enable one to progress peacefully towards the ultimate existence, to reach the Absolute. They sanctify a person throughout the important stages of life. They lay the foundations of a harmonious society. The rules of *karma* invite us to conform to *varnashrama*, *samskaras* and prayers:

> A person who reaches the *karma-kanda* stage must become firmly situated in *varnashramadharma* and develop the desire to reach the *jnana* stage. That is his duty. He must remain within the *varnashrama* system as long as he has some attachment for material activities...To receive the Lord's mercy, the Vaishnava (householder) who still has some material attachment must accept the natural order of *varnashrama* and follow with his wife the principles of *dharma, artha, kama, moksa*, to stay alive. Thus he will manage to transform his attachment.
>
> Through *samskaras* we can sanctify relations between parents and children, between husband and wife, between master and disciple, between humans on earth, between men and the deceased, between men and demigods, the sages and God. *Samskaras* drive away the evil influences of the visible and the invisible worlds and attract the blessings of the sages, demigods and God Himself. In the absence of *samskaras*, life's activities become mundane. (Prema Rasa Dasa and Sandipani Muni Dasa 1997, pp.xiii-iv)

According to Prema Rasa Dasa and Sandipani Muni Dasa ISKCON devotees follow two paths. The first is *Pancharatrika-vidhi*, a combination of Vedic and tantric systems (ibid. p.30). The *Hari-bhakti-vilasa* and *Sat-kriya-sara-dipika* of Srila Gopala Bhatta Goswami which refer to Vedic, tantric and Pancharatric texts are basic works for Gaudiya Vaishnava rituals. The second is the path of *Srimad Bhagavatam*, pure love of godhead revealed by Chaitanya. Vaishnava rituals imply union with one God and in that sense for Vaishnavas they reveal the hidden meaning of the Vedas.

The principal *samskaras* are those performed traditionally by all Hindus and they are believed by Vaishnavas to purify and protect body and mind. They are *vivaha* (marriage); *garbhadhana* (purification of the act of conception); *pumsavana* (rite for begetting a male child); *simantonnayana* (parting the wife's hair for healthy/male children, good fortune, long life); *sosyanti* (rite for safe child birth); *jata-karma (*birth ceremony to produce intelligence in the child*)*; *niskramanam* (taking the child outside for the first time); *nama-karana* (name-giving ceremony); *pausti-karma* (ceremony for the continued health of the child*)*; *mundana* (first hair-cutting ceremony*)*; *anna-prasana* (first grains ceremony); *putra-murdhabhighranam* (smelling the son's head); *karna-vedha* (piercing the ears); *cuda-karana* (hair-cutting ceremony); *vidyarambha* (beginning education); *upanayana* (rite of initiation*)*; *samavartana* (graduation ceremony); *antyeshti-kriya* (funerary rites). Vedic astrology recommends that each *samskara* should be performed at particular auspicious times (see Goswami 1997, pp.259-69). Those who perform ritual are urged to give *dakshina* (offerings) to all initiated Vaishnavas and all Vaishnava *brahman*s and *prasadam* to all devotees and guests (ibid. p.170). Prema Rasa Dasa and Sandipani Muni Dasa are persuaded that it is only when ISKCON devotees set up the system of *varnashramadharma* that the exhaustive performance of the *samskara*s, which includes the resort to astrology, will be possible.[47] "Vedic rules are part of the primeval and eternal universal Tradition which will always prove invaluable regardless of time and circumstances, and even in the gloomy theatre of Kali-yuga" (ibid. p.63).

My (limited) research indicates that, of the 16 or so *samskara*s recommended by texts such as the *Sat-kriya-sara-dipika*, few are regularly performed in the UK and Ireland. Easily the most popular *samskara* is that of marriage, followed by that of *mundan*, the shaving of a young child's head. *Sannyasi*s sometimes give the children of their disciples a name, but this naming is devoid of the usual Hindu ritual procedures for *nama-karana samskara*. Vedic weddings have been performed from the foundation of ISKCON, but marriage itself has been treated with some ambivalence. After Prabhupada's death the dominance of the ascetics meant that marriage was devalued and involved a loss of status, especially for men (Rochford 2001, p.2). Rasamandala Das notes interestingly that in the past the marriage *samskara* was viewed as a "fall-down." He writes (1995, p.90): "As a young *brahmachari* the author was recommended to completely avoid an ISKCON wedding ceremony, described to him as a 'funeral'." From the 1980s however ISKCON has become far more family-oriented and household based, and Rochford (2001, p.6) urges ISKCON to promote family life as the very foundation of its future.

Interviews with four priests indicate that other *samskara*s, and particularly death ritual, are being developed in ISKCON. Collectively ISKCON priests (generally Gujarati *pujari*s) in the UK perform about 30 funerals a year in London, Watford, Birmingham, etc. Members of the congregation generally turn to their local Asian communities at the time of death, while Western devotees often have mainstream funerals or cremations with Vaishnava elements.[48] There is continuing devotional and scholarly exploration of the spiritual and pastoral resources available in ISKCON for those who are dying or grieving, but many devotees remain uncertain about Vaishnava liturgy or procedure at the time of death. There are also competing theological explanations of tragic or untimely deaths.[49] One of the most interesting aspects of the funerary rituals of death is that ISKCON converts have usually grown up within a culture from which the dead are largely absent.[50] While ISKCON teaching is that extended death rituals are unnecessary for the pure Vaishnava and that worship of the *devta*s and *pitri*s is erroneous, many within the lay congregation still perform *shraddha* rituals for the ancestors. Kripamoya Das (personal communication) offered the perceptive insight that the life of the Vaishnava is a permanent *shraddha*:

> Love of God takes care of everything. No subsidiary appeasement is necessary. With increasing purity there is less need to perform death rituals. The souls of the dead will be delivered as a result of *your* devotion. This is a permanent *shraddha*.

ISKCON's Priests

In seeking to interview practising priestly *brahman*s I spoke to Shaunaka Rishi Das and Kenneth Valpey (Krishna Kshetra Das) who are now attached to the Oxford Centre for Hindu Studies but who spent many years as respected Vaishnava priests. They recommended that I rely particularly on the vast experience and knowledge of Kripamoya Das who has been performing *samskara*s for over 20 years. Kripamoya Das's experience of living with Gujaratis in East Africa inspired him with a desire to perform service for families by developing *samskara*s. As a householder he knew the value of the *grihastha* rites of passage. He explained to me that *samskaras* help people to remember God because they are "witnessed and solemnised before God."[51]

Kripamoya Das comments of his own role: "My job in performing *samskara*s is to bring others into the presence of God, to bring sacred space where there is profane and to bring people who have no belief into belief." If he is performing a marriage ceremony in a hotel for example, he creates a state of ritual purity by putting on priestly dress (*dhoti*, mid-cloth, *chadar*, shirt and *gumsha*) and marking out the boundaries of a sacred space. Before the ceremony he gathers together all the *puja* items used in worship and draws up an astrological chart.[52] The performance of any *samskara* has an essential ritual core to which he adds on appropriate local or family customs. The marriage ceremony for example necessarily includes all the traditional ritual – *kanya dan*, circumambulation of the fire, *sapta padi*, etc. – but in Britain it will probably also include a speech by the best man, the exchange of rings and the cutting of a cake. The spiritual advice given to the bride and groom in the UK is very little different from that given by any sympathetic minister whether Christian, Hindu, Sikh or even humanist. Kripamoya Das explains his own position as follows:

> When I worship personally I act as a Vaishnava. When I perform service for someone else my identity is subsumed into that of a priest. My duty is to help them on their emotional, social and spiritual journey according to the beliefs they hold...When I perform rituals for others I allow myself to be a co-celebrant.

ISKCON priests bring their own very personal approach to the performance of rituals, but any job specification would have to include the ability to put people at ease, a keen sense of humour and a relaxed manner. In many Indian marriage ceremonies Kripamoya Das must be able to hold the attention of 600 or more wedding guests for two hours, explain each of the 60 different rituals in English and cope with microphones and video technology. He emphasises the need to interpret ritual to third and fourth generation British Asians whose first language is English and who are less in touch with Vedic culture.

The majority of British Asians are Gujarati (70 per cent), a statistic reflected in the weekly congregation which attends Bhaktivedanta Manor (about 1000-1200 people). Priests differentiate loosely between three groups who may require ritual services. Affiliated members who attend regularly and who think of Bhaktivedanta Manor as "their own" temple; the extended congregation; the (Hindu) population at large. Today the *pujaris* of Bhaktivedanta Manor conduct worship and perform marriages in homes and temples throughout the UK. The only formal stipulation is that couples before the ceremony observe a period of vegetarianism. Many of the weddings are inter- and intra-religious.[53] Young British Hindus (and Sikhs) want non-Asian friends to feel happy and comfortable, and Bhaktivedanta Manor seems the perfect setting. In 2004 British-born filmstar Nitin Ganatra chose to get married at Bhaktivedanta Manor for just these reasons. His "best man" was Sanjeev Bhaskar, actor star of the TV series "Goodness Gracious Me" and "The Kumars at No. 42."[54]

Kripamoya Das performs as many as 50 or so weddings a year, most of them within the summer holiday months. ISKCON priests who perform ritual within the temple are treated as employees. Outside the temple they receive *dan* and *dakshina* (gifts and offerings). As is the *brahmanical* custom there are no fixed charges. I was interested to discover that while the ISKCON priest never demands money, he will have a proper respect for the office of priest. A marriage party which consults Kripamoya Das as to how much they should give, may be gently challenged: "What am I worth to you?" "Am I worth as much as the DJ?" "As the chef?"

Training for Priesthood

ISKCON leaders have been prescient in developing programmes of ministerial and pastoral training and in systematically exploring the rich medieval heritage of Gaudiya Vaishnavism (cf. Klostermaier 2000a, p.126). Scholars have long raised the question as to whether ISKCON will become an ethnic Hindu church. A puzzle more relevant to this chapter concerns the "clergy." Now that Krishna Consciousness is a global movement how broadly or narrowly do priests construe their pastoral and ritual duties? In terms of the core of initiated devotees? The Asian congregation? The general public? The answer, as far as I could ascertain, is that they feel a strong responsibility to all who require their services, of any faith and none.

The criteria for qualified priests are set out in *The Book of Samskaras*. We are told that not everyone can perform a *yajna* or *samskara*. To perform such rites, one must fulfil certain criteria:

1) Take shelter at the feet of a spiritual master;
2) Receive both initiations (*harinama-grahane* and Vaishnava *mantra-diksha*);
3) Be authorised to perform such rites by one's spiritual master;
4) Study the performance of such rites from a qualified Vaishnava;
5) Behave in an exemplary way;
6) Show enthusiasm for serving guru, Sri Gauranga and Vaishnavas;
7) Be in good health;
8) Be of a pleasant disposition;
9) Wear a *sikha*;
10) Follow the regulative principles.

As in Hinduism generally the officiating priest is believed to take on some *karma* which is hard to digest. He must therefore be exemplary in his spiritual practices when he performs *karmakanda*. By chanting the Holy Names he reduces this *karma*. Similarly the priest should be a householder. Only the *upanayana samskara* (initiation) may be performed by a *sannyasi* or *brahmachari*.

There has been in recent decades in ISKCON a move away from simple recruitment. The focus now is on training and graduation. Education and training programmes offered to devotees include the study of the theology, history and practices of Vaishnavism. Rasamandala Das (1995, p.91) reports that the VTE (Vaishnava Training and Education) recommends that for managers, ministers and priests, training lasts for a minimum of five years. The VTE is developing courses, including teacher training, management and leadership, communications, missionary practice, scripture, pastoral care and care for the sick and dying. By working in co-operation with British educational consultants and government agencies, it is moving towards official accreditation for many of its courses. Programmed and certifiable training in *karmkand*, Sanskrit education, etc. are becoming essential requirements. This is in accord with the global growth of

Hindu priestly traditionalism accompanied by the adoption of increasingly modernist values and attitudes (see Fuller 2003, p.152).

The development of the Oxford Centre for Hindu Studies, an independent academy at Oxford University, suggests the value placed now on rigorous scholarship. The Centre is interested in initiating a new kind of studies which includes practitioners who will become academically accredited. The Centre's first two doctoral students graduated from Oxford University in 2004. Both Ravi M. Gupta (Radhika-ramana Dasa) and Kenneth Valpey are scholars and practitioners of Hinduism who focused their studies on various aspects of the Hindu tradition. Kenneth Valpey's decision to study the deity (or *murti*) worship of Lord Krishna was motivated by almost three decades as a *pujari* or ritual priest. During that time he played an important role in composing a two-volume manual for Vaishnava deity worship. Among outstanding scholars invited to be Director of Academic Affairs have been Thomas J. Hopkins (1998-9), Klaus Klostermaier (2000-1), Francis X Clooney, S.J., (2002-3), Pratap Kumar (2004-5) and Gavin Flood (2005). Bhaktivedanta College in Belgium which is affiliated with the University of Wales, Lampeter, teaches theology and religious studies but today devotees are studying Vaishnava theology and practice in mainstream universities.[55]

Liturgy and Translations

After the death of Chaitanya in 1534 his disciples carried on his work. In addition to stressing the most important Vaishnava scriptures, the *Bhagavad Gita* and the *Bhagavata Purana*, the early disciples produced a number of important manuals and treatises, in Bengali and Sanskrit. Knott (1986) comments:

> Perhaps the most important of these – at least from the perspective of the Hare Krishna movement – were Sanatana Goswami's *Hari-bhakti-vilasa*, a manual of ritual, the *Bhakti-rasamrita-sindhu*, a theological treatise by Rupa Goswami (translated into English by Prabhupada and entitled *The Nectar of Devotion*, considered to be the law book of the Krishna Consciousness movement), and Krsnadasa Kaviraj's *Vaitanya-caritamrita*, a biography.

Songs, prayers and scriptural readings continue to be sung, recited, and read in Sanskrit or Bengali, while Prabhupada's translations and commentaries on the *Bhagavata Purana*, the *Bhagavad Gita*, the *Caitanya-caritamrita*, the *Bhakti-rasamrita-sindhu* and the *Isopanishad* are foundation texts. However, now devotees have access to the many translations of Vaishnava texts and numerous monographs on Vaishnava history and theology published by Western scholars. Vaishnava texts published outside ISKCON are held by Bhaktivedanta Library Services (BLS) in Belgium. Devotees have been engaged in translating key Vaishnava texts including the *Sat-kriya-sara-dipika* of Srila Gopala Bhatta Goswami, the authorised Vedic *yajna* and *samskara* manual for the Vaishnava community. Gopala Bhatta Goswami gives detailed descriptions of the rituals for the performance of fire sacrifices and *samskaras* according to the *vaishnava-smriti*, and enunciates principles of *yajna-vidhi* which are standard for deity installations, festivals and *samskaras*. He writes for surrendered souls, substituting worship of Vishnu and his associates for worship of Ganesha, the material *sakti*s and the planetary deities, and replacing references to the demi-gods with *mahajana*s from the *Bhagavata Purana*.

Reflections

This chapter celebrates the Western transmission of Vaishnava ritual, the punctilious maintaining and monitoring of spiritual standards and worship and the translation and study of ritual texts. It acknowledges a wide spectrum of perspectives about the practice of *sadhana bhakti* but suggests that on the whole devotees see strictness in ritual practice as the bedrock of ISKCON's mission (cf. Valpey 2004, pp.46, 52). I have emphasised Prabhupada's priestly role as founder-*acharya*, his emphasis on *vidhi* and the *brahmanical* or priestly dimension in ISKCON because they have too often been neglected or regarded as insignificant. Priestly values permeate all *ashram*s, whether ascetic or householder (Kripamoya Das: personal communication: 12.10.04). Moreover, historical contextualisation is vital. It is quite remarkable that devotees with educated, non-*brahmanical*, non-Hindu backgrounds have year after year maintained forms of deity worship that are alien to the surrounding culture. Kripamoya Das points out:

> In a medieval religious culture with (too) many rituals, reformers like Chaitanya and his followers could stress spiritual emotions over ritual; in a Western context however, where there (are) decreasing levels of any religious ritual, for ISKCON merely to stress such emotion is to encourage forms of antinomianism. Cultural context influences religious practice and vice versa. (personal communication)

Devotees believe that theology dictates the rituals: "To change the theology changes the rituals." However, if we reverse that view and regard liturgical and ritual language as a lens through which to view ISKCON's theology and its relationship to its founder any changes or transformations become significant (cf. Waterhouse 2004). It has been claimed (cf. Shinn 2004, p.xviii) both that the authentic practices of ISKCON attracted devotees, and also that they caused the society to stand out in contrast, and even opposition, to Western religious and cultural values, engendering fundamental tensions between ISKCON and its adopted culture in the West. I take a more nuanced view. Internal changes within ISKCON, within British society and globally have led to a shifting spectrum of understandings. Men and women devotees have not only had to encounter contradictions between Eastern and Western lifestyles and cultures, but now, perhaps more challengingly, a revisioning of their own neo-traditionalism (their articulate ideological commitment to the authority and legitimacy of tradition) within the context of a theological and philosophical engagement with modernity.

There are liberal devotees who inspire ISKCON's inter- and intra-faith conversations with other theological traditions (including other Hindu schools) and who advocate a progressive, non-literal understanding of Prabhupada's teachings. There are also devotees who fear being swallowed up by mainstream Hinduism or secular humanism, and who are concerned with strict authenticity of text and ritual. "Back to Prabhupada" is the battle cry of the disillusioned. There are those who are on the fringes of the movement or who have joined one of the many Gaudiya Vaishnava groups which have sprung up. Many devotees, perhaps the great majority, float or toss in the waves of mingling currents.

The context in which ISKCON finds itself today in Britain differs radically from the situation 40 years ago. Language, thought-forms, expectations and culture have changed. ISKCON itself has been transformed. An examination reveals rapid indigenisation. Terms like priest, liturgy, sacrament and even "God" are widely used and understood easily by the wider population, creating new hybrid meanings. The very concept of liturgy reflects a blurring of cultural and linguistic horizons. In many "new" and diasporic traditions (cf. Waterhouse 2004) ritual is translated into English, abbreviated and its doctrinal content reduced. In ISKCON the capacity of gurus and priests to interpret sacramental action in terms that young British people understand and find relevant has been vital to the success of the movement. Prabhupada and his successors simply continue the tradition of the great medieval preachers of *bhakti* who used vernacular languages to get their message across: Tamil, Avadhi, Brajbhasha, Bengali, Mahratti, Gujarati etc. (Klostermaier 2000b, p.4). The turn to indigenous comprehensible language may be simply a passing phase. Nevertheless, it has enabled ISKCON to address new generations of Hindus and to become a powerful force for multifaith, antiracist education.

The Indianisation of ISKCON and the Iskconisation of British Hinduism have huge implications for the future of both. Attempts to distinguish ISKCON as a universal religion from "Hinduism" still occupy the thoughts of some devotees, but ISKCON leadership has long since distanced itself from the robust exclusivist theology of 40 years ago. Scholars and devotees (e.g. Rochford 1985, p.262; Goswami 1998, p.263) have for some decades pondered whether the growth of the Indian congregation poses a dilemma for ISKCON. While there are devotees who interpret Prabhupada's mission as primarily to the West and feel that the mission may be diverted by the compelling need to provide ritual and pastoral care to the wider South Asian congregation, the great majority of devotees recognise the vital contribution (financial and political) of the Hindu community to ISKCON, and their own reciprocal duties of pastoral care and nurture. This is leading to specialised ministries in which priests like Kripamoya Das make contemporary sense of medieval rituals and puranic stories for young British Hindus. Since a Hindu sense of identity and belonging is expressed through rites of passage, this priestly ministry will become an ever more crucial and recognised aspect of ISKCON's mission.

My brief incursions into the complex areas of *varna* and gender have led me to conclude that the ambiguities of the relationship between *varnashramadharma* and *bhagavat-dharma* given the authority of scripture and guru *are* irresolvable in an absolute sense. However, in practice ISKCON literature prudently uses the term *varna* to refer to the development of individual potential and aptitude. Similar tensions surround the spiritual advancement and material participation of women. My research indicates that in its inspiring and hardworking women devotees ISKCON has a remarkable spiritual resource. A principled and feminised reinterpretation of tradition and philosophy should inevitably lead to priestly leadership becoming a vocation exercised by men and women alike, a development which can only strengthen the mission of Krishna Consciousness.

The institutional life of Britain necessarily shapes the way ISKCON presents itself publically.[56] Political, legal, educational and funding structures exert irresistible pressures on the development of all faith communities in the UK. In turn ISKCON's success means that it is able to influence (even at times to control) the construction of Hinduism in Britain. ISKCON has the cultural, social and economic capital that enables devotees to speak on behalf of Hinduism and the Hindu community. Several gurus have commented to me that British Hindus have not yet developed a collective tradition of self-reflexity or self-promotion, and acknowledge the danger that ISKCON may present its own teachings as "pure" *sanatan* or *Vedic dharma* or even pure Vaishnavism. The development of institutions like the Oxford Centre for Hindu Studies and Bhaktivedanta College in Belgium which have policies of ecumenicism and critical textual and ritual scholarship are intended to counter sectarian representations.

Research has born out the commonsense view that many currents within the wider society are affecting ritual performance. Although Prabhupada arguably preached an exclusivity of worship to his young followers, in Britain ISKCON is served by priests whose approach is inclusive, inter-religious and dialogic. Partly as a result of their intense labours and self-reflexivity festivals and rituals once regarded as "exotic" now inspire public confidence and even affection. Priests who perform family *samskaras* tend to accept all the traditional Hindu ways of *karma* and *bhakti*, and to celebrate sanctified diversity, an acknowledgement that each devotee brings a highly personalised and highly individualised approach to worship and ritual. The importance of time, place and circumstance is accepted. Liberal practitioners accept that there is a multiplicity of paths to Krishna and that He evokes different *rasa*s in different devotees. "Krishna, the Supreme Personality of Godhead manifests according to the heart of the worshipper. For some Krishna is the Torah, for some He is the divine White Light into which we move, for others He is a dear son or lover. He possesses an infinity of ways to relate to us."

I conclude that while ISKCON is becoming increasingly catholic and ecumenical, it is also becoming more diverse. While ISKCON leaders and scholars are increasingly knowledgeable about the richness of their Brahma-Gaudiya-Vaishnava ritual tradition and *siksha sampradaya*, this tradition is being shaped, as well as challenged, by many other influences: the pastoral needs of diasporic Hindus, the values and structures of the wider British community, the deepening commitment to inter-faith dialogue, the transfer of congregational celebrations to Sundays, the opportunities for devotees from all over the world to meet, interact and share ideas.

The future for ISKCON in Britain looks exciting. ISKCON's dialogue with contemporary trends in scholarship and society will ensure that it retains intellectual vibrancy and relevance. Scholarly devotees whose faith is undisputed have for a decade or more been applying perspectives derived from the wider society – postmodernist, feminist, pluralist, textual-historical, etc. – to Prabhupada's transplanted and literalist tradition (e.g. Goswami and Valpey 2004). Meanwhile ISKCON is continuing to diversify; to develop new projects; to safeguard and translate texts; to support scholarly and devotional study; to train clergy; to exercise an expanded pastoral role in ways that value individuality and initiative; and to advocate a vegetarian, ecologically sustainable and non-violent life style. Devotion in practice, *vidhi bhakti sadhana*, has been crucial to the Mission's success. Exemplariness in ritual training and pastoral care enables devotees to become bearers of tradition within a worldwide Hindu diaspora. Krishna *bhakti* can only thrive where Krishna is worshipped. To paraphrase Goswami (1983, p.210), "From the grammar of *brahmanical* ritual flows the poetry of *bhakti*."

PART 4

Identity and Perception

9

ISKCON'S SEARCH FOR SELF-IDENTITY:
Reflections by a Historian of Religions

Thomas J. Hopkins

The Beginning

I first became aware of ISKCON in 1966, a few months after A.C. Bhaktivedanta Swami, as he then was known, had moved into his storefront headquarters at 26 Second Avenue in New York. I had been teaching at Franklin and Marshall College in Lancaster, Pennsylvania, since 1961, offering mainly courses on Indian religion. One day in the fall of 1966, a student from New York brought me a copy of the *Village Voice*, which regularly reported on new happenings in the city, and showed me an article about New York's latest phenomenon: an Indian swami who was singing and chanting with a group of young followers in Tompkins Square Park on the Lower East Side.

My student was puzzled, and asked me, "What is this all about?" I read the article, which didn't help much to answer the question. Tompkins Square Park had long been known as the social centre for the surrounding multi-cultural community in lower Manhattan, and by then it had also become a gathering place for the newly emerging population of hippies in the area. Even by these eclectic standards, however, the swami and his activities stood out. The author of the *Village Voice* article had no real understanding of what he had seen, but he knew that the swami in Tomkins Park was quite different from the swami who headed the long-established Vedanta Society in central Manhattan. In an inspired moment, he coined the terms "uptown swami" and "downtown swami" to distinguish the two.

I knew about the highly Westernised Vedanta Society and the sophisticated "uptown swami" who led its New York chapter, but the "downtown swami" who was singing, dancing, and chanting in the park was a mystery. He was described as an older man who wore an ochre robe and looked Indian, but the young people with him seemed to be typical New York hippies. Who was this lively, smiling senior citizen in a robe, where had he come from, and what was he doing in NewYork's Lower East Side? And who, moreover, were the young Americans who seemed to be his followers? What was going on?

At this point, I had to admit that I couldn't explain what this was all about, but the *Village Voice* article about the "downtown swami" had sparked my curiosity even if it could not answer my questions. In particular, it started me thinking about what kind of religious event the reporter had witnessed, and where it might fit into what I assumed was an Indian and probably Hindu tradition of origin. Reading between the lines of the article, it seemed to be describing some kind of group devotional activity, and if so, then I had at least some idea where it might have come from.

I had done my PhD dissertation at Yale some five years earlier on Vaishnava devotionalism in the *Bhagavata Purana*, and in the course of my research had studied various Hindu religious movements that emphasised devotion to Vishnu, especially in his incarnation as Krishna. One of the most important of those movements was what is known as Gaudiya Vaishnavism, a tradition established in Bengal by the saint Chaitanya (1486-1533) that practiced a form of group devotional singing and chanting known as *sankirtana*. The activities in Tompkins Square Park seemed to fit the pattern of *sankirtana* as I understood it from my reading, so it seemed at least possible that the "downtown swami" came from the Gaudiya or Chaitanya tradition.

I decided to go to New York to see if I could find out more. I had no way to get to India for research at that point, but I thought that if I were lucky I might learn something about Vaishnava devotionalism from this new Indian swami. With no more than a hunch to guide me, I applied for a small travel grant from my college and set out for New York City.

By the time I set out for New York, an article about the Tompkins Square Park phenomenon had appeared in *The East Village Other*, another New York newspaper, this time with the swami's name and the address of his new headquarters. I now knew that I was looking for A.C. Bhaktivedanta Swami at 26 Second Avenue, and I also knew from the article that he was indeed a devotee of Krishna. Now somewhat better informed about where I was going, but unsure of what I would find, I headed for Second Avenue.

Bhaktivedanta Swami's headquarters, as all students of ISKCON's early days know, was a former storefront curiosities shop with the wonderfully apt words "Matchless Gifts" painted above the large plate-glass window that faced the street. I don't remember what was in the window on my first visit, but typically when I visited later there would be a large painting of Chaitanya dancing with his companions and notices of A.C. Bhaktivedanta Swami's coming lectures and talks. The notices further stated that Bhaktivedanta Swami's programmes were under the auspices of what was called the "International Society for Krishna Consciousness," a name that had also appeared in *The East Village Other* article, but that meant little to me when I first walked into 26 Second Avenue for my first encounter with ISKCON.

That first encounter was both auspicious and inauspicious for my intended purposes. It was auspicious because just inside the door was a table with a selection of books for sale, and among those books was a three-volume set of Bhaktivedanta Swami's translation and commentary on the First Canto of the *Bhagavata Purana*. This excited me because when I had done my dissertation research a few years earlier I could find only two translations of the *Bhagavata Purana* anywhere in the USA: one at Yale and the other at Harvard. Now here was a third, or the First Canto of a third, on a table in a storefront on the Lower East Side – and it was apparently for sale. So far, so auspicious.

Auspiciousness continued when I entered the main room of the storefront and was told by a young man who was there that the books out front were in fact for sale. "Do you want to buy something?," he asked, as if mine was a strange request. "Yes," I said, "I'd like to buy those three volumes of the *Bhagavata Purana*. How much are they?" "The *Bhagavata Purana*?," he replied, "Is that the same thing as the *Bhagavad Gita*?" "No," I said, "it's a different scripture. I'll show you what I want to buy." I led him to the table and showed him three volumes covered by Indian dust-jackets with names and images of Vishnu's incarnations, a scene of Vishnu reclining on the cosmic ocean, and a picture on the front showing the cowherd Krishna with Radha in Vrindavan. "Those," I said.

I don't remember what I paid for the set, but it wasn't much. What I do remember is the conversation that surrounded and followed the purchase. It was not auspicious. When I pointed out the books I wanted, each with the title *Srimad Bhagwatam* and the name A.C. Bhaktivedanta Swami on the cover, the young man said, "Oh yeah. Those are books that Swami brought from India. When I asked where the swami had come from in India, he looked at me in puzzlement. "India," he said, as if that were as specific as one could get, and as much information as I could possibly need.

"Did you ever hear him mention Bengal?", I asked, still hoping to find a connection to Gaudiya Vaishnavism. "Bengal? What's that?" "It's a state in Eastern India, a region of India," I said, hope sinking. "No, I never heard Swami mention it," he concluded, making it clear that wherever A.C. Bhaktivedanta Swami came from was of no great interest to him. He had also, I soon learned, never heard of Chaitanya, and I was sure by then that he had never heard of Gaudiya Vaishnavism. I was right; he had not, and even the term Vaishnavism seemed unfamiliar to him. But at least he had heard of the *Gita*, I thought, and that was a good start.

It was of course, as we know now, a much better start than I realised at the time. Even then, however, before I had met Bhaktivedanta Swami or talked to other followers, I had a sense that something important was happening in that unpretentious little storefront with what seemed its very pretentious claim to be the home of an international society. That claim seemed much less pretentious after I met the society's founder and saw his impact on those around him, but even after months of visiting the temple, participating in the lively *bhajan* (hymn) sessions that Bhaktivedanta Swami led, and listening to his compelling lectures, I could never have imagined what happened over the next few years as ISKCON more than lived up to the promise of its name.

How are we to understand the dramatic growth of ISKCON over its first few years from a simple storefront temple on 26 Second Avenue in New York to a complex international movement that rapidly acquired a world-wide following and captured the imagination of a generation? And how are we to understand also the equally dramatic struggles it has gone through since A.C. Bhaktivedanta Swami left his mortal body in 1977?

The simple answer to these questions is of course that Bhaktivedanta Swami – or Prabhupad, as he is now more often called – was physically present as the unquestioned leader of the movement during its first dozen years and has not been physically present since 14 November 1977. Like most simple answers, however, this one raises many further questions.

The Transition

There is no doubt about the central importance of Prabhupad in ISKCON's first dozen years. I have described my own first contact with ISKCON in some detail because this experience has served ever since as my benchmark for measuring the movement's development. The young man whom I met in the temple that day was certainly not the most advanced of Bhaktivedanta Swami's followers, but he was fairly typical of most whom I met during my early visits. The most knowledgeable disciple I met in that early period was Brahmananda, the temple president and all-purpose organiser, but even he and other senior disciples – most of them initiated during September of 1966 – were just beginners in Vaishnava devotion.

"Senior" is definitely a relative term in this context, because the oldest of the early disciples, Umapati, was only in his early 30s; most of the early leaders such as Brahmananda, Hayagriva, Satsvarupa, Kirtanananda, Damodara, Gargamuni, and Raya Rama were in their mid-20s; and some of the initial disciples such as Jadurani and Acyutananda were in their late teens. Prabhupada by contrast was 70, at least 40 years older than all but one of his new initiates and steeped in the tradition he was just beginning to reveal to his new followers.

It was Prabhupad who conceived ISKCON; it was he who knew what Krishna Consciousness was and how to achieve it; and it was he who had the charismatic authority to draw others into what to all of them was a totally unfamiliar tradition. He also had the skill and patience to teach his young disciples what they needed to know to practice Krishna devotion, and for some time – at least for the first few years of ISKCON's existence – he was the only one who knew enough about the tradition to know what needed to be taught.

This is why he worked so tirelessly to translate and write commentaries on the essential devotional texts, and why one of his first goals was to publish devotional material for his disciples and others: first by producing the journal *Back to Godhead*, which was initially run off on a mimeograph machine at 26 Second Avenue; then by establishing the ISKCON Press in Boston; and finally by incorporating the Bhaktivedanta Book Trust in 1970 to oversee all of ISKCON's publications. As initiating and teaching guru, translator, commentator, publisher, and organisational leader, he did it all, and there is no question that ISKCON could never have existed – much less prospered– without his guidance and ceaseless effort for ISKCON's first 12 years.

This essential role continued up to the time of Prabhupad's final days, and it is not surprising that his departure in 1977 left a great vacuum in the organisation he had worked so hard to establish. There had been internal problems before then, but he had always been available to guide his followers through the rough patches. It is obvious, however, from the accounts of many members, that the intimacy and frequent interaction that characterised the early period at 26 Second Avenue did not survive into the period of expansion that followed during the next two years. ISKCON's only temple in 1966 was the one at Second Avenue.

In early 1967, Prabhupad went to San Francisco to establish a second temple and initiate a large number of new disciples, and by the end of that year some of his early disciples had established temples in Montreal and Los Angeles. Prabhupad himself returned to New York after nearly three months in San Francisco, but two months later, in the midst of a flurry of activity, he suffered a serious heart attack that required a hospital stay and several weeks of rest. He returned to San Francisco at the end of June with Kirtanananda, one of his earliest initiates, but he and Kirtanananda left within a month to fly to India. There they stayed for the next four and a half months while Prabhupad recuperated, and it was there that he initiated Kirtanananda as the first ISKCON *sannyasi* (renouncer).

In retrospect, one can see that 1967 marked a decisive turning point in ISKCON's development. No longer a New York movement based in a simple storefront temple, it had leaped the continent to the fertile recruiting ground of California's lively counterculture scene in San Francisco and was soon to expand south to Los Angeles. Prabhupad's return to India, though mainly for reasons of health, allowed him to lay the foundation for an eventual expansion of ISKCON back to his homeland, and his initiation of Kirtanananda as a *sannyasi* was the first step toward creating a leadership cadre that could oversee the rapidly increasing numbers of ISKCON centres and devotees that soon stretched well beyond the boundaries of North America. By the end of the year, ISKCON was truly living up to its name as an international society.

These developments had permanent consequences for ISKCON as a religious movement. In classic sociological terms, ISKCON was no longer a small intimate community of disciples dependent on the inspiration and physical presence of a charismatic leader. Prabhupad was certainly still the charismatic leader and source of inspiration for ISKCON, but there was no longer a single intimate community and Prabhupad was only occasionally physically present to most of his disciples. As ISKCON expanded, many who came to local temples had never seen

Prabhupad in person and even many initiated disciples had seen him only briefly. More and more of the actual contact with members was carried out by senior disciples, and this pattern increased as Prabhupad initiated more of them as *sannyasis* and gave them new administrative and preaching roles.

One effect of these organisational changes was that Prabhupad could no longer give as much personal instruction and guidance to his disciples as he did during the early days in New York. This was a serious problem, because there was so much his disciples needed to learn in terms of both content and conduct if they were to become proper devotees. Prabhupad's age and health problems made everyone aware that he had a limited time to achieve this through his own effort; so he chose to focus increasing amounts of his time and energy on his writing as the best way to ensure that his teaching would be carried forward no matter what happened to him personally. He continued to maintain a demanding travel programme to visit new centres, initiate new disciples and new *sannyasis*, and continue his personal guidance of the senior leaders who soon were scattered around the world, but writing and the publication of his writing took on increasing urgency.

Prabhupad had already started a translation of the *Bhagavata Purana* with his own commentary or "purport" before he came to New York, but only a limited supply of the first three volumes of this work had been published in India in 1965 by the League of Devotees, an organisation that Prabhupad had started in 1953 as the first step in what he hoped would be an international Krishna Consciousness society. The immediate need of his disciples in the West, however, was for a more accessible grounding in the principles of Vaishnava belief and devotion to Krishna.

Prabhupad had used the *Bhagavad Gita* for this purpose in the Second Avenue temple, guiding his new disciples through the text with lectures and his own translation and commentary. The only easily available Sanskrit text for his students to use, however, was in a paperback edition of the *Gita* that included not only the Sanskrit text but also a translation and commentary by Sarvepalli Radhakrishnan, an Indian philosopher whose interpretation of the text was heavily influenced by Shankara's Advaita Vedanta (*mayavada*) teachings. This was an unacceptable situation for Prabhupad, who saw Shankara and other mayavadins or "impersonalists," including Radhakrishnan, as opponents of Krishna devotion.

It was in this context that Prabhupad worked to complete his own *Gita* translation and commentary, *Bhagavad Gita As It Is*, which he started during his first year in New York and completed during his stay in San Francisco in 1967. With this work finished, though not yet published, he started on a translation of the *Caitanya-caritamrita*, the great 17th century account of the life and teachings of the Bengali saint Chaitanya who founded the Gaudiya Vaishnava tradition, a translation project that was finally completed only in 1975.

By the end of 1968, however, he had also started work on two additional works on Krishna devotion: *The Nectar of Devotion*, a "summary study" Of Rupa Goswami's famous exposition of the principles of devotion, the *Bhakti-rasamrita-*

sindhu, and another "summary study," *Krishna, the Supreme Personality of Godhead*, which was Prabhupad's own exposition of the story of Krishna as it is told in the Tenth Canto of the *Bhagavata Purana*. Both of these works were published in 1970, the latter with an introduction by George Harrison of Beatles fame, and made an important body of teaching on devotion available to disciples.

Parallel to all of these writings, Prabhupad was also continuing his translation and commentary on the *Bhagavata Purana* (the *Srimad Bhagavatam*) itself, working through this mammoth text canto by canto at a slow but steady pace and publishing each section when it was complete. The First Canto, which had been published in India in 1965, was published in a new edition by the Bhaktivedanta Book Trust in 1972 along with the newly completed Cantos Two and Three and the beginning of Canto Four. The rest of Canto Four followed in 1974 and Canto Five in 1975, and the work continued in this way until Prabhupad's departure in 1977. Parts of Canto Ten and Cantos Eleven and Twelve, still unpublished at that point, were completed with the use of his draft manuscript by his disciple Hridayananda.

This brief summary gives some indication of the importance Prabhupad placed on his writings and how much time and effort he devoted to them. This time and effort, moreover, was in addition to the attention he had to give to personal guidance of his disciples and to the increasingly complex administrative issues that faced what had become an international organisation with temples throughout the world. He typically carried out these other activities during the day and evening and did most of his writing very early in the morning, because even with his age and uncertain health he was unwilling to sacrifice his writing time for extra rest.

There were very good reasons for this urgency, especially with the rapid expansion of ISKCON centres and a corresponding flood of new members. Each of these new members, it must be remembered, was little better off in terms of knowledge than the one that I encountered on my first visit to Second Avenue. In the beginning, Prabhupad could guide such a novice directly by personal instruction and example, but the new circumstances made this impossible. There were too many followers, in too many different places, for Prabhupad to give any one – or even any single group – more than brief personal attention. Education in devotional practice, in the relevant scriptures, and in the Chaitanya tradition as a whole, all had to come either from Prabhupad's writings – because most of the relevant texts were not otherwise available in English or other Western languages – or from senior disciples whom Prabhupad had personally trained.

This was the crux of the problem, because most of Prabhupad's senior disciples, even those who had been granted status as *sannyasis*, simply did not know enough about the scriptures and tradition and did not have enough devotional maturity to do the necessary job. They were trying hard and were learning rapidly, but ISKCON was effectively missing a generation of mature and traditionally educated devotees between Prabhupad, now nearing 80, and his under-40 senior disciples. These senior disciples, moreover, were unable to do what relatively new disciples would have done in the traditional Indian system –

i.e. live for years with their teacher, study under his direction, and learn devotional practice by being with others who were further along the path than they were.

Prabhupad's early initiates had started that way, though with far less background than new disciples would typically have had in India and with only one more advanced devotee – Prabhupad – to provide an example. But now, within a few years of their initiation, many of the most advanced of them had been initiated as *sannyasis*, skipping the traditional stage of marriage and family life that Prabhupad himself had followed in India before he became first a renunciant and then, in 1959, a *sannyasi* – 41 years after his marriage in 1918, and 27 years after his initiation by his own spiritual master, Bhaktisiddhanta Sarasvati, in 1932.

Instead of studying at the feet of their guru, however, or living for years in a community of committed experienced devotees, these young *sannyasis* were travelling around the country and the world as teachers in their own right, establishing temples and ministering to the religious and institutional needs of communities of new followers – in consultation with Prabupad certainly, but almost always at a distance and only intermittently. In practice, in a way that would almost never happen in India, they had become in less than ten years essentially independent gurus.

Prabhupad's Legacy

This was still the situation when Prabhupad departed in 1977, leaving the further development of his disciples dependent on what he had made available to them up to that point. This is not to ignore the guidance they might also receive from Krishna Himself, but the ability to perceive and understand that guidance, much less submit to it, depended on the level of their spiritual development. Prabhupad was well aware of the problems that might arise because of his disciples' relative immaturity both in age and devotional experience, but he did not have either the time or circumstances to give them the traditional training. Instead, he tried to provide in his writings the resources that his disciples and ISKCON would surely need in the future.

The result was the major works he published or completed in manuscript form between 1967 and 1975. His work on these writings followed a clear set of priorities based on what he considered his disciples needed most. *Bhagavad Gita As It Is* provided the philosophical and theological framework for devotion to Krishna, and with Prabhupad's commentary it also provided an introduction to the Chaitanya devotional tradition. *The Nectar of Devotion* gave access to Gaudiya Vaishnavism's most important theological treatise on devotion, and *Krishna: The Supreme Personality of Godhead* laid out the account of Krishna from the *Bhagavata Purana* that provides the images and stories central to Krishna devotion.

Prabhupad's two major additional writing projects were the completion of this body of essential teachings that he bequeathed to his disciples. I once asked him in a conversation in Philadelphia in 1975 how he viewed the relationship of the *Gita*, the *Bhagavatam*, and the *Caitanya-caritamrita*, and he said that the *Gita* provided the basic education on Krishna devotion, the *Srimad Bhagavatam* was like graduate study, and the *Caitanya-caritamrita* was like post-graduate education for the most advanced devotees because it presented an intimate account of Chaitanya and his devotional life with his companions.

It was no doubt with this understanding that Prabhupad undertook his translations and commentaries on the latter two great scriptures. He had already started work on the *Bhagavata Purana* in India, and continued that work even as he started working on the *Caitanya-caritamrita*. The latter was completed first, in 1973-74, both because it was a shorter text and because it was written in Prabhupad's native language, Bengali, with which he was more proficient than with the famously difficult Sanskrit of the *Bhagavatam*. Only the first four cantos of the *Bhagavatam* had been completed and published by 1975, but work speeded up from that point onward and the text and commentaries were substantially complete when Prabhupad departed in 1977.

This collection of works opened up the riches of the Gaudiya Vaishnava devotional tradition to Prabhupad's disciples by providing English translations of the most important works in the tradition with his own interpretations and commentaries. The three main works, moreover, the *Bhagavad Gita*, the *Srimad Bhagavatam*, and the *Caitanya-caritamrita*, contained not only Prabhupad's verse-by-verse commentaries ("purports") on the texts but also the original Sanskrit texts for the first two and the Bengali text for the third, each with a word-by-word translation and explanation of each verse along with the translation of the verse as a whole. His disciples were thus not only introduced to the traditional Indian commentary form in these publications, but were also given a starting point for learning Sanskrit and Bengali, the languages that would give access to all of the tradition's texts and writings.

All of this amazing production was in place when Prabhupad departed except for the completion of the *Srimad Bhagavatam*, and his achievement is further evidenced by the fact that he had disciples trained by that time to complete the job. Some of his disciples were already doing advanced work in Sanskrit by then, and many more knew the Sanskrit texts that he had provided with his translated works.

Knowledge of Bengali was slower to develop. The *Caitanya-caritamrita* was published later than the *Gita* and the early cantos of the *Bhagavatam*, and there were fewer resources available in the West for studying Bengali. There were nonetheless Western disciples in Bengal by 1977 who were beginning to learn the language, inspired not only by Prabhupad's publication of Chaitanya's biography but by a growing awareness of the depth of the Gaudiya Vaishnava tradition and the variety of devotional materials available in Bengali as well as Sanskrit.

Prabhupad's achievements by the time he departed can best be measured by a comparison of where ISKCON stood in 1977 as compared to where it was at the time of its incorporation in 1966. There is no doubt that Prabhupad already had an international vision for his newly incorporated Society for Krishna Consciousness, but that vision was then still almost entirely in his own mind.

Certainly few of his new followers in the storefront on Second Avenue could have imagined that they were taking the first steps in the direction of a worldwide religious movement, or that they would soon be in charge of communities of devotees in Europe, Central and South America, Africa, and even in India.

Most of Prabhupad's early followers, moreover, had no idea where this movement had come from, as my first visit to the Second Avenue temple indicated, and they certainly had no working knowledge of the languages in which the tradition had largely been transmitted before Prabhupad began his publications in India. Gaudiya Vaishnava texts and teachings had in fact been published in English by the 19th century leader Bhaktivinoda Thakura (1838-1914), the father of Prabhupad's spiritual master Bhaktisiddhanta Sarasvati and the originator of the modern effort to carry Krishna devotion to the whole world. Prabhupad's early disciples, however, knew of this background mainly from learning the names of the disciplic succession in which he stood – names that were recited as part of the formal structure of every devotional service, but names that at first were only names in a list.

All of this background had to be gradually transmitted to the new ISKCON disciples by Prabhupad himself, since he was the only one available to do it. The process of transmission began as personal instruction to a small group of disciples who effectively started from scratch with regard to scriptural teachings and devotional practices and had even less knowledge of the historical antecedents that Prabhupad was drawing on. He could basically assume nothing but willingness to learn on the part of his disciples, and took it for granted that he would have to teach them everything they needed to know.

The transmission process speeded up as soon as Prabhupad was able to publish his writings. One of the first things he did in the Second Avenue temple was to start publishing articles in *Back to Godhead*, a publication he had started in India and revived in New York, first as a mimeographed pamphlet and then as an illustrated magazine, *The Magazine of the Hare Krishna Movement*. Many of Prabhupad's writings appeared first in *Back to Godhead* before they were published in book form, putting teaching material in the hands of his disciples almost as soon as it was completed.

Even with transmission speeded up, however, the process of learning an entirely new tradition still had to be repeated with each new ISKCON member. More knowledgeable senior disciples could soon help with the teaching, but there was a limit to how fast the learning could be carried out. The senior disciples, moreover, were often teaching at the limits of what they knew, and were only slowly realising how much more there was to learn once they had acquired the necessary background and tools to do so. The gap between Prabhupad and his disciples was probably nowhere so evident as in this area, and there was no way it could be bridged before Prabhupad's departure. As in so many other areas, his departure left much to be done to fulfil his vision for ISKCON.

ISKCON on Its Own

Prabhupad left his body on 14 November 1977, in his room in the Krishna-Balarama Mandir, the magnificent temple built by ISKCON in Vrindavan, India, the boyhood home of Krishna. He had been living in Vrindavan as a *sannyasi* in 1962 when he began his work on the *Srimad Bhagavatam*, and it was there that he had made his decision to carry the *Bhagavatam*'s message of Krishna Consciousness to America. He had been nearly 70 years old when he first arrived in New York City in 1965 with almost no money and uncertain what his mission would achieve. Now, at 81, he had come full circle back to Vrindavan to complete his mission with what was later described as his "last lesson," his surrender to Krishna and return to Godhead.

Prabhupad was surrounded in his final days by a group of disciples whose efforts had helped bring the Krishna-Balarama Mandir into being some two and a half years earlier, several of whom had been with him since the beginning of his mission. It was now these and the other senior disciples who would have to carry that mission forward, for the first time without his personal guidance. Prabhupad had taught them all that he could over the past 12 years, and had left them with a massive body of resources: his personal letters to them, his lectures and talks, his writings, translations, and commentaries, and beyond that the entire tradition of Gaudiya Vaishnavism to which he had given them access. It was now up to them to use these resources to ensure the continuing success of ISKCON's mission.

The future of the mission at that point looked very promising. ISKCON had been little more than a vision a dozen years earlier; now it was an international religious organisation with nearly 100 centres and a dozen farms worldwide. At the time of Prabhupad's departure, there were some 34 centres in the USA, 21 in Latin America, 11 in Europe, and 21 in Asia, including three in Australia and 11 in India. The movement was drawing new followers from every race and religion, and was beginning to attract a following of Hindus both in India and abroad. In England and America especially, Indian immigrants were drawn to ISKCON's temples and activities as a way to maintain their religious identity as they adjusted to a new culture, and they in turn added an established multi-generational Hindu householder community to ISKCON's membership.

The leadership of ISKCON also seemed to be in good shape, thanks to Prabhupad's creation in 1970 of a Governing Board Commission made up of 12 senior disciples. These designated members of what was known as "the GBC" would serve as "zonal secretaries" during his lifetime to relieve him of direct management duties. This system was in place for seven years before Prabhupad's departure, and except for occasional problems that he had to resolve it seemed to be an adequate solution to ISKCON's ongoing leadership needs.

It was assumed that there would be some difficulties when Prabhupad was no longer there to give personal guidance, but there was general confidence that the systems in place would be able to deal with the new situation. This confidence, however, was clearly misplaced. Anyone who has followed ISKCON's history since Prabhupad's departure knows only too well how badly things went without him. This is not the place to review ISKCON's problems over the past 30 years, or to assign blame for who or what created the discord within ISKCON and the opposition to the movement from outside. Many factors were involved, the situation has been very fluid, and the pattern has not been the same in all of the many regions or "zones" in which ISKCON has been active.

Just describing, much less explaining, the past three decades of ISKCON's history following Prabhupad's departure will be a task for future scholars with access to data on all of ISKCON's many branches and leaders, their activities, their financial and membership records, their correspondence, their legal battles, etc. – a daunting task that will take years of effort even to assemble the needed material. For the moment, we can only try to understand what happened after Prabhupad's demise in more general terms, and see if we can put ISKCON's situation in a clearer perspective.

It is important in such an undertaking to recognise what is not the best path to understanding ISKCON's troubles after 1977: namely, blaming individuals for what happened. It is certainly tempting to do so, and one need only look at the website of the ISKCON Revival Movement or the many discussions of the so-called "ritvik" issue at that site, or the large number of sites that a Google search for "ISKCON ritvik" will turn up, to see how many have yielded to the temptation. The widespread nature of ISKCON's troubles, however, and the large number of individual leaders involved in various types of problems, suggest that the causes were more structural than individual.

This is not to say that individual ISKCON leaders were not responsible for questionable judgments and ill-advised actions that led to many of the movement's troubles. It is to say, however, that these leaders were placed in a situation that they were not prepared to handle, and that their judgments and actions can be better explained by the situation than by their individual flaws. It certainly seems to me initially more useful to try to understand that situation than to try to assign individual blame to those who were placed in it.

The most significant feature of the new situation was of course the absence of Prabhupad. All of the leaders had been his personal disciples from the time they first joined ISKCON; they had committed themselves to him, and he had always been available to them for guidance and advice. He had inspired them, criticised them, supported them, and challenged them, and had in every sense been their spiritual master. Now that he was gone, there was no one to take his place, because there was no older generation of mature devotees in ISKCON.

Prabhupad had been 81 at the time of his departure, while few of his senior disciples were as old as 40. The gap between Prabhupad's age and that of his disciples had been a significant factor in the authority he exercised over them and the willingness on their part to accept his authority. When he departed, the leadership role suddenly fell on a group of disciples who were all not only two generations younger but also all more or less the same age. Instead of accepting authority from an experienced devotee who was old enough to be their grandfather, the situation was now more like having one's brothers in charge – with all of the possibilities for sibling rivalry that that opened up.

Prabhupad had always thought of ISKCON as Krishna's organisation, and had emphasised Krishna's guidance throughout his years of effort in India and then in America to establish ISKCON as a vehicle for Krishna devotion. Prabhupad's disciples, however, had known Prabhupad longer than they had known Krishna, and certainly knew him better, since their disciplic service to Prabhupad was more advanced than their devotional practices to Krishna. It was natural, therefore, that they thought of ISKCON primarily as Prabhupad's organisation, and thought of their new leadership duties as a continuation of their disciplic service to Prabhupad.

It is important to keep in mind in this context that when Prabhupad created the GBC in 1970, his first initiates into ISKCON – those who were then his "senior" disciples – had been with him for scarcely more than four years. They were the most experienced disciples he had, but were hardly experienced in terms of traditional Vaishnava guru-disciple relationships – and moreover had little knowledge of such traditions, just as they had little knowledge of historical Vaishnava or Hindu culture in general.

Similarly, when Kirtanananda was initiated as a *sannyasi* in 1967, less than a year after his disciplic initiation, few of Prabhupad's Western followers recognised what a dramatic departure from tradition it was for someone newly initiated as a disciple – or, in traditional terms, as a *brahmachari* or celibate student – to be initiated almost immediately as a *sannyasi* without having been a married householder for many years. And it was not just Kirtanananda who was given this status; there were soon many more new *sannyasi*s, none of whom had gone through the mandatory householder stage called for in traditional texts on *varnashramadharma* ("duties of class and stage of life"), such as The Laws of Manu.

It was not as if Prabhupad himself was unaware of how he was departing from tradition. He had, after all, done something that many orthodox Hindus considered improper just by going overseas to America, and to compound that he had given formal initiation to young men – and young women – who did not come from Hindu families and had not gone through traditional childhood religious rituals to prepare them for initiation as disciples. There was precedent in the Chaitanya tradition for what he was doing, but it was not traditionally orthodox.

Prabhupad knew, moreover, that he himself was not following all of the traditional rules for *sannyasi*s, as he made clear at a wedding I attended in the Second Avenue temple. Before the ceremony, which was one of the first he performed, he said publicly that he was not supposed to be doing this as a *sannyasi*, since only a married householder priest was allowed to perform marriage rituals. The couple, however, were his disciples, he said, and they had asked to be married: "so what am I to do; I must help my disciples." Then, with that confession out of the way, he proceeded to perform the ritual as a priest/*sannyasi*, filling the crowded storefront with flames and billowing smoke as he poured ladles of ghee over the sacrificial fire in the centre of the temple floor.

This was a good example of Prabhupad's willingness to break traditional rules for the sake of his disciples or to serve the needs of ISKCON, and a good example also of his awareness of what he was doing and why. There were dangers in such a departure from traditional *varnashramadharma*, however, especially in the example it set for his own *sannyasi* disciples. Although he certainly never intended it, some of his appointed *sannyasi*s got the message that it was all right to break traditional rules in the cause of devotional service or to benefit ISKCON – and none of them had his experience and maturity of judgment to know where to draw the line.

The unfortunate consequence of this was that some *sannyasi*s began to develop an attitude of superiority over other disciples, especially over married householders, and began to consider *sannyasi*hood as an essential qualification for leadership. Some of this attitude had already emerged in the years before Prabhupad's departure, and he did his best to contain it. He needed the *sannyasi*s for ISKCON's preaching services, however, and they were increasingly also given leadership roles such as heads of temples and service on the GBC, so he was inclined to correct them kindly rather than recognising that they were a potential danger to ISKCON's future health.

That danger became evident when Prabhupad was no longer present to help counteract the increasing influence of ISKCON's *sannyasi* leaders on the movement's cultural values. All of the *sannyasi*s were male, and all had taken vows of celibacy when relatively young. They were not the *sannyasi*s assumed in the traditional *varnashramadharma* system who, as *The Laws of Manu* VI.2 famously says, take up a renunciate life only when their skin is wrinkled, their hair has turned white, and they have seen the sons of their sons.

These *sannyasi*s had never been married, much less seen their sons and grandsons. My wife used to refer to the more zealous groups of travelling *sannyasi* preachers as "the Dartmouth boys," comparing them to the smug and immature male chauvinists from an all-male college whom she had encountered as an undergraduate. Her assessment reflected the fact that many of these *sannyasi*s treated women with contempt, and it was clear that they considered it a mark of their own superiority that they had leap-frogged over the householder stage of life.

This was very different from Prabhupad's attitude toward women, as evidenced by his relationship to female devotees such as Jadurani. As a former householder, a mature long-time *sannyasi*, and an advanced devotee, Prabhupad clearly did not feel threatened by women, and it was Prabhupad himself who had sanctioned marriage within ISKCON by performing the first weddings for his disciples. It seemed by contrast that many of the newly-initiated *sannyasi* preachers were contemptuous of women because of their own insecurity, and they seemed threatened by sexual matters in general.

It is not at all uncommon for new young celibates in any religion to feel this way, but they usually remain for years under the supervision of older mentors who can help them acquire more mature attitudes. The young *sannyasis* in ISKCON had no such guidance after 1977, and some of the more ambitious of them soon gained widespread influence and claimed more and more authority by virtue of their *sannyasi* and guru status. Not all of the ISKCON *sannyasis* sought managerial authority, and many if not most of them followed the more traditional path of spiritual growth as true renunciates. The influence of the few soon came to overshadow the piety of the many, however, and *sannyasi* rule became for a critical period the ISKCON norm.

The most damaging immediate result of this development was the marginalising of women, and married devotees within ISKCON as *sannyasis* assumed the most important roles, activities, and offices. The long-term result was equally serious, at least for ISKCON's claims to a higher morality, because many of the *sannyasis* who held important leadership positions could not maintain their celibacy and "blooped," disillusioning their disciples and bringing disdain on ISKCON in general. Having acquired organisational authority, too many of ISKCON's *sannyasi* leaders seem to have lost their spiritual bearings.

Hidden beneath the surface during this period was the fact that some of these same *sannyasis* were also mainly responsible directly or indirectly for the child abuse and wife abuse that became a tragic feature of some ISKCON communities that they led, creating problems for the movement and its members that are still in the process of being resolved. The failure of a significant number of ISKCON's more prominent *sannyasis* in this regard put the whole movement in jeopardy and had serious consequences for the leadership structure – especially the GBC – that had tacitly allowed this to happen. It is again important to recognise, however, that these problems were at their root more a by-product of flaws in ISKCON's leadership structure than the result of individual leaders' wickedness. There can be no excuse for what individuals did or allowed to be done to those over whom they had authority, but it is important to recognise that many of ISKCON's leaders – especially, one might say, those who sought and were given the greatest authority in the aftermath of Prabhupad's departure – were simply not ready to exercise their authority responsibly.

Most of the *sannyasis* initiated by Prabhupad were ardent devotees committed to his mission, and it is no doubt the case that most of those who caused the most trouble were acting in what they thought was the best way to promote that mission. The problem was that as devotees too many had learned to talk the talk, as the saying goes, but had not yet learned to walk the walk. They were often charismatic devotees, but not yet mature ones, and they were forced by circumstance – Prabhupad's departure – to take on responsibilities for which they were not prepared in terms of either experience or spiritual growth. Other ISKCON leaders – including the numerous responsible *sannyasis* who had successfully met the challenges – had to pick up the pieces.

The task of picking up the pieces has been going on within ISKCON since the mid-1980s, gaining special intensity after the conflicts between the GBC and Kirtanananda that led to his expulsion from ISKCON in 1987. The process of recovery has involved among other things making organisational and attitudinal changes to guard against future abuses, dealing with lawsuits and trying to improve relations with disaffected former devotees. It has been a slow process, but ISKCON seems to have moved beyond the most difficult period and now is better able to carry out its central mission of devotion to Krishna.

There are still many problems to be faced, however, not least of which is defining ISKCON's identity more clearly in terms of both its past history and its future goals. This is not primarily an organisational issue to be solved by management decisions, but rather a basic theological concern that can only be resolved by intensive intellectual effort and spiritual insight over a period of time. At stake are ISKCON's fundamental values and basic commitments, the core identity or self-identity that must be understood and accepted by all of its members before the central mission can be properly carried out.

The Search for Self-Identity

The search for self-identity has already started on one level in the passionate exchanges of arguments and counter-arguments, charges and defences, on ISKCON-related internet sites, which help identify some of the critical issues. Discussions at this level, however, typically generate more heat than light and seldom resolve any issues of real importance. What is needed is a long-term commitment by ISKCON to the kind of theological enterprise that is at the heart of most religious traditions: a continuing critical assessment of the tradition's sources of authority, both personal and scriptural, to gain further insights into their meaning, and a continuing evaluation of its institutions and practices to find the best ways to respond to current circumstances.

The issues involved in such an enterprise are typically not at the level of facts but at the level of values, interpretations, and priorities. Many of the disagreements within ISKCON, by contrast, involve claims that "Prabhupad said this" versus claims that "Prabhupad said that." This is the kind of literalist proof-texting that characterises Christian and Muslim fundamentalists, and it basically settles nothing because the "proof" presented on both sides is all on the same level – i.e. it is one quote versus another, with no systematically applied exegetical principles to determine their relative authority.

The situation is if anything even worse in ISKCON than in these other traditions, because the volume of Prabhupad's statements and writings over the years is so great, and they have been so carefully recorded and made available, that a careful search of the cumulative records – an activity at which ISKCON's various factions have been very adept – can usually turn up something to prove almost any point. This makes it even more important to have an exegetical system that can help determine the relative importance of various statements in different contexts and circumstances. Without this, there is a tendency to treat every statement as if it had *ex cathedra* authority, which is a claim that is not even made about the Pope.

Beyond the question of the relative authority of Prabhupad's statements with regard to each other is the question of their authority in relation to Vaishnava scriptures and to other teachers within the Chaitanya tradition. ISKCON in the beginning had no authority except Prabhupad, because all of its access to the tradition he represented came through him. This continued even after he translated many of most important scriptures and writings of the tradition, since his translations and his commentaries gave them all his personal authority.

Is Prabhupad's authority absolute for all time, and does ISKCON accept only his authority? Prabhupad himself gave ultimate authority to Krishna, but does ISKCON believe that Krishna's guidance is available only through Prabhupad's presentation of him? Does Krishna have no independent or superior authority, or is his authority limited to what Prabhupad taught about him? Can Krishna not speak for Himself through others? Can others not speak with authority about Krishna?

These are all serious theological questions, and one could easily come up with many more. They have to do with ISKCON's core values: its interpretation of tradition and authority, the way it determines what to accept of the earlier tradition, the role it gives to its various sources of authority, and the institutional and ritual structures it employs to support and promote devotion to Krishna. How ISKCON answers these questions defines its identity, and how it goes about answering them will be an important factor in determining how well it can carry its mission forward.

This is of course not a situation unique to ISKCON, but one that is central and determinative in every tradition. "Tradition" means literally "what is passed down," so what keeps a tradition alive is how well it handles the process of transmission. The handing down process always involves change as people and circumstances change, so a tradition that survives and prospers over time must balance transmission and change so it can keep its core identity while responding to new conditions.

But what is a tradition's core identity? That's the problem. No matter how clearly a tradition's identity may have been defined at one time, transmission and change require constant redefinition over time. Collective self-identity requires a collective effort, and there is almost never complete agreement within a tradition. Answering the question "Who are we?" thus requires internal negotiation, and that process must continue as long as the tradition continues. There may be times when the process is more or less urgent than at other times, but the need to answer the question never goes away.

How can a tradition resolve the question of its self-identity? Or, more specifically, how can ISKCON do so? The history of religions suggests that this is not easy for a new tradition, because it requires first recognising the problem and then finding ways to resolve it. But since every new tradition has had to struggle with the problem, we can learn a great deal by seeing how religious traditions of the past have worked out their own solutions over time.

The most useful comparison for ISKCON is probably the Christian tradition, because like ISKCON it was a missionary devotional religion that crossed cultural boundaries and had to find ways to maintain ties to its origins while shaping a new identity to meet new religious needs. I often had the feeling in the early days of ISKCON that I was watching a replay of the origins of Christianity, and that impression has continued over the years not just in spite of but to some extent because of ISKCON's problems. There are obvious differences between the two traditions, of course, but there are also some instructive similarities.

The problem of self-identity typically emerges when a religious movement begins to think self-consciously about its distinctive qualities in relation to other traditions. The followers of Jesus, for example, saw themselves as a movement within Judaism for the first decade after his death, and only began to change their self-identity when their early churches began attracting large numbers of Gentiles. By this time, around 40 CE, the Christian movement had spread beyond its original homeland and leaders like the apostle Paul were beginning to formulate a theology that distinguished them from mainstream Jews. According to *Acts* 11:26, it was in the Greco-Roman culture of the Roman Empire that the term "Christian" was first used, and it was in this situation that "Christians" began to create their own self-identity.

The earliest evidence we have of this effort is the letters written by Paul to new churches in the Mediterranean region. Paul, who was a citizen of the Roman Empire, was a Jew from Asia Minor who was converted to faith in Jesus as the Christ around 34 CE, four years after Jesus' death. He then spent nearly 30 years as a missionary to the new Christian churches until his death in 62 CE, and during that time corresponded with churches in Asia Minor, Greece, and Rome about issues of belief and practice in the fledgling communities.

Paul's letters, the earliest texts in *The New Testament*, are the first written evidence of how the Christian tradition was gradually shaped by its interaction with both Jewish and Greco-Roman culture. As a Jew who grew up in the Hellenistic culture of the Roman Empire, Paul was uniquely qualified to deal with the many conflicts between Jewish and Gentile values that threatened the unity of the early churches. Resolving these conflicts was necessarily a trial-and-error process, however, and we can learn much about the ways in which traditions are transmitted and transformed over time by seeing how Paul and his fellow Christians went about it.

In his situation, Paul insisted that all of the traditions competing for a place in the new churches had to be tested against the central Christian faith in Jesus as the crucified and risen Christ. Thus, although Paul himself was a Jew, and although the Jewish scriptures were considered authoritative by early Christians, Paul recognised that many traditional Jewish religious practices were not essential for Christians. He therefore argued, against the so-called "circumcision party" within the church, that Gentiles should not have to accept the obligations of Jewish law before they could become Christians (*Galatians* 2, I *Corinthians* 7). In Paul's view, Jews could thus continue to follow Jewish practices and also be

Christians, as was the case with Paul himself, but these practices were not essential to what it meant to be a Christian. Both Jewish and Gentile practices could thus become part of the Christian tradition, but only after careful evaluation against non-negotiable Christian standards; "passing down" meant also passing each item through a filter that screened out what did not meet those standards or was not considered important to the developing Christian communities.

It is Paul's filter that we know best because of his early and well-preserved writings, but other filters were also at work that reflected different values and standards – i.e. different interpretations as to what was most authentically "Christian" or most consistent with what was considered the significance of Jesus' life and teachings. Although we have relatively few details about the sources of these filters, their results are evident in the diversity of early Christian traditions, perhaps most strikingly in the various presentations of Jesus that circulated in the early Christian period.

Questions about Jesus' life were apparently not important in the first decades after his crucifixion. Early disciples such as Peter must have passed on oral accounts of what they had seen and heard, and collections of Jesus' teachings were apparently in existence in some form soon after his death. The earliest surviving texts that give an organised presentation of Jesus' life and teachings, however, known collectively as the Gospels, date only from after the deaths of both Paul in 62 CE and Peter around 64 CE.

Disputes over belief and practice had been common in the rapidly expanding Christian community, as we know both from Paul's letters and from accounts in *The Acts of the Apostles* that describe how he and Peter worked to resolve emerging conflicts, but these conflicts seem not to have involved the person and teachings of Jesus. A generation later, however, with Peter and Paul gone and with large numbers of Gentile members who knew little about Jesus' background or his activities in Galilee and Judea, the churches wanted an authoritative presentation of who Jesus was, what he did, and what he taught.

What they got was not one presentation, but many, reflecting the fact that by the time the Gospels were written there were already different interpretations of Jesus in different Christian communities. The first of the Gospels, *The Gospel According to Mark* – literally, the "Good News" according to Mark – was written about 70 CE, and was followed over the next 20 years by Gospels ascribed to Matthew, Luke, and John, each telling a somewhat different story about Jesus with different selections of teachings and different emphases. There were, moreover, many more Gospels – especially the so-called Gnostic Gospels – written later and with much more radical views of Jesus, representing various other factions within the Church.

The first four Gospels were eventually given canonical status alongside the letters of Paul and a few other early writings, but it was not until the late fourth century that the mainstream Roman Church could finally agree on all the contents of what became *The New Testament* – and by then, several branches of the original church had either been expelled or had withdrawn over various doctrinal issues.

Even the mainstream churches did not agree on all issues, and preserved differences that in several cases eventually led to further splits within the church.

This brief survey suggests that ISKCON need not be too concerned that it has not yet resolved all of its internal disputes, because it is in good company. Christianity has not resolved all of its internal disputes either, and it has been working at this for 2,000 years. Christians have never fully agreed on the nature of Jesus Christ, on the relation of Jesus to God the Father, on the means of salvation, on the organisation of the Church, or on the relative authority of the scriptures, the Church, and personal religious experience. It is fair to say that they will never fully agree on all of these, and will no doubt continue to find new areas of disagreement.

What Christians have learned to do, however, although it took centuries to achieve, is to be able to define areas of disagreement systematically and determine their relative importance in light of what the particular church considers its core identity. There have been attempts at various times in Christian history to enforce a policy of "one Church, one faith, one practice," almost always with negative results. Whether the motivation is to enforce authority or demand rigid orthodoxy, one or another faction is inevitably driven away or driven underground for no good reason. If you absolutise everything, nothing has greater priority than anything else.

It has proved much better in the long run to define the non-negotiable core values, the essential self-identity, and allow a fairly wide range of options on less essential matters. "Don't sweat the small stuff" is a good theological principle as well as a good guide to human relations. The key is to be sure about the essentials, to know what their relative priorities are and how they relate to each other, and to be confident enough about less important matters to allow a range of freedom and variety.

ISKCON could learn from this Christian experience, and could in fact use it to understand better its own past history. Much of the success of ISKCON in its early years is because Prabhupad understood the difference between core identity and non-essentials, what one could never let go of and what could be altered or set aside. He was adamant about the central importance of devotion to Krishna, for example, but was willing to deviate from orthodox *varnashramadharma* rules when he considered it necessary to further the propagation of devotion.

In this and other respects, Prabhupad was following the tradition of Chaitanya and of his Gaudiya Vaishnava predecessors such as Bhaktivinoda Thakura and Bhaktisiddhanta Sarasvati, all of whom placed the demands of devotion far above the demands of orthodox social or even ritual regulations, including regulations dealing with such matters as initiation. All of them also, of course, knew the rules of orthodoxy well enough, and knew devotion well enough, to know exactly what they were doing and why.

A further lesson that ISKCON could learn from the Christian experience and from its Vaishnava predecessors as well is how to get beyond immediate issues to more basic doctrines, scriptures, or teachings. In Christianity, this is the task of

Biblical theology and systematic theology, the former to identify and interpret scriptural authority and the latter to develop consistent theological systems on the foundation of that authority. In the Vaishnava tradition, this task is typically carried out by means of commentaries on authoritative scriptures to show how they apply to current issues or how they can be interpreted/reinterpreted to have broader or different meaning.

This latter activity is what Prabhupad was consistently doing with his translations and commentaries, presenting not only the basic scriptural text but also – though usually unidentified – the interpretations of earlier Vaishnava commentators as well as his own interpretation of the "purport" of the text. This is how the Vaishnava tradition has historically solved the problem of transmission, preserving scriptural authority while at the same time allowing the flexibility needed to meet new circumstances. Almost everything that Prabhupad passed on to ISKCON went through this process, and it was this process – the English translations, the commentaries, the interpretations, and the applications to daily life – that made it possible for the members of ISKCON to receive the tradition he handed to them.

As ISKCON seeks its self-identity, it has to decide whether this process is part of its core principles or whether the process stopped with Prabhupad. Are Prabhupad's words the end of revelation, or can others receive revelation from the scriptures or from Krishna directly without going through Prabhupad? Or to put it another way, to what extent does ISKCON's self-identity depend on Prabhupad alone, and to what extent does it also include the Gaudiya Math, Gaudiya Vaishnavism, or Vaishnavism in general?

Certainly devotion to Krishna is central, but to what extent is that devotion limited to what Prabhupad was able to transmit and to what extent does it include other Vaishnava traditions or aspects of the Gaudiya tradition that Prabhupad did not pass along to ISKCON? Is ISKCON based on the premise that Prabhupad transmitted everything of importance with regard to Krishna devotion, or does it assume that there is more about Krishna devotion yet to be revealed either through the scriptures or through the experience of other devotees?

Like all the other questions about ISKCON's self-identity, these are questions that only ISKCON can answer. As the Christian example indicates, it will undoubtedly take time and probably much controversy to work through the issues and come up with answers, and there will always be more work to do. The only way that ISKCON can be the Society for Krishna Consciousness that Prabhupad wanted it to be, however, is to take up the task of figuring out exactly what that means and to include all of the devotees in the process.

Krishna tells us in the *Gita* (9:26) that he will accept whatever is offered with devotion. In his purport on this verse in *Bhagavad Gita As It Is*, Prabhupad says, "The only qualification required in this connection is to be a pure devotee of the Lord. It does not matter what one is or where one is situated. The process is so easy that even a leaf or a little water or fruit can be offered to the Supreme Lord in genuine love and the Lord will be pleased to accept it. No one, therefore, can be barred from Krishna consciousness, because it is so easy and universal."

As a starting point for ISKCON's self-identity, this could hardly be improved on. It is up to ISKCON to figure out where everything else fits in around this essential centre.

10

Thealogising Radha:
The Feminine and Feminist Dimensions of Deity

Anna S. King

Introduction

This chapter explores the position of Radha in ISKCON and the paradoxes she embodies for aspiring devotees. She is both present and absent, ultimate and submissive, visible and occluded. It is argued that feminism represents for many devotees a mistaken focus on the material world and even a threat to divinely-given patterns of life. However, a thealogy of Radha by exploiting the resources of the Vaishnava tradition could complement a human rights approach by exploring the essential equality of all living beings and by emphasising the profoundly personal and reciprocal ethics of Vaishnava teaching. The chapter suggests that the emphasis on the root and branch transmission of ISKCON to the West has neglected the originality and unique character of ISKCON. It also concludes that theology has been largely the preoccupation of male gurus and scholarly devotees and suggests that a thealogy of Radha could balance the orientation to the male divine and incorporate the devotional experience of women. A revisioned emphasis on the loving pastimes of Radha-Krishna would support an ethics of mutuality, justice and compassion.

In this chapter Krishna Consciousness constructions of gender (both complementarian and egalitarian) are compared with feminist visions of personhood. A feminist understanding of ISKCON's spiritual culture is unlikely to recommend itself to aspiring devotees. Devotees find deeply problematic the argument that what Schweig calls "intimism" implies an ethics of virtue and relationship, and that an esoteric or erotic mysticism based on reciprocity develops ethics based on respect for others, freedom, justice and equality. My approach may also be challenged by students of religious studies or anthropologists since it implies a kind of trans-religious principle (cf. Gross and Radford Reuther 2001, p.13). It crosses the boundary between religious studies and theology, and assumes that ethical behaviour is as important as theological process. I accept that in general we should leave the questioning of patriarchal elements in other traditions to their practitioners, particularly women, and that ISKCON at 40 years of age has many devotees, both women and men, in the UK with profound and applied knowledge of Srila Prabhupada's teachings. It is difficult for an outsider, however well-intentioned, to present an essay that will not be perceived by devotees as stereotypical. Nevertheless, I argue that an acceptance of the irreducibility of cultural and religious diversity need not lead to the adoption of ethical neutrality. I agree with Ursula King (2004) that the time has come to explore new ways of co-operation between men and women.

Western deeply-entrenched stereotypes of "oppressed Indian women" and monolithic, denigrating portrayals of non-Western women are culturally reversed in ISKCON. For aspiring devotees it is Western culture ("materialism") that consumes and abuses women. They learn that, in opposition to secular Western modernity, "Indian" or Vaishnava spiritual culture gives a space where women can flourish "according to their nature", freed from the pressures of a society in which sex is commodified, families fragmented and women exploited. It is my argument that, as devotees move beyond these stereotypes, a liberating and transforming thealogy of Radha and Krishna devoid of hierarchy will emerge.

Scholarly Feminism and the Feminine Divine

While Western goddess movements have celebrated powerful goddesses as highly affirmative of women's power, scholars have pondered as to whether the presence of the feminine divine in India has helped or hindered women's liberation: the right to freedom, justice and equality. In other words, is the Goddess a feminist? This rhetorical question assumes that the Goddess has some kind of intrinsic essence which exists beyond the changing attitudes of her devotees. More fundamentally it implies very general connections between religious symbols and social and cultural behaviour. The view that the fiercer goddesses encourage the independence of women has until recently been accepted uncritically. Kali, armed with the weapons of the male gods, strung about with a necklace of severed male heads and astride an ithyphallic Siva is an extraordinarily powerful image. Western feminists disenchanted with a Judeo-Christian monotheistic male God have celebrated such goddesses, often distinguishing between goddesses who empower and those like Sita, Parvati, Radha or Lakshmi who encourage traditional social roles. Malevolent and benevolent goddesses whose character is shaped by relationships as wives or consorts are contrasted with goddesses who are supreme, comprehensive and independent. Wendy O'Flaherty (Doniger) writes, "The goddesses of breast who are generally role models of Hindu women embody maternal qualities of generosity and graciousness, subservient to their husbands, while the goddesses of tooth are independent" (1996, p.174).

Hiltebeitel and Erndl (2000) rightly caution us against such simplistic theories, arguing that the question of relationships between Indian goddesses and women is multi-faceted and complex, frequently leading to contradictory answers. Many recent writers have adopted a hermeneutic of suspicion, suggesting that there is no necessary correlation between a symbol and its interpretation and that even where powerful female divinities are worshipped, male attitudes towards women remain repressive (cf. Pintchman 1994). Others interpret India's goddess traditions as male traditions in which the goddess's symbolism is employed to express the interests, anxieties and religious experiences of South Asian men (e.g. Young 1993, p.xix). Young suggests that women are often associated with evil qualities, such as bloodthirstiness or death (Kali, Durga) because of a male fear of sexuality. Kripal (2000, p.241) notes the element of male desire in the embodiment of Hindu deities and argues that the interest of Western men in Hindu goddesses in general and Tantric goddesses in particular may be driven by the search for a heterosexually coded male mysticism. Caldwell (2001) concludes that Kali is very much a product of male fears. It is interpretations such as these that have caused right-wing Hindus to react fiercely to Western psycho-spiritual theories.[1]

The goddess Radha has never figured in the panegyrics of Western feminists. Yet Radha retains her appeal for diverse groups of Hindus which is why, like Sita, she continues to hold sway in the popular imagination (cf. Kishwar 2005). The initial companionship and joyful togetherness of Sita-Ram become in the Radha-Krishna story the total self-surrender of love. The dance of divine love (*Rasa Lila*) offers images of male and female nature which include a sexuality which is not destructive but reciprocal. *Shringara* or *madhurya rasa* (amorous love) reveals the intimacy of God in relationship and the dimension of divine tenderness.

ISKCON Devotees Speaking

ISKCON converts and second generation devotees have at the heart of Godhead, a female divinity who is unconnected with maternal absorption or with decapitation and sacrifice. She is Lover rather than Mother. She symbolises *madhurya* (erotic love), a love which leads to bliss (*ananda*). Yet the question whether Radha (or Radharani) can be genuinely liberative for Western devotees living in contemporary pluralist contexts is generally answered negatively; scholarly accounts of Radha seldom explore the implications of Radha for women devotees except in the context of the "feminine" service attitude, which is simply to give pleasure to Krishna.

When I began to speak to devotees of my interest in Radha, many were shocked. Their surprise was the result of what they perceive to be the delicacy, difficulty and confidentiality of the subject. Even advanced devotees speak and write of Radha cautiously, submissively and with the greatest humility. Devotees believe that it is entirely impossible for anyone to comprehend Radha's *lila (sport or play)* without prior understanding of all the sacred texts (particularly the *Gita* and the *Puranas*), the authoritative works of Swami Prabhupada, the guidance of spiritually advanced devotees and above all sincere faith. One devotee remarked that first you have to go to Krishna and Radha through Chaitanya, to Chaitanya through the six Goswamis of Vrindavan, to the Goswamis through Bhaktisiddhanta Swami, to Bhaktisiddhanta Swami through Prabhupada, etc. Years of steady practice are required before, by Krishna's grace, one might be sufficiently purified of sensual attachment to be vouchsafed some small insight into the radiant complexity of Radha. As for seeing the spiritual world as a model for the material world this, too, is impossible since the spiritual and material worlds are absolutely distinct. Feminism itself is held to constitute a denial of ISKCON's one-pointed focus upon Krishna.

I was interested in talking to devotees of all ages and persuasions and felt humbled by the enjoyment they showed in discussions, their patience and their absolute insistence that without serious and committed practice nothing of Radha could be known. I illustrate these views by quoting directly firstly from conversations with devotees mature in their practice, and secondly with two young devotees. Our subject was the nature of Radharani's love for Krishna and its implications for men and women in the material world.

Bhakti Rasa Das, a householder, kindly agreed to respond to the first draft of this paper.[2] He accepted that there was an important application for increasing the profile of Radharani within limits, and "provided that it is done expertly by devotees who have a firm appreciation of the highly rarefied and nuanced dynamics of Radha-Krishna. These are eternal truths which can be rightly appreciated on many levels of understanding but cannot be tampered with to anyone's benefit. Inappropriate or premature introduction of Radhacentric, *madhurya bhava* conceptions constitute a form of such tampering." Bhakti Rasa Das also stated firmly that *raganuga bhakti* (spontaneous, loving devotion) is advocated by ISKCON "proportionate to the devotee's stages of development."

Radha Mohan Das, a committed devotee who works for ISKCON's UK Communications department, similarly pointed out to me that ISKCON does not promote the concept of physically doing nothing all day and then thinking of these *lila*s:

> If one does not perform service, then such *lila*s are not necessarily manifest to us and may be approached from a mundane point of view. ISKCON is…a preaching movement too, and such activities are understood to increase one's ability to absorb these *lila*s. In fact significantly, preaching/outreach projects are generally viewed as preferable to rituals alone.

Radha Mohan Das expanded this idea by saying that persons who are after sense gratification (a materialistic life) should not try to imitate *raganuga* devotional service:

> Srila Prabhupada has elaborately explained in his book *The Nectar of Devotion* the progress of the devotee from *sadhana-bhakti*, or the execution of regulative principles, to *raganuga-bhakti* (also known as *vidhi bhakti*), or service executed in love of Godhead. When a pure devotee follows the footsteps of a devotee in Vrindavana, someone close to Lord Krishna, he/she develops *raganuga-bhakti*. However, one can never enter straight into *raganuga-bhakti*.

I met Gopa Kumar Das and Radhika Devi Dasi, two enthusiastic young devotees, at Bhaktivedanta Manor on 30 March 2005. Gopa Kumar Das has received *brahmanical* initiation and is engaged to be married to another devotee; he has therefore removed himself from the *brahmachari ashram* and wears the white robes of the *grihastha*. He explained that Radha and Krishna together are the original form of Godhead, *adi-rasa*. We should never try to imitate them. Their relationships are *prema*, transcendental love. These are reflected in the physical world as *kama* (lust). Human love is always tinged with selfish desire, whereas the cowherd girlfriends of Krishna (*gopi*s) desire only to satisfy Krishna. Their only desire is for His pleasure. If, for example, Krishna desires the company of another *gopi* then Radha will facilitate their encounter.

I asked Gopa Kumar Das whether Krishna's love for another does not arouse Radha's jealousy or give her pain. He answered:

> Krishna also submits to Radha. We cannot bring in mundane conceptions. Feminist conceptions are embedded in thoughts of the material world. In Gaudiya Vaishnavism there is only one *Purusha* (Cosmic Man), *MahaPurusha*. All other living entities are female. There is *purusha* and *prakriti* (divine female creative energy) which is subordinate. Krishna and Radha are one person, but separate eternally for the purpose of enjoying pastimes.
>
> Radha is above Krishna because her love never wavers and she controls Krishna with her devotion. The physical and spiritual worlds are totally separate. *Prakrta Sahajiyas* (mundane lust) merge the spiritual with the material. Men put on saris. Mistakenly. The duties of the body and the duties of the soul are distinct. The affairs of the soul lie in surrendering, chanting, reading scriptures...

If there is equality on the spiritual platform, why is gender relevant in the material world?

> The devotee just accepts Prabhupada's authority. In *varnashrama* (socio-religious organisation) people have different duties. There are duties for

men and duties for women. Most women want to be in the shelter of a man. Why else would they get married?...Western culture may stress equality but is it a good thing that women have aspirations that take them away from their children?

Why is *raganuga bhakti* not advocated by ISKCON for all devotees?

We have faith in Prabhupada and practise humility. The *bhakti* process is one of realisation by service to the guru and Krishna. We also gain realisation of subject matter in books. ISKCON teaches *vidhi bhakti* because you can't institutionalise *raganuga bhakti*. We gradually elevate the soul. Prabhupada's mood was to serve the mission and to introduce Krishna Consciousness to fledgling disciples. There are *anarta* – unwanted qualities. Lustiness, greed and envy. To approach Radha and Krishna we have to be pure. We are not qualified to approach them in our present condition.

Radhika Devi Dasi from Bulgaria also spoke to me of the impossibility of understanding such a difficult subject. She commented that Radha was very special, more special than Krishna, but it was impossible to comprehend her nature without years of practice and the advice of advanced devotees:

I was amazed, really amazed, to hear you asking about Radha! No one has before asked questions about such matters. But you must begin cautiously. In the spiritual world there is only one man, all the rest are feminine. The Lord is the enjoyer. We are the enjoyed. We are meant to serve the Lord. Radha is the best of servants. She has unlimited capacity to serve. This is in the spiritual world; in the material world the body doesn't matter. Men and women are no different. There are only certain rules and regulations to be observed and a structure to follow. We are all the same. We are aspiring to self-realisation.

Why then is there gender difference in ISKCON?

Now we don't know better than the body. Women are more emotional. This is the conditioning of the material world. How much can we perceive with our tiny little brains? Krishna is so vast. Radha is even more complicated. She loves Him so much. She thinks, "if my suffering brings pleasure to Krishna, then my suffering becomes a pleasure."

If someone is practising really seriously then little spiritual secrets are revealed slowly. If we *hear* about a wonderful drink we cannot form a real understanding but if we are given a taste then we will slowly, slowly, begin to understand. The Lord is so kind that he gives us portions of spiritual truth. Only when he sees our true desire and serious endeavour will He give us as much as we want...

Radha is special to the Lord and special to the devotees. You have to start from the basics! "What is the soul?" "Who is the Lord?" "What are we doing here?" You must be very careful not to take transcendental things on a mundane level. The spiritual world is a tree; the material world is a reflection of that tree in the water…The material world is everything upside down – lusty desires, bad relationships. There everything is at the highest level; here it is gross and disgusting. In the spiritual world all souls focus on Krishna; their only desire is to please, to serve Krishna. Here we put ourselves at the centre, "me" and "my" activities and desires. There are so many sufferings, misunderstandings, no true love. The Lord is not at the centre. It takes time to understand because we are in the material condition, going through millions of years of births as animals, as trees, as insects. It takes time. If you manage to please the Lord then by His grace everything becomes clear. Nothing seems so complicated. If you want to understand Radha you must pray, try to please the devotees, practise and serve the Lord. Slowly, slowly everything becomes clearer.

Both Radhika Devi Dasi and Gopa Kumar Das seek to immerse themselves in Prabhupada's spiritual worldview. Radhika Devi Dasi showed me her *Gita* which was full of puzzled notes. She told me that sometimes she asks so many questions of advanced devotees that they suggest she should occupy her time better, perform service for Krishna, get hold of a mop, clean the floor, etc. Her replies to me indicate that she sees bodily distinctions as unimportant, a matter of conditioning, but spiritual souls as eternally "female." Gopa Kumar Das also was absorbed in the study of ISKCON's texts. Both told me that they loved to speak about such spiritual matters. Both understood Prabhupada as stating that the worship of Krishna with his eternal companion Radha had nothing to do with mundane sexuality. Only the advanced or fully-realised devotee who has purified himself or herself from the slightest taint of lust or sex desire can even contemplate the divine pastimes. On the other hand, both devotees were eager to give me those books which Srila Prabhupada had written on the subject of *Radha-Krishna lila* and were very happy to speak to me as someone who was genuinely interested in Radharani. This paradoxical veiling and exposure shows obedience to Srila Prabhupada who sent his books round the world for everyone to read but who simultaneously advocated caution.

ISKCON and the Construction of Gender

It has long been recognised by devotees that scholars have played a supportive and interactive part in ISKCON's proselytising mission by favourably legitimating its "authenticity", its wholesale transmission of "Vaishnava culture." This almost universal approbation has, however, been radically qualified in the area of gender (cf. Judah 1974; Daner 1976; Mangalvadi 1977; Whitworth and Shiels 1982, Rochford 1985; Shinn 1987; Lipner 1994; Flood 1995; Knott 1995, 2004). Puttick writes that Prabhupada "allowed women disciples but was ambivalent about their status, alternating between a mystical concept of spiritual equality with male disciples and a conservative Hindu belief in female inferiority" (1997, p.76). "ISKCON is unliberated even by Indian standards" (ibid. p.173). "(T)he link between celibacy and misogyny is particularly clear in ISKCON" (ibid. p.109).

Haddon's excellent ethnography (2003) emphasises, not ISKCON's fidelity to the past, but the uniqueness and originality of its mission.[3] This is also my position. I consider that ISKCON's spiritual culture must be understood in its own terms rather than as a root and branch transmission of Vaishnavism. In order to take ISKCON's theology seriously we must turn primarily to Prabhupada, not his lineal predecessors, to discover how beliefs about the eternal identities of souls translate into empowering or oppressive spiritual and social practices. He is the first, last, and foremost authority on any subject for members of ISKCON (cf. Sivarama Swami 2000, p.xviii). Even then the growing heterogeneity of ISKCON, and the individual experience of gender mediated through cultural or ethnic context, guarantees fiery, and sometimes acrimonious, debates over exactly what Swami Prabhupada taught. Swami Prabhupada's commentaries and purports are read authoritatively within a community of devotees, but the contrary and sometimes inflammatory uses which they have served suggests that the needs and values of the devotees become as much a source of norms as the texts themselves.

The expectations of the large Indian congregation, Gujarati, Bengali, Punjabi, etc. also have complex implications for the ways in which gender identities are marked in ISKCON. Increasingly integrated into the educational mainstream and enjoying middle class affluence and life-styles, many British Hindus nevertheless honour Western devotees precisely because of their fidelity to "Vedic" culture – their ritual punctiliousness, their *dhotis* and saris, concept of *stri dharma* (a woman's socio-religious role) vegetarian diet, sexual abstinence and the presence of ascetics and *brahmacharis*. Western converts who respect an ancient tradition of ascetic altruism are perceived to be "better" Hindus than the wider congregation they serve. Indeed, many diasporic Hindus interpret Bhaktivedanta Manor as an inclusive pilgrimage centre with a high standard of ritual performance. One Gujarati grandfather from Kenya who came to the Manor with his entire extended family told me: "This temple is for everyone. Everyone is welcome here. Hindus, Christians, Muslims. There are many paths but God is one." A Hindu lady accompanying visiting Indian relatives on a rapid tour of Hindu sites arrived just in time for *arati* (worship) and *mahaprasadam* (sanctified food). She exclaimed breathlessly that they had come from the Swaminarayan temple in Neasden, north London, "a museum", to the temple at Bhaktivedanta Manor, "a real Hindu temple." Yet Haddon points out that ISKCON's externals are signs not of Indianisation, but of mimesis of a transcendental culture. Diasporic Hindus are fascinated to see "white" devotees adopting "ethnic" Indian/Hindu culture and etiquette. However, the devotees themselves understand ISKCON's Vedic spiritual culture and *varnashramdharma* as divinely authorised, as more "authentic" than the practices and beliefs of the Hindu congregation. Devotees position ISKCON in total opposition to many aspects of modern Hinduism and in particular to "caste *brahman*ism", the treatment of *dalit*s (untouchables), etc.: "We are completely against the principle of untouchability and our definition of *varnashrama* is very different indeed. This anti-caste-ism is quite fundamental to ISKCON's approach. That...is something important for you to understand: (t)here is no *dalit* class in ISKCON."

The early demonisation of Western society also contributes to the complex processes of identity and gender construction among converts. Converts, many from Christian or Jewish backgrounds, embodying plural identities, speak of the intensity of spiritual life and practice in ISKCON as one of its most appealing features. Yet opposition to the world is less a "flight" and more an unending struggle with conflicting messages about the construction of love and sexual identity. Devotees must battle continuously against the complex and subtle influences of the material world. There are therefore conflicting pressures within the movement to conserve, to adapt, to integrate and to innovate. These pressures are reflected in inflammatory debates in websites, journals and discussion groups around the world (e.g. *www.chakra.org; www.vaisnavi.com; www.vnn.org; www.galva108.org; www.iskcon.com*).

Can Radha be re-envisioned as an empowering role model within a positive intercultural context? It seems doubtful since devotees disclaim any idea that Radha could be "read" in ways that would affirm Western feminist ideals of gender equality. The narratives of Radha are accessible only to the fully-realised soul. "Fledgling" devotees' understanding of Radha comes not principally from Indian social and cultural dynamics, but from Prabhupada's cultural translations, and particularly *Krsna: The Supreme Personality of Godhead*, which is glossed by Prabhupada as "A Summary Study of Srila Vyasadeva's *Srimad Bhagavatam*, Tenth Canto" and the longer translation of the Tenth Canto of the *Srimad Bhagavatam* itself. Prabhupada's instructions about the importance of mission, humility, asceticism and strict standard of sexual segregation are taken deeply to heart. "Conversion" presumes a slow, and very gradual immersion in ISKCON's spiritual culture which ultimately will develop the concept of *rasa*, the whole aesthetic that underlies Vaishnava spirituality or *bhav*, a deeply felt receptivity of mind, heart, and soul towards a manifestation of the divine (Cave 2000, p.5).

The Grace of Radha

Radha is the most powerful exemplar for all *bhakta*s (devotees). To perform devotional service means to follow in her footsteps. Devotees put themselves under the care of Radha (the internal potency of Krishna) in order to achieve perfection in their devotional service. Devotional service therefore attracts even Krishna Himself (Prabhupada 1970 [1982], p.16). It is also the grace of Radha that enables devotees to enter a world which is non-different from the spiritual world of Vrindavan. As Haddon points out:

> To enter the space of a temple for the first time is a rare and ultimately auspicious event for the individual living entity (*jiva*) – a cumulative result of lifetimes of karmic evolution. Most significantly for the devotee of Krishna, to enter the space of a temple means that Srimati Radharani, or Radha, has invited you to witness her intimate *lila* with Krishna in the spiritual world. (2003, p.43)

While some Hindus worship the gods as symbols pointing to an ultimate oneness beyond *maya* (illusion), ISKCON devotees encounter the reality of the deities in this world. To the surrendered devotee the passionate love of Radha demonstrates how Krishna wishes to be worshipped. Without Radha and the *gopis*, Krishna's attraction to the *parakiya-rasa* of Vraja would not be known. Only through attaining Radha-like absolute dedication and devotion can humans understand Krishna's nature and their own eternal identity. Radha's is the language of Krishna-*bhakti*. Men must take women for their guides in nurturing their "feminine" qualities. Knott, a very sympathetic observer, writes:

> It is the constitutional nature of the soul to be a servant of God. The perfection of this natural role is exemplified by Radha, the beloved consort of Krishna, and it is only through her that devotees, both male and female, ultimately can approach Him. All devotees, whether female or male in body, must adopt a "feminine" attitude to spirituality. This "feminine" approach is essentially an attitude – spiritual, mental and physical – of surrender and service to others, and ultimately to Krishna who manifests a "masculine" approach. Femininity and masculinity, as manifested transcendentally in Radha and Krishna, are eternal values, not merely cultural constructions. The spiritual role model for devotees is "female" and the "feminine" approach of surrender and service is recommended for all. (2004, p.294)

In the greater Vaishnava tradition Radha is the devotional focus of a refined aesthetic and a complex theology. In the Chaitanyite tradition Radha is beloved as Krishna's favourite *gopi*. She is the Supreme Goddess but also Krishna's supreme *shakti* or divine energy, his pleasure principle, his co-equal, his female dimension, his ideal worshipper and Krishna Himself. Radha and Krishna are in fact inseparable, two aspects of the same being. Cave remarks that the theme of inseparability is represented in many ways:

> ...sentimentally in song, dramatically with the two intertwined in dance, artistically in drawings of a being half-Krishna and half-Radha, theologically in the understanding of Sri Caitanya Mahaprabhu's nature, and

philosophically in the fundamental principle of Caitanyite Vaishnavism: *achintyabhedabheda*, inconceivable difference in nondifference. (2000, p.115)

Radha *Lila*

If Kali is more a goddess of male fears and anxieties than she is a goddess *for* women (Kripal 2000, p.241), is Radha any more likely to empower her female devotees? It seems at first unlikely. Radha, unlike Kali, does not transgress in order to transcend (ibid. p.261). Radha is never spontaneously mentioned by devotees in the context of women's rights, her erotic and assertive playfulness is occluded publicly and where expressed hedged around with all kind of disclaimers. She is relatively unknown to thealogians in the West except in the context of Krishna-centred *bhakti*.[4] While Krishna stands out as a distinct personality Radha is known primarily through her relationship to Him. She is not worshipped independently. Radha, the favourite companion of Krishna's adolescence, is another's (*parakiya*), not "his own" (*svakiya*); theirs is a bond of pure love (*prema*). It is, as Hawley (1996, p.13) says, a relationship without children and free from the confines of family. Whereas Krishna is regarded in later life as an exemplary householder whose wives and children are numbered in the thousands, Radha abandons her family for Krishna. Krishna's cosmic salvic role in history is not shared by Radha.[5] His later life, his marriage with Rukmini and Satyabhama, his role in the great war of Kurukshetra and his death are known in detail. We know that Radha is the wife of Abhimanyu, daughter of the cowherd Vrishabhanu and his wife Kamalavati, granddaughter of Paurnamasi, great granddaughter of Mukhara, daughter-in-law of Jatila, but her life is bound up with that of Krishna. When Krishna departs from Vraj Radha is left in Vrindavan to grieve. Prabhupada presents her as devastated by Krishna's infidelities and broken-hearted when he finally departs for Mathura to slay the demon-King Kamsa.

Thealogically too, this story presents dilemmas in a post-Enlightenment, post-Christian, post-feminist and post-Freudian Western context. Radha's relationship with Krishna may be that of ultimate identity, but, humanly speaking, its language is that of the beloved to lover, woman to man, devotee to deity. This interrelationship of social and spiritual issues is disputed by devotees who view the pastimes as purely transcendental. In ISKCON Radha's qualities of all-consuming love and desire for Krishna merge into the more "feminine" virtues of self-effacing devotion and loyalty.

The light-hearted pastimes of Radha and Krishna on earth are affected by the tears of separation and the anguish of longing. Just as Sita experiences the pain of rejection, Radha experiences the pain of absence and indeed of inconstancy. It is her unwavering fidelity and desire to please Krishna that makes her greater than Krishna himself. Her story, ostensibly a narrative of joy and longing, could be read as exposing the sharp pain of many generations of women. Radha's experience of desertion and abandonment, even of infidelity, makes her an emotionally powerful but ambivalent figure. Her changing emotions (*mana*) – anger, hurt, jealousy and deep longing at Krishna's betrayal – are lovingly depicted by male poets and dramatists and make her a deeply sympathetic, even wronged, figure (cf. Hawley and Wulff 1996, p.321). However, in ISKCON's spiritual vision Radha's pain is temporary and only serves to inflame her longing and love. There is little exploration of separation as a dark night of the soul, or of divine absence.[6] For Prabhupada it is an episode within an eternal *lila*. Radha's pain disappears with the knowledge that in reality Radha belongs to Krishna eternally.[7]

Pati-Bhav and Gopi-Bhav

The question whether female practitioners of Vaishnavism will eventually benefit from the secret pre-eminent position of the goddess in the Vaishnava tradition has puzzled commentators (e.g. Rosen 1996, p.2). However it has generally been argued (cf. Brzezinski 1996, p.60) that Vaishnava traditions have fewer resources for women's independence and leadership than Shaiva or Shakta traditions. Many women have devoted their lives to Krishna and have considered themselves married to Krishna. Nevertheless, they have not usually challenged gender or caste hierarchies. Even an exemplary devotee like Mirabai, the embodiment of absolute devotion to Krishna, can be read as reinforcing social inequalities by transposing the human relationship of husband and wife to the divine-human realm (cf. Martin 1996, p.13). Moreover, the practice of *pati bhav* – the worship of Krishna as husband and Lord,[8] is not one of the relationships with the divine sanctioned by many sects devoted to Krishna. The roles of a servant, friend, parent, or lover of God, or a *manjari* or *sakhi* of Radha are encouraged, but not that of a wife to a divine husband (Martin 1996, p.38).[9] Just as Krishna in ISKCON theology is not an ordinary human, but the Supreme Personality of Godhead, Radha is emphatically *not* a worldly model for devotees whose sexuality is domesticated within marriage or renounced completely. Indeed, Radha as mistress appears to contradict the Hindu ideal that regards mundane marriage as of prime importance for women. Sita, not Radha, is the ideal *pativrata*, the woman whose faithful observance of *dharma* is held to be exemplary. Krishna Himself instructs women on the importance of chastity, affirming the ideals and goods of marriage (cf. Prabhupada 1970 [1996], p.285). In practice devotion to Krishna for women is more or less inextricably linked with devotion to a human (male) guru or with marriage. Mira in her own time was not regarded as a safe role model for women. ISKCON accepts the authority of Vaishnava texts and Prabhupada's purports, which teach that women are to be controlled by men for their own protection and dignity. Spiritually advanced men, according to Rosen (1996, p.5), "rise beyond the materialistic conceptions of women and in fact treat them with the deepest respect, honouring them as representative of the Cosmic Mother and perhaps even a *gopi* or one who is dear to Krishna."

Radha in the Cumulative Tradition

From ISKCON's perspective Radha simultaneously exists eternally in the spiritual realm while manifesting in this world as a person at the end of the Dvapara Yuga. Devotees place the birth (divine descent) of Sri Krishna and Radha 5,000 years ago in 3,000 BCE. Prabhupada notes that Krishna stayed on this earth for 125 years and played exactly like a human being, but His activities were unparalleled (1970 [1996], p.xiv). He has appeared and disappeared on the earth innumerable times over millions and billions of years. Aspiring devotees worship Radha as the eternal divine associate of the intimate Supreme Deity. From this vantage point the fact that historical analysis of Indic traditions does not find deities called Krishna or Radha anywhere in the oldest corpus of Vedic texts (cf. Delmonico 2004, p.33) and that in the Puranic and Epic texts deities other than Krishna lay claim to the status of supreme absolute God is irrelevant. Vedic knowledge is the only knowledge worth knowing. However, that devotion (an appeal to the heart), and critical scholarship (an appeal to the mind) can be fruitfully combined is demonstrated by Prabhupada's grandguru, Kedarnath Datta Bhaktivinoda (cf. Shukavak N. Das 2004. pp.97-111).[10]

Wulff (1996), employing historical methods of textual criticism, argues that Radha may have come out of the songs of the Abhirs, a cattle-herding community of North India, and comments that the earliest sources, a succession of stray verses in Sanskrit, Prakrit and Apabramsa from about the third century CE that celebrate her love with Krishna, are not explicitly devotional. In the *Harivamsa* (2nd or 3rd century CE) we find accounts of Krishna's youth when he infatuates the girls of the cowherds (Hardy 1994, p.273). Ecstatic *bhakti* with its typical depiction of "love in separation" was incorporated into the *Bhagavata Purana*, a Sanskrit text produced in South India about CE900.[11] Its longest section, the Tenth Canto, is devoted to Krishna who was born in Mathura. Radha is not mentioned by name in the *Bhagavata Purana* but she is usually identified with the foremost of the *gopis*. In *bhakti* literature she becomes much more than a milkmaid; she becomes the eternal partner in Krishna's *lila* and the exemplification of pure love, of love-in-separation and ecstatic union. In art and literature Radha is depicted in the *lila* of love; by turns diffident and audacious, shy and passionate, playful and resourceful. Krishna's love for Radha is celebrated in the relatively late 12th century *Gitagovinda* of Jayadeva, and later in the poetry of Candidas and Vidyapati (14th century). Their poetry, written from the viewpoint of Radha, expressed her deep emotional longing for Krishna (Flood 1996, p.138). In some of the later literature of the Goswamis Radha is assertive and demanding while Krishna is submissive. This feistiness is not reflected in ISKCON narratives.

Radha through the Eyes of Personal Faith: Presence and Absence

How significant in ISKCON's spiritual culture is Radha? Krishna with Radha is worshipped as the highest level of divine intimacy, the supreme *shakti*. Schweig states uncompromisingly that, "in Radha are found all the *Gopi*s, and all other goddesses as well; indeed, she is understood to be the supreme Goddess, the embodiment of all divine women (Schweig 2004, p.19)." Radha is even more attractive than Krishna. She is *Madana-mohana-mohani* – the attractor of the attractor of Cupid (Prabhupada 1970[1982], p.16). Radha is supremely beautiful: "Her eyes defeat the attractive features of the eyes of the *cakori* bird. When one sees the face of Radharani, he immediately hates the beauty of the moon, her bodily complexion defeats the beauty of gold. Thus, let us all look upon the transcendental beauty of Srimati Radharani" (Prabhupada ibid. p.354).

Devotees, like many Hindus, say that Radha is honoured *before* and *above* Krishna. Her name precedes Krishna's (*Radha-Krishna, Radhe-Shyam*), most importantly in the chanting of the *mahamantra*, "Hare Krishna", where *Hare* is identified with Radha. It is significant, too, that the devotee first requires the blessings of Radha before being accepted by Krishna (Radha Mohan Das: personal communication: 11.01.05). Radha is the conveyer of divine grace. The title *Shree* or *Shrimati Radharani* invariably used of Radha shows respect and affection. However, in ISKCON the greeting *Hari Bol* is more frequently heard than the Vaishnava salutation *Radhe, Radhe*!

Radha Gokulananda, the deities of Bhaktivedanta Manor, are referred to as *Their Lordships*, and daily worship – *bhog* and *arati* – is offered to both Radha and Krishna with the same devotional intensity. Radha's co-equal position at the altar with Krishna honours women but also indicates her position in the spiritual world itself. By performing devotional service to Radha-Krishna devotees engage in the same activity performed by fully realised souls in the spiritual world. The Sri Tulasi *kirtana* sung at Tulasi *arati* every morning in every ISKCON temple includes this prayer:

> O Tulasi, beloved of Krsna, I bow before you again and again. My desire is to obtain the shelter of Sri Sri Radha and Krsna. Whoever takes shelter of you has his wishes fulfilled. Bestowing your mercy upon him will make him a resident of Vrindavana. My desire is that you will also grant me a residence in the pleasure groves of Sri Vrindavana-dhama. Thus within my vision I will always behold the beautiful pastimes of Sri Sri Radha and Krsna. I beg you to make me a follower of the cowherd damsels of Vraja. Please give me the privilege of devotional service and make me your own maidservant. This very fallen and lowly servant of Krishna prays, "May I always swim in the love of Sri Sri Radha and Govinda!"

As the ritual cycle of the year progresses Radharani takes part in many *lila*s – the joyful festivities of Holi, the swing festival of the monsoon season,

Govardhan *puja*, Diwali, etc. Devotees assert that where Krishna is, there is
Radha.[12] Yet Radha is clearly far less central to the ritual year than Krishna, and
much of the worship – *japa*, *kirtana*, *bhajan*, etc. – reinforces Krishna's
predominance.

Visually Radha is omnipresent in ISKCON's art. Dominating the iconographic
imaginations of devotees, the presentation of the deity is a window into the
intimate world of the highest deity of the godhead. It is neither simply
metaphorical nor allegorical. Schweig states that: "This iconocentric conception
of the deity...sharply contrasts with our own (W)estern iconophobic and
iconoclastic conceptions of God from the Abrahamic traditions" (2004, p.26).
The Deities or temple forms of Radha and Krishna are incarnational forms of the
divine (cf. Knott 2004, p.107). The sculptures, paintings, posters, internet images,
*rasalila*s, are forms in which divinity can be known, see and be seen (*darshan*). They
should evoke in devotees feelings of absorbed bliss and beauty.[13]

Krishna is depicted in multiple roles: as the protector of cows, the flute player,
the younger brother of Balarama, the leader of his cowherd friends and, most
importantly, as the lover of Radha. Radha on the other hand is depicted focused
entirely upon Krishna, radiating blissful happiness in the beauty of their mutual
love. The divine couple are shown by day seated in forests of flowering trees and
running streams, and at night under a full moon scented by blossoming jasmine
and lotus. Radha is portrayed as essential to Krishna even where Krishna is
surrounded by other women. The masculine ordering of this Vraja paradise from
feminist perspectives indicates a form of eroticised male culture. To ISKCON
devotees it symbolises, not romantic wish-fulfilment, but the (feminine) soul's
surrender to the (masculine) God. That Krishna is always at the centre of an
adoring group of women simply illustrates the reality of the divine-human
relationship. The very human dilemmas of love-in-separation point to the
ultimate goal of the return to Godhead.

Haddon argues that in the context of scriptural instruction, narrative practice
and the spiritual practice of *shravana* ("hearing"), Radha is absent. Haddon states
that the question, "Who is Krsna?" actually becomes dissociated from its
correlative, "Who is the girl with Krsna?" He suggests that the notable absence of
stories about Radha and Krishna from formalised narrative practice in ISKCON
also stands in contrast to the regular presence of such stories (known as *katha*) in
orthodox Gaudiya-Vaishnavism (2003, p.196):

> The process of "hearing" the intimate *lila* of Radha and Krishna as revealed,
> for instance, in the Tenth Canto of the *Bhagavatam*, is a traditional religious
> practice in Gaudiya-Vaisnavism. In ISKCON, however, this same practice
> has become subject to strict censorship, and has been effectively closed as a
> legitimate path to salvation for those who wish to follow the letter of
> Prabhupada's teachings under the spiritual auspices of ISKCON.

Haddon recalls (2003, p.220) that in 1976 Swami Prabhupada became very angry when he heard that a group of his disciples was reading portions of the *Caitanya-caritamrita* that describe Radha and Krishna's intimate pastimes (cf. Goswami 1998, pp.322-5). Prabhupada warns that Krishna's conjugal pastimes can only be understood by highly advanced devotees and that premature attempts to enter such esoteric topics would end in mundane lust. Indeed, Prabhupada seems to suggest that the form and logic of *raganuga*, even in the form of "hearing", is *sahajiyism* (mere lust) and should therefore be banned as heretical practice.

Haddon's research in Australia suggests that ISKCON literature focuses on Krishna to such an extent that ISKCON comes close to a male monotheism. It is certainly true that Radha is absent in all but name from many devotional accounts of spiritual life in ISKCON (e.g. Gelberg 1989). However, Prabhupada's own writings are more profoundly ambivalent than Haddon's conclusions suggest. While Prabhupada emphasised that the service attitude of a devotee should be that of separation from Krishna, he encourages devotees to read and study the pastimes of Krishna as a principal means of developing Krishna Consciousness, as solace for those devotees feeling separation from Krishna and as auspicious and purifying.[14]

Prabhupadanuga Bhakti: Prema and Kama

Prabhupada introduced to the West "a tradition that revels in the unlimited forms, or omnimorphism, of the supreme deity" (Schweig 2004, p.26). Scholarly devotees are now studying and translating the texts of the wider Gaudiya Vaishnava tradition, the theological literature left by the Six Goswamis and their followers. They are also themselves writing about the divine *lila* (e.g. Sivarama Swami 2001; Schweig 2005). However in the early years Prabhupada's translations and purports were almost the only source of devotees' knowledge: principally his translations of the *Bhagavata Purana* and the *Bhagavad Gita*. Swami Prabhupada's commentaries are authoritative for his followers and transport them into a Vaishnava world of devotion, a world in which the unlimited divine takes limited form as an act of grace and transcendent power. Prabhupada taught that souls in this world dwelled originally with God and then fell to this world where they became entangled in the body and materiality. These beliefs imply the radical separation of the body from the sense of self, fostering the growth of dualism, asceticism and sexual renunciation. Prabhupada's writings and commentaries contrast the exquisite transcendental pastimes of Radha-Krishna with the degradation of life in the world in the Kali Yuga. His teachings about Western and Indian society, Hindu modernity, human embodiment and the position of women have implications for his treatment of Radha, women and the embodied self. They inevitably therefore carry very mixed cultural messages for Western devotees.

Prabhupada's translations and amplifications of Vaishnava texts are regarded by devotees as timeless truths which illuminate the spiritual path back to Godhead and set out in exact detail the divine pattern for social existence. Nevertheless, it is impossible to read Prabhupada's commentaries without becoming aware of their historical context – that of Hindu revival and mission. Like many Hindu gurus Prabhupada was deeply influenced by constructions of Vedic culture as the "Golden Age", a civilisation which is also primordial and eternal. He was anti-rational and idealist in his writings, revering *brahmanical* traditions of learning as superior to Western knowledge and science. He had little understanding of Christian theology, the humanistic and naturalistic sources of European culture or the methods of the empirical sciences. He wanted to reintroduce global *varnashrama* and *brahmanical* elitism as necessary aspects of spiritual culture. The *brahmanical* model and the reformed *varna* system are contrasted with the uncontrolled sexuality and depravity of the outer world. The "real" India is equated with the innocent traditions of Vrindavan and the non-modern communities of *gopi*s.

Prabhupada taught that Krishna is the intimate Supreme Godhead with the cosmic Vishnu as his amplification. Krishna's supremacy was "drilled" into his disciples, yet Prabhupada wanted his followers to encounter and ultimately participate in the realm of Krishna's intimacy (Valpey 2004, p.161).[15] Krishna is more merciful than Rama because he became an ordinary cowherd boy. He is supreme and yet a plaything in the presence of the pure devotee. He is pleased with pure affection and love rather than reverence. Nevertheless, Prabhupada does not neglect the Krishna of the *Gita*. He rejects the views of those who out of "lusty feelings" consider that Krishna's dealings with the Pandavas are less important than his dealings with the *gopi*s (1970, p.418).

Prabhupada refers to Radha specifically in *Krsna: The Supreme Personality of Godhead*, *The Nectar of Devotion: The Complete Science of Bhakti Yoga* and *Caitanya-caritamrita*. He follows the Chaitanyite tradition, teaching that Radha is the Supreme Goddess who controls Krishna with her love and that Krishna manifests himself as Radharani in order to exhibit His internal pleasure potency. This pleasure potency is the foremost and chief of many extensions, expansions and incarnations. Radha is Krishna's *hladini* principle, the power by which God enjoys pleasure. It is also the potency by which the servants of God enjoy the highest spiritual pleasure. The essence of love of God is *bhava*, or intense spiritual emotions, the ultimate development of which is *mahabhava*. Lord Krishna enchants the world, but Sri Radha enchants Him. Therefore, she is the Supreme Goddess, above all others. She is the *purna-shakti*, the full power.

The pastimes of Radha and Krishna are the ultimate goal of the devotee but dangerous and forbidden for the neophyte. There is therefore a hierarchy of access. The best way to approach Krishna is through his recognised devotees. One should not try to establish the relationship directly. The serious student (of *rasa*) should receive the message of *Bhagavatam* in the chain of disciplic succession from Srila Sukadev Goswami. Yet Prabhupada quotes Srila Sukadev Goswami that every conditioned soul should engage himself in hearing and chanting the transcendental pastimes of the Lord (1970 [1996], p.1008). Hearing the attractive pastimes of Lord Krishna's different incarnations is a chance for liberation for the conditioned soul and "by hearing His pastimes one is sure to get salvation and be transferred home, back to Godhead" (1970 [1996], p.1006).[16] Prabhupada exclaims:

> The transcendental pastimes of the Supreme Personality of Godhead, Krsna, are so powerful that simply by hearing, reading and memorising this book, Krsna, one is sure to be transferred to the spiritual world, which is ordinarily very difficult to achieve. The description of the pastimes of Lord Krsna is so attractive that it automatically gives us an impetus to study repeatedly, and the more we study the pastimes of the Lord, the more we become attached to Him. This very attachment to Krsna makes one eligible to be transferred to His abode, Goloka Vrindavana. (1970 [1996], p.1007)

Prabhupada struggles to find appropriate and dignified English equivalents for Krishna's relationships and as a result his language sounds archaic and ponderous.[17] He divides conjugal love into two categories – conjugal love as husband and wife, and conjugal love as lover and beloved. Both feel grief in separation.[18] This conjugal love for Krishna is not limited to women. Men too can develop such sentiments (1970 [1982], p.129). However, Prabhupada's purports reveal that Krishna himself lived as a king with many wives, children, servants and animals. They assume the obedience of wives to their husbands. Krishna's household is hierarchically ordered. Males control females, and elders their children. The women-subordinating axis of purity and pollution is frequently stressed:

> The queens at Dvaraka were *svakiya* or duly married wives, but the damsels of the Vraja were young friends of the Lord while He was unmarried…These girls, as well as queens, underwent severe penances by taking vows, bathing and offering sacrifice in the fire, as prescribed in the scriptures.[19] The rites are means to attain to the highest stage of *svarupa* to render constitutional transcendental service to the Lord…The kissing of the Lord, either by His wives or His young girl friends who aspired to have the Lord as their fiance, is not of any mundane perverted quality. (ibid. p.11)

Prabhupada distinguishes radically between "sex life in the diseased material condition and spiritual sex life" (1989, p.51). Mundane sex is always "abominable." Human desire is simply lust, a way of treating another person as an object to be used for self-gratification. Indulgence in sex is not Krishna-*bhakti* but *prakrita-sahajiya* – materialistic lust. Radha-Krishna display their pastimes through Krishna's internal energy. Because we are part and parcel of Krishna, the pleasure potency is within us also, but we try in vain to display that pleasure potency in matter. While this teaching indicates dis-ease with physical embodiment, for aspiring devotees it is much more about Krishna Consciousness, about practice and discourse constrained by tradition, about the recognition of the eternal relationship between humans and God, and therefore about self-realisation and surrender.

While Radharani in Prabhupada's summary study of Srila Rupa Goswami's *Bhakti-rasamrita-sindhu* is shown under the influence of love for Krishna as angry, ashamed, bashful, confused, crying, dizzy, ecstatic, embarrassed, intoxicated, jealous, tearful and trembling, sometimes this emotional, all too human, Radha is eclipsed by a more dignified divine alter ego. Prabhupada's translation of *Srimad Bhagavatam* canto 2.3.23 purport, reads:

In Vrindavana all the pure devotees pray for the mercy of Srimati Radharani, the pleasure potency of Lord Krsna. Srimati Radharani is a tender hearted feminine counterpart of the supreme whole, resembling the perfectional stage of the worldly feminine nature. Therefore, the mercy of Radharani is available very readily to the sincere devotees, and since She recommends such a devotee to Lord Krishna, the Lord at once accepts the devotee's admittance into His association. The conclusion is, therefore, that one should be more serious about seeking the mercy of the devotee than that of the Lord directly, and by one's doing so (by the good will of the devotee) the natural attraction for the service of the Lord will be revived. In fact, it is only the love of Radharani that can control Krishna, therefore she is more powerful than Him!

While participation in the *lila*s of Krishna and Radha is the supreme goal for the pure devotee, Prabhupada is ever uneasy that the transcendental pastimes of Radha and Krishna will be treated irreverently or lustily (e.g. 1989, p.46). He advocates the "regulative principles" and the institutionalised path to *bhakti*, dismissing *prakrita-sahajiya* as "a pseudosect of so-called Vaisnavas" (1970 [1982], p.127). The mass of devotees are required to follow the standard way of service (*vidhi bhakti*). It is partly for this reason that theologically ISKCON remains Krishnacentric, and the thealogy of Radha is undeveloped and ambivalent.

Chaitanya

Prabhupada traces ISKCON's lineage back to Sri Krishna Chaitanya ("he who awakens consciousness of Krishna"),[20] who was born in Mayapur, West Bengal in 1486. ISKCON's devotional literature refers to him as an incarnation of Krishna who descended to this world to spread the chanting of the Holy Names of God and to deliver everyone from material bondage.[21] Chaitanya underwent a relatively sudden conversion when he went to Gaya to perform memorial rites for his father. He was initiated into the worship of Krishna and on his return home began to sing devotional songs about the love of Krishna and Radha and to have periods of ecstasy and trance. He became a *sannyasi* and moved from Bengal to the great pilgrimage centre of Puri, the seat of the Jagannath temple where he was more and more overtaken by Radha *bhava*, the ecstasy associated with Radharani's essence. Among his followers the view emerged that Chaitanya was an *avatara* of Krishna or a manifestation of Krishna and Radha in one body or in the mood of his own devotee. Vaishnavas believe that Krishna became incarnate in the form of Chaitanya, assuming the fair complexion and the emotions of Radha but dressed in the yellow clothes of Krishna. Chaitanya as manifest divinity thus elevates Radha to a pre-eminent position in the worship of Krishna. In Krishna *lila* Krishna was the subject and Radharani the object. They were separated; they still had two distinct bodies. Chaitanya or Mahaprabhu's story echoes the events in Krishna's life with this exception. He experiences within one body the bliss of union with his *shakti* (divine energy). Moreover Chaitanya's disciples who were all male aspired to have the consciousness of the *sakhis*, Radha's female friends. They became symbolically female (homoerotic) in their encounters with Krishna. Radha's status as a married woman is used to develop an elaborate analogy, suggesting that the worshipper should overcome all such mundane obstacles to achieve union with the deity. Chaitanya himself is said finally to have merged with the image of Krishna in the form of Sri Jagannatha in Puri and disappeared from the world.[22]

ISKCON devotees believe that Chaitanya incarnated in order to experience the love of Radha himself but also specifically to proselytise, to spread the love of Radha. Rosen comments that Chaitanya Mahaprabhu descended to introduce a "unique" *sthayi-bhava*, *Bhavollasa-rati* or that state wherein one's love for Radharani supercedes one's love for Krishna. "This, indeed, is the 'inner woman' that Gaudiya Vaisnavas seek to get in touch with" (Rosen 1996, p.118). However, while ISKCON devotees describe themselves as following Chaitanyite practices, they often declare that Swami Prabhupada's "mood" was not that of Chaitanya. One devotee reminded me that "Prabhupada's mission was to explain to those ignorant of Indian spiritual culture the basics of Krishna Consciousness, not to confuse them with accounts of confidential, secret pastimes."

Prabhupada's Teachings: the Confidential Pastimes

Devotees understand Gaudiya *bhakti* devotion as rooted in the ecstatic experience of Chaitanya and the entire heritage of Vaishnava *bhakti*. The pastimes that form the goal of the devotee's meditation are regarded as "secret", "private" or "confidential."[23] Yet aspiring devotees assert that in fact all ISKCON devotees revere Radha even more than Krishna. She shows that the devotee can control Krishna by his or her love. She remains steadfast in her love and loyalty whereas Krishna as the Personality of Godhead appears fickle. Krishna's love can never match that of Radha or the *gopis*. Devotee Shaunaka Rishi told me that in this sense Radha is more important than Krishna. Many devotees have ecstatic dreams or mystical visions of Radha. However, they do not reveal them. To the world they continue to fulfil all the demands of *vidhi bhakti* (Shaunaka Rishi: private communication: 29.11.04). Indriyesha Das, director of ISKCON Educational Services, remarked to a group of visiting Year 2 undergraduates, "We don't talk much about Radha because she's Lord Krishna's girlfriend and you don't talk about that sort of thing in public!" He commented:

> Krishna's birthday was 5,000 ago and Radha was born two weeks later. Radha is the boss. There is both female and male. *Yin* and *yang*. The female performs receptive service. She serves Krishna. So Krishna says: "I can never repay you. I serve you." But we don't talk about it. The soul is female. By serving Krishna we take the female role. Radha is Krishna's girlfriend. As female, we are submissive.

Vaishnavism becomes for some devotees a type of Shaktism wherein the *purna-shakti*, or the most complete form of the divine feminine energy, is worshipped as the pre-eminent aspect of divinity, eclipsing even the male Godhead in certain respects. Rosen comments (1996, p.113) that the "ultimate goal of Caitanyite Vaisnavism is to realise one's inner identity as the servant of the servant of Radharani's maidservants, and by doing so develop love for God in the feminine mood of the well-known *gopi*s of Braj." The mood of the *gopi*s is the highest spiritual achievement for both men and women (Rosen 1996, p.114).

It is men, according to John Stratton Hawley, who have to undergo a social devaluation in two ways by adopting the role of a woman. Firstly they have to become cowherds and leave behind pretensions of caste, literacy and learning, and secondly they leave behind their maleness and become women. Men suffer a further loss when they become not merely low-caste and rural but women who are adulterous. To be a *gopi* in relation to Krishna brings not only humility but social opprobrium (quoted in Rosen 1996, p.114).

Many prominent Vaishnava authorities bring out the special significance of *Manjari-bhava*, the state of selfless service to Radharani in the mood of a cowherd girl. The ecstasy associated with such spiritual selflessness is said to exceed that of Radharani herself. Among those "most confidential devotees", the *gopi*s, there are those who are especially given to this *Manjari-bhava*. Rosen identifies the different groups. There are firstly the eight principal *gopi*s, the most intimate associates of Radha. These eight, though friends of Radha, also have intimacy with Krishna and sometimes Radha arranges their pastimes. Then there are the *priya-sakhi*s who are subordinate to the primary eight *gopi*s. There are 64 of these particular kinds of *sakhi*s and then innumerable other *sakhi*s who have their own encounters with Krishna. Either they love Krishna intensely or they love Radha and Krishna equally. Then there are the *prana-sakhi*s and the *nitya-sakhi*s, an extraordinary group of *sakhi*s whose love for Radha is supreme, and who only have the desire to bring Krishna and Radha together. They savour an emotion known as *Radha* *snehadhika*: their love for Radha stands supreme (*Bhavollasa rati*). This is *Manjari-bhava*.

> The *manjari* is a beautiful young *gopi* who is resplendent with all charming qualities. She is always pre-pubescent or, at most, thirteen years of age. This is so because, according to Vaishnava canon, this age is one of innocence and emotional intensity…In some ways *manjaris* are considered superior to regular *sakhis*. For example, when Radha and Krishna desire to engage in their most intimate transcendental *lila*, the regular *sakhis* cannot gain entrance…In these private moments, the *manjaris* serve the needs of the divine couple. The types of service rendered by the *manjaris* include fetching water, serving betel nut, fanning Radha and Krishna, combing and braiding the divine couple's hair, decorating their bodies, massaging their limbs, and entertaining them with food and dance. Thus, only the *manjari* witnesses and relishes the most intimate *lila* of the Lord. The *manjaris* are ultimately the most fortunate of all *gopis*. (Rosen 1996, p.120) [24]

Gelberg, now an ex-devotee, reflects:

> According to Gaudiya-Vaisnava theology, the various *rasas* or spiritual sentiments with which souls experience and relate to God, including the male-female model (*madhurya-rasa*), are applicable only to full liberated souls who have transcended bodily identification and, with it, attraction to corporeal sexuality. These mystical *rasas* are not something that can be casually experienced by worldly people…
>
> Although certain aspects of the Radha-Krishna relationship may externally resemble romantic sensuality, they are understood theologically to be utterly pure, spiritual and eternal. Although Sri Caitanya was himself a very strict and ascetical *sannyasi*, he advocated Radha's devotion for Krishna as the most exalted and sublime form of theistic devotion. In some Sahajiya sects, devotees ritually assume the roles of Radha and Krishna and engage in ordinary sexual exploits. These sorts of left-handed tantric tendencies have affected even certain lines coming from Sri Caitanya. Mainline Vaisnavas consider this sort of thing as an abomination. (Gelberg 1983, p.33)

Prabhupada's stern warnings to his devotees were authoritative (cf. Joseph 2004, p.242). Particularly in the sexually freer culture of the West *raganuga bhakti* could encourage "lustiness." Thus the embryonic Hindu missionary movement maintained an orderly community life focused on deity-worship and service. Chastity and continence became defining ideals that shape the lives of committed devotees, and an important source of spiritual energy and direction. Those members of ISKCON who wanted to emphasise the esoteric aspect of *bhakti* were often branded as heretical (Goswami 1997). A number split off from ISKCON in order to join other Gaudiya movements, some headed by ex-guru *bhai*s ([god-]brothers) of Prabhupada who stress the mood of *raga*. One of the major schisms in ISKCON relate to Narayana Maharaja's delight in relating the Krishna-Radha *lila*s. Today there are many Vaishnava groups that compete for devotees' allegiance, and it is important to be aware that ISKCON contextually positions itself in opposition to other contemporary forms of Chaitanya Vaishnavism and to charismatic Gaudiya teachers outside its own jurisdiction. Fidelity to *Prabhupadanuga lila* becomes its essential defining characteristic.

There are a growing number of devotees and scholars who are writing on the nature of devotional love. Among the most inspiring are Graham Schweig, an editor of the *Journal of Vaishnava Studies*, and the author of *Dance of Divine Love – India's Classic Sacred Love Story: The Rasa Lila of Krishna* (2005), and Sivarama Swami, a member of the GBC who is responsible for leading ISKCON's mission in the United Kingdom and Hungary. Sivarama Swami claims that Srila Prabhupada intended his disciples to write creatively and that it is permissible to narrate the loving pastimes of Sri Krishna in order to inspire devotees. His literary, but well researched, trilogy seeks to resolve many of the paradoxes inherent in Prabhupada's ambivalent treatment of the pastimes. *Na Paraye Ham: I am Unable to Repay You* (2000), is based upon the teachings of *Srimad Bhagavatam, Sri Caitanya-caritamrita* and the commentaries of Visvanatha Cakravarti Thakura. Sivaram Svami asks: "To what goal should devotees be inspired?" His single-word reply is, "*Prema*" (Love) (2000, p.1). He notes Srila Prabhupada's translation of *Srimad Bhagavatam* 10.32.22, where he emphasises Krishna's inability to repay the *gopi*s: "I cannot repay your continuous love…," "It is impossible to repay you…" and "…it is not possible for Me to repay My debt to you" (*Krsna* Book, 1, p.308). Here Sivaram Swami expands this idea of Krishna's debt to Radha and the *gopi*s and suggests why He is unable to match the love of His devotees. He argues that in the form of Gauranga (the "golden-limbed" one), Krishna adopts the single-pointed love of Radha and thus liquidates the debts occurred during the *vraja-lila*. He identifies the sorrow of separation from Krishna (*vipralambha-bhava*) as a misery accompanied by a myriad of melancholy symptoms, yet also as a symptom of *prema*, the supremely glorified goal of life. Meeting and separation are inseparable aspects of one principle – love. He also explains the nature of the *parakiya-bhava* of Vraja, the divine ecstasy of unwedded love, why it is superior to all other forms of love and why its mood finds perfection in Sri Radha. It is little wonder then that some long term women devotees have reported that readings of Sivarama's trilogy have given them "feminine affirmation and pleasure" (Bhakti Rasa Das: personal communication: 01.06.05).

Madhurya Bhav

Many converts are drawn to Radha precisely because she embodies *madhurya bhav*, the emotional stance of erotic love towards Krishna and of *viraha*, longing and love in separation. All in the presence of Krishna are *gopis*. Radha is the archetype for the devotee's self-giving love. It is the dimension of human relationality between Krishna and Radha that allows women as well as men to value "feminine" qualities and experiences. Radha captivates Krishna in the intimacy of love and the devotee understands through her that Krishna will not abandon those who love him. Radha brings to her relationship with Krishna steadfast warmth and intimacy. She abandons her inhibitions and reveals herself. She expresses the freedom experienced in love. Her unashamed and unselfconscious self-giving becomes a model for love unabashed by societal reaction. Devotees learn not to be cold or distant in their relationships. They are to be kind and loving in their dealings with others. The perfect Vaishnava attitude is to appreciate the activities of other devotees and to exhibit humility as part of the surrendering process. Srila Prabhupada, for example, in ISKCON is regarded as both a perfect spiritual master and pure devotee (cf. Knott 1997, p.63).

Gender: Equality and the Body

Prabhupada framed the traditional Vaishnava worldview within a deeply anti-secular, anti-science and anti-modern rhetoric. The radical denigration of the rationality of science, an insistence on a literal reading of scripture and polemical rhetoric against *mayavadins* or impersonalists and other religious traditions created a community initially isolated from mainstream scientific, philosophical and religious currents. Prabhupada attracted followers from the counterculture, partly because they were disillusioned by the pluralistic relativism of modern living and partly because of his own piety and strict regimen of discipline and study. The very demi-gods (e.g. Kali and Durga) who now fascinate Western feminists and scholars are described by him as abhorrent. He insisted that his disciples follow strict ritual and dietary rules. And while contraception has enabled millions of people to separate sexual activity from procreative activity, in ISKCON sexuality is linked with procreation alone. All sexual activity is confined to married heterosexual couples. Chastity is recommended for all outside and within marriage. Asceticism marks the final stage of self-denial and austerity. Issues of contraception, abortion, homosexuality, bisexuality, transexuality, have therefore scarcely arisen publicly. ISKCON, like many other religious traditions, rejects all non-heterosexual practices. Only by embracing chastity can women and men transcend their fleshly, material nature. While devotees understand their active asceticism as symbolically and materially rising above material desires, Prabhupada's rejection of "illicit" sex and anxiety to control active adult sexuality seem to reflect very traditional psychosocial patterns of Indian culture which regard sexual pleasure as the prime cause of the soul's bondage.[25]

For early devotees Prabhupada's teachings and example heralded a global return to Vedic culture in which men served God through their spiritual masters and women served God through the men who protected them. Prabhupada's idealisation of the Vedic period creates the idea that gender roles, like *varna* functions, have become profoundly disturbed and dysfunctional in the modern period. In the degraded Kali Yuga spiritual and moral perfection can only be reached through *bhakti-yoga*, the sublime process of Krishna Consciousness. Men and women are equal on the spiritual platform but are fundamentally different in their natures. Women are obedient, receptive and passive, and their lives are characterised by service: it is men who are the initiators and actors.[26] Women always need the shelter of a man, and female respectability is preserved "more elegantly" where women are kept separate. The sexes should not mix unrestrictedly (e.g. 1970, p.582). Women's advantage lies in their ability to transcend their nature because of their soft hearts and qualities of surrender and submission (ibid. pp.997-8). Women, by virtue of their natures are better practised in this loving approach or attitude than men. This glorification of women as exemplars of submission is however offset by their role as sexual temptresses:

Maya has many activities, and in the material world her strongest shackle is the female. Of course in actuality we are neither male nor female – for these designations refer only to the outer dress, the body. We are all actually Krishna's servants. In conditioned life, however, we are shackled by the iron chains which take the form of beautiful women. (1988, p.3)

Prabhupada is hostile to the women's liberation movement because he expects women to be shy, chaste, faithful and submissive, and men to be responsible and protective. Men and women have essentially complementary and equally essential roles in *varnashramadharma*. While Prabhupada and ISKCON see spiritual equality as the overriding issue, feminist theologians require this spiritual equality to be reflected in ways that change the actual power structures. For Prabhupada there is social disruption when women are *not* subordinate to men (Indian Continental Committee 2005, p.20). Women who are not supported, protected and guided by their husbands lack happiness:

So-called equal rights for women means that the men cheat the women. Suppose a woman and a man meet, they become lovers, they have sex, the woman becomes pregnant, and the man goes away. The woman has to take charge of the child and beg alms from the government, or else she kills the child by having an abortion. This is the woman's independence. In India, although a woman may be poverty-stricken, she stays under the care of her husband, and he takes responsibility for her. When she becomes pregnant, she is not forced to kill the child or maintain him by begging. So, which is real independence – to remain under the care of the husband or to be enjoyed by everyone?

Just like in the Western countries, the women declare that "Why we should not have equal rights with the man?" But by nature it is different. The man is the enjoyer, and the woman is the enjoyed. That is the position. Bhokta and bhogya. There are many social problems in your country – I do not wish to discuss – but it is very grave problems. (Prabhupada quoted in Indian Continental Committee 2005, pp.3-4)

Prabhupada accepted that women have souls which are eternally gendered and equal but he thought that due to natural differences women should never share equal rights with men. They lack rationality, self control and the capacity for independent existence. Prabhupada encouraged his devotee "daughters" to remain submissive in the temple, but aggressive in *sankirtana*. "A lamb at home, a lion in the chase."

Western devotees, aware of the wider impact of Prabhupada's controversial statements about women, rapidly drew my attention to ways in which Prabhupada might have seemed a revolutionary to his contemporaries. They pointed out that he opened his movement to women, initiated them as *brahman*s, gave them access to the priesthood and the scriptures, offered them special responsibilities and included them within the communal spheres of the temple, ritual, performance and even scriptural study. In a letter to Silavati Devi (14 June 1969) Prabhupada writes:

Caitanya Mahaprabhu has said that anyone who knows the science of Krishna, that person should be accepted as Spiritual Master, regardless of any material so-called qualifications; such as rich or poor, man or woman, or *brahmana* or *sudra*.

In a conversation on 18 June 1976, Toronto, Prabhupada is recorded as saying:

There are so many Western women, girls, in our society. They are chanting, dancing, taking to Krishna consciousness. Of course, because superficially, bodily, there is some distinction, so we keep women separately from men, that's all. Otherwise, the rights are the same.

Professor O'Connell then asks:

Is it possible, Swamiji, for a woman to be a guru in the line of disciplic succession?

Srila Prabhupada:

Yes. Jahnava devi was Nityananda's wife. She became. If she is able to go to the highest perfection of life, why is it not possible to become guru? But, not so many. Actually, one who has attained the perfection, she can become guru...In our material world, is it any prohibition that woman cannot become professor? If she is qualified, she can become professor. What is the wrong there? She must be qualified. That is the position.

Women who became Srila Prabhupada's close disciples directed their energy, not in asserting their interests as women, but as activists in creating a global institution. They propagated Hindu *dharma*, values and lifestyles in cultures in which they believed modesty had been eroded and women sexually exploited. They preached the sanctity of chastity within the family and the community. They submitted to the guru's control of their sexuality. Knott suggests that close women devotees of Prabhupada found it possible to accept the principles of *bhakti-yoga* on the one side and *varnashrama* on the other, the *varnashrama* system with its home-centred role for women and the progressive model for women in *bhakti-yoga*. Yamuna Devi Dasi (2000, p.6) remarks that she was a strong and independent woman when she met Prabhupada in 1966 and took initiation in 1967. He did not demand conformity to orthodox rules for women as a condition of surrender but rather lovingly encouraged and engaged women in the *sankirtana* movement and consistently revealed himself to be *panditah samah-darsinah* – equal to all:

He trained me, urged me to accept more and more responsibility, and regularly asked me to lead *kirtana*s, give classes, arrange programmes, manage departments, provide comforts for visiting devotees, meet with leaders and actively promulgate Krsna consciousness.
(2000, p.6)

Western and Indian feminisms over the last decades have drawn attention to existing gender divisions, inequalities and oppressions and have increasingly understood that women's voices are not homogeneous. In ISKCON while some women are boldly moving from the advocacy of spiritual equality to the language of equal rights and human rights, many devotees respect Prabhupada's defence of family and community values, regarding motherhood as the primary sacred duty of women. Such women devotees draw on scriptural images of Radha to celebrate women's aptitudes for service and negation of the self, discovering great joy in their lives as women and wives and mothers. These women are often critical of the world outside ISKCON, finding a focus in the beauty and spirituality of traditional Vaishnava practice. I interviewed young second-generation women devotees who argued that feminist approaches generate division between men and women. They emphasise that spiritual equality is central to the Vaishnava tradition but not economic and social sameness. Women by nature are not fit for (male) leadership roles but for family life. They claimed that a truly feminist theology subverts the natural order and the authority of guru and tradition. On the other hand, I also interviewed women who were working in everyday jobs, had children and successfully integrated Krishna Conscious practice into the daily practices of family and work.

Contrary Voices

Lorenz (2004, p.121) argues that Prabhupada's own personal amplifications of Vaishnava teachings diverge from those of previous Vaishnava gurus. Prabhupada exalts the spiritual master as good, beyond sexuality, and superior to all; "women and sex are dangerous and bad." Lorenz regards Prabhupada's writings as polemical and as habitually denigrating women and sex. According to his calculations, 80 per cent of all statements made by Prabhupada about women are negative: they involve restrictions, list bad qualities, group women within socially inferior classes, or treat them as sex objects that have to be avoided:

> When Bhaktivedanta Swami speaks about women in the context of *varnashrama*, he inevitably brings up the topics of bad population, adulteration, prostitution, *varna sankara*, women's lesser intelligence, and the lifelong control of women by men. (2004, p.379)

Prabhupada's attitudes towards independent women can be illustrated by his vilification of Indira Gandhi (quoted in Lorenz 2004, p.379):

> PRABUPADHA: And Indira was doing that. Indira and company...She is a prostitute; her son is a gunda...
> TAMALA KRISHNA: She seems to have been one of the worst leaders so far.
> PRABUPADHA: She (Indira Gandhi) is not leader, she is a prostitute. Woman given freedom means prostitute. Free woman means prostitute. What is this prostitute? She has no fixed-up husband. And free woman means this, daily, new friend.

Prabhupada advises his disciples:

> And being the weaker sex, women require to have a husband who is strong in Krishna consciousness so that they may take advantage and make progress by sticking tightly to his feet. (2004, p.380)

Lorenz insists that Prabhupada cannot be exempted from blame for past abuses and that the spiritual culture of ISKCON denigrates women and positive feminine principles. Prabhupada's teachings introduce concepts of women's powerlessness and dependence, which have led to human rights violations and cycles of violence. They contributed to the humiliation and devaluation experienced by women devotees and to physical, sexual and psychological abuse suffered by many children in ISKCON's *gurukulas* (schools) (Lorenz 2004; Wolf 2004; Deadwyler 2004).

Few devotees or scholars have been bold enough to suggest that Prabhupada's teachings led directly to the strikingly asymmetrical relationship of women to men in ISKCON. Many devotees exempt Prabhupada from responsibility by interpreting the period of ascetic dominance before and following his death as introducing a new male-oriented, misogynistic element. Nori J. Muster, an ex-devotee, argues with bitterness that in a system in which the structure of authority is formed by gender and seniority, women have little or no real power.[27] She recalls details of molestation and humiliation of women by gurus and male leaders, of schools which taught girls to be ashamed of their bodies and female minds and of a culture of wife-beating. The practice of arranging marriages continued. Celibacy was idealised and privileged, and child sexual abuse ignored. She says (2004, p.319): "In the thirty-seven-year history of ISKCON, women have married, divorced, had children and grandchildren, lost loved ones, aged, and suffered their humiliations in silence. In my opinion, ISKCON's policies towards women have been unacceptable."

Many devotees deny that this is a balanced or accurate picture of ISKCON's past. It depicts all men as abusers and all women as victims. We are reminded that the abuse that took place in ISKCON's schools in Dallas and elsewhere was perpetrated by women as well as men, and that the problems that arose were often the result of inexperience. They were related, not primarily to gender, but to bad communication, lack of training, absence of pastoral care and monitoring, fanaticism and to neglectful mothers as well as fathers. The schools were also run by men "who are less sensitive to children than women are." In general the difficulties of that time are attributed to the overly monastic element of the movement, the lack of *varnashramadharma* and a negative view of marriage. Radha Mohan Das questions whether a higher profile for Radharani at that time in those communities would have made much difference (Radha Mohan Das: personal communication: 08.04.05).

Feminine and Feminist Approaches

Since the 1970s and 1980s there has been great scholarly interest in the feminine divine in all religious traditions, nourished in the West by feminisms of all kinds, New Age goddess spirituality and ecological feminism. Feminists like Carol Christ have asserted that religions centred on the worship of a male God generate conditions that keep women in a state of dependence on males and legitimate the political and social authority of men (e.g. Christ 1983, p.234). They emphasise the importance of creating or recovering empowering female symbols to combat the ones that support patriarchy. Gross points out that the enormous rise in the number of publications on Hindu goddesses correlates with the more general rise of feminist scholarship (cf. Gross 1994; 1998). Some writers also stress the rich source of Goddess symbolism as being an ancient and unbroken tradition of Goddess worship in which the Goddess proliferates in ever new forms (see Hawley 1996, p.2). Hinduism's popular and scholarly appeal is that it can be used as "a resource for the contemporary rediscovery of the goddess" (Gross 1994). There is a particular connection between feminism and research exploring the symbolism of strong goddesses. Feminists from traditions that lack goddesses have turned to goddesses who in India have often been the recipients of blood sacrifice and who are represented as full of transforming sexual energy and potency. Individual Western women have found such goddesses, particularly Kali, to be potent mythic models and therapeutic symbols.[28] Goddesses associated with tantric worship and the symbolism of transgression have been appropriated and extolled. On bookshelves all over the world there are semi-scholarly explorations of Hindu Tantra which have fed into Western psychotherapies of sacred sex.

The study of world religions, gender and sexuality is now firmly established on the curriculum in universities, colleges and schools throughout the world. Feminist scholars have over recent decades articulated a powerful protest against deep-rooted hierarchical and patriarchal structures of oppression. In so doing they have transformed the study of religion. The concept of women and men as different but spiritually equal in many religious traditions has been shown often in practice to legitimise the moral subjugation of women; religious cultures that consider women spiritually equal have often assigned them inequality socially and politically.[29] Similarly the vindication of particular feminine qualities – receptivity, humility, sacrifice – has often compounded women's powerlessness and kept women subdued. Almost every mainstream religion today is struggling with complex issues to do with sex and sexuality, linking domination in sexual relations in part to oppressive religious power.[30]

ISKCON has transformed over the last two decades. It has adopted detailed processes of self-examination and reform, acknowledging openly historical problems linked with authority, gender attitudes and theology.[31] Charges of historical abuse of women and children in ISKCON (Lorenz 2004; Knott 2004; Muster 2004) have been publicly examined. Gradually the issue of women's second-class status has been brought out into the open. Sudharma Dasi was able to form the ISKCON Women's Ministry in 1996 when she attained guest status on the GBC (Knott 2004, p.303). Women in ISKCON were increasingly vocal in appealing for fundamental human rights (e.g. Radha Devi Dasi 1998) and respect for individuality (e.g. Urmila Devi Das 1998). In March 2000 nine women spoke to the assembled GBC representatives, the first time in the movement's history. Some spoke movingly of the sufferings of the past, of sexist and inhumane behaviour, of the abuse and neglect of women. As a result the GBC offered their humble apologies to ISKCON's women, and adopted a series of resolutions aimed at recognising the value of women of ISKCON and ensuring their right fully to participate in the Society according to their abilities and wishes. Since then women devotees have mobilised even more strongly and overcome many institutional barriers to serve and advance in ISKCON. In 2005 for example, the GBC accepted the principle that women could take on the role of initiating guru. Among some liberal male devotees there is the positive recognition of Srila Prabhupada's own example in applying the spirit of the law according to time, place, person and circumstance. All the hagiographical literature shows how skilfully Prabhupada applied his teachings to fit the global context he found himself in during the 1960s and 1970s. Bhakti Rasa Das from Newcastle suggests that ISKCON needs to follow Prabhupada's model primarily by continuing "to re-structure politically on GBC/temple management, policy level and socially in the areas of promoting a common understanding of proper Vaishnava etiquette regarding women, taken from within the context of a re-dressed balance between vedic/*varnashrama* models and progressive 21st century international *sankirtana* culture. This can be most effectively served by a re-reading of Srila Prabhupada's text and hagiography."

Liberating Radha

It has become a commonplace for feminist analysts to state (cf. Brzezinski 2004) that the history of Hinduism shows that the presence of a divine consort or Supreme Goddess does not automatically mean that women's social, economic or political independence is guaranteed or valued, or that the symbolism of the divine couple or of goddesses negates conservative or androcentric tendencies. Radha's visual presence in the temple does not mean that gender hierarchy is not a part of ISKCON's theology and ethic. It does not necessarily lead to liberationist strategies for women or the emergence in ISKCON of women of spiritual authority. For devotees mimesis of *Prabhupadanuga lila* is fundamental. Yet ISKCON's conservatism on matters of gender has appeared oppressive, even misogynous, to women both outside and inside the movement. Its spiritual culture has suggested an underlying fear of women and of the body which emphasises and perpetuates women's weakness.[32] Radha's passionate love gets turned against women.

If the Goddess's loving devotees are not necessarily feminists, is the feminine at the heart of Godhead itself liberating? Gross argues that goddesses can be seen to promote the humanity of women: "...the first function of Goddesses is not to provide equal rights or high status, but to provide psychological comfort...nothing is more basic to psychological comfort than the presence of positive female imagery at the heart of a valued symbol system" (Gross 2000, pp.106-7). Basham sees Krishna as meeting nearly every need of men and women:

Krishna, probably even more popular than Rama, is a divinity of a rare completeness and catholicity, meeting almost every need. As the divine child, he satisfies the warm maternal drives of Indian womanhood. As the divine lover, he provides romantic wish fulfilment in a society still tightly controlled by ancient norms of behaviour which give little scope for freedom of expression in sexual relations. As charioteer of the hero Arjuna on the battlefield of Kurukshetra, he is the helper of all those who turn to him, even saving the sinner from evil rebirths, if he has sufficient faith in the Lord. (1983, p.17)

Where does this eulogy leave Radha? Devotees distinguish her from all other goddesses, identifying Radha alone as part of the Supreme Personality of Godhead. They also hasten to disassociate her from the triumphant transgressions of mother goddesses like Kali. And while Radha's story apparently subverts conventional Hindu ethics, orthodox Vaishnavas have cherished every facet, mood and nuance of her relationship with Krishna. While the presence of Radha may encourage the development of women's spiritual self-esteem, a divine-human relationship to Krishna modelled upon that of Radha might seem to lead inevitably to the theological legitimation of female submission and the ethics of passive obedience. Male and female devotees are encouraged spiritually to identify with the role of Radha, a woman in love. For men the adoption of feminine attitudes teaches them the virtues of submission, sensitivity, moral intuition, altruism, nurturing, humility and service but does not exclude them from leadership. It is men, partly because gurus are expected to be renunciants (or *sannyasis*), who have a virtual monopoly on spiritual and teaching roles. While Western feminists have fought to throw off a label that defines them exclusively in terms of relationship, the playful freedom of Vrindavan has often required from women self sacrifice: long hours of drudgery and menial work and lifetimes spent in *seva* to male gurus.

This leads us to consider ISKCON's radically ambivalent attitudes to the material world, to women and to human sexuality. Male and female sensuality are represented in many ways. Some representations affect women adversely and are male-centred, others are tender and celebratory. Prabhupada himself teaches a dualism of body/soul and of gender. He considers sexuality and spirituality as conflicting opposites, lust as disordered desire. Sexual desire is a metaphor for longing for God but also a powerful subversion of that longing. Self-restraint is the dominant virtue in sexual ethics, together with a body-rejecting model of sexuality. ISKCON spirituality therefore presupposes a cultural system that denies, displaces and sublimates sexualities. Behind the veil of *rasa* puritan (and misogynist) values are hidden. While these may appear to offer points of reference in a postmodern world, they also imply that gender inequality is divinely revealed.

Rita Gross argues that the triadic model of the Hindu pantheon obscures the significance of goddesses by incorrectly locating the major division within the Hindu pantheon along gender lines (Gross 1998). According to Gross, this model gives the impression that male deities are more important and popular than female deities. She suggests that here we have co-operating androcentrisms – Hindu and Western. Androcentrism and a text-elite bias against popular religion, powerfully combine to justify a model of the Hindu pantheon that seriously obscures its goddesses (cf. Gross 1998, p.320). In fact female and male deities are interdependent and dominance "flutters back and forth between them."

From the inter-religious and feminist perspectives Radha's Western trajectory should facilitate genuine encounters between women and men, open opportunities, provide women with choices and allow them to make decisions about their own lives. Radha's example of service should enable women to choose orthodoxy, to be at the heart of the ISKCON family and the nurturers of its soul. On the other hand, her ultimacy should guarantee the right of female gurus to confer *diksha* and reverse the traditional bias against female embodiment.

Feminist Hermeneutics

A feminist hermeneutics of Radha would address the historically neglected dynamics of religion, power and gender. It would initiate a dialogue between theology and feminine/feminist reflection. There is a danger that ISKCON presents itself as a male monotheism and monopoly which preserves the letter of ritual rather than the spirit of *rasa*. Feminist and feminine perspectives of Radha would lead to re-readings of Prabhupada's hagiography and texts in ways that support the spiritual concerns of women as lovers, mothers and friends. If it is true that Radha and Krishna are equivalent then this truth should effect political and social transformation.

Thealogical theory should be embedded in practice. ISKCON's valorisation of the feminine dimension of the divine has often coincided with extreme religious orthodoxy and staunch support of male authority. The critical task then for feminists would be to confront the Chaitanya tradition wherever the historical perpetuation of unjust, exclusionary practices that have legitimated male superiority are found. The transformative task would be to re-appropriate the central symbols, texts and rituals so as to incorporate and affirm the neglected experiences of women, and to show how the divine feminine relates to and supports the spiritual concerns of women. The understanding of God as both female and male implies a recognition of the principle of spiritual egalitarianism. Otherwise the combined male and female Deities duplicate gender-stereotyping, leaving dominant male divine power intact. Any social, personal or economic discrimination which women suffer because of their sex would be challenged on thealogical grounds. Beliefs that sustain and reinforce the notion of male supremacy would be rejected as thealogically offensive. Prabhupada's commentaries about Radha and women could be scrutinised for resources that are ultimately liberating for both sexes. The equivalence of Radha and Krishna could be employed to undercut the vilification of female sexuality and the portrayal of women either as evil, dangerous temptresses or male projected ideals of virginity and motherhood. Offensive attitudes and discriminatory policies towards women could be rebutted from within the resources of the Vaishnava tradition to create new meanings and symbols. At present the male authorship, transmission, canonisation and translation of Vaishnava scriptures is recognised; scripture is received and designated authoritative by the (male) bona fide guru. The ideal of the submissive woman and the profoundly ambiguous image of femininity would be opposed by a positive feminine hermeneutics.

Many women who left ISKCON did so because they felt estranged from its androcentric tradition and culture. ISKCON has often been profoundly uncomfortable with female intellectual assertiveness, failing to bring out the diverse feminine and feminist thoughts of Vaishnava women. The symbolism of Radha as inclusive and liberating for ISKCON communities has to be continually rediscovered. Radha represents radical freedom from oppressive structures.

A Vaishnava "Feminine" Approach

As I suggested in my introduction, it is unlikely that feminist approaches would be acceptable to devotees. They challenge the foundations of ISKCON's theology. However, I believe that the revisioning of Radha to move beyond gender inequalities can be resourced from within ISKCON's tradition itself. Devotees accept the spiritual feminisation that the Vaishnava tradition offers, bringing a degree of security and stability. Radha is the spiritual role model for *all* devotees and her approach of surrender and service is recommended for *all*. The relationship between Radha and Krishna, that of beloved and lover, has been exalted by many Hindus as the highest form of intimacy, whether divine or human. Krishna is a personal god, always accessible and unfailingly responsive. He, the supreme object of devotion, worships the highest devotee, Radha. The *lila* of love takes as its reality the relationship between subject and object, and its goal is not liberation, but a full realisation of this relationship (cf. Case 2000, p.70). A theaological understanding would emphasise the interdependence and interplay of Radha and Krishna, the feminine and masculine dimensions of both and their androgynous status.

A theology of Radha thus offers both affirmative and subversive possibilities. The presence of Radha as the feminine aspect of Krishna (*purna shakti*) has already enriched ISKCON with an attitude of *seva*, a sacramental life style, strong same sex friendships and bonding, the celebration of dance, music, chanting, art, cooking, festivals and feasting, an aesthetic of beauty, sensitivity, delight and joyfulness. A confident theology of Radha would go further in promoting mutual relationships of rights and duties, encouraging all devotees to feel religiously valued, and developing structures and policies which would enable women as well as men to develop skills of leadership.

Radha also "queers" *dharma*. She could be read as facing sorrow, shame and humiliation, passionately and freely choosing social obloquy over convention.

Gelberg (2004, p.398) suggests that ISKCON's prohibition against "illicit sex" results in "sexy celibacy." He says:

> To be frank, there is something very sad, tragic even, in the spectacle of sincere spiritual aspirants endlessly struggling against and denying sexual feelings, continually berating themselves for their lack of heroic detachment from the body, seeking dark corners in which to masturbate, or, finding themselves 'attached to' another devotee, planning and scheming 'illicit' encounters. All this cheating and hypocrisy, guilt and shame, denial and cover-up, make a pathetic sham of ISKCON's ascetical conceit.

Yet Radha's story recalls the pastimes of Krishna and affirms the divine preference for intimacy and the human need for the warmth of real human relationships. Radha and Krishna are seen at play, delighting in doing and enjoying things. They show us that spiritual life is fundamentally relational: not primarily an intellectual experience but a personal one which is mutual and non-exploitative. It is this bond of love and intimacy between Radha and Krishna which delights and absorbs Vaishnavas, linking them across the world in common devotion, creating a community out of the dynamics of interconnection.[33]

We do not yet know whether women devotees will take up the task of thealogising Radha. Most of the writing about Radha today is still being done by men. However, such a dynamic "feminine" revisioning could explore in a Western context the love of which Krishna speaks in the *Gita*. Bryant and Ekstrand (2004, p.14) characterise the Krishna movement as "theistic intimacy" or "intimism." "The word implies, drawing from its Latin origins, a vision of God that presents his 'innermost' relations within the godhead, his 'nearest' or 'closest' relationships of love." Radha captivates Krishna by her love but in turn is loved. A revisioned thealogy would amplify Vaishnava tradition in ways that affirm and include women's experience and which render women less invisible in their daily, material reality. If human identity lies in the stories we tell and in our actions and practice then the story of Radha is crucial to the ISKCON community. The female model for God as Lover, if understood non-hierarchically, suggests human flourishing, connectedness, empathy, tenderness and compassion rather than masochistic self-sacrifice and voluntary powerlessness.

Scholars often compare Radha's relationship with Krishna with Christian thought. The love of the lover for his beloved, of wife for husband, of the soul for the Lord pervades the writings of many Christian saints and mystics, Marian devotion, the Song of Songs, the bridal metaphor used of the entire church, etc. There is a similar use of erotic language to suggest mystical relationships and the loving nature of God. Nevertheless, in Vaishnava theology the erotic element is far stronger. The love between Radha and Krishna is at the heart of Godhead. Radha's love is returned in full by Krishna and forms a model for love, for attachment, rather than detachment, for ethics which are passionate and relational.

Radha as a female image expresses intimacy, inclusivity, partnership and mutuality within the divine and between humans and the divine. She remains a figure of mystery within ISKCON because of her ultimacy. But she is additionally ambiguous because ISKCON's teachings still remain significantly at odds with modern concepts of human embodiment and social and sexual justice, and with the Vaishnava tradition which elevates *rasa* above ritual. Prabhupada theologically implies an explicit demarcation between the world of spirit and the world of matter – between the transcendent and the mundane, the self and the body – exalting the former and devaluing the latter.

Reflections

The first women converts were not birth-Hindus. Many found a sense of belonging and connectedness in the sacramental life of an ISKCON community. They accepted Prabhupada's guidelines on chastity and purity, and rejoiced in the space and time they offer to pursue spiritual ideals. They saw themselves as rooted in timeless truths beyond the material world, and as women nurturing and protecting goodness and *dharma*. Most importantly they considered themselves the carriers of tradition within the community and the family. They strove to embody the gentleness, purity and virtue that tradition ascribes to women. This position often has the advantage of providing a confident sense of self and a hallowing of the past.

Today the core of devotees who live a life of renunciation and community are outnumbered by congregational Hindus. At Bhaktivedanta Manor, as in many other large Western temples, there are about 1,500 regular Sunday worshippers who are born Hindu. Many of these accept that Krishna or Vishnu-*tattva* is higher than that of Shiva-*tattva* or other "demi-gods" even as the "in-house" ISKCON devotees do (many of whom now are also Indian). Amongst the Indian community who attend the very large Manor festivals such as Janmashtami (60,000), many will worship a plurality of gods, and have varying levels of commitment to ISKCON. According to Radha Mohan Das (personal communication: 12.04.05), "(T)he nearer you get to ISKCON's 'core', whether Indian or Western, the more likely they will put Radha and Krishna at the top."

In the UK there may not be such a wide theological difference between the regular "Indian" worshippers and the "Westerners" as Haddon suggests (2003). However, my argument that many devotees and congregational Hindus work in the material world, educate their children in state schools and share a public culture of equality still stands. A strong thealogy of Radha could offer critical but constructive perspectives to combat the "nightmarish images of the world looming outside the walls of ISKCON" (Gelberg 2004, p.402). Few women devotees, one suspects, would actually prefer to return to an ideal Vedic society privileging a small *brahmanical* (male) elite serviced by a large class of *shudras* and an underclass of women. The future of ISKCON depends upon the strength and abilities of women devotees, and the good will of male devotees. Women living active lives in the world need to be comfortable with the choices open to them. They have to feel that the central symbols of ISKCON speak to them. Many young women may choose to remain within the tradition that gives them their identity, but only if it responds to their own concerns and prepares them to live and work in the secular world if they choose to do so.

Gelberg describes ISKCON as a "woman-fearing, woman-hating, woman-exploiting institution" (2004, p.399). That is not the argument of this chapter. However, it is the argument that the creative exploration of Radha as the feminine divine has been predominantly male and that a reflexive and dialectical thealogy encompassing ritual action and *madhurya bhav* could hold in creative tension the power of traditional Hindu feminine ideals of self-sacrifice and duty *and* feminist affirmations of female sexuality, freedom and embodiment. Feminist and feminine re-readings of Radha would campaign for the recognition of women as leaders and gurus, the implementation of women-oriented rituals, scriptural classes and liturgies, an ethic of care, connectedness and interdependency. They would also campaign for the liberation of men devotees, caught as they are between the "feminine" attitude of devotion and the heavy responsibilities of the male householder.

The Radha-Krishna *lila* has been understood by poets, artists and in popular culture as giving a spiritual dimension to human playfulness, as a celebration of life, desire and joy. Theologians have explored it as a vision of spiritual hope and integration. If Radha is understood as promoting a shared humanity as the epitome of reciprocal love and mutuality, an ethics of passionate engagement and commitment and a connection with all living things could emerge. In this case she will carry all Krishna's devotees beyond the distinctions of gender to a tectonic shift in which men and women work together (King 2004). In this sense perhaps theological reflection on the interrelatedness of Radha and Krishna and the interrelatedness of female and male identities might become central and support ISKCON's male and female devotees as they co-operate in an inclusive philosophical thinking about the future.

NOTES AND REFERENCES

Introduction

1.   For a list of works (books, published lectures, conversations and other writings) by His Divine Grace A.C. Bhaktivedanta Swami Prabhupada, see the Appendix to this book. For photographic images of the Hare Krishna movement's founder, as well as some of his followers, see the book's Plates.

2.   The term "Vaishnavism" denotes a particular set of Indian religious schools in which Vishnu, the preserver of the universe, is traditionally held to be incarnated in a variety of forms, including the form of Krishna, to help living entities during times of strife or struggle. However, while in the older Vaishnava schools Vishnu is venerated as the ultimate deity, with Krishna worshipped merely as a derivative manifestation, in Chaitanya Vaishnavism (or Gaudiya Vishnavism) the relationship is reversed. Thus, in the Hare Krishna movement it is Krishna not Vishnu who is viewed as the Supreme form of Godhead, and it is Krishna rather than Vishnu who is the object of devotion, worship and service.

3.   Major and frequently cited scholarly texts on the Krishna Consciousness movement include works by the following: Bromley, D.G. and L. Shinn (1989) (Eds.) *Krishna Consciousness in the West* (London and Toronto: Associated University Presses); Brooks, C. (1989) *The Hare Krishnas in India* (New Jersey: Princeton University Press); Gelberg, S.J. (1983) (Ed.) *Hare Krishna, Hare Krishna: Five Distinguished Scholars on the Krishna Movement in the West* (New York: Grove Press); Knott, K. (1986) *My Sweet Lord: The Hare Krishna Movement* (Wellingborough: Aquarian Press); Rochford, E.B. Jr (1985) *Hare Krishna in America* (New Jersey: Rutgers University Press); Rosen, S.J. 1992 (Ed.) *Vaisnavism: Contemporary Scholars discuss the Gaudiya Tradition* (New York: Folk Books); Shinn, L. (1987) *The Dark Lord: Cult Images and the Hare Krishnas in*

America (Philadelphia: Westminster Press); Stillson, J.J. (1974) *Hare Krishna and the Counter Culture* (New York: Wiley). For a more recent study of the Hare Krishna movement, see Malory, N. (2001) *Multiculturalism and Minority Religions in Britain: Krishna Consciousness, Religious Freedom and the Politics of Location* (London and New York: RoutledgeCurzon); for other major articles authored by academics and by key figures within the Hare Krishna movement itself, see *ISKCON Communications Journal* and the *Journal of Vaishnava Studies*

4.   Bryant, Edwin F. and Maria L. Ekstrand (2004) (Eds.) *The Hare Krishna Movement: The Postcharismatic Fate of a Religious Transplant* (New York: Columbia University Press).

5.   See Bryant and Ekstrand's "Concluding Reflections," in Edwin F. Bryant and Maria L. Ekstrand (2004) (Eds.), *The Hare Krishna Movement: The Postcharismatic Fate of a Religious Transplant*, pp.431-41 (New York: Columbia University Press).

6.   For assessment and crticism of Bryant and Ekstrand's edited work, see F. M. Smith's 2004) review of Edwin F. Bryant and Maria L. Ekstrand (2004) (Eds.) *The Hare Krishna Movement: The Postcharismatic Fate of a Religious Transplant* (New York: Columbia University Press), in *Journal of Vaishnava Studies* 13 (1): 179-89; see also L. N. Das's (2004) review of Edwin F. Bryant and Maria L. Ekstrand (2004) (Eds.)*The Hare Krishna Movement: The Postcharismatic Fate of a Religious Transplant* (New York: Columbia University Press), in *Journal of Vaishnava Studies* 13 (1): 191-210.

Chapter 1

1.   This chapter is a revised version of a paper by Steven J. Rosen (Satyaraja Dasa) and Bruce Scharf (Brahmananda Dasa) (1998), which first appeared in the *Journal of Vaishnava Studies* 6 (2). The original paper was based on a premise explored in my earlier book: Rosen, S.J. (1992) *Passage From India: The Life and Times of His Divine Grace A.C. Bhaktivedanta Swami Prabhupada*, pp.57-64 (Delhi: Munshiram Manoharlal).

2.   Thakura, Vrindavandas, Antya-Lila, in *Chaitanya-Bhagavata*, 4.126.

3.   See, Bhagavata-Mahatmya, in *Padma Purana*, Uttara-Khanda, especially Text 51: "Bhakti said: 'Leaving this place (Vrindavan) I will travel to foreign lands.' " It is interesting that the passive verb *gamyate* is used in this verse, implying that she (Bhakti) will be carried by someone to foreign shores. Regarding translating *videshan* as "foreign shores," see Shrivatsa Goswami, in S. Gelberg (1983) *Hare Krishna, Hare Krishna: Five Distinguished Scholars on the Krishna Movement in the West*, pp.244-5 (New York: Grove Press).

4.   Thakura, Bhaktivinoda (1885) Nityananda Suryodoy, in *Sajjana-Toshani*, pp.4-5.

5.   Ibid.

6.   Melton, J.G. (1989) The Attitude of Americans toward Hinduism from 1883 to 1983 with Special Reference to the International Society for Krishna Consciousness, in David G. Bromley and Larry Shinn (Eds.), pp.90-1 *Krishna Consciousness in the West* (Lewisberg: Bucknell University Press).

7.   Ibid.

8.   Karnow, F.S. (1983) *Viet Nam: A History*, p.415 (New York: The Viking Press).

9.   Text of Speech to Non-Christian Groups in Bombay, in *The New York Times*, 4 December 1964, p.24.

10.   Abbott, W.M. (1966) (Ed.) The *Documents of Vatican II*, pp.661-2 (New York: Guild Press).

11.   Ibid.

12.   Ibid. p. 659.

13.   Vatican Councils: Vatican II, in *Encyclopedia of Religion*, vol. 15, pp.199-206.

14.   Roman Catholicism, in *Encyclopedia of Religion*, vol. 12, pp.429-45.

15.   Commentary on the Documents of Vatican II, in *Encyclopedia of Religion*, vol. 3, p.1

16.   Ibid. p.137.

17.   Ellwood, R.S. (1989) ISKCON and the Spirituality of the 1960s, in David G. Bromley and Larry Shinn (Eds.), p.102 *Krishna Consciousness in the West* (Lewisberg: Bucknell University Press).

18.   Gelberg, S. (1983) *Hare Krishna, Hare Krishna: Five Distinguished Scholars on the Krishna Movement in the West*, p.153 (New York: Grove Press).

19.   Stillson, J.S. (1974) *Hare Krishna and the Counterculture*, p.16 (New York: John Wiley & Sons).

20.   Gelberg, S. (1983) *Hare Krishna, Hare Krishna: Five Distinguished Scholars on the Krishna Movement in the West*, p.154 (New York: Grove Press).

21.   Cox, H. (1980) Foreword, in Satsvarupa Dasa Goswami *Srila Prabhupada-Lilamrita*, vol. 1 p.viii (Los Angeles: Bhaktivedanta Book Trust).

22.   See Dhanurdhara Swami's (2004) review of Edwin F. Bryant and Maria L. Ekstrand (2004) (Eds.) *The Hare Krishna Movement: The Postcharismatic Fate of a Religious Transplant* (New York: Columbia University Press), in the *Journal of Vaishnava Studies* 13 (1)

23.   See Lakshmi Nrisimha Das's (2004) review of Edwin F. Bryant and Maria L. Ekstrand (2004) (Eds.) *The Hare Krishna Movement: The Postcharismatic Fate of a Religious Transplant* (New York: Columbia University Press), in the *Journal of Vaishnava Studies* 13 (1).

Chapter 2

1.   For a recent study of the expansion of Chaitanya's mission within the Gaudiya Math, see B.A Paramasvaiti Swami (1999) Our family the Gaudiya Math – A Study of the Expansion of Gaudiya Vaisnavism and many Branches Developing around the Gaudiya Math, pp.18-9,
      http://www.consciousart.de/galleries/literature/documents/paramadvaiti-swami/family.pdf

2.   In 1896 Bhaktivinoda Thakura printed a booklet written in Sanskrit under the title *Sri Gauranga-lila-smarana-mangala-stotram*, with a commentary by Srila Sitikantha Vacaspati of Nadia. The introduction in English was called Caitanya Mahaprabhu, His life and Precepts. It was also reviewed in the *Journal of the Royal Asiatic Society* by Mr. F.W. Fraser, an erudite British scholar.

3.   Goswami, Satsvarupa Dasa (1998) *Srila Prabhupada Lilamrta: A Biography of His Divine Grace A.C Bhaktivedanta Swami Prabhupada*, One Volume Edition, p.39 (Los Angeles: Bhaktivedanta Book Trust).

4. Ibid. pp.1-8.

5. Ibid. p.8.

6. In the *Brahma-Vaivarta Purana* (Forth Part, Krsna-Janma-Khanda, chapter 129, verses 50-59) Lord Krishna foretold that after 5,000 years the chanting of His names would spread all over the world, beginning the 10,000 year Golden Age. According to ISKCON devotees, we are currently around the early stages of the Golden Age, which took a significant step forward when Srila Prabhupada came to the West. However, it is understood that it initially began with the advent of Lord Chaitanya in 1486. In his purport to the *Srimad Bhagavatam* 8.5.23, Srila Prabhupada writes: "When Sri Caitanya Mahaprabhu appeared, He ushered in the era for the *sankirtana* movement." He also states in the purport that "for ten thousand years this era will continue."

7. These shared remembrances at Bhaktivedanta Manor in June 2003 were recorded by the author. One can find similar published statements by Syamasundar Das, in Danavir Goswami (2003) *Remembering TKG and George*, vol. 6, pp.25-9 (India: Rupanuga Vedic College).

8. Ibid.

9. Ibid.

10. The rules included the "Four Regulatory Principles": no meat eating, no intoxication of any kind, no gambling and no illicit sex. It is also required of temple residents to rise at 4 a.m. to attend a series of ceremonies, including meditation and scripture classes. In addition, members were expected to chant the Hare Krishna *mantra* at least 1,728 times a day on beads, shave their heads and wear the dress of a Vaishnava. Especially in the earliest days of the movement, showers had only cold water; temple devotees had little money of their own and very few personal possessions.

11. This statement was given by Kripamoya Das in April 2004 (personal communication).

12. Ordinarily, it would not be appropriate to utter the informal name of A.C Bhaktivedanta Swami Prabhupada (viz. Srila Prabhupada) whilst using the formal title of a junior (in this case Tamal Krishna Goswami). However, for consistency and easier reading the author has maintained Srila Prabhupada's informal name.

13. Lord Chaitanya Mahaprabhu, believed to be an incarnation of Radha and Krishna combined, was born in Mayapur, Navadwip, West Bengal, on the banks of the holy Ganges river in February 1486. Therefore, ISKCON's world headquarters were established there.

14. This period in Srila Prabhupada's life is documented in detail; see Tamal Krishna Goswami (1998) *TKG's Diary – Prabhupada's Final Days* (Dallas Texas: Pundits Press).

15. Ibid. p.170.

16. Goswami, Tamal Krishna (June 1997) The Perils of Succession: Heresies of Authority and Continuity In the Hare Krishna Movement, *ISKCON Communications Journal* 5 (1), *http://iskcon.com/icj/5_1/5_1perils.html*

17. *Diksha*: Sanskrit, from the verbal root *diksh* to "consecrate or dedicate oneself." *Ksha* means "destruction of sins." It has been a tradition for *diksha* gurus to whisper a

private *mantra* to a new disciple. In ISKCON a similar process takes place during the second initiation, when the Gayatri *mantra* is imparted.

18. On 9 July 1977, on Srila Prabhupada's behalf, Tamal Krishna Goswami wrote a letter to ISKCON leaders, listing 11 devotees who were to initiate on Srila Prabhupada's behalf. The IRM position is that the word "henceforward" that appears in the letter meant that anyone initiating from that point on would be Srila Prabhupada's direct disciple even after his demise. In contrast, the ISKCON position is that "henceforward" applied only up to the point of Srila Prabhupada's departure. It is most significant that the actual writer of the letter, Tamal Krishna Goswami, later stated he meant the ISKCON interpretation to be correct.

19. Swami, Jayapataka (inspired by) (1991) *100 Deviations of Ritvikism* (Los Angeles: Bhaktivedanta Book Trust).

20. See Collins' chapter in Edwin F. Bryant and Maria L. Ekstrand (2004) (Eds.), *The Hare Krishna Movement: The Post Charismatic Fate of a Religious Transplant*, pp.213-37 (New York: Columbia University Press).

21. Letter to Rupanuga Tirupari, 28 April 1974, *The Bhaktivedanta Vedabase* CD Rom (1998).

22. Recorded during an interview conducted by the author in May 2004.

23. Recorded during an interview conducted by the author in April 2004.

24. For details, see *www.statistics.gov.uk/census2001*

25. The National Council of Hindu Temples (NCHT), founded in 1978, is an umbrella body of about 90 temples across Britain.

26. Vertovec, Steven (2000) *The Hindu Diaspora: Comparative Patterns*, p.88 (London and New York: RoutledgeCurzon).

27. Nye, Malory (June 1996) Hare Krishna and Sanatan Dharma in Britain: The Campaign to save Bhaktivedanta Manor, *ISKCON Communications Journal* 4 (1), *http://www.iskcon.com/icj/4_1/nye.html*

28. Nye, Malory (1997) ISKCON and Hindus in Britain: Some Thoughts on a Developing Relationship, *ISKCON Communications Journal* 5 (2)*http://www.iskcon.com/icj/5_2/5_2nye.html*

29. Ibid.

30. Nye, Malory (June 1996) Hare Krishna and Sanatan Dharma in Britain: The Campaign to save Bhaktivedanta Manor, *ISKCON Communications Journal* 4 (1), *http://www.iskcon.com/icj/4_1/nye.html*

31. Recorded in an interview conducted by the author in March 2004.

32. Bhaktivedanta Manor Foundation (1996) *Victory for Bhaktivedanta Manor – The Completion of an Historic Campaign* (Watford: New Direction).

33. The quotation is taken from a speech delivered by Annutama Dasa in April 1998 at the Conference on Religious Freedom and the New Millennium in Washington; for further details, see *http://www.religiousfreedom.com*

34. Das, Rasamandala (2002) *Heart of Hinduism: A Comprehensive Guide for Teachers and Other Professionals* (Aldenham: ISKCON Educational Services).

35. This statistic was given by Kripamoya Das in April 2004 (personal communication).

36.   Knott, Kim (1986) *My Sweet Lord: The Hare Krishna Movement*, p.19 (Wellingborough: Aquarian Press).

37.   Recorded during an interview conducted by the author in April 2004.

38.   Ibid.

Chapter 3

1.   It is important to recognise that these values may not have found deliberate expression but were implicit within ISKCON culture.

2.   The author joined the Society in 1973 and to him and his colleagues it was unthinkable – practically inconceivable – that ISKCON could do anything but expand quite perceivably.

3.   The term "congregational member" does not automatically imply that such a devotee is of lower spiritual standing than a "core member." This misunderstanding may be at the root of some of ISKCON's problems, particularly regarding its system of validation and reward. The use of geographical situation as a means of demonstrating spiritual status is obviously subject to flaw. Nevertheless, it seems that all except the most spiritually advanced devotees need the support of external indicators of a person's status. In the "Vedic" model, these include locational pointers (i.e. the temple in the centre surrounded by the *brahmans*, then the *kshatriya* class and so on). What becomes evident from analysis is that ISKCON has placed the temple as central but that also under this nomenclature fall aspects of ISKCON which are far from exemplary (as they need to be in such a central position). This includes trainees whose status is actually only tentative and should be recognised as such (as in our proposed model for phase three). This problem could also be addressed by establishing a more assertive enrolment policy.

4.   The Asian Hindu community may have been considered significant in terms of making Life Members and raising funds. Still, its contributions may not always have received appropriate appreciation from the more austere temple residents.

5.   Meaning, more or less, outside of the ISKCON temple.

6.   Conversely, it may be argued that the structural development of ISKCON was the symptom of such a world view. I would suggest that both statements are true –the cause and effect being somewhat interchangeable.

7.   Devotees now realise that the Hare Krishna movement extends well beyond the temple (though the special role of the temple is not to be under-estimated).

8.   I am not suggesting there is no truth in the authorised statements, which ostensibly underpin certain dualistic attitudes in ISKCON, the devotee/demon opposition being an example of this. What I wish constructively to confront is our understanding and application of such principles. Ravindra Svarupa Dasa (1994) has written: "What I now know is that the line that separates the godly from the ungodly is not congruent with the line dividing ISKCON from non-ISKCON."

9.   This chapter is not a criticism of the Society. The phases through which the Society has passed, and the associated phenomena, are natural and certainly not exclusive to ISKCON (even though it has its unique features). The Society cannot be legitimately

blamed for its immaturity and concomitant shortcomings, but it does have the responsibility to learn from them and move forward. What is more, whilst the value systems of the past were, with hindsight, somewhat naive they were also highly effective (and perhaps absolutely necessary) in laying down roots for the future.

10. The reader may also consider whether or not devotees imported certain values from their previous lives, i.e. from their social, familial or religious backgrounds.

11. Again the author does not dispute the Gaudiya Vaishnava theology which extols the virtues of unmotivated and uninterrupted devotional service. Nevertheless, he poses the question, "How can ISKCON best operate to evoke these natural tendencies from its members"?

12. The author joined ISKCON in 1973.

13. The author does not intend to question the value of learning to depend on Krishna. Nevertheless, the reader may consider (a) whether or not this precludes making plans ourselves and (b) in the case of it being inappropriate to consider one's personal future (as may be the case in the student stage of life) whether or not devotee leaders should be concerned for the future of their charges and thus make the appropriate arrangements.

14. For an excellent study of these topics, and indeed the whole development of ISKCON, the reader may consult Ravindra Svarupa Dasa (1994).

15. With usually nothing but the best intentions.

16. Beginning in the UK in March 1982.

17. The author suggests that the tension between liberality and purity is central to ISKCON's development. The synthesis of these apparently conflicting needs obviously cannot be achieved through the phase one model (where the only acceptable means of socialisation was living in the temple and getting a new name). Rather, it requires the definition of a progressive hierarchy of standards applicable to the respective sections of membership. For more information on this subject, the reader may consult Ravindra Svarupa Dasa (1994).

18. "United Kingdom Life Membership", a term now out of date.

19. Fading out was usually due to sensual weakness and/or difficulties relating to the devotees within Section A. (It is highly significant that very few of these devotees abandoned their belief in the theology of Krishna Consciousness. This points to the need for support beyond merely exhorting purity from the *vyasasana*). Although such devotees usually kept some regular connection with ISKCON (unlike many of the "blooped" devotees of the 1970s) there was often considerable unease and uncertainty with regard to their relationship with temple residents.

20. There are many issues to be addressed here, not least the fact that the marriage *samskara* has been viewed as a "fall-down." As a young *brahmachari* the author was recommended completely to avoid an ISKCON wedding ceremony, described to him as "a funeral." The reader may consider whether or not ISKCON has somewhat confused the *brahmachari ashram* with the fourth stage of life (specifically in respect of the values and attitudes it should impart). The reader may also consult and consider *Bhagavad Gita* (chapter 2 verse 40) and the Bengali proverb, *ghute pore*

gobarhase: "When the dry cow dung is burning in the fire, the soft cow dung laughs" (Rohininandana 1990).

21. One of the greatest difficulties, the author suggests, is with devotees who become (prematurely) intimate with the Society and then fall away. Even if their behaviour is on par with that of a *nama hatta* member, the lapsed "temple devotee" is viewed with greater suspicion and given less validation. One possible solution is to be more selective about who is eligible for residential training and to initially discourage involvement demanding a high degree of renunciation. In other words, spiritual progress and the recognition of this, should as far as possible be steady, and continuous throughout one's life. "Going retrograde" should be avoided, both in real terms and in respect of perceived spiritual progress.

22. The reader may find interest in studying ISKCON's system of validation. What do we reward in our devotees? The ability to produce short-term results or commitment to a lifetime in Krishna Consciousness? Willingness to conform or ability to demonstrate initiative (within clearly communicated standards)? Does the Society's system of validation promote on-going spiritual development or the shooting-star phenomenon? Furthermore, is our system of validation commensurate with the values endorsed by scripture, or is it a reaction to circumstances?

23. Purity is not ensured by trying to bring everyone to the highest platform immediately but by "filtering out" those who cannot and validating their interaction with the Society at the appropriate level.

24. The VTE (Vaishnava Training and Education) recommends that for managers, ministers and priests this lasts for a minimum of five years. Bhaktivedanta Manor already has structured training courses for the first three years of residential studies.

25. Srila Prabhupada, in *Srimad Bhagavatam* (1.9.26, purport), writes: "The *brahmacari ashram* is especially meant for training both the attached and the detached."

26. Increasingly this will occur from the congregation, i.e. those who have had some defined interaction with the Society.

27. The author suggests that this category will feature an important sub-group consisting of lay-preachers. In fact, the training and education department at Bhaktivedanta Manor has already organised training seminars for leaders and teachers from within *nama hatta* groups.

28. Hence the amendment at this stage to our definition of "core membership."

29. Traditionally, one of the duties of the *grihastha* is to generate wealth and to support members of the other three *ashrams*. Significant to ISKCON's development has been the temple's dependence on students for fund-raising and the lack of financial support from householders (for various reasons which, the author suggests, are worthy of further exploration). In this connection, the VTE (1994) has written: "Householders who value their training are more likely to voluntarily contribute towards the Society, freeing students from the debilitating constraints of fund-raising." It also adds: "If our Society is to flourish, its members must give esteem to the *grihastha ashram*." This latter statement points towards the need for mutual appreciation between the student and householder *ashrams* and for the necessity of developing appropriate values and attitudes within trainees.

30. The author has used this term somewhat loosely to refer either to self-contained rural communities or to householders integrated within the broader society.
31. What is evident here is the need for individualisation. Rather than debating the merits of the different *ashrams* and trying to establish a single set of standards according to our personal preference, there can be different emphases for different students, at least at a more mature stage of training.
32. For example, the VTE in Europe and Bhaktivedanta Manor in England. Though the author has no detailed information, he has heard of similarly successful projects in Mumbai and South Africa.
33. The author suggests that both these are essential. Even if emphasis is given to congregational expansion, as some devotees propose, this gives rise to the need for highly trained "ministers." Such training is perhaps best organised through residential courses.
34. The reader may have had the experience of attending a meeting and formulating an excellent plan of action, only to be balked by the task of identifying the people with the necessary skills to fill the newly-created posts.
35. Figures derived from the author's personal calculations whilst living and working in the ISKCON community in the UK.

Baumann, G. (1996) *Contesting Culture: Discourses of Identity in Multi-Ethnic London* (Cambridge: Cambridge University Press).

Carey, S. (1987) The Indianisation of the Hare Krishna Movement in Britain, in R. Burghart (Ed.), *Hinduism in Great Britain: the Perpetuation of Religion in an Alien Cultural Milieu* (London: Tavistock).

Dasa, Ravindra Svarupa (1994) Clearing House and Cleaning Hearts: Reform and Renewal in ISKCON – Part One, *ISKCON Communications Journal* 3.

Das, Rasamamdala (1997) Towards Principle and Values: An Analysis of Educational Philosophy and Practice within ISKCON, *ISKCON Communications Journal* 5 (2).

Dasa, Rohininandana (1990) *Vaishnava Verse Book* (Los Angeles: Bhaktivedanta Book Trust).

Davies, S. (1997) Education and ISKCON: Some Reflections from an Interested Observer, *ISKCON Communications Journal* 5 (1).

Prabhupada, A. C. Bhaktivedanta Swami (1985) *Srimad Bhagavatam* 12 cantos (Los Angeles: Bhaktivedanta Book Trust).

Prabhupada, A. C. Bhaktivedanta Swami (1986) *Bhagavad Gita As It Is* (Los Angeles: Bhaktivedanta Book Trust).

Vaishnava Training and Education (1994)*The Vaishnava Training and Education Syllabus for Stage One* (Oxford: Vaishnava Training & Education).

Vaishnava Training and Education (2002) *Leadership and Management Course* (Oxford: Vaishnava Training & Education).

Vaishnava Training and Education (2005) *Grihastha Training Course* (Oxford: Vaishnava Training & Education).

Chapter 4

1.   I wish to thank all the devotees at Bhaktivedanta Manor who provided much help and information, which made the research I carried out possible. Devotees to whom I am especially grateful include Radha Mohan Das, Shalini Amrit, Jaya Krishna Dasa, Bimal Krishna Das, Bhakti Mati Devi Dasi, Bhakta Craig, Damayanti Devi Dasi, Vaikuntha Krishna Das, and Indriyesya Das. I would like to acknowledge the tremendous assistance and help of Radha Mohan Das in particular. He facilitated my research at the Manor in a variety of crucial ways, giving up much of his time in order to ensure I had access to much valuable computer software and library materials, as well as providing me with key ISKCON publications and arranging important introductions to the Manor's devotees. Radha Mohan Das equally provided valuable comments on an earlier version of this chapter. For all this and for much more besides, I am most grateful to him. For other helpful comments on an earlier version of this chapter I also wish to thank Anna King at the Centre for the Study of Theology and Religion, University of Winchester. Finally, as much of this chapter was originally published in the *Journal of Beliefs and Values* (see, *http://www.tandf.co.uk*), I am grateful to the editors and publishers of the journal for their permission to draw from this work.

2.   Draupadi Devi Dasi and Brajisma Das are two devotees based in Malaga, Spain who are currently researching the phenomenon. The prospective title given to their forthcoming work on dreams, entitled *Prabhupada Now*, which indeed seems most apt, is awaited with interest. Yet another ISKCON devotee, Ananta Shakti Das, also offers some valuable accounts of dreams of Prabhupada in the May/June 2004 issue of the *Vaishnava Connection*, an independent newsletter of the ISKCON UK community.

3.   I have chosen not to use pseudonyms for the cases discussed in this chapter. This is because respondents, not only stated they had no objections to their own names actually being used, but also because some of them told me they were happy to be associated with the research, especially if it helped to promote greater understanding of devotional life in the Hare Krishna movement as well as augment understanding of Prabhupada's on-going centrality to it.

4.   The celibacy rule was often said by *brahmachari* informants at Bhaktivedanta Manor to be the most difficult one to maintain, with temptation to break the rule being an ever-abiding difficulty.

Berger, P. and T. Luckmann (1967) *The Social Construction of Reality* (Harmondsworth: Penguin).

Bowman, M. (1992) Phenomenology, Fieldwork and Folk Religion, *Occasional Papers*, pp.1-21, British Association for the Study of Religions.

Brockington, J. (1991) *The Sacred Thread: Hinduism in its Continuity and Diversity* (Edinburgh: Edinburgh University Press).

Bryant, E.F. and Ekstand, M.L. (2004) (Eds.) *The Hare Krishna Movement: The Postcharismatic fate of a Religious Transplant* (New York: Columbia University Press).

Das, Ananta Shakti (2004) Dreaming of Prabhupada, *Vaishnava Connection* 7 (4): 8-9.

Dasa, Drutakarma (2002) Gurus, Disciples, Initiations, and Karma: What Srila Prabhupada Taught, in Drutakarma Dasa (Ed.), *Plain Vanilla: Selected Essays*, pp.7-19 (Delhi: Lal).

Dasa, Ravindra Svarupa (2004) Cleaning House and Cleaning Hearts: Reform and Renewal in E.F. Bryant and M.L. Ekstrand (Eds.), *The Hare Krishna Movement: The Postcharismatic fate of a Religious Transplant*, pp.149-69 (New York: Columbia University Press).

Dwyer, G. (2003) *The Divine and the Demonic: Supernatural Affliction and its Treatment in North India* (London and New York: RoutledgeCurzon).

Gelberg, S.J. (Subhananda Dasa) (1985) ISKCON after Prabhupada, *ISKCON Review* 1 (1): 7-14.

Goswami, Satsvarupa Dasa (1993 [1980]) *Srila Prabhupada-Lilamrta*, 6 vols. (Los Angeles: Bhaktivedanta Book Trust).

Goswami, Tamal Krishna (1997) The Perils of Succession: Heresies of Authority and Continuity in the Hare Krishna Movement, *ISKCON Communications Journal* 5 (1): 10-27.

Husserl, E. (1964) *The Idea of Phenomenology*, trans. W.P. Alston and G. Nakhnikian (The Hague: Nijhoff).

Husserl, E. (1967) *Cartesian Meditations*, trans. D. Cairns (The Hague: Nijhoff).

Freud, S. (1998 [1900]) *The Interpretation of Dreams*, trans. J. Strachey (New York: Avon Books).

Knott, K. (1986) *My Sweet Lord: The Hare Krishna Movement* (Wellingborough: Aquarian Press).

Knott, K. (1997) Insider and Outsider Perceptions of Prabhupada, *ISKCON Communications Journal* 5 (1): 1-11.

Krishnapada, Swami (1996) *Spiritual Warrior: Uncovering Spiritual Truths in Psychic Phenomena* (Largo: Hari-Nama Press).

Muster, N.J. (1997) *Betrayal of the Spirit: My Life behind the Headlines of the Hare Krishna Movement* (Chicago: University of Illinois).

Prabhupada, A.C. Bhaktivedanta Swami (1972-80) *Srimad Bhagavatam* 12 cantos (New York, Los Angeles: Bhaktivedanta Book Trust).

Rochford, E.B. Jr (1985) *Hare Krishna in America* (New Brunswick: Rutgers University Press).

Schutz, A. (1967) *Collected Papers* 1. Edited by M. Natanson (The Hague: Nijhoff).

Schutz, A. (1970) *On Phenomenology and Social Relations.* Edited by H.R. Wagner (Chicago: University of Chicago Press).

Shinn, L.D. (1987) *The Dark Lord: Cult Images and the Hare Krishnas in America* (Philadelphia: Westminster Press).

Shinn, L.D. (1996) Reflections on Spiritual Leadership: The Legacy of Srila Prabhupada, *ISKCON Communications Journal* 4 (2): 1-4.

Swami, Jayananda (2002a) Where the Rtvik People are Wrong, in Drutakarma Dasa (Ed.), *Plain Vanilla: Selected Essays*, pp.37-70 (Delhi: Lal).

Swami, Jayananda (2002b) Where the Rtvik People are Wrong Again, in Drutakarma Dasa (Ed.), *Plain Vanilla: Selected Essays*, pp. 71-98 (Delhi: Lal).

Swami, Jayananda (2002c) "Plain Vanilla" Made Plainer, in Drutakarma Dasa (Ed.), *Plain Vanilla: Selected Essays*, pp. 99-107 (Delhi: Lal).

Chapter 5

1.   I wish to thank all the devotees at Bhaktivedanta Manor who facilitated my research. Radha Mohan Das' comments on an earlier draft of this chapter have been especially valuable. For these comments and for much more besides, I am grateful to him. For other helpful comments on an earlier version of the chapter I would like to thank Anna King at the Centre for the Study of Theology and Religion, University of Winchester. I also wish to thank the editors and publishers of the *Journal of Beliefs and Values* (see, *http://www.tandf.co.uk*) for their permission to reproduce here earlier work of mine originally published in the journal.

2.   Radha Mohan's own understanding of how the images or phenomena of dreams are anchored in the actualities of the lived-in world was pertinently illustrated by him during one interview in which my informant discussed the image of a golden mountain and other similar fantastic images. He stated that when one dreams of such an object one simply conjoins in the dream the idea of mountain and the idea of gold, each of which the dreamer has encountered or seen in the actual experience of wakefulness. And to elaborate the point further, he mentioned a relevant extract in the writings of Bhaktivedanta Swami Prabhupada: "We have seen gold, and we have also seen a mountain, so in a dream we can see a golden mountain by combining the two ideas" (Prabhupada 2002 [1970], p.12). The quotation concerning dreams in fact also captures much of the essence of what Sartre has written about regarding the nature of the imaginary consciousness (see Sartre 2001, p.156 and *passim*). However, it must equally be pointed out that, although there seems to be agreement between ISKCON and Sartre here, it would be incorrect to see the two positions as entirely identical (and Prabhupada himself has offered some criticism of Sartre's existentialism, criticism targeted particularly at Sartre's atheistic stance [see Bhaktipada *et al.* 1985, pp.478-89]). As Radha Mohan insisted during interviews with him, because in ISKCON divine beings are understood to have existence independent of the human world or the world of ordinary human experience, it is quite erroneous to treat dreams of deities simply in epiphenomenal terms; that is to say, while such dreams in one sense may be said to have an anchor in the lived-in world, the appearance of divine entities in dreams cause the dreamer not merely to have experience of that which lies beyond this world but also to have experience of that which is fundamentally irreducible and which can never be grasped in terms of the actualities of everyday life.

Bhaktipada, K.S. *et al* (1985) *Dialectic Spiritualism: A Vedic View of Western Philosophy* (Moundsville: Prabhupada Books).

Brockington, J. (1991) *The Sacred Thread: Hinduism in its Continuity and Diversity* (Edinburgh: Edinburgh University Press).

Castaneda, C. (1993 [1931]) *The Art of Dreaming* (London: Aquarian Thorsons).

Dufrenne, M. (1973) *The Phenomenology of Aesthetic Experience* (Evanston: Illinois, North Western University).

Dwyer, G. (2003) *The Divine and the Demonic: Supernatural Affliction and its Treatment in North India* (London and New York: RoutledgeCurzon).

Freud, S. (1998 [1900]) *The Interpretation of Dreams*, trans. J. Strachey (New York: Avon Books).

Husserl, E. (1970) *The Crisis of European Sciences and Transcendental Phenomenology: An Introduction to Phenomenological Philosophy*, trans. D. Carr (Evanston, Illinois: North Western University).

Jung, C.G. (1978) *Man and His Symbols* (London: Picador).

Jung, C.G. (1979 [1961]) Symbols and the Interpretation of Dreams, in *The Collected Works*, part 2, vol. 18. Edited by H. Read, M. Fordham and G. Adler, trans. from German by R.F.C. Hull (London: Routledge).

Jung, C.G. (1995 [1938]) *Dream Analysis, Parts 1 and 2: Notes of the Seminar given in 1928-1930 by C. G. Jung*. Edited by W. McGuire (London: Routledge).

Kapferer, B. (1997) *The Feast of the Sorcerer: Practices of Consciousness and Power* (Chicago: University of Chicago Press).

Kilborne, B. (1987) Dreams, in M. Eliade (Ed.), *The Encyclopedia of Religion*, 4, pp. 482-92 (London and New York: Collier Macmillan).

Knott, K. (1986) *My Sweet Lord: The Hare Krishna Movement* (Wellingborough: Aquarian Press).

Lalitavistara Sutra: The Voice of the Buddha, The Beauty of Compassion, vol. 1 (1983), trans. from French by G. Bays (Berkeley: Dharma Publishing).

Prabhupada, A.C. Bhaktivedanta Swami (1982 [1970]) *The Nectar of Devotion: The Complete Science of Bhakti Yoga* (New York: Bhaktivedanta Book Trust).

Prabhupada, A.C. Bhaktivedanta Swami (2002 [1970]) *Krsna: The Supreme Personality of Godhead* (New York: Bhaktivedanta Book Trust).

Sartre, J-P. (2001 [1940]) *The Psychology of the Imagination* (London: Routledge).

Scruton, R. (1995) *A Short History of Modern Philosophy: From Descartres to Wittgenstein* (London and New York: Routledge).

Warnock, M. (2001) Introduction in J-P. Sartre *The Psychology of the Imagination*, pp.ix-xvii (London: Routledge).

Chapter 6

1. *Markine Bhagavata-dharma*/Preaching *Bhagavata-dharma* in America, in Prabhupada, A.C. Bhaktivedanta Swami (1991) *Songs of the Vaisnava Acaryas: Hymns and Mantras for the Glorification of Radha and Krsna*, p.29 (Los Angeles: The Bhaktivedanta Book Trust, 1991). All materials cited from Bhaktivedanta Book Trust publications are also accessible in *The Bhaktivedanta VedaBase*, the searchable database published by the Bhaktivedanta Archives, Sandy Ridge, NC, *www.prabhupada.com*

2. See World Pacifist and the *Bhagwat Gita*. Meeting with the Governor of Bihar, in *The Bhaktivedanta VedaBase*. An archivist at the Bhaktivedanta Archives described the work as a "typescript carbon with handwritten marginal corrections." It is undated. Since Prabhupada gives his name in the report as Abhay Charanarvindo

Bhaktivedanta, without the title of Swami, it would have been written before 1959, the year he took *sannyasa* initiation.

3.   Prabhupada, A.C. Bhaktivedanta Swami (1962) *Srimad Bhagavatam.* First Part, p.i (Vrindavan and Delhi: The League of Devotees). When the first three volumes were later republished in America, devotees under Prabhupada's direction edited them to conform to standard American usage. This improvement had the downside of breaking up the characteristic rhythm of Prabhupada's writing, his long rhetorical periods, which weakened some of the power of his original voice.

4.   All quotations from Prabhupada's letters, recorded lectures, and recorded conversations are from *The Bhaktivedanta VedaBase.*

5.   See Prabhupada, A.C. Bhaktivedanta Swami (1988) *Srimad Bhagavatam: With the Original Sanskrit Text, Its Roman Transliteration, Synonyms, Translation and Elaborate Purports*, 12 cantos (Los Angeles: The Bhaktivedanta Book Trust). The same publication can also be found in digital form in *The Bhaktivedanta VedaBase.*

6.   The sonnet "O Friend! I know not which way I must look" (1807).

7.   Prabhupada, A.C. Bhaktivedanta Swami (1982 [1970]) *The Nectar of Devotion: The Complete Science of Bhakti-Yoga*, p.115 (Los Angeles: The Bhaktivedanta Book Trust).

8.   Dasa, Hari Sari (1992) *A Transcendental Diary: Travels with his Divine Grace A.C. Bhaktivedanta Swami Prabhupada*, vol. 1, November 1975-April 1976, pp.415-6 (San Diego, CA: HS Books, 1992). This work is also in *The Bhaktivedanta VedaBase.*

9.   Ibid. pp.423-4.

10.   Prabhupada, A.C. Bhaktivedanta Swami (1973) *Elevation to Krsna Consciousness*, p.87 (Los Angeles: The Bhaktivedanta Book Trust). Also see, *The Bhaktivedanta VedaBase.*

11.   For a recent compendium of ISKCON's woes, see Edwin F. Bryant and Maria L. Ekstrand (2004) (Eds.) *The Hare Krishna Movement: The Postcharismatic Fate of a Religious Transplant* (New York: Columbia University Press).

Chapter 7

1.   For the purpose of this essay I will refer to ISKCON's teachings as "Vedic", which is how Srila Prabhupada defined them. I do, however, recognise that many modern scholars do not consider the *Bhagavad Gita* and the *Puranas* to be Vedic texts.

2.   Prabhupada, A.C. Bhaktivedanta Swami (1989) *Srimad Bhagavatam* 1.5.11. (Los Angeles: Bhaktivedanta Book Trust). This of course is a peaceful, bloodless revolution that aims to change our worldview rather than our political affiliations.

3.   Ibid. 1.2.1

4.   From a poem that Prabhupada wrote while on board the ship Jaladuta, at the Commonwealth Pier, Boston, Massachusetts, 18 September 1965 – the day he arrived in America. See, Satsvarupa Dasa Goswami (1993 [1980]) *Srila Prabhupada Lilamrita* (Los Angeles: Bhaktivedanta Book Trust).

5.   For these articles authored by Prabhupada see, *Back to Godhead* 1, part 2 (1944), 1, part 8 (1952), and 3, part 4 (1956). *Back to Godhead* is the magazine of ISKCON that Prabhupada started in 1944. From reading these and other similar articles, of which there were many, it is plain that Prabhupada was a man very much in touch with the

issues of his day, which he never hesitated to address, offering his Krishna Consciousness solutions.

6. *Srimad Bhagavatam* 1.17.38.

7. *Srimad Bhagavatam* 10.2.34. For Prabhupada, human society was only human in truth if it was spiritually progressive, and in his and indeed the Vedic view this began with the institution of *varnashramadharma*.

8. *Srimad Bhagavatam* 5.19.19.

9. From these descriptions, and from reading statements such as the previous one quoted and many others like it, one might wonder if ISKCON has political ambitions to become leaders of government. This could perhaps be the subject of a whole study by itself, especially as there is not at present any clear consensus on this even within ISKCON. Some statements made by Prabhupada might seem to support such a view, but overall he indicated that ISKCON should primarily be *bramin*ical, and that *brahmans* were not usually administrators of the state; rather they were spiritual advisors. Again, as stated above, ISKCON seeks a spiritual revolution rather than a political one, in which society's values change and along with that will come all other changes, including the leadership.

10. *Srimad Bhagavatam* 1.1.11. Prabhupada made a number of statements along these lines, but these are offset by many more in which he clearly called for the establishment of a *varnashrama* society, beginning in ISKCON itself. His point here is that it is not possible perfectly to institute *varnashrama*, with all the traditional duties and their many regulations, but certainly he wanted at least the basic framework. (*Kali-yuga* is the current age in which we live, as defined in Vedic chronology. It is considered to be a dark age, filled with quarrel and hypocrisy.)

11. *Srimad Bhagavatam* 4.14.20.

12. Conversation between Prabhupada and Lieutenant Mozee, 5 July 1975, Chicago, in Prabhupada, A.C. Bhaktivedanta Swami (1983) *The Science of Self-Realisation* (Los Angeles: Bhaktivedanta Book Trust).

13. Conversation between Prabhupada and Mayor Evanston, 4 July 1975, Chicago, in Prabhupada, A.C. Bhaktivedanta Swami (1983) *The Science of Self-Realisation* (Los Angeles: Bhaktivedanta Book Trust). Although unsuccessful on this occasion in convincing the Mayor, Prabhupada could be very persuasive in these discussions. His disciple Mukunda Goswami, a member of ISKCON's Governing Body, reports that after meeting with Prabhupada on one occasion, Senator Jackie Vaughan of Michigan said: "I am completely convinced that this is not simply theoretical and that this movement can solve all problems of life."

14. *Srimad Bhagavatam* 1.16.6. The theological idea here is that everything is ultimately the divine energy of God, but when it is used for non-godly purposes it loses its divine nature and becomes mundane. However, when it is again used in God's service it is once more connected with him and therefore "regains" its spiritual nature.

15. Prabhupada letter to Caru, Bombay 9 May 1974, in Anon. (1987) *Letters From Srila Prabhupada* (Culver City: The Vaishnava Institute).

16. Das, Kurma (2001) *The Great Transcendental Adventure* (Melbourne: Kurma Books).

17. *Srimad Bhagavatam* 1.17.5. "Twice-born" refers to spiritual initiation, considered to be a second birth in Vedic circles. In *varnashrama* society this second birth takes place for *brahmans*, *kshatriyas* and *vaishyas*. Only the *shudra* or working class do not receive this initiation.

18. *Srimad Bhagavatam* 1.7.37.

19. Goswami, Satsvarupa Dasa (1993) *Prabhupada Lilamrita* (Los Angeles: Bhaktivedanta Book Trust). It should be understood that when Prabhupada referred to *brahmans* he did not mean a hereditary class, i.e. *brahman* by birth. Rather he meant actually qualified *brahmans* as defined in Vedic texts, i.e. clean, sense-controlled, truthful, tolerant, wise, etc.

20. Prabhupada Lecture, Hyderabad, 23 November 1972, in Anon. (2003) *The Complete Teachings of A.C. Bhaktivedanta Swami Prabhupada* (Sandy Ridge, North Carolina: Bhaktivedanta Archives).

21. See, Wonderful Prasadam, in *Back to Godhead* 30 (3) (2000) (Los Angeles: Bhaktivedanta Book Trust). The story is told of how Prabhupada, when in Calcutta, was watching a group of hungry children sifting through a rubbish pile, looking for food. Moved by compassion he then said that within ten miles of all ISKCON temples no one should go hungry. See also, The Maha Mantra Research Project, in *Back to Godhead* 34 (1) (2000), an article in which mention is made of the "modes" of ignorance, passion and goodness and how Vedic knowledge describes the influence of material nature on the soul. These three modes combine together in various permutations to produce many kinds of behaviour, with of course pure goodness being the best. Vedic teachings say that chanting God's names gradually elevates one to pure goodness, and thence to transcendence.

22. Das, Dhira Govinda (1990) *A Second Chance* (Los Angeles: Bhaktivedanta Book Trust).

23. See, A Life of Purity and Purpose, in *Back to Godhead* 13 (8) (1978). ISKCON members, of course, take a vow to abstain from all forms of intoxication when they receive initiation from a spiritual master. The other vows are to abstain from illicit (extra marital) sex, gambling and meat-eating.

24. *Back to Godhead* 15 (3) (1980).

25. See, Prospectus for the League of Devotees, written by Prabhupada in 1962. Prabhupada originally set up this organisation in India in 1953, but it never found the same success as ISKCON.

26. Prabhupada, A.C. Bhaktivedanta Swami (1983) *The Science of Self-Realisation* (Los Angeles: Bhaktivedanta Book Trust). Prabhupada wanted his disciples to "go everywhere" and issue challenges to modern scientists to prove their claims that life is a material product. "Bring some chemicals and restore a dead man to life."

27. *Back to Godhead* 14 (2) (1979).

28. The Seven Purposes of ISKCON, adopted at the Society's incorporation in New York, July 1966.

29. Prabhupada Conversation, 5 July 1975, Chicago, in Anon. (2003) *The Complete Teachings of A.C. Bhaktivedanta Swami Prabhupada* (Sandy Ridge, North Carolina: Bhaktivedanta Archives).

30. *Srimad Bhagavatam* 1.8.40.

31. Prabhupada Conversation, 27 May 1974, in Anon. (2003) *The Complete Teachings of A.C. Bhaktivedanta Swami Prabhupada* (Sandy Ridge, North Carolina: Bhaktivedanta Archives). A key tenet of ISKCON's teachings is: "Simple living, high thinking", which means keeping life's necessities to a minimum so that one's time can be maximised for spiritual practices. The "taste" or happiness derived from those practices is said by Vedic knowledge to more than adequately compensate for any restriction of sensual pleasures. Prabhupada wanted this to be demonstrated on ISKCON projects and there are now some 50 ISKCON communities around the world working toward this end.

32. Prabhupada Conversation, 11 January 1977, in Anon. (2003) *The Complete Teachings of A.C. Bhaktivedanta Swami Prabhupada* (Sandy Ridge, North Carolina: Bhaktivedanta Archives). It is certainly a major challenge to show that, rather than making advancement, human society is currently going backwards. But again, it is a question of values. Vedic teachings consider a society to be progressive when it is advancing in spiritual principles and values, not in materialism.

33. Prabhupada Conversation, 15 Marchm 1974, in Anon. (2003) *The Complete Teachings of A.C. Bhaktivedanta Swami Prabhupada* (Sandy Ridge, North Carolina: Bhaktivedanta Archives). Prabhupada often spoke of unemployment being caused by industrialisation, and how it meant that a few men enjoyed at the expense of many. He would speak of the Vedic alternative as "spiritual communism", with God at the centre rather than "Marx or Lenin."

Chapter 8

1. Authorised texts claim that by worshipping Krishna one gains the full benefit of worshipping demi-gods, performing *shraddha* and *tarpana* for the ancestors, austerities, penances (*prayaschitta*), sacrifices, *homas*, charity, vows, etc. Wealth should only be used for the service of Krishna and His devotees. However, many devotees say that it *is* permissible to worship Ganesh and other *devtas* at a lower level provided that one acknowledges Krishna as Supreme Godhead. *Puja is* offered to Ganesh in ISKCON *samskaras*.

2. See, for example, the 2004 ISKCON Communications UK booklet entitled *ISKCON and Interfaith: ISKCON in Relation to People with Faith in God*, Oxford. Moreover, the 2004 World Parliament of Religions was held in Barcelona, Spain. As in previous years, and following an increasing appreciation of the need for inter-religious dialogue, there were a number of ISKCON members present and involved in various presentations. Shaunaka Rishi Dasa, Executive Director of the Oxford Centre for Hindu Studies, is an executive member of the Northern Ireland Interfaith Forum, based in Belfast. See also Saunaka Rsi Dasa 1999.

3. What is of value in this chapter is due entirely to the kindness of friends and devotees met at Bhaktivedanta Manor, the Soho Temple and Govinda's Restaurant and the Centre for Hindu Studies in Oxford. I also draw from Prabhupada's translations and commentaries, liturgical texts and the writings of and conversations

with colleagues and devotees. I acknowledge with gratitude the advice, wisdom and encouragement of Kripamoya Das, Shaunaka Rishi Dasa, Dr Kenneth Valpey (Krishna Kshetra Dasa), Indriyesha Das, Rasamandala Das, Radha Mohan Das and Dr Graham Dwyer.

4.   Kripamoya Das notes (personal communication) that this tension mirrors the split in Sri Vaishnavism between the Tenkalais and the Vatakalais. The *vatakalai* emphasised the Sanskrit scriptures and salvation through traditional *bhakti-yoga*, that is devotion to the temple icon, while the *tenkalai* emphasised the Tamil scriptures and surrender to the Lord by his grace (cf. Flood 1996, p.137).

5.   Prabhupada writes that Sukadeva Goswami teaches in the *Srimad Bhagavatam* that "what was achieved in the Satya-yuga by this meditational process (*yoga*), and in the following *yuga*, the Treta-yuga, by the offering of great sacrifices, and in the next *yuga*, the Dvapara-yuga, by temple worship, would be achieved at the present time, in this Kali-yuga, by simply chanting the names of God, *hari-kirtana*, Hare Krsna."

6.   Prabhupada (1997, p.11) adds that Chaitanya taught that in Kali Yuga all *yajnas* (sacrifices) are forbidden because they are useless attempts by foolish men. Devotional service is the highest goal of human life.

7.   A typical example of devoted service is reported in the Bhaktivedanta newsletter (2003-4, p.5). It declares that, "Mother Kulangana, a senior disciple of Srila Prabhupada, has been making Mangal-arati sweets at the Manor for over 16 years. A selfless servant of Radha Gokulananda, she is always absorbed in cooking and caring for their Lordships."

8.   On one visit to Govinda's Restaurant on 19 September 2004, a devotee passed me balancing several *thalis* and a water jug, she smilingly murmured: "Cleaning, cleaning, cleaning. We are always cleaning."

9.   "Janmashtami was celebrated in the House of Commons with over 333 political leaders and representatives from the Hindu community on 7 September. Hosted by Tony McMulty MP and Abhay Lakhani. The programme was supported by ISKCON and the National Council of Hindu Temples UK. The event was attended by Deputy Prime Minister John Prescott, MPs, Peers, the Indian High Commissioner, and London Mayor Ken Livingstone…It consisted of speeches, the swinging of a deity of baby Krishna, traditional dances, and *bhajans*" (*Bhaktivedanta Manor Newsletter*, October 2004). A British cover story (2004, p.1) features a BBC sponsored name-giving ceremony (involving fire sacrifice, accompanied by live *kirtana*) for a baby elephant at Whipsnade Zoo. There is also report of a devotional exercise (ibid. p.4) in February in which 6,000 trees and shrubs were planted around the estate. "James Clappison MP of Hertsmere with his family, and Hertsmere Mayor Eddie Roach, took part in an ancient Vedic ceremony of planting the first two trees. With *mantras* chanted by Romapada prabhu, the ceremony included the sprinkling of Vrindavan dust and the pouring of Ganges water." Other stories describe the ritual installation of deities, and festivals like Snana Yatra, the *abhishek* (bathing) of Sri Jagannath, Baladev and Subhadra dressed in elephant masks (*Hathi Vesha*), a festival which takes place before London Ratha Yatra. Diwali was attended by the Deputy Prime Minister and other MPs. Global events are also reported. For

example, the advent in Mayapur of Pancha-Tattva, Sri Chaitanya and his associates (February 2004) was celebrated internationally with detailed accounts of the two-day installation ceremony and huge fire sacrifice.

10.   Brockington (2004, p.40) notes that the Bhakti movement has always interacted with the learned orthodox tradition and made deliberate use of the sanctity and prestige of Sanskrit to establish its respectability.

11.   Shinn (1987, p.97) remarks that what began as a fairly simple and informal spiritual programme consisting of *kirtana, japa,* and altar worship has developed, over the years, into a much more evolved and regularised spiritual regimen. Shinn also notes that deity worship became standardised throughout ISKCON, with old Sanskrit religious texts becoming the foundation of the *arati* ceremony.

12.   Doktor (2002, p.31) suggests that a higher tension with the social environment produced by the early connection with the counterculture may have been diminished by a meticulousness in following prescribed rituals.

13.   Nesbitt describes ethnography as a "discipline of deep listening and close reflective observation" (2004, p.5). She also suggests that faith communities are only perceived as homogeneous and "different" by outsiders (ibid. p.2). Whereas to the outsider boundaries may appear solid, insiders are likely to see distinctions and differences. My research demonstrates that the insider may at one and the same time unconsciously present an idealised, textual or "orthodox" form of the religion, *and* emphasise the inevitable diversity of lived experience.

14.   Prabhupada gradually increased the level of ritual performance over the years, preparing his followers for higher degrees of ritual discipline. Some devotees (like Kripamoya Das) were attracted to Swami Prabhupada precisely because of his "authentic" Sanskritic scholarship and practice. Prabhupada attacked the *brahman* class who during the Moghul and British periods oppressed and exploited the poor by their rituals and superstitions, and who abandoned the lowest castes, leaving them bereft of spiritual guidance. As a result Hindus in their thousands converted to Islam or Christianity.

15.   The Soho temple is closed daily while devotees with buckets of water clean the floor and the prayer mats.

16.   This is in keeping with Prabhupada's teaching that knowing how to die is important. Only those remember Krishna or Narayana at the time of death will go back to Godhead.

17.   British Hindus (numbering 559,000 in the 2001 Census) have diverse patterns of settlement and differentiated regional, sectarian and caste traditions. Nevertheless, they are usually referred to by ISKCON as "the Hindu community."

18.   Leslie (2003, p.66) explores the fact that Hindus in Britain when they arrived were divided by ethnicity, caste, sect and, especially language.

19.   See *Bhaktivedanta Manor Newsletter* October 2004, 4 -5.

20.   Prabhupada himself argued that it is only out of ignorance that people worship the demi-gods as though they are God. Such worship is improper and should be avoided. Only Vaishnavism or *sanatana dharma* contains the whole truth (see Baird 1999, p.528 ff). While many Western devotees used the term "demi-god", none of

the Indian visitors or volunteers I spoke to did so spontaneously. One young professional explained that all gods were created by Krishna, but Shiva was in an anomalous position: neither a god nor a demi-god but somewhere between the two.

21.   The same literature claims that at any time there are up to 50 resident trainees drawn from all sections of British society, including the Gujarati community.

22.   Knott (1986, p.24) points out that in Britain the majority of Hindu temples established by the Indian community are dedicated to the worship of Lord Krishna.

23.   The growth of a prosperous middle class which is prepared to spend money on rituals is also significant. Major patrons and sponsors of ISKCON temples are now predominantly Asian.

24.   Youth ministers communicate through a network of youth databases, websites, newsletters, email groups, etc.; represent inter-generational needs and concerns at youth gatherings and leadership meetings; organise youth festivals, reunions, *harinama sankirtana* bus tours, gatherings, events; educate and train youth ministers, temple presidents, and ISKCON leaders in the art of reaching out to, guiding, engaging, and integrating youth; develop and implement ISKCON Youth Minister Training Courses worldwide; produce books, brochures, and websites to assist current and future youth ministry work in ISKCON.

25.   It has often been pointed out that the term "Governing Body Commission" (GBC) was in fact the name of the governing board of the British-established Indian railways (Ravindra Svarupa Dasa 1999, p.10; Flood 1995, p.13).

26.   *All* Prabhupada's writings reflect the scriptural understanding of the *varnashramadharma* system as divinely established. Krishna states in the *Bhagavad Gita* (4.13) that this ordering is generated by God, in such a way that each person is naturally disposed toward a particular category by virtue of *guna* (the controlling mode of nature) and *karma* (specialised activity and means of livelihood).

27.   Prabhupada's goal is a socially harmonious order in which people follow differentiated but equally valued occupations. He wanted his disciples to create properly structured communities in which everyone's purpose is to please Lord Krishna (cf. Sivarama Swami 1999, p.144). Prabhupada attacks almost every aspect of modern urban civilisation: Western "rascal" materialism, politics, factories, urban living, cars, hippies, etc. His practical solution is local self-sufficiency based on cow husbandry and agriculture, farm projects and sustainable development. A strong work ethic underlies all Prabhupada's writings, and his advocacy of simple living, high thinking lends itself to the *varna* layering of society.

28.   In India today the great majority of *brahmans* follow secular occupations. However, *brahmans* are the traditional priests of Hinduism. Their superiority within the caste structure depends upon their traditional command of learning as given by their right to learn (*adhayayana*) and teach (*adhyapana*), to sacrifice (*yajna*) and to preside over the sacrifices of others (*yajna*), and to give (*dana*) and receive gifts (*pratigraha*). *Brahmans* have come to be partly assimilated with renouncers so that the *brahman* who carries out rituals for others and who receives gifts or payments is often seen as inferior to the *brahman* who does not serve at all or is a scholar or teacher. The ideal *brahman* should lead an austere life and regard ritual and teaching as a form of worship rather

than as a livelihood or business. There are therefore constraints in the matter of earning by *yajna* and *pratigraha*. Moreover, teaching should be practised as *vidya-dana* (the gift of learning) and its divine aspect safeguarded (cf. Chandrasekharendra Sarasvati 1991, p.68).

29. Bhaktivinoda Thakura refused to acknowledge caste distinctions among devotees and in particular opposed the wearing of the sacred thread by *brahman*s as a sign of superiority. According to Hopkins (1983, p.49), Bhaktisiddhanta Sarasvati gave the sacred thread to every candidate accepted for initiation, regardless of his caste background.

30. Prabhupada (1989, p. 391) views the *brahman* order of society as the spiritually advanced caste or community which was always held in great esteem by the other, subordinate castes (the administrative kingly order, the mercantile order and the labourers). However, he frequently refers to *brahman*s who display sinful activities and debauched habits.

31. Anyone wishing to be initiated as a *brahman* would have to pass the *Bhakti-sastri* examination. Candidates would have to study the following books: *Bhagavad Gita*, *Nectar of Devotion*, *Nectar of Instruction*, *Isopanishad*, *Easy Journey to Other Planets*, and all other small paperbacks, as well as *Arcana-paddhati* (a book to be compiled by Nitai Prabhu based on *Hari-bhakti-vilasa* on Deity worship).

32. Prabhupada teaches that the actual perfection of human life lies in being always Krishna Conscious and always being aware of Krishna while performing all types of activities. Devotional practices are one way of controlling and purifying the mind, and achieving spiritual peace and happiness.

33. Ravindra Svarupa Dasa (1999a) in "ISKCON and Varnasrama-Dharma: A Mission Unfulfilled" recalls a moment in the early 1970s when Prabhupada had arrived in New York and was interviewed by the press. In a reply to a question about his mission, Prabhupada said: "I have come to give you a brain. Your society is headless." He asserted that modern Western society was malformed: "There are a few *vaisya*s and everyone else is *sudra*." Prabhupada notes: "Modern civilization is considered to be in advance in the standard of the mode of passion. Formerly, the advanced condition was considered to be in the mode of goodness" (*Bhagavad Gita* 14.7, purport).

34. "Any proposal, therefore, for establishing *varnashramadharma* in ISKCON, and even in the society at large, is first of all to take the first step and do everything needed to form a proper community of *brahman*s. According to the *Bhagavad Gita* (18.42), two of the traits evinced by *brahamanas* are *jnana* and *vijnana*, that is, they have genuine knowledge of the Absolute Truth and they possess the wisdom to apply that knowledge appropriately. If this first step is taken, and ISKCON is thus given a brain, then I am sure we shall be in a better position to know where to go further."

35. Gelberg (1989, p.150) offers one of the most detailed accounts of the spiritual practices proper.

36. After responsive recitation of the day's verse (led first by the instructor, then by volunteers) and responsive recitation of the word-for-word, Sanskrit-to-English, translation, the instructor reads the full English translation of the verse followed by

Prabhupada's commentary. The instructor then presents his own extended comments on the subjects raised in the verse and commentary. After a question and answer discussion period, class comes to an end with the offering of obeisance.

37.   "The spiritual master is as good as the Supreme Personality of Godhead..." In ISKCON the theological difference between *sakshad Hari* and *sakshad Hari-tva* is subtle but of enormous importance. *Sakshad Hari* means "as Hari" and *sakshad Hari-tva* means "as good as Hari" (Kripamoya Das: personal communication 12.10.04).

38.   Devotees should respect *siksha-gurus* in the form of Krishna and Chaitanya and their incarnations, energies and holy names. They worship the teachings of the Vedas and the *acharyas*, the Six Goswamis and ISKCON's founder-*acharya* and *siksha-guru*, Srila Prabhupada, the *vartma-pradarsaka-guru*, any devotee in a position of responsibility, *sannyasis*, *brahmans*, seniors, elders, parents, god-brothers and godsisters, teachers, the *diksha-guru*, an advanced devotee, non-devotee instructors and non-humans (cf. Sivarama Swami, 1999, pp.162-4).

39.   Sivaram Swami argues that transmitting *siksha* is the primary function of the *guru parampara* but in practice there is a *diksha*-culture in which initiating gurus are revered while the many *siksha-gurus* are neglected. Other gurus maintain that *siksha* and *diksha* are equally important.

40.   Sri Prahlad Dasa and Braj-Sevaki Devi Dasi (2004, pp.30-8) address this paradox by suggesting that while meditation, deity worship and *yajnas* (sacrifices) are less relevant methods of worshiping the Lord in Kali Yuga, when employed in subordination to the chanting of the holy name they make a powerful impression that purifies the mind and senses.

41.   Full-time devotees are expected to dedicate 24 hours a day to developing their own spiritual purity and to helping others through preaching activities. To maintain individual and collective purity, devotees take life-long vows at initiation to comply with four rules: (i) to abstain from all meat, fish or eggs; (ii) to avoid all intoxication (including tea, coffee and tobacco); (iii) to abstain from gambling; (iv) to engage in sex only for the procreation of children within marriage.

42.   Ales Crnic reports that in Slovenia there are considerably more men than women with second initiation and women generally have been initiated for a shorter period than men. This he attributes to the generally lower position of women in ISKCON (Crnic 2002, p.43).

43.   The nature of the *sampradaya* is such that offerings go straight to the temple organisation. Thus the ambivalence surrounding gifts in mainstream Hinduism (cf. Raheja [1998], Parry [1994]) is muted. I was told by Syamasundara Das that each month ISKCON has to refuse gifts of cows (*godan*) because the land available cannot support them.

44.   Women like *shudras* and untouchables were traditionally ineligible to hear the recitation of the Vedas. They were not invested with the sacred thread and have rarely exercised a priestly role (but see Pintchman 2000, p.194).

45.   One prominent guru commented that Westerners did not understand the Indian cultural context: in reality women held all the power. When I asked why in that case women could not take *sannyasa*, he replied in traditional terms that a life of

wandering was dangerous for women even in the 21st century. More personally he remarked that his own Catholic upbringing and Vaishnava training had instilled in him ineradicable attitudes of protection.

46. See also in this volume Rasamandala Das's essay, which offers some analysis of ISKCON Membership in the UK.

47. There are devotees like Rasamandala Das who work as astrologers and cast horoscopes.

48. Western converts who are active in the temple are often young (aged 20 to 25). Others may move on and not ask for *samskaras*. Kripamoya Das mentioned however that some Western converts had followed Chaitanya's example and visited Gaya to perform *shraddha*.

49. The concept of the good Vaishnava death was the focus of Tamal Krishna Goswami's thinking before he himself so tragically died. His work was taken over by Graham Schweig (2004). See also the paper by Hari-Dhama Dasa (1998) Spiritual Need, Pain and Care: Recognition and Response, in *ISKCON Communications Journal* 6 (2): 51-60.

50. A point kindly made by Dr Shirley Firth (personal communication).

51. See the website: Kripamoya.com

52. In a marriage Kripamoya Das gathers together coconut, grains, barley, sesame, rice, ghee, camphor, wood, *samagri*, *kumkum*, *var-mala*, *sindoor*, almonds/sugar candy, garlands, red strings, *kansar* sweets, incense, ghee wicks, leaves, banana, sand, greenery, flower petals, *koduja* pots, tealight candles, astrological details and *sankalpa* sheet, puffed rice for *mangala-fera*, *antarpat*, etc.

53. On 5 October 2004 I met a wife and husband, one Hindu, the other Sikh, who had come to Bhaktivedanta Manor to arrange the wedding of their daughter with a Canadian from a Christian background. They themselves were not members of the congregation. They told me that their daughter wanted her fiancee's friends to feel comfortable.

54. Cf. Radio 4 Archives, *Poetry Please*, Rites of Passage, features Nitin Ganatra, his wife and Kripamoya Das's choice of poetry for marriage.

55. Tamal Krishna Goswami had almost completed a PhD at Cambridge when he so tragically died in 2002. Other devotees are now completing doctoral degrees in Theology and Religious Studies in departments at Lancaster, Warwick, etc.

56. For example major festivals and especially the annual Jagganath Ratha Yatra in London involves liaising with the police, the media, politicians and public health officials.

Baird, Robert D. (1995) Swami Bhaktivedanta and Ultimacy, in Robert D. Baird (Ed.), *Religion in Modern India*, pp.515-41 (New Delhi: Manohar).

Barker, E. (1982) (Ed.) *New Religious Movements, Studies in Religion and Society*, vol. 3 (New York and Toronto: The Edwin Mellen Press).

Basham, A. (1983) Interview with A.L. Basham, in Steven J. Gelberg (Ed.), *Hare Krishna, Hare Krishna: Five Distinguished Scholars on the Krishna Movement in the West*, pp.162-95 (New York: Grove Press).

Baumann, G. (1992) Ritual Implicates "Others": Rereading Durkheim in a Plural Society, in D. de Coppet (Ed.), *Understanding Rituals*, pp.97-116 (London: Routledge).

Baumann, M. (1999) The Hindu Diasporas in Europe and an Analysis of Key Diasporic Patterns, in T. S. Rukmani (Ed.), *Hindu Diaspora: Global Perspectives*, pp.59-79 (Montreal: Department of Religious Studies Concordia University).

Bhaktivedanta Manor Newsletter, Souvenir Issue 2003-2004 (contact *nima@pamho.net* or *www.krishnatemple.com*).

Black, Brian (2004) The "True Brahmin" and the Implications of Brahminhood, in Julia Leslie and Matthew Clark (Eds.), *Creating a Dialogue: Text, Belief and Personal Identity* (Proceedings of the Valmiki Studies Workshop), pp.11-4 (London: SOAS, University of London).

Brockington, J. L. (1991) *The Sacred Thread: Hinduism in its Continuity and Diversity* (Edinburgh: University of Edinburgh Press).

Brockington, J. L. (1992) *Hinduism and Christianity* (London: Macmillan Press).

Brockington, J. L. (2004) The Epics in the Bhakti Tradition, in Anna S. King and John Brockington (Eds.), *The Intimate Other: Love Divine in Indic Religions*, pp.31-53 (Delhi: Longman Oriental).

Bromley, David G. and Larry D. Shinn (1989) (Eds.) *Krishna Consciousness in the West* (Toronto: Bucknell University).

Case, M. (2000) *Seeing Krishna* (New York: Oxford University Press).

Cracknell, Kenneth (2000) ISKCON and Interfaith Dialogue, *ISKCON Communications Journal* 8 (1): 23-32.

Clooney, F. (1994) Hindu-Christian Studies as Necessary Luxury in the Context of Today's Pluralism, *Hindu-Christian Studies Bulletin* 7: 39-44.

Crnic, A. (2002) Devotees of Krsna in Slovenia, *ISKCON Communications Journal* 10: 35-49.

Dasa, Gopiparanadhana (2001) Srila Prabhupada and the Vaishnava Tradition of Scriptural Commentary: Serving the Words of His Predecessors, *ISKCON Communications Journal* 8 (2): 1-8.

Dasa, Prema Rasa and Sandipani Muni Dasa (1997) *The Book of Samskaras: Purificatory Rituals for Successful Life* (New Delhi: Bhaktivedanta Book Trust).

Dasa, Ravindra Svarupa (1999a) ISKCON and Varnasrama-Dharma: A Mission Unfulfilled, *ISKCON Communications Journal* 7 (1): 35-44.

Dasa, Ravindra Svarupa (1999b) Pillars of Success: The Principles and Practices of Reform, *ISKCON Communications Journal* 7 (2): 1-12.

Dasa, Saunaka Rsi (1999) ISKCON in Relation to People of Faith in God, *ISKCON Communications Journal* 7 (1): 1-9.

Dasa, Sri Prahlad and Braj-Sevaki Devi Dasi (2004) Matter to Spirit: The Anatomy of a Deity Installation, in *Back to Godhead*, Nagaraja Dasa (Ed.), July/August: 30-38.

Dasi, Radha Devi (1998a) Fundamental Human Rights in ISKCON, *ISKCON Communications Journal* 6 (1): 31-41.

Dasi, Radha Devi (1998b) Participation, Protection and Patriarchy: An International Model for the Role of Women in ISKCON, *ISKCON Communications Journal* 6 (2): 7-14.

Dasi, Urmila Devi (2001) A Response to: Women in ISKCON; Presentations to the GBC, March 2000, *ISKCON Communications Journal* 8 (2): 79-80.

Dasi, Visakha Devi *et al* (2001) Women in ISKCON: Presentations to the GBC, March 2000, *ISKCON Communications Journal* 9: 1-22.

Deadwyler, G. (Yudisthira Dasa) (2001) Fifteen years Later: A Critique of Gurukula, *ISKCON Communications Journal* 9: 13-22.

Doktor, T. (2002) Psychological Characteristics of ISKCON Members, *ISKCON Communications Journal* 10: 25-34.

Ellwood, R.S. (1973) *Religious and Spiritual Groups in Modern America* (Englewood Cliffs: Prentice Hall).

Ellwood, R. S. (1983) Foreword, in Steven J. Gelberg (Ed.), *Hare Krishna, Hare Krishna: Five Distinguished Scholars on the Krishna Movement in the West*, pp.11-3 (NewYork: Grove Press).

Flood, G. (1995) Hinduism, Vaisnavism, and ISKCON: Authentic Traditions or Scholarly Constructions?, *ISKCON Communications Journal* 3: 5-15.

Flood, G. (1996) An *Introduction to Hinduism* (Cambridge: Cambridge University Press).

Fuller, C. J. (2003) *The Renewal of the Priesthood* (Princeton and Oxford: Princeton University Press).

Gelberg, S. J. (1983) (Ed.) *Hare Krishna, Hare Krishna* (New York: Grove Press).

Gelberg, S. J. (1989) Exploring an Alternative Reality: Spiritual Life in ISKCON, in David G. Bromley and Larry D. Shinn (Eds.), *Krishna Consciousness in the West*, pp.139-62 (Lewisburg, PA: Bucknell University Press).

Gelberg, S. J. (1991) The Call of the Lotus-Eyed Lord: The Fate of Krishna Consciousness in the West, in Timothy Miller (Ed.), *When Prophets Die: The Postcharismatic Fate of New Religious Movements*, pp.149-64 (Albany: State Universityof New York Press).

Goswami, Srila Gopala Bhatta (1997) *Sat-kriya-sara-dipika*, trans. Bhannu Svami (Mayapura: Bhaktivedanta Academy).

Goswami, Srivatsa (1983) Interview with Srivatsa Goswami, in Steven J. Gelberg *Hare Krishna, Hare Krishna: Five Distinguished Scholars on the Krishna Movement in the West*, pp.196-258 (New York: Grove Press).

Goswami, Tamal Krishna (1998) *A Hare Krishna at Southern Methodist University, Collected Essays 1995-1997* (Texas: Pundits Press).

Hopkins, T. J. (1983) Interview with Thomas J. Hopkins, in Steven J. Gelberg (Ed.), *Hare Krishna, Hare Krishna: Five Distinguished Scholars on the Krishna Movement in the West*, pp.101-61 (New York: Grove Press).

Jarrow, E.H. (2003) The Good Death, *Journal of Vaishnava Studies* 11 (2): 61-76.

Klostermaier, K. (1998) *Hinduism: A Short Introduction* (Oxford: Oneworld).

Klostermaier, K. (2000a) *Hinduism: A Short History* (Oxford: Oneworld).

Klostermaier, K. (2000b) *Hindu Writings: A Short Introduction to the Major Sources* (Oxford: Oneworld).

Knott, Kim (1986) *My Sweet Lord: The Hare Krishna Movement* (Wellingborough: Aquarian Press).

Knott, Kim (1995) The Debate about Women in the Hare Krishna Movement, *ISKCON Communications Journal* 3 (2): 33-49.

Knott, Kim (1996) The Debate about Women in the Hare Krishna Movement, in Steven J. Rosen (1996) (Ed.), *Vaisnavi: Women and the Worship of Krishna*, pp. 87-111 (New Delhi: Motilal Banarsidass).

Knott, Kim (2004) Healing the Heart of ISKCON: The Place of Women, in Edwin F. Bryant and Maria L. Ekstrand, *The Hare Krishna Movement: The Postcharismatic Fate of a Religious Transplant*, pp.291-311 (New York: Columbia University).

Melton, J.G. (1989) The Attitude of Americans toward Hinduism from 1883 to 1083 with Special Reference to the International Society for Krishna Consciousness in *Krishna Consciousness in the West*, in David G. Bromley and Larry D. Shinn (Eds.), pp.79-101 (Lewisburg: Bucknell University Press).

Nye, Malory (1997) ISKCON and Hindus in Britain: Some Thoughts on a Developing Relationship, *ISKCON Communications Journal* 5 (2): 5-13.

Pandey, Raj Bali (1969) *Hindu samskaras: socio-religious study of the Hindu sacraments* (Delhi: Motilal Banarasidass).

Parry, J. (1994) *Death in Banaras* (Cambridge: Cambridge University Press).

Prabhupada, A.C. Bhaktivedanta Swami (1974) *Caitanya-caritamrita* 17 vols. (Los Angeles: Bhaktivedanta Book Trust).

Prabhupada, A.C. Bhaktivedanta Swami (1982) *The Nectar of Devotion: The Complete Science of Bhakti-Yoga* (Los Angeles: Bhaktivedanta Book Trust) Angeles: Bhaktivedanta Book Trust).

Prabhupada, A.C. Bhaktivedanta Swami (1983) *The Bhagavad Gita As It Is* (Los Angeles: Bhaktivedanta Book Trust).

Prabhupada, A.C. Bhaktivedanta Swami (1999) in *Srila Prabhupada on Varnasrama and Farm Community Development, Vol. 1, Speaking about Varnasrama*, compiled by Hare Krsna-Devi Dasi, edited by Suresvara-Dasa (Los Angeles: Bhaktivedanta Book Trust).

Raheja, G.G. (1988) *The Poison in the Gift: Ritual, Prestation, and the Dominant Caste in a North Indian Village* (Chicago: University of Chicago).

Rasamandala Das (1997) Towards Principles and Values – An Analysis of Education Philosophy and practice within ISKCON, *ISKCON Communications Journal* 5 (2): 1-11.

Rochford, E. Burke Jr (1985) *Hare Krishna in America* (New Brunswick: Rutgers University Press).

Rochford, E. Burke Jr (1997) Family Formation, Culture and Change, *ISKCON Communications Journal* 5 (2): 61-82.

Rochford, E. Burke Jr (2001a) ISKCON and Interfaith Dialogue, *ISKCON Communications Journal* 9: 23-32.

Rochford, E.Burke (2001b) The Changing Face of ISKCON: Family, Congregationalism, and Privatisation, *ISKCON Communications Journal* 9:1-11.

Rosen, Steven J. (1991) *The Six Goswamis of Vrindavan* (New York: Folk Books).

Rosen, Steven J. (1992) *Vaisnavism: Contemporary Scholars Discuss the Gaudiya Tradition* (New York: Folk Books).

Rosen, Steven J. (1996) (Ed.) *Vaisnavi: Women and the Worship of Krishna*, pp.87-111 (Delhi: Motilal Banarsidass).

Rosen, Steven J. (1996) Raganuga Bhakti: Bringing Out the Inner Woman in Gaudiya Vaishnava Sadhana, in Steven J. Rosen (Ed.), *Vaisnavi: Women and the Worship of Krishna*, pp.113-32 (Delhi: Motilal Banarsidass).

Rustau, H. (2003) The Hindu Woman's Right to Sannyasa: Religious Movements and the Gender Question: The Sri Sarada Math and the Ramakrishna Sarada Mission, in Antony

Copley (Ed.), *Hinduism in Public and Private: Reform, Hindutva, Gender, and Sampradaya*, pp.143-72 (New Delhi: Oxford University Press).

Sarasvati, Svami Chandrasekharendra (1991) *Voice of the Guru: The Guru Tradition* (Bombay: Bharatiya Vidya Bhavan).

Schweig, Graham M. (2004) Dying the Good Death, in Anna S. King and John Brockington (Eds.), *The Intimate Other: Love Divine in Indic Religions* (Delhi: Longman Oriental).

Shinn, L.D. (1985) Conflicting Networks: Guru and Friend in ISKCON, in Rodney Stark (Ed.), *Religious Movements: Genesis, Exodus and Numbers* (New York: Paragon House).

Shinn, L .D. (1987) *The Dark Lord: Cult Images and the Hare Krishnas in America* (New Brunswick: Rutgers University Press).

Swami, Sivarama (1999) *The Siksa-guru: Implementing Tradition within ISKCON* (Hungary: Bhaktivedanta Institute).

Van der Velde, P. (2004) What do we look at? About the "true" nature of Krishna's lila and the Dalai Lama's secret paradise, in Bocken, I, Dupre W and P van der Velde (Eds.), *The Persistent Challenge: Religion, Truth and Scholarship: Essays in Honour of Klaus Klostermaier*, pp.121-45 (Maastricht: Uitgeverij Shaker Publishing).

Warrier, M. (2003) The *Seva* Ethic and the Spirit of Institution Building in the Mata Amritanandamayi Mission, in Antony Copley (Ed.), *Hinduism in Public and Private: Reform, Hindutva, Gender, and Sampradaya*, 254-289 (New Delhi: Oxford University Press).

Waterhouse, H. (2004) unpublished paper given at the 2004 BASR conference.

Whitworth, J. and Shiels, M. (1982) From Across the Black Water Two Imported Varieties of Hinduism – The Hare Krishnas and the Ramakrishna Vedanta Society, in Eileen Barker (Ed.), *New Religious Movements: A Perspective for Understanding Society* (New York: Edwin Mellen).

Vertovec, Steven (2000) *The Hindu Diaspora: Comparative Patterns* (London: RoutledgeCurzon).

Young, K. (2002) Women and Hinduism in A. Sharma (Ed.), *Women in Indian Religions*, pp.3-37 (New Delhi: Oxford University Press).

Chapter 9

Doniger, W. and B.K. Smith (1991) trans. *The Laws of Manu* (London: Penguin).

Prabhupada, A.C. Bhaktivedanta Swami *Back to Godhead: The Magazine of the Hare Krishna Movement* (First published in Calcutta in 1944 by Srila Prabhupada himself, then published in 1966 in Los Angeles by Bhaktivedanta Book Trust).

Prabhupada, A.C. Bhaktivedanta Swami (1970) *The Nectar of Devotion: The Complete Science of Bhakti-Yoga*, A Summary Study of Srila Rupa's Bhakti-rasamrita-sindhu (Mumbai: Bhaktivedanta Book Trust).

Prabhupada, A.C. Bhaktivedanta Swami (1970) *KRSNA the Supreme Personality of Godhead* 2 vols. (Los Angeles: Bhaktivedanta Book Trust).

Prabhupada, A.C. Bhaktivedanta Swami (1972) *Bhagavad Gita As It Is* (Los Angeles: Bhaktivedanta Book Trust).

Prabhupada, A.C. Bhaktivedanta Swami (1974) *Caitanya-caritamrita* 9 vols. (Los Angeles: Bhaktivedanta Book Trust).

Prabhupada, A.C. Bhaktivedanta Swami (1988) *Srimad Bhagavatam* 12 cantos (Los Angeles: Bhaktivedanta Book Trust).

Chapter 10

1. Malhotra (cf. *rajiv.malhotra@worldnet.att.net*) argues that Hinduism is being mocked, and quotes Sardar who declares that "the realities of (non-Western cultures)…are for sale in the supermarket of postmodern nihilism" (Malhotra 2004, p.2). Malhotra suggests that even Krishna *bhakti* may not escape the superimposition that *tantra* equals sex. It is true that all researchers are to some degree connected to, and a part of, the object of their research (Charlotte Aull Davies 1999). Scholars, however self-reflexive and transparent, are inevitably inspired partly by their own cultural debates and personal quests.

    Wendy O. Doniger, Paul Courtwright, Jeffrey Kripal and David Gordon White have been attacked violently for their psychoanalytical interpretations. Western scholars have offered counter-arguments. David Smith (2003, p.101), for example, argues that scholars within the West are colonised by the Indian imagination. Wendy Doniger claims that no culture can be "owned" and asserts that it is possible for individuals to be simultaneously orthoprax and heterodox – they remain within their cultural norms, e.g. following their religion's rituals, while benefiting "in their heads" from the myths of many cultures (1999, p.344). Many contemporary writers on Hinduism as a living religion are women who are not birth Hindus and non-native speakers but who have attempted to enter the real world of Indian women to explore the nature of *vrats* (vows), rituals, etc. Some have been deeply influenced by the Indian women's movement and journals like Madhu Kishwar's *Manushi*.

2. STIMW Symposium held at Newcastle University on 17 May 2005.

3. Suhukavak N. Das maintains that if Chaitanya Vaishnavism is to have a lasting position in and a positive impact on the West, then it must begin to develop new forms of intellectual expression and perspectives that are a part of the Western intellectual and academic traditions (2004, p.109).

4. The approaches of Western scholars to Radha reveal much about their own preoccupations. Donna Marie Wulff suggests (1996) that the story of Radha at the most simple level has been read in the West as an allegorical love story: mirroring a universal human search for wholeness. It is a desire for union which involves not the majesty and awe of god and servant but the sweetness of loving intimacy. Radha's intense longing for Krishna both represents and inspires the yearning of the human soul for the divine. Radha's story is ultimately a story of hopefulness. For humans in the world it offers the reassurance that their lives are not doomed to fragmentation and alienation. They can be made whole. David Kinsley, on the other hand, interprets Radha and Krishna's love affair as light and playful. Krishna becomes the ringmaster of a festival of love: "By means of his flute he beckons the

women of Vrndavana to that separate world of his where intoxication and abandon, joy and rollicking sport reign supreme" (1977, p.52).

5. Krishna in the *Bhagavad Gita* says that whenever the world experiences a decline of *dharma* or righteousness, he will incarnate himself in earthly form to destroy the evil threatening the world order, and to redress the imbalance between right and wrong.

6. Contemporary young Hindus in internet chat rooms interpret the relationship of Radha Krishna in many ways: as adulterous; as pure, divine love uncontaminated by sexuality; as a human story of love, desire, passion, adultery and sex. Thus, one reads: "The eternal meaning of true love;" "The relationship of Radha and Krishna in the end is too unjust…she should be married to Krishna only – only to Krishna;" "What a male fantasy; all those *gopis*, all those thousands of wives and a loving mistress as well – what a lot of **."

7. Radha's real grief at separation and longing for union has been presented by some scholars as a kind of "dark night of the soul" experienced by Christian mystics and powerfully presented in the writings of St John of the Cross and St Theresa of Avila.

8. According to the official biography of Mata Amritananda produced by the Mission, she came to realise her innate divinity at the age of 21 when she gained mystic union first with Krishna and subsequently with Devi, the goddess.

9. Krishna does not marry until he leaves Braj, allowing no place for a marital relationship in the Braj *lila*. Devotion to Krishna as husband leaves almost no space for human gurus or mortal husbands.

10. Since Bhaktivinoda makes the distinction between the cumulative tradition and faith, he is able to keep the door open for continued empirical study of the cumulative tradition (Shukavak N. Das 2004, p.109). Bhaktivinoda employed the methodology of modern religious scholarship, maintaining that religion is both the cumulative religious tradition *and* pure religious faith. This mirrors Wilfred Cantwell Smith's understanding of religion as two complementary categories, one, the historical cumulative tradition, and the other, the personal faith of the individuals who take part in that tradition.

11. ISKCON devotees do not date the *Srimad Bhagavatam* to CE 900. They may accept that such ancient works go through stages in history when they are written "on paper" to ensure their survival but understand as authoritative Srila Prabhupada's dating of the original spoken *Srimad Bhagavatam* to 5,000 years ago (ie. 3,000 BCE).

12. "Radhastami, the appearance day of Shrimati Radhani, took place on 21st September. Radha and Krishna are forever bound in love for one another and worshipping them is the goal of life for all devotees. On Radhastami, devotees will especially seek Radha's favour so that She will recommend them to Krishna. Special classes and a feast were held at Bhaktivedanta Manor, and Radharani was offered 108 food preparations, many gifts, and a dress made of flowers. This year Their Lordships were offered three new dresses in one day" (*Bhaktivedanta Manor Newsletter* October 2004, p.1).

13. Their pre-industrial Vedic setting symbolises Radha and Krishna's association with plant life and fertility but also harmonises with ISKCON's contemporary mission –

cow protection, organic farming and sustainable agriculture, vegetarianism and ecological concern.

14. Prabhupada rhetorically asks why Krishna manifests the pastimes with the *gopis*, which are "disturbing to the so-called moralists of the world." His answers are various. He suggests for example that Krishna dances only with the spiritual bodies of Radha or the *gopis* (1970 [1996], p.321) or that He does so in order to captivate the conditioned soul and to show special mercy to men and women who are very much attracted to sex (1970 [1996], p.320).

15. He teaches that: "Those who follow (*vidhi*)-*sadhana-bhakti* go to Vaikuntha, and those who follow *raganuga-sadhana-bhakti* go to Vrindavan." He remarks, "Generally the followers of Lord Chaitanya go to Vrindavan" (Valpey 2004, p.162). "Lord Krishna wants to make known that He is more attracted by *raga-bhakti* than *vidhi-bhakti*, or devotional service under scheduled regulations" (quoted by Rosen 1996, p.117).

16. Prabhupada's *Krsna* contains all the much loved stories of Krishna – Krishna attracting the *gopis* by playing the flute, His stealing of their clothes, the *Rasa* Dance, the *Gopis'* feelings of separation – but equally it narrates the stories of Krishna's kidnapping of Rukmini, the birth of Pradyumna, and Krishna's marriages with 16,108 queens and the birth of 161,080 sons. Prabhupada explains that the *original* Krishna is the Krishna of Vrindavan and that some of his different pastimes are manifested by his expansions (1970 [1996], p.987). While Krishna was living at Dvaraka, for example, he displayed all his opulences of wealth and beauty, enjoying 16,000 beautiful wives simultaneously. "Although Krsna had grandchildren and great-grandchildren, neither Krishna nor his queens looked older than sixteen or twenty years of age." His pastimes are "eternal, never-ending occurrences, whereas in the material world they are simply impermanent perverted reflections" (1970 [1996], p.991). Prabhupada describes both the *gopis* and queens as achieving the highest salvation, which it is impossible for great sages and saintly persons and ascetics to achieve.

17. He refers to Krishna's sublime dealing with His conjugal associates the *gopis*, as well as with His married wives at Dvaraka.

18. He notes (1970 [1996], p.523) the inconsolable grief felt at Krishna's departure. After His separation from Vrndavana from the innocent rural cowherd boys, girls, ladies and others, they all felt shock throughout their lives, and the separation of Radharani, the most beloved cowherd girl, is beyond expression. "Once they met at Kuruksetra during a solar eclipse, and the feeling which was expressed by them is heartrending." His thousands of wives are similarly devastated when He leaves them. The departure of Lord Krishna for Dvaraka is also attended by the weeping ladies of Hastinapura.

19. Altogether Lord Krishna had 16,108 queens at Dvaraka, and in each of them He begot ten children. All these children grew up and each had as many children as the father. The aggregate number of the family numbered 10 million (Prabhupada 1970 [1996], p.547).

20. Chaitanya taught that God is a person who has a name, a form, qualities and pastimes, but who is nonetheless absolute and transcendental, beyond our

experience in this material world. Chaitanya also taught that all living beings are eternal spiritual parts of Krishna.

21. "In the age of Kali the incarnation of the Lord always chants the holy name 'Krishna' in the company of His associates. His complexion is not blackish (like Krishna) but golden. The wise worship Him by chanting His name in congregation" (*Srimad Bhagavatam* 11.5.32).

22. Krishnadasa Kaviraj in *Sri Caitanya-caritamrita* adds another reason for Krishna's descent to earth as Chaitanya. He says that: "The Lord's desire was born for two reasons. He wanted to taste the sweet essence of the mellows of love of God (as exhibited by Sri Radha), and he wanted to propagate service in the world on the platform of spontaneous attraction (*raganuga*). Thus he is known as supremely jubilant and as the most merciful of all" (Prabhupada quoted in Rosen 1996, p.116). In their theological treatises Rupa and Jiva Goswami explain that Krishna has a three-fold divine energy (*shakti*). The highest and most essential (*svarupa*) of these aspects is his blissful energy, his *hladini shakti*, which is Radha. In their understanding then Radha is an essential and exalted part of the godhead. Chaitanya expounded the precepts of Krishna Consciousness to Srila Goswami and Sanatana Goswami, great ascetics who later produced devotional writings; to Sarvabhauma Bhattaracarya and Prakashananda Sarasvati, leading "impersonalist" philosophers and to Ramananda Raya. A hymn by Jiva Goswami, a follower of Chaitanya, plays on the inseparability of Radha and Krishna:

1) For Krishna, Radha is love embodied; for Radha, Krishna is love made real. While I live and when I die, Radha-Krishna is my destiny.

2) Radha's treasure trove is Krishna, Krishna's treasure trove is Radha. While I live and when I die, Radha-Krishna is my destiny.

3) Radha is his breath of life, Krishna is her living breath. While I live and when I die, Radha-Krishna is my destiny.

4) The joy of Krishna's being fills her to the brim, he is drowning in the joy of Radha's being. While I live and when I die, Radha-Krishna is my destiny.

5) Krishna lives in Radha's heart, she's the pleasure of Krishna's heart. While I live and when I die, Radha-Krishna is my destiny.

6) In Krishna's consciousness stays Radha, in Radha's consciousness he's fixed. While I live and when I die, Radha-Krishna is my destiny.

7) Radhika is dressed in blue, Sri Krishna's decked in yellow silk. While I live and when I die, Radha-Krishna is my destiny.

8) Vrndavana's empress – Radhika, Vrndavana's master – Sri Krishna. While I live and when I die, Radha-Krishna is my destiny. *Sri Srijivagosvamipada Viracita Sriyugalastakam*

23.   Prabhupada emphasises that Chaitanya wanted to keep his ecstasies secret:

> Please rest assured that I have nothing to hide from you, Lord Caitanya
> told Ramananda. Even if I do try to hide from you, you are such an
> advanced devotee that you can understand all My secrets. I request that
> you please keep this a secret and do not disclose it to anyone. If it were
> revealed, everyone would consider Me a madman. The facts which I have
> disclosed to you cannot be understood by materialistic people. When they
> hear of this, they will simply laugh at Me. You can understand this yourself
> and keep it to yourself. From a materialistic point of view, a devotee
> becomes mad in his ecstasy of love for Krsna. Both you and I are just like
> madmen. So please don't disclose these facts to ordinary men. If you do
> they will surely laugh at Me. (1988, p.346)

24.   Rosen argues that *Manjari-bhakti* is the pre-eminent mood in Gaudiya Vaishnavism:

> Gaudiya Vaisnavas are distinct among Vaisnavas of the other *sampradayas*
> in their pursuance of Manjari-bhav, although the Nimbarkas, Vallabhites,
> and Harivamsas also have some interest in the subject. Following in the
> footsteps of exemplary *manjaris* is natural for those in the line of
> Mahaprabhu, for this was the mood exhibited by Lord Caitanya's closest
> associates. The original Six Goswamins were themselves manifestations of
> six primary *manjaris*, as were Lokanatha Goswamin, Krsnadasa Kaviraja
> Goswamin, and virtually every prominent *acarya* in the Gaudiya line. This
> means that, throughout history, the greatest teachers of Gaudiya
> Vaisnavism – who were predominantly male – labored to bring out 'the
> inner woman' (albeit in an extremely spiritual sense) through meditation
> on their spiritual form as *manjaris*. (Rosen 1996, p.121)

25.   Prabhupada (see Lorenz 2004, p.116) interprets *Bhagavata Purana* 7.12.1 as teaching
       that the guru exerts complete control over his married male disciples:

> If the spiritual master's orders allow a *grihastha* to engage in sex life at a
> particular time, the *grihastha* may do so; otherwise, if the spiritual master
> orders against it, the *grihastha* should abstain. The *grihastha* must obtain
> permission from the spiritual master to observe the ritualistic ceremony of
> *garbhadhana-samskara*. Then he may approach his wife to beget children,
> otherwise not. A Brahmin generally remains a *brahmacari* throughout his
> entire life, but although some Brahmins become *grihasthas* and indulge in
> sex life, they do so under the complete control of the spiritual master.

26.   Prabhupada, like Aristotle and Aquinas, regards women as incapable of many
       virtues. Women in general are unable to speculate like philosophers, but they are
       blessed by the Lord because they believe at once in the superiority and almightiness

of the Lord and offer obeisances without reservation (1970, p.395): "Women as a class are no better than boys, and therefore they have no discriminatory power like that of a man;" "Women, merchants and laborers are not very intelligent, and thus it is very difficult to understand the science of God or to be engaged in the devotional service of the Lord;" "They are more materialistic, but by engagement in the service of the Lord they become pure souls eligible to enter into the kingdom of God" (Prabhupada 1970, p.548).

27. Muster writes: "Although there were some bright spots and good friendships, we women lived under a cloud of chauvinism and outright hatred of our gender. I look back on my ten years in the movement with regret" (2004, p.312). She says:

> *Sannyasis* received all the advantages, while women generally got the worst accommodations, waited at the end of the food line, and prayed at the back of the temple. When these changes took place in the mid-1970s, people who resisted were either silenced or forced out. By the time I joined, the controversy was settled: women's place as second-class citizens was cemented and thoroughly institutionalised. (2004, p.315)

28. Hinduism attracts such interest because, as in Paganism and earth religions, goddesses attract devotion and prayer in their own right (1994). Not only is Devi worshipped by millions of Hindus as ultimate ruler and creatrix, but, as Gross (1998, p.325) points out, in the Hindu pantheon there are not only gods and goddesses. Female dimensions of deity are important in both the Vaishnavite and Shaivite systems while male dimensions of deity are important in Shakta systems.

McDermott reports (1996) that whereas in Bengal Kali is predominantly conceived as a kind and beautiful maternal force, in the West it is Kali's connection with time, death and sexuality that is emphasised. She is depicted eating the entrails of a corpse or is imaged in pagan terms as the third stage of womanhood – the hag. She becomes a feminist icon as she dances on the prostrate ithyphallic corpse of Shiva (*shava*), wearing garlands of skulls and carrying weapons.

29 Religion itself has been deconstructed by some feminists to be a creation or projection of male concerns and imagery. Throughout history men have formulated the beliefs of religions, composed and transmitted the sacred writings and been their sole interpreters, created the religious and secular institutions of their societies and controlled worship and other important rituals. They have written the history.

Moreover, during the past 150 years feminist movements have been numerous in the USA and Europe. Women have battled to be ordained ministers and rabbis. Feminist theorists have reinterpreted God or gods in terms of female experience, use gender neutral or feminine language in liturgy and reclaim stories and images of women who have been forgotten by history. Finally, there has been an attempt to discover within Western religion a Goddess or to appropriate strong Goddess figures from elsewhere and to start a process of indigenisation.

30. Womanist theology has emerged to articulate the experience of Afro-American Christian women. Mujerista theology articulates the theological reflection of

Hispanic American feminists. Asian feminists, African feminists, Latin American feminists, lesbians and disabled women are drawing attention to the differences among women (including power differences).

31.　It accepts that ISKCON's treatment of women has drawn criticism from anti-cult groups, rights organisations and even governmental bodies. Julius Lipner writes: "ISKCON needs all the help it can get in the years ahead. Unless it succeeds in convincing the female devotees that they have an equally important role to play – not only physically, but also intellectually and spiritually if they so desire, ISKCON's hope for the future will be seriously undermined. It seems to me…that the role of women must be reconstructed in ISKCON" (Lipner 1994, p.24).

32.　Servants of the goddess and indeed women in general can transmit very orthodox teachings that perpetuate women's weakness. However, Rita Dasgupta Sherma, for example, observes that it does not appear that Hindu Goddess worship has given women autonomy or greater authority, but argues that it is in subtle ways that Hindu women can identify with the female deities. Hindu women if devoted wives, are aligned with Lakshmi and if self-sacrificing, referred to as Sita (Sherma 2000, p.25). Even those devotees who still regard feminism as a subversion of the natural order and who accept that their primary identities are as self-sacrificing mothers and wives, gain the strength to demand that men perform their paternal protective role.

33.　The heart of a devotee is considered to be the residence of Lord Krishna. The essence of his existence Krishna. Therefore, a devotee sees everything in relation to the Supreme Personality of Godhead. Padmapani Das (2004) writes that "(the devotee) has no enemies; politics and diplomacy have no place in the person of a Vaisnava. His only motivation is to please Krsna, being always absorbed in His loving devotional service. So when truly advanced Vaisnavas interact with one another, the atmosphere is surcharged with spiritual bliss."

Brzezinski, Jan (2004) Charismatic Renewal and Institutionalization in the History of Gaudiya Vaishnavism and the Gaudiya Math, in Edwin F. Bryant and Maria L. Ekstrand (Eds.), *The Hare Krishna Movement: The Postcharismatic Fate of a Religious Transplant*, pp.73-96 (New York: Columbia University).

Brockington, J. (1992) *Hinduism and Christianity* (Basingstoke: Macmillan).

Bryant, Edwin F. and Maria L. Ekstrand (2004) (Eds.) *The Hare Krishna Movement: The Postcharismatic Fate of a Religious Transplant* (New York: Columbia University Press).

Bryant, Edwin F. and Maria L. Ekstrand (2004) Concluding Reflections, in Edwin F. Bryant and Maria L. Ekstrand (Eds.), *The Hare Krishna Movement: The Postcharismatic Fate of a Religious Transplant*, pp.431-41 (New York: Columbia University).

Caldwell, S. (2001) *Oh Terrifying Mother: Sexuality, Violence and Worship of the Goddess Kali* (New Delhi: Oxford University Press/Oxford India Paperbacks).

Coburn, Thomas B. (1985) *Devi Mahatmya: The Crystallization of the Goddess Tradition* (Delhi: Motilal Banarsidass).

Coburn, Thomas B. (1991) *Encountering the Goddess: A Translation of the Devi-Mahatmya and a Study of its Interpretation* (Albany: SUNY Press).

Daner, F. (1976) *The American Children of Krsna* (New York: Holt, Rinehart and Winston).

Das, Bhakti Rasa (2005) Comments on paper given by Anna S. King at STIMW, Newcastle University, May 17.

Dasa, Ravindra Svarupa (1994a) Cleaning House and Cleaning Hearts: Reform and Renewal in ISKCON, Part One, *ISKCON Communications Journal* 3.

Dasa, Ravindra Svarupa (1994b) Cleaning House and Cleaning Hearts: Reform and Renewal in ISKCON, Part Two, *ISKCON Communications Journal* 4.

Dasa, Ravindra Svarupa (1991) The Position of Women in ISKCON Today, parts 1-2, ISKCON European Communications Seminar.

Das, Shuhavak N. (2004) Bhaktivinoda and Scriptural Literalism, in Edwin F. Bryant and Maria L. Ekstrand (Eds.), *The Hare Krishna Movement: The Postcharismatic Fate of a Religious Transplant*, pp.97-111 (New York: Columbia University).

Davies Aull, Charlotte (1999) *Reflexive Ethnography: A Guide to Researching Selves and Others* (London: Routledge).

Deadwyler, Gabriel (Yudhishthira Das) (2004) Fifteen Years Later: A Critique of *Gurukula*: Personal Story II, in Edwin F. Bryant and Maria L. Ekstrand (Eds.), *The Hare Krishna Movement: The Postcharismatic Fate of a Religious Transplant*, 345-6 (New York: Columbia University).

Delmonico, Neal (2004) The History of Indic Monotheism and Modern Chaitanya Vaishnavism, in Edwin F. Bryant and Maria L. Ekstrand (Eds.), *The Hare Krishna Movement: The Postcharismatic Fate of a Religious Transplant*, pp.31-4 (New York: Columbia University).

Dasi, Radha Devi (1998) Participation, Protection and Patriarchy: An International Model for the Role of Women in ISKCON, *ISKCON Communications Journal* 6 (1): 31-41.

Dasi, Radha Devi (1998) Fundamental Human Rights in ISKCON, *ISKCON Communications Journal* 6 (2): 7-14.

Dasi, Visakha Devi, Sudharma Dasi, Sitala Dasi, Yamuna Devi Dasi, Kusa Dasi, Saudamani Dasi, Sudharma Dasi, Rukmini Devi Dasi (2000) Women in ISKCON: Presentations to the GBC, *ISKCON Communications Journal* 8 (1): 1-22.

Dasi, Yamuna Devi (2000) Srila Prabhupada's Transcendental Sweetness and Beauty, in Visakha Devi Dasi, Sudharma Dasi, Sitala Dasi, Yamuna Devi Dasi, Kusa Dasi, Saudamani Dasi, Sudharma Dasi, Rukmini Devi Dasi, Women in ISKCON: Presentations to the GBC, *ISKCON Communications Journal* 8 (1): 6-7.

Doniger O'Flaherty, W. (1975) *Hindu Myths*, trans. (London: Penguin).

Erndl, Kathleen M. (1993) *Victory to the Mother: The Hindu Goddess of Northwest India in Myth, Ritual and Symbol* (New York: Oxford University Press).

Flood, Gavin (1995) Hinduism, Vaishnavism, and ISKCON: Authentic Traditions or Scholarly Constructions?, *ISKCON Communications Journal* 3 (2): 5-15.

Flood, Gavin (1996) *An Introduction to Hinduism* (Cambridge: Cambridge University Press).

Gelberg, Steven J. (1983) (Ed.) *Hare Krishna, Hare Krishna: Five Distinguished Scholars on the Krishna Movement in the West* (New York: Grove Press).

Gelberg, Steven J. (1991) The Call of the Lotus-Eyed Lord: The Fate of Krishna Consciousness in the West, in T. Miller (Ed.), *When Prophets Die: The Post Charismatic Fate of New Religious Movements* (Albany: SUNY Press).

Gross, Rita M. (1994) Hindu Female Deities as a Resource for the Contemporary Rediscovery of the Goddess, in Carl Olson (Ed.), *The Book of the Goddess: Past and Present*, pp.217-30 (New York: Crossroad).

Gross, Rita M. (1998) Toward a New Model of the Hindu Pantheon: A Report on Twentysome Years of Feminist Reflection, *Religion* 28: 319-327.

Gross, Rita M. and Rosemary Radford Ruether (2001) *Religious Feminism and the Future of the Planet: A Buddhist-Christian Conversation* (London: Continuum).

Haddon, Malcolm (2003) *The Nectar of Translation: Conversion, Mimesis, and Cultural Translation in Krishna Consciousness*, doctoral thesis submitted on 30 July, 2003, to Macquarie University, the Department of Anthropology, Division of Society, Culture, Media and Philosophy.

Hardy, Friedhelm (1994) *The Religious Culture of India: Power, Love and Wisdom* (Cambridge: Cambridge University Press).

Hawley, John Stratton and Donna Marie Wulff (1982) (Eds.) *The Divine Consort: Radha and the Goddesses of India* (Berkeley: Berkeley Religious Studies Series).

Hawley, John Stratton (1996) The Goddess in India, in John Stratton Hawley and Donna Marie Wulff (Eds.), *Devi: Goddesses of India*, pp.1-28 (Berkeley: University of California Press).

Herzig, Thomas (Tamal Krishna Goswami) and Kenneth Valpey (Krishna Kshetra Das) (2004) Revisioning ISKCON: Constructive Theologizing for Reform and Renewal, in Edwin F. Bryant and Maria L Ekstrand (Eds.), *The Hare Krishna Movement: The Postcharismatic Fate of a Religious Transplant*, pp.416-30 (New York: Columbia University).

Hiltebeitel, Alf and Kathleen M.Erndl (2000) *Is the Goddess a Feminist? The Politics of South Asian Goddesses* (Sheffield: Sheffield Academic Press).

Indian Continental Committee (subcommittee) A Social Model for ISKCON, *http://www.salagram.net/SOC-Iskcon.html*, pp.1-21, accessed 15.03.2005.

Jeffery, Patricia and Amrita Bas (1998) (Ed.), *Appropriating Gender: Women's Activism and Politicised Religion in South Asia* (New York: Routledge).

Judah, J.S. (1974) *Hare Krishna and the Counterculture* (New York: Wiley).

King, U. (2004) Response to a paper at the conference of the British Association for the Study of Religions, Oxford.

Kinsley, David (1977) *The Sword and the Flute: Krsna, Dark Visions of the Terrible and the Sublime in Hindu Mythology* (Berkeley: University of California Press).

Kinsley, David (1986) *Visions of the Hindu Divine in Hindu Religious Tradition* (New Delhi: Penguin).

Kishwar, Madhu (1999) Yes to Sita, No to Ram!: The Continuing Popularity of Sita in India, in *Off the Beaten Track: Rethinking Gender Justice for Indian Women*, pp.234-49 (New Delhi: Oxford University Press).

Knott, Kim (1995) The Debate about Women in the Hare Krishna Movement, *ISKCON Communications Journal* 3 (2): 33-49.

Knott, Kim (1996a) The Debate about Women in the Hare Krishna Movement, in Steven J. Rosen (Ed.), (1996) *Vaisnavi: Women and the Worship of Krishna*, pp. 87-111 (New Delhi: Motilal Banarsidass).

Knott, Kim (1996b) Hindu Women, Destiny and Stridharma, *Religion* 26: 15-35.

Knott, Kim (1997) Insider and Outsider Perceptions of Prabhupada, *ISKCON Communications Journal* 5 (1): 59-71.

Knott, Kim (2004) Healing the Heart of ISKCON: The Place of Women, in Edwin F. Bryant and Maria L. Ekstrand (Eds.), *The Hare Krishna Movement: The Postcharismatic Fate of a Religious Transplant*, pp.291-311 (New York: Columbia University).

Kripal, Jeffrey K. (2000) A Garland of Talking Heads for the Goddess: Some Autobiographical and Psychoanalytic Reflections on the Western Kali, in Alf Hiltebeitel and Kathleen M.Erndl (Eds.), *Is the Goddess a Feminist? The Politics of South Asian Goddesses*, pp.239-68 (Sheffield: Sheffield Academic Press).

Leslie, Julia (1991) (Ed.) *Roles and Rituals for Hindu Women* (London: Pinter Publishers).

Lipner, Julius (1994) ISKCON at the Crossroads?, *ISKCON Communications Journal* 3.

Lorenz, Ekkehard (2004) The Guru, Mayavadins, and Women: Tracing the Origins of Selected Polemical Statements in the Work of A.C. Bhaktivedanta Swami, in Edwin F. Bryant and Maria L. Ekstrand (Eds.), *The Hare Krishna Movement: The Postcharismatic Fate of a Religious Transplant*, pp.112-28 (New York: Columbia University).

Lorenz, Ekkehard (2004), Race, Monarchy and Gender: Bhaktivedanta Swami's Social Experiment, in Edwin F. Bryant and Maria L. Ekstrand (Eds.), *The Hare Krishna Movement: The Postcharismatic Fate of a Religious Transplant*, pp.347-90 (New York: Columbia University).

Malhotra, Rajiv (2004) *rajiv.malhotra@worldnet.att.net*, 1-3, accessed 20.12.2004.

Mangalvadi, V. (1977) *The World of the Gurus* (Delhi: Vikas).

McDermott, Rachel Fell (1996) The Western Kali, in John Stratton Hawley and Donna Marie (Eds.), *Devi: Goddesses of India*, pp..281-313 (Berkeley: University of California Press).

Martin, Nancy (1996) Mirabai: Inscribed in Text, Embodied in Life, in Steven J. Rosen (Ed.), *Vaisnavi: Women and the Worship of Krishna*, pp.7-46 (New Delhi: Motilal Banarsidass).

Midgley, M. (1996) *Utopias, Dolphins and Computers* (London: Routledge).

Muster, Nori (2004) Life as a Woman on Watseka Avenue, in Edwin F. Bryant and Maria L. Ekstrand (Eds.), *The Hare Krishna Movement: The Postcharismatic Fate of a Religious Transplant*, pp.312-20 (New York: Columbia University).

Padmapani Das (2004) The Heart of a Devotee: personal communication.

Pintchman, Tracy (1994) *The Rise of the Goddess in Hindu Tradition* (Albany: SUNY Press).

Prabhupada, A.C. Bhaktivedanta Swami (1969) *Sri Isopanishad* (Los Angeles: Bhaktivedanta Book Trust).

Prabhupada, A.C. Bhaktivedanta Swami (1970) *Srimad Bhagavatam*, First Canto-Part Two (New York: ISKCON Press).

Prabhupada, A.C. Bhaktivedanta Swami (1970 [1982]) *The Nectar of Devotion: The Complete Science of Bhakti-Yoga. A Summary Study of Srila Rupa's Bhakti-rasamrita-sindhu* (Mumbai: Bhaktivedanta Book Trust).

Prabhupada, A.C. Bhaktivedanta Swami (1970 [1996]) *Krsna: The Supreme Personality of Godhead* (Mumbai: Bhaktivedanta Book Trust).

Prabhupada, A.C. Bhaktivedanta Swami (1988) *Teachings of Lord Caitanya* (Los Angeles: Bhaktivedanta Book Trust).

Prabhupada, A.C. Bhaktivedanta Swami (1989) *Srimad Bhagavatam*, First Canto-Part One (Australia: Bhaktivedanta Book Trust).

Prabhupada, A.C. Bhaktivedanta Swami (1990) *Conversations with Srila Prabhupada*, vol. 22, Toronto, 6.18.76 (Los Angeles: Bhaktivedanta Book Trust).

Puttick, Elizabeth (1997) *Women in New Religions: In Search of Community, Sexuality and Spiritual Power* (New York: St Martin's Press).

Rosen, Steven J. (1992) (Ed.) *Vaisnavism: Contemporary Scholars Discuss the Gaudiya Tradition* (New York: Folk Books).

Rosen, Steven J. (1996) (Ed.) *Vaisnavi: Women and the Worship of Krishna* (New Delhi: Motilal Banarsidass).

Rosen, Steven J. (1996) Raganuga Bhakti: Bringing out the Inner Woman in Gaudiya Vaisnava Sadhana, in Steven J. Rosen (Ed.), *Vaisnavi: Women and the Worship of Krishna*, pp.113-32 (New Delhi: Motilal Banarsidass).

Schweig, Graham (2004) Krishna, the Intimate Deity, in Edwin F. Bryant and Maria L. Ekstrand (Eds.), *The Hare Krishna Movement: The Postcharismatic Fate of a Religious Transplant*, pp.13-30 (New York: Columbia University).

Schweig, Graham M. (2005) *Dance of Divine Love – India's Classic Sacred Love Story: The Rasa Lila of Krishna* (Princeton: Princeton University Press).

Shinn, L.D. (1987) *The Dark Lord: Cult Images and the Hare Krishnas in America* (Philadelphia: Westminster Press).

Sivarama Svami (1999) Venu-Gita, *Krsna in Vrndavana*1 (Hungary: Bhaktivedanta Institute).

Sivarama Svami (2000) Na Paraye 'Ham: I am Unable to Repay You, *Krsna in Vrndavana* 2 (Hungary: Lal Kiado).

Stuart, Elizabeth and Adrian Thatcher (1997) *People of Passion: What the Churches Teach about Sex* (London: Mowbray).

Urmila Devi Dasi (1998) Fundamental Human Rights in ISKCON, *ISKCON Communications Journal* 6 (2): 15-26.

Valpey, Kenneth (Krishna Kshetra Das) (2004) Krishna in Mleccha Desh: ISKCON Temple Worship in Historical Perspective, in Edwin F. Bryant and Maria L. Ekstrand (Eds.), *The Hare Krishna Movement: The Postcharismatic Fate of a Religious Transplant*, pp.45-60 (New York: Columbia University Press).

Wulff, Donna Marie (1996) Radha: Consort and Conqueror of Krishna, in John Stratton Hawley and Donna Marie Wulff (Eds.), *Devi: Goddesses of India*, pp.109-34 (Berkeley: University of California Press).

Young, Serenity (1993) (Ed.) *An Anthology of Sacred Texts by and About Women* (New York: Crossroad).

NOTES ON CONTRIBUTORS

Kenneth Anderson (Krishna Dharma Das) is the author of the world's most popular editions of India's great epics: the *Ramayana: India's Immortal Tale of Adventure, Love and Wisdom* (1998, New Delhi: Torchlight) and the *Mahabharata: The Greatest Spiritual Epic of All Time* (1999, New Delhi: Torchlight). He is a regular radio broadcaster and a frequent contributor to the press. For the last 25 years he has offered lectures and seminars on the Vedas and their associated disciplines. In 1986 he established an ISKCON temple in Manchester, England, which he ran until 2001. He currently lives with his wife and three children in Hertfordshire.

Ross Andrew (Rasamandala Das) is an initiated disciple of His Divine Grace A.C. Bhaktivedanta Swami Prabhupada. He has some fifteen years experience in education and teacher training, runs an educational consultancy in Oxford, and he is also co-ordinator of ISKCON Educational Services. He has authored both articles on the Hare Krishna movement as well as a book, entitled *The Heart of Hinduism: A Comprehensive Guide for Teachers and Professionals* (2002, Aldenham: ISKCON Educational Services), a book widely used in schools throughout the UK.

Richard J. Cole (Radha Mohan Das) became a full time temple resident within the International Society for Krishna Consciousness in 1993 at the age of 23, after completing a BA in Media and Performance at Salford University. Today he continues to reside in ISKCON temples as a *brahmachari* (celibate monk), following all the principles of Krishna Consciousness. He is firmly established at Bhaktivedanta Manor, the headquarters of ISKCON in the UK and works as the Secretary of ISKCON UK's Communications

Department, which deals with all aspects of internal and external media as well as with political VIPs, interfaith, websites, European affairs and many academic enquiries regarding ISKCON and Hinduism at large. He was a major researcher for the lead-title by Joshua Greene (Yogesvara Dasa), *Here Comes The Sun: The Spiritual and Musical Journey of George Harrison* (2006, New York: Wiley & Sons). He also regularly makes presentations on Krishna Consciousness but has a specialisation in writing and performing dramas. In this connection he regularly writes and performs plays based on India's Vedic scriptures to modern audiences in Europe, the USA and India.

William H. Deadwyler (Ravindra Svarupa Dasa) received a B A in Philosophy from the University of Pennsylvania in 1966 and a Ph D in Religion from Temple University in 1980. In 1971 he became an initiated disciple of Srila Prabhupada as well as the president of ISKCON's Philadelphia temple. He has also served as a writer, lecturer, and researcher with ISKCON's Bhaktivedanta Institute and as a writer and editor for *Back to Godhead* magazine. In 1987 he was elected to ISKCON's Governing Body Commission. He has published a number of scholarly articles about Gaudiya Vaishnava philosophy and about ISKCON. The Bhaktivedanta Book Trust has published a selection of his *Back to Godhead* articles under the title Endless Love.

Graham Dwyer has a BA in Religious Studies and Sociology from the University of Lancaster and received his M St and D Phil in Social Anthropology from the University of Oxford. He is Honorary Research Fellow at the Centre for Theology and Religious Studies, University of Winchester and Lecturer in Social Sciences at Greenwich Community College, London. He has carried out research on popular Hinduism in Rajasthan, concentrating on spirit possession and exorcism, and has authored both articles and, more recently, a book on the topic: *The Divine and the Demonic: Supernatural Affliction and its Treatment in North India* (2003, London and New York: RoutledgeCurzon). His interest in the International Society for Krishna Consciousness (ISKCON), an interest he has had since being befriended by Hare Krishna monks over 30 years ago, became the major focus of Dwyer's research in 2002. Besides the work in which he has been engaged organising as well as contributing to the present collection of essays on ISKCON, he has also authored articles on the Krishna Consciousness movement.

Thomas J. Hopkins has a Ph D from Yale University in Comparative Religions (1962). He taught Religious Studies at Franklin and Marshall College for 34 years, retiring as Emeritus Professor in 1996. He is the author of *The Hindu Religious Tradition* (1972, Belmont: Wadsworth), entries in *The Encyclopedia of Religion* and other reference sources, and numerous articles on aspects of Vaishnava devotionalism and ISKCON. His interest in the Krishna Consciousness movement dates back to 1967, when he visited the 2nd Avenue temple in New York and met A.C. Bhaktivedanta Swami and his early disciples, and he has followed the movement's history since then.

Anna S. King is Senior Lecturer in the Centre for Theology and Religious Studies, University of Winchester. She trained as a social anthropologist at the Institute of Social and Cultural Anthropology, Oxford. Her research interests have focused on the sacred city of Hardwar in North India and the Kumbha Mela. She is the contributing editor with John Brockington of *The Intimate Other: Love Divine in Indic Religions* (2004, Delhi: OrientLongman). Her articles include ISKCON: A Society in Transition, in C. and J. Erricker (Eds.), *Contemporary Spiritualities: Social and Religious Contexts* (2001, New York: Continuum International); The Guru-Disciple Relationship in ISKCON, with particular attention to Tamal Krishna Goswami, *Journal of Vaishnava Studies* : 173-186, S. J. Rosen (Ed.) (March edition, 2003); Dalit Theology: a Theology of Outrage, in I. Bocken, W. Dupre, P. van der Velde (Eds.), *The Persistent Challenge: Religion, Truth, and Scholarship, Essays in Honour of Klaus Klostermaier*, pp.53-78 (2004, Masstricht: Uitgeverj Shaker). She is Convenor of the Oxford Spalding Symposium on Indian Religions and of the Ritual and Devotion Research Group of the Dharam Hinduja Institute of Indic Religions, Cambridge University.

Steven J. Rosen (Satyaraja Dasa) is an initiated disciple of His Divine Grace A.C. Bhaktivedanta Swami Prabhupada as well as founder and editor-in-chief of the *Journal of Vaishnava Studies*, an academic quarterly esteemed by scholars around the world. He is also a contributing editor to *Back to Godhead, the Magazine of the Hare Krishna Movement*. An author of some 20 books in several languages, his more recent work includes *Gita on the Green: The Mystical Tradition Behind Bagger Vance* (2000, New York: Continuum International); *The Hidden Glory of India* (2001, Sweden: The Bhaktivedanta Book Trust); and *Holy War: Violence and the Bhagavad Gita* (2002, Hampton, Virginia: Deepak Heritage Books). He has also contributed to Edwin F. Bryant and Maria L. Ekstrand (Eds.) *The Hare Krishna Movement: The Postcharismatic Fate of a Religious Transplant* (2004, New York Columbia University Press) and authored the popular book *Holy Cow: The Hare Krishna Contribution to Vegetarianism and Animal Rights* (2004, New York: Lantern Books). He lives with his family in the New York area.

APPENDIX
List of Works by His Divine Grace A.C. Bhaktivedanta Swami Prabhupada

Books and Articles Authored by Bhaktivedanta Swami Prabhupada

Prabhupada, A.C. Bhaktivedanta Swami *Back to Godhead: The Magazine of the Hare Krishna Movement* (First published in Calcutta in 1944 by Srila Prabhupada himself, then published in 1966 in Los Angeles by Bhaktivedanta Book Trust).

Prabhupada, A.C. Bhaktivedanta Swami (1968) *Introduction to Bhagavad Gita* (Los Angeles: Bhaktivedanta Book Trust).

Prabhupada, A.C. Bhaktivedanta Swami (1969) *Sri Isopanisad* (Los Angeles: Bhaktivedanta Book Trust).

Prabhupada, A.C. Bhaktivedanta Swami (1970) *Nectar of Devotion: The Complete Science of Bhakti Yoga* (Los Angeles: Bhaktivedanta Book Trust).

Prabhupada, A.C. Bhaktivedanta Swami (1970) *Nectar of Instruction* (Los Angeles: Bhaktivedanta Book Trust).

Prabhupada, A.C. Bhaktivedanta Swami (1970) *KRSNA the Supreme Personality of Godhead* 2 vols. (Los Angeles: Bhaktivedanta Book Trust).

Prabhupada, A.C. Bhaktivedanta Swami (1970) *Easy Journey to other Planets* (Los Angeles: Bhaktivedanta Book Trust).

Prabhupada, A.C. Bhaktivedanta Swami (1972) *The Perfection of Yoga* (Los Angeles: Bhaktivedanta Book Trust).

Prabhupada, A.C. Bhaktivedanta Swami (1972) *Message of Godhead* (Los Angeles: Bhaktivedanta Book Trust).

Prabhupada, A.C. Bhaktivedanta Swami (1972) *Bhagavad Gita As It Is* (Los Angeles: Bhaktivedanta Book Trust).

Prabhupada, A.C. Bhaktivedanta Swami (1972) *The Path of Yoga* (Los Angeles: Bhaktivedanta Book Trust).

Prabhupada, A.C. Bhaktivedanta Swami (1972) *The Transcendental Teachings of Prahlada Maharaja* (Los Angeles: Bhaktivedanta Book Trust).

Prabhupada, A.C. Bhaktivedanta Swami (1972) *Krishna Consciousness: The Topmost Yoga System* (Los Angeles: Bhaktivedanta Book Trust).

Prabhupada, A.C. Bhaktivedanta Swami (1972) *Krsna: The Reservoir of Pleasure* (Los Angeles: Bhaktivedanta Book Trust).

Prabhupada, A.C. Bhaktivedanta Swami (1973) *Raja Vidja: The King of Knowledge* (Los Angeles: Bhaktivedanta Book Trust).

Prabhupada, A.C. Bhaktivedanta Swami (1973) *Elevation to Krishna Consciousness* (Los Angeles: Bhaktivedanta Book Trust).

Prabhupada, A.C. Bhaktivedanta Swami (1974) *Caitanya-caritamrita* 9 vols. (Los Angeles: Bhaktivedanta Book Trust).

Prabhupada, A.C. Bhaktivedanta Swami (1974) *The Matchless Gift* (Los Angeles: Bhaktivedanta Book Trust).

Prabhupada, A.C. Bhaktivedanta Swami (1974) *On the Way to Krishna* (Los Angeles: Bhaktivedanta Book Trust).

Prabhupada, A.C. Bhaktivedanta Swami (1975) *Lord Caitanya in Five Features* (Los Angeles: Bhaktivedanta Book Trust).

Prabhupada, A.C. Bhaktivedanta Swami (1977) *The Teachings of Lord Kapila* (Los Angeles: Bhaktivedanta Book Trust).

Prabhupada, A.C. Bhaktivedanta Swami (1978) *The Teachings of Queen Kunti, the Son of Devahuti* (Los Angeles: Bhaktivedanta Book Trust).

Prabhupada, A.C. Bhaktivedanta Swami (1979) *The Path of Perfection* (Los Angeles: Bhaktivedanta Book Trust).

Prabhupada, A.C. Bhaktivedanta Swami (1979) *Life comes from Life* (Los Angeles: Bhaktivedanta Book Trust).

Prabhupada, A.C. Bhaktivedanta Swami (1980) *The Teachings of Lord Caitanya* (Los Angeles: Bhaktivedanta Book Trust).

Prabhupada, A.C. Bhaktivedanta Swami (1982) *Beyond Birth and Death* (Los Angeles: Bhaktivedanta Book Trust).

Prabhupada, A.C. Bhaktivedanta Swami (1983) *Intellectual Animalism: A Penetrating Insight into the True Nature of Modern Civilisation* (Los Angeles: Bhaktivedanta Book Trust).

Prabhupada, A.C. Bhaktivedanta Swami (1983) *Perfect Questions, Perfect Answers* (Los Angeles: Bhaktivedanta Book Trust).

Prabhupada, A.C. Bhaktivedanta Swami (1983) *The Science of Self Realization* (Los Angeles: Bhaktivedanta Book Trust).

Prabhupada, A.C. Bhaktivedanta Swami (1984) *Light of the Bhagavata* (Los Angeles: Bhaktivedanta Book Trust).

Prabhupada, A.C. Bhaktivedanta Swami (1984) *Coming Back: the Science of Reincarnation* (Los Angeles: Bhaktivedanta Book Trust).

Prabhupada, A.C. Bhaktivedanta Swami (1988) *Srimad Bhagavatam* 12 cantos (Los Angeles: Bhaktivedanta Book Trust).

Prabhupada, A.C. Bhaktivedanta Swami (2002) *The Hare Krishna Challenge: Exposing a Misdirected Civilisation* (Los Angeles: Bhaktivedanta Book Trust).

Books Authored by Bhaktivedanta Swami Prabhupada in Bengali

Prabhupada, A.C. Bhaktivedanta Swami (1975) *Geetar-gan* (Mayapur: Bhaktivedanta Book Trust).

Prabhupada, A.C. Bhaktivedanta Swami (1976) *Bhakti-ratna-boli* (Mayapur: Bhaktivedanta Book Trust).

Prabhupada, A.C. Bhaktivedanta Swami (1977) *Buddhi-yoga* (Mayapur: Bhaktivedanta Book Trust).

Prabhupada, A.C. Bhaktivedanta Swami (1977) *Vairagya Vidya* (Mayapur: Bhaktivedanta Book Trust).

Lectures, Conversations and Other Writings of Bhaktivedanta Swami Prabhupada Compiled by Devotees after Prabhupada's Demise

Prabhupada, A.C. Bhaktivedanta Swami (1981) *Search for Liberation* (Los Angeles: Bhaktivedanta Book Trust).

Prabhupada, A.C. Bhaktivedanta Swami (1982) *Chant and be Happy: The Story of the Hare Krishna Mantra* (Los Angeles: Bhaktivedanta Book Trust).

Prabhupada, A.C. Bhaktivedanta Swami (1985) *Dialectic Spiritualism: A Vedic View of Western Philosophy* (West Virginia: Prabhupada Books).

Prabhupada, A.C. Bhaktivedanta Swami (1991) *The Laws of Nature: An Infallible Justice* (Los Angeles: Bhaktivedanta Book Trust).

Prabhupada, A.C. Bhaktivedanta Swami (1991) *Civilisation and Transcendence* (Los Angeles: Bhaktivedanta Book Trust).

Prabhupada, A.C. Bhaktivedanta Swami (1991) *Narada-Bhakti-Sutra* (Los Angeles: Bhaktivedanta Book Trust).

Prabhupada, A.C. Bhaktivedanta Swami (1991) *A Second Chance* (Los Angeles: Bhaktivedanta Book Trust).

Prabhupada, A.C. Bhaktivedanta Swami (1991) *Preaching is the Essence* (Mumbai: Bhaktivedanta Book Trust).

Prabhupada, A.C. Bhaktivedanta Swami (1992) *Mukunda-Mala-Stotra* (Los Angeles: Bhaktivedanta Book Trust).

Prabhupada, A.C. Bhaktivedanta Swami (1992) *Facts for Life: Conversations with: His Divine Grace A.C. Bhaktivedanta Swami Prabhupada* (Los Angeles: Bhaktivedanta Book Trust).

Prabhupada, A.C. Bhaktivedanta Swami (1992) *Renunciation through Wisdom* (Mumbai: Bhaktivedanta Book Trust).

Prabhupada, A.C. Bhaktivedanta Swami (1992) *Nectarean Instructions from the letters of His Divine Grace A.C. Bhaktivedanta Swami Prabhupada* (Los Angeles: Bhaktivedanta Book Trust).

Prabhupada, A.C. Bhaktivedanta Swami (1993) *Collected Lectures on Srimad Bhagavatam* 14 vols. (Los Angeles: Bhaktivedanta Book Trust).

Prabhupada, A.C. Bhaktivedanta Swami (1994) *Collected Teachings of His Divine Grace A.C. Bhaktivedanta Swami Prabhupada* 7 vols. (Los Angeles: Bhaktivedanta Book Trust).

Prabhupada, A.C. Bhaktivedanta Swami (1995) *Collected Lectures on Bhagavad Gita* 7 vols. (Los Angeles: Bhaktivedanta Book Trust).

Prabhupada, A.C. Bhaktivedanta Swami (1997) *The Quest for Enlightenment* (Los Angeles: Bhaktivedanta Book Trust).

Prabhupada, A.C. Bhaktivedanta Swami (1997) *The Journey of Self Discovery* (Los Angeles: Bhaktivedanta Book Trust).

Prabhupada, A.C. Bhaktivedanta Swami (1998) *Dharma: The Way to Transcendence* (Los Angeles: Bhaktivedanta Book Trust).

Prabhupada, A.C. Bhaktivedanta Swami (1999) *Beyond Illusion and Doubt: A Vedic Perspective on Western Philosophy* (Los Angeles: Bhaktivedanta Book Trust).

Prabhupada, A.C. Bhaktivedanta Swami (1999) *Srila Prabhupada on Varnashramadharma*, compiled by Hare-Devi Dasi, edited by Suresvara Dasa (Los Angeles: Bhaktivedanta Book Trust).

Prabhupada, A.C. Bhaktivedanta Swami (2004) *Bhakti: The Art of Eternal Love* (Los Angeles: Bhaktivedanta Book Trust).

GLOSSARY OF SANSKRIT TERMS
(as Employed and Understood in ISKCON)

acharya	elevated spiritual master who teaches by his own example
achintya bhedabheda tattva	inconceivable simultaneous oneness and difference (with Krishna)
arati	rite of worship typically involving the clockwise circling of a ritual object (e.g. lamp, incense stick, conch shell) before the image of a deity
ashram	monastic institution or community; stage of life of which there are four orders: celibate student life, householder life, retired life, and renounced life (cf. *brahmacharya, grihastha, vanaprastha* and *sannyasa*)
avatara	incarnation of God
Bhagavad Gita	literally, "Song of the Divine One"; a major episode in the great epic Sanskrit work *Mahabharata* and a text in which Krishna as the Supreme Personality of Godhead appears in order to give instruction to the warrior Arjuna
Bhagavata Purana	Sanskrit text celebrating the life of Krishna, His various incarnations and devotees (cf. *Srimad Bhagavatam*)
bhajan	hymn; devotional song
bhakta	devotee
bhakti	loving devotion to Godhead
bhakti-yoga	the path or way of devotion

Bhaktisiddhanta Maharaja	the spiritual master or guru of Bhaktivedanta Swami Prabhupada
Bhaktivedanta Swami Prabhupada	founder of ISKCON, the Hare Krishna movement
bhava	ecstatic spiritual emotion
bhog	food offering made to God (cf. *prasadam*)
brahmachari(n)	celibate student/monk (nun)
brahmacharya	celibate student life; first stage of life
brahman	ritual technician or priest (cf. *pujari*)
Caitanya-caritamrita	biography/hagiography of Chaitanya
Chaitanya Mahaprabhu	15th-16th century ecstatic held in ISKCON to be non-different from Krishna and Radharani combined
darshan	viewing; the act of seeing and in turn being seen by a deity through the medium of the deity's image
dharma	virtue, morality, order, righteousness, religion; socio-religious duty
diksha	initiation
Gaudiya Vaishnavism	the tradition of Vaishnavism inaugurated by Chaitanya; known also as Chaitanya Vaishnavism
GBC	Governing Body Commission, ISKCON's ruling power base, possessing ultimate authority and formed by the founder of ISKCON in July 1970
gopi	female cowherd; a cowherd girl friend of Krishna
grihastha	householder life; the second stage of life
gurukula	religious school for young students
guru parampara	unified, unbroken succession of gurus or spiritual masters (cf. *parampara*)
havan	sacred fire; used for purposes of sacrifice or oblation
ISKCON	International Society for Krishna Consciousness, the Hare Krishna Movement
japa	*mantra* or sacred verse uttered repetitively
kirtana	devotional chanting of a *mantra* (cf. *sankirtana*)
Krishna	the Supreme Personality of Godhead in Gaudiya Vaishnavism of which ISKCON is a branch
lila	divine sport or play, pastimes of a deity
mayavada	a synonym of Advaita Vedanta, the non-dualistic or monistic philosophy propounded by the 8th-9th century teacher Shankara (or Shankaracharya); an impersonalist theology thoroughly rejected in ISKCON
mayavadin	an adherent of *mayavada* philosophy

mahamantra	the Hare Krishna *mantra.* *Hare Krishna, Hare Krishna, Krishna Krishna, Hare Hare, Hare Rama, Hare Rama, Rama Rama, Hare Hare*
moksha	salvation; liberation from the cycle of rebirth and redeath
murti	image of a deity
parampara	lineage of spiritual masters
prasadam	sacred remains of food left by God distributed to the public
puja	worship
pujari	priest; one who carries out ceremonial acts, especially the congregational rite of worship
Purana(s)	stories of the ancient past involving humans and deities and considered in ISKCON to be historical narratives rather than chronicles of mythological events
raganuga (sadhana) bhakti	spontaneous service or devotion to God as opposed to rule-governed devotion (cf. *vidhi [sadhana] bhakti*)
ritvik	the guru's representative viewed in ISKCON as one who has been given authority to act on behalf of the guru for the purpose of initiation while the guru is still living
sadhana	ritual method or spiritual practice
sampradaya	established doctrine transmitted from one guru or teacher to another; lineage of gurus
samskara	rite of purification; rite of passage
samsara	endless cycle of rebirth and redeath
sankirtana	congregational chanting of a *mantra*
sannyasa	renounced life; fourth stage of life
sannyasi	renouncer; one who has renounced all worldly ties and duties
seva	service, task or duty performed as an act of devotion to god
shakti	divine energy, the power possessed by a deity
Srimad Bhagavatam	Bhaktivedanta Swami Prabhupada's English transalation of, and commentary on, the *Bhagavata Purana*
stri dharma	women's socio-religious duties
Vaikuntha	abode of Vishnu or Vishnu's heaven; spiritual realm
Vaishnava	a devotee of Vishnu, Lord Krishna
vanaprastha	retitred life; third stage of life
varnashrama/ varnasharamadharma	socio-religious organisation in ancient India comprised of four categories of person, viz., priest/teacher (*brahman*), warrior/leader/administrator (*kshatriya*), farmer/merchant (*vaishya*), and servant/labourer (*shudra*)
yajna	sacrifice; sacrificial rite or ceremony
Vedanta	theological articulation of the Vedic tradition and the most influential of the six schools of orthodox Indian philosophy

Veda(s)	scriptures regarded as ancient divine revelation rather than of human authorship and communicated by God to the sage Vyasa (or Vyasadeva)
vidhi (sadhana) bhakti	standard devotional service; study and meditation; the four regulative principles: (1) to abstain from all meat, fish or eggs; (2) to avoid all forms of intoxication (including tea, coffee and tobacco); (3) to abstain from gambling; and (4) to avoid sex except for the purpose of procreation within marriage
Vishnu	the supreme deity in Vaishnavism and considered to be a manifestation of Krishna in Gaudiya Vaishnavism
yatra	pilgrimage

INDEX